Growing the Productivity of Government Services

Growing the Productivity of Government Services

Patrick Dunleavy

London School of Economics and Political Science, UK

Leandro Carrera

Pensions Policy Institute, King's College, London, UK

Edward Elgar

Cheltenham, UK • Northampton, MA, USA

Published by
Edward Elgar Publishing Limited
The Lypiatts
15 Lansdown Road
Cheltenham
Glos GL50 2JA
UK

Edward Elgar Publishing, Inc.
William Pratt House
9 Dewey Court
Northampton
Massachusetts 01060
USA

A catalogue record for this book
is available from the British Library

Library of Congress Control Number: 2012947334

ISBN 978 0 85793 498 7 (cased)
        978 1 78195 610 6 (paperback)

Typeset by Servis Filmsetting Ltd, Stockport, Cheshire
Printed and bound by MPG Books Group, UK

Contents

Preface

At root, productivity is a fairly simple performance measure. It is calculated as the ratio of all the outputs produced by a given organization divided by all the inputs or the resources used in producing those outputs. In the private sector, the measurement of firms' productivity, and the analysis of the factors causing productivity growth, have developed a great deal. However, this is not the case in the public sector and for government agencies. The main reason for the lack of reliable productivity estimates for government services has been that public sector outputs do not have a price, unlike those in the market sector, so we cannot use prices to weight the different outputs produced by a given organization. Until the late 1990s this led to public sector outputs being measured by their inputs, that is, by the cost of producing them. This approach was equivalent to assuming that productivity in the public sector is always completely flat and unchanging.

Methodological advances since the late 1990s now allow us to estimate productivity ratios for government services by using the costs of producing each type of outputs to weight them. So where a government department does many things, we can now arrive at a useful overall measure of its outputs. In addition, the increasing availability of government services' activity data in the UK now allows us to compare productivity ratios for different government services, and to begin assessing the different factors that may be systematically related to productivity growth. This book aims to fill the large gap in the existing literature by providing a practical, organization-level approach to measuring productivity in the public sector. We show how productivity data over time and across comparator organizations can be combined with rich qualitative information about departments and agencies so as to begin analysing the different factors that may be related to government agencies' productivity growth.

Developing reliable productivity estimates for government services, and showing in detail how productivity trends relate to organizational changes, are not just of interest from an academic point of view. For public managers these steps forward are vital if they are to know how their organization performs compared to others. Productivity estimates may also usefully inform policy-makers' decisions on how to organize or restructure key government services, paying special attention to ensure that service levels are not affected. Better information on public sector productivity could also help citizens to hold policy-makers and public managers more accountable for the provision of government services, and to counteract the otherwise strong tendencies for government service costs to rise relative to those of other economic sectors. We also show that productivity change in government is integrally linked to innovation, much more closely so than in private industries. So focusing on continuous productivity advance also entails a lot more than simple cost-cutting, and innovations can also be very positive for enhancing the modernity and usefulness of government services.

The book has three parts. The longest, Part I, focuses on the analysis of nationally provided services, looking in detail at the processing of goods for customs, the collection of taxes, the processing and payment of social security benefits, and two aspects of government regulation (passports and driver/vehicle registration). The analysis of such services in productivity terms has been especially difficult because they are administered by large departments or agencies that are unique in each country. We show in every case a strong interaction between advances in information and communication technologies (ICTs, or IT) on the one hand, and cultural resistance to change in long-lived bureaucracies on the other. This dialectic can explain why contemporary productivity outcomes in national government bodies have varied a lot, but overall have tended to remain broadly flat or grow only slowly over long periods of time.

Part II shifts focus to government services where there are multiple providers, so allowing us to look across productivity levels in different organizations and to track down the factors that explain variations, using regression or other analyses that control for multiple variables. One main problem here has been that services with multiple providers are often more complex and professionally delivered. They are less standardized, and hence quality variations can have far more direct and substantial importance for the accurate measurement of outputs. A second problem has been that previous studies have made only limited progress in measuring organizational factors that may have a bearing on overall organizational performance, again especially ICT changes and management innovations. We look at the measurement of productivity across NHS trusts in England and Wales, and apply a new approach (a web-census) to develop data on the use of management techniques and ICT and their links to productivity performance.

Part III steps back from the empirical analysis to draw out some of the key lessons across all our chapters for government organizations. To shift from previous erratic or slow progress, and to move instead towards serial innovations and sustainable productivity advances, year in and year out, entails a wide ranging set of changes:

- embracing digital change enthusiastically but realistically;
- really understanding innovation in government organizations, so as to best foster it;
- shedding the managerialist obsession with reorganizations;
- engaging public sector workers more in promoting change; and above all
- focusing hard and continuously on productivity levels.

We welcome comments on and enquiries about this work:
E-mail: p.dunleavy@lse.ac.uk

Leandro Carrera
Patrick Dunleavy

LSE Public Policy Group
Government Department
London School of Economics
May 2012

Acknowledgements

It took more than five years to undertake the research involved in this book, and two more years to write up the analysis. It was only made possible through the generous help of many dozens of public policy practitioners in government and the outsourcing industries, without whose active engagement and unstinting cooperation it could not have been undertaken.

Our biggest debt is to the systems integrator company EDS, and later Hewlett Packard after it took over EDS. They most generously funded and supported this research for five years as the main research project undertaken by LSE Public Policy Group (PPG) for the EDS-LSE Innovation Research Programme. We could not have developed this project without the far-sighted and no-strings funding that the company donated. And the analysis would have been much poorer without the active support and engagement of a large number of EDS and later EDS-HP executives and senior managers in the UK. They attended more than 15 major seminars and mini-conferences held during 2005–09, and also helped to involve dozens of senior government civil servants and local government and NHS staff in these key events. We owe a special debt to the late and much missed Charles Cox, and to Sheelagh D. Whittaker, two outstanding and intellectually committed business executives, who first helped the Innovation Research Programme get launched. We also learnt a great deal about practical government computing, public administration and ICT change issues from a large number of EDS and EDS-HP executives responsible for liaison with the project over the years, and who commented on earlier version of papers presented at different seminars, which subsequently became part of this book. We are especially grateful to Craig Wilson and later James Johns for their unstinting and generous help, while others (including David Rimmer and Michael Gough) provided valuable specific inputs. We should double stress, however, that none of these EDS or HP people have read or approved any part of this book, and nor have they in any way agreed to or signed off the analysis. The responsibility for everything written here and for all the judgements made, is ours alone – reflecting a complete intellectual and analytic independence that was always fully respected by the company and its staff.

Our second greatest debt is to a huge range of civil servants, local government and NHS staff who have worked with LSE Public Policy Group teams on a wide range of in-depth projects from 1998 to 2009, some for academic work and many undertaken for the National Audit Office. Most especially for this book we are grateful to staff in the productivity analysis sections of HM Revenue & Customs (HMRC) and the Department for Work and Pensions (DWP): without their exemplary work in assembling and weighting outputs data, and commitment to transparency, the project would not have been feasible. At HMRC, we received support and key activity data from the members of the KAI Strategic Analysis and Coordination team. We are also thankful to senior HMRC staff who provided useful feedback during seminars on customs and tax productivity held at the HMRC in 2009, and to the dozens of HMRC and Treasury staff who attended a seminar at the Treasury on 'Inherently Digital Public Services' in summer 2010. At the DWP we are particularly thankful for the support provided by Dave Barnbrook and Heather Turnpin, at the Business Modelling and Analysis Division, who provided data on activity measures used in Chapter 5. We thank Sir Richard Mottram, now a Visiting Professor at LSE, but in the noughties a key figure in the transformation of DWP as its permanent secretary: we have had many debates with him about what was and was not accomplished in this period – which are sure to continue! Lord Michael Bichard (Permanent Secretary at the Department of Social Security before 2000, and latterly Chair of the Institute for Government for several years) also contributed most helpfully.

In July 2008 an LSE conference (supported by the LSE's Higher Education Innovation Fund or HEIF) led to valuable contacts with experts and practitioners at the Office for National Statistics (ONS). We received useful feedback from Aileen Simkins, head of the UK Centre for the Measurement of Government Activity (UKCeMGA). Mike Phelps, also from UKCeMGA provided very useful comments and suggestions in different seminars and conferences at which we presented early versions of this research. We are grateful for this input, and to be able to draw on the broader stream of impressive ONS findings and method developments.

Throughout the gestation and most of the undertaking of this research LSE Public Policy Group worked closely with an outstanding UK agency, the National Audit Office (NAO) on contracted research for value for money (VFM) and other studies. We are intensely grateful for many great suggestions and comments to Michael Whitehouse (now Chief Operating Officer at NAO), Jeremy Lonsdale and David Raraty across many projects – surely these must be three of the most intellectually involved officials in any public agency anywhere in the world. A wide range of other NAO staff were also unstinting in their help on individual projects, including Mark Davies, Chris Lambert, Leon Bardot, Rob Prideaux, Liane Hinds, Theresa Crowley, Elena Bechberger and many others. Sir John Bourne, head of NAO for many years and Amyas Morse who succeeded him as Comptroller and Auditor General, both provided valuable ideas and encouragement. Finally, the intellectual debt that we owe NAO staff over more than a decade and a half can be traced in the large number of references to the organization in our bibliography. NAO reports are a treasure trove of information, for far too long neglected by British university researchers.

Turning to academia itself, Patrick Dunleavy has intellectual debts impossible to quantify to Helen Margetts (now Director of the Oxford Internet Institute), and to Jane Tinkler and Simon Bastow from LSE Public Policy Group. We draw extensively on previous joint work with all three on British central government and on government ICT systems, throughout Chapters 3 to 6. We thank too Chris Gilson, who especially contributed to much of the second half of Chapter 9. The close involvement of these four authors was a constant in a dozen or so projects undertaken between 1998 and 2009, to which a wide range of former PPG staff also contributed in one or more studies. Key people here include (in rough chronological order) Steve John (now at BUPA), Don McCarthy (now at the Independent Institute), Hala Yared, Ruth Callaghan, Patricia Bartholomeou, Oliver Pearce (now at Christian Aid), François Boucek (now at Queen Mary College, London), Nihan Akyelken (now at Oxford University), Edward Towers (now at Accenture), Sofia Goldchluk (now at Consumers International), Camila Aguilar (now working in Columbia's government) and Anne White (now working in Ontario government). All these co-authors provided invaluable help at different stages of this research, helping to make a reality of a rich concept of 'organizational productivity' in government. Elsewhere in LSE, colleagues from the Centre for Economic Performance provided useful suggestions and some initial data for Chapter 8 on productivity in the NHS, and Joachim Wehner advised us on regression methods.

Some early versions of papers that now form part of this book were presented at academic seminars and conferences. In particular, Helen Margetts, Christopher Hood and others commented helpfully at seminars held at the Oxford Internet Institute in early 2010 and in spring 2012. We also received most useful comments and insights from participants at a panel organized at the 2010 Annual Conference of the American Political Science Association in Washington, DC. We are most grateful also to Dee Compson-Wragg for all her help on improving the book manuscript.

A project of this scale and duration inevitably has mostly adverse implications for the families and personal friends of its authors, for whom we hope the finished book is some slender compensation. Leandro Carrera records his grateful thanks to Jen, Esther, Cecilia and Carlos, for all their help and support. Patrick Dunleavy thanks Sheila, who gives real meaning to the much misused concept of co-production.

Glossary and abbreviations

*	multiply by
AA	Attendance Allowance
ACCORD	consortium of computer firms
AEI	Average Earnings Index
ANPR	automatic number plate recognition
BA	Benefits Agency
BBC	British Broadcasting Corporation
BPO	business process outsourcing
CHIEF	'Customs Handling of Import and Export Freight', the main computer system used from 1994 onwards by HMCE and HMRC for handling customs checks on freight
CSA	Child Support Agency (UK)
CSP	Community Systems Provider
DCS	Disability and Carers' Service (UK)
DEA	data envelopment analysis
Defra	Department of Environment, Food and Rural Affairs (UK)
DEG	digital era governance
DfEE	Department for Education and Employment (UK)
DfT	Department for Transport (UK)
DHSS	Department of Health and Social Security (UK)
DLA	Disability Living Allowance
DMUs	decision-making units
DMV	Department of Motor Vehicles (USA)
DoH	Department of Health (UK)
DSS	Department of Social Security
DWP	Department for Work and Pensions (UK)
ECA	European Court of Auditors, the Supreme Audit Institution for the European Union
EDI	electronic data interchange
EDS	major computer firm
ESA	Employment Services Agency
FCO	Foreign and Commonwealth Office (UK)

FTE	full-time equivalent staff numbers
GAO	Government Accountability Office, the USA's Supreme Audit Institution at federal government level
GST	goods and services tax
HCC	Health Care Commission
HMCE	Her Majesty's Customs and Excise (UK)
HMRC	Her Majesty's Revenue & Customs (UK)
ICT/IT	information and communication technology/information technology
ITO	Information and Technology Office
ITSA	Information Technology and Support Agency
IPS	Identity and Passport Service (UK)
IR	Inland Revenue (UK)
IRS	Inland Revenue Service (USA)
IS	Income Support
IVR	intelligent voice recognition
JCP	Jobcentre Plus
JSA	Job Seeker's Allowance
KPI	key performance indicators, indices selected and announced as significant indicators of the performance of a system, organization or set of organizations
MLAs	micro-local agencies
MOD	Ministry of Defence (UK)
NAO	National Audit Office (UK), the UK's Supreme Audit Institution
NATOE	Nodality, Authority, Treasure, (basic) Organization and (organized) Expertise – the five basic tools of government
NDPB	non-departmental public body
NHS	National Health Service (UK)
NI	National Insurance
NIC	National Insurance Contributions
NICO	National Insurance Contribution Office
NIRS	National Insurance Register System
NPfIT	National Programme for IT, a centralized IT investment programme in the NHS that operated from 2005 to 2011
NPM	new public management
NPS	New Payments System for income tax
OCR	optical character reader technology

OPRA	Occupational Pensions Regulatory Authority (UK)
PAYE	pay as you earn tax system
PAYGO	pay as you go welfare systems
PCs	personal computers (now any modern computer desktop or laptop)
PCT	Primary Care Trust, a type of trust, part of the NHS in England
PFI	Private Finance Initiative
PRA	Passports and Records Agency (UK)
PRIME	property sale and re-lease deal
QGAs	quasi-government agencies
R&D	research and development
RPI	Retail Price Index
systems integrator	large IT firm acting as main contractor for implementing major computing/networking projects
SAI	Supreme Audit Institution, the top-level auditing body at national government level
SSA	Social Security Administration (USA)
TFP	total factor productivity
UKPA	United Kingdom Passport Agency
VAT	value-added tax
VED	vehicle excise duty
VFM	value for money

1. Introduction: why has government productivity been so neglected in economics and public management?

In advanced industrial societies, public sector activities account for substantial shares of total economic activity. In the UK, for instance, the government's share of final consumption represented almost 24 per cent in 2009 (Office for National Statistics, 2010a). So it matters a great deal to national competitiveness and to overall economic welfare how well government sector production activities are organized. For many decades, the conventional wisdom has been that government is a low productivity sector where improvements in the organization of activities always take place with a slower tempo than in the private sector, creating a significant drag on changes in the rest of the economy.

Many observers argue that the public sector performs far worse than this, constituting a huge zone of the economy where productivity increases hardly at all, and may even move negatively over a long period. For instance, a well-known centre-right UK think-tank, the Centre for Economics and Business Research, claimed in mid-2009:

> In a little noticed revision slipped out on 14 August, the Office for National Statistics let on that the *public sector's productivity performance had been even worse than earlier admitted, with a decline of 3.4% from 1997 to 2007*. At the same time productivity in the market sector rose by 27.9%, so *had productivity in the public sector moved in line with that in the market sector, productivity would have been 32.4% higher*. On the other hand . . . over the whole period from 1997 to 2007 pay in the public sector rose by slightly less [than the private sector]. So in looking at the cost of public expenditure it is probably fairer to use the unit labour cost comparison which shows public sector costs rising by 30.5% relative to the market sector. This productivity calculation . . . applies to General Government Final Consumption Expenditure . . . [which] amounts to about £250 billion a year. So *had costs risen in line with the market sector, this would have cost £58.4 billion less*. (Centre for Economics and Business Research, 2009, original emphasis)

Seeking to evaluate the worth of such apparently dramatic claims, we quickly run into the difficulty that no one seems to know at a more detailed organizational level what the productivity of government organizations is.

A whole swathe of analysis that has been developed over more than four decades in the analysis of private sector industries and firms remains in its infancy in the public sector. A start has recently been made on the macro-analysis of government productivity, at the level of national statistics, which we review in Chapter 2. But at the level of individual government departments and agencies the norm is still that managers have little systematic information on how productivity *at an organizational level* has changed in recent years, or how their performance in achieving improvements compares with other similar agencies.

In this chapter we first show how difficulties in the analysis of government sector productivity have led to the neglect of an important set of tools for improving the available data on government organizations' performance. As a result, little systematic progress has yet been made on analysing the factors that condition improvements or lack of improvement in how government carries out its activities *at the level of individual organizations* – a deficit that cries out for explanation. The second section briefly reviews how organizational productivity has been studied in the private sector over recent decades, showing what the key influences seem to have been on modern productivity growth. Lastly, we show how this analysis has begun to be slowly extended into the public sector, beginning with organizations operating in decentralized delivery systems (discussed in detail in Part II of this book). Analysis has been least effective for national or federal government departments and agencies (which are the focus of Part I).

1.1   BARRIERS TO ANALYSING GOVERNMENT PRODUCTIVITY

Productivity is defined as the ratio of outputs divided by inputs, and at first glance it seems to be a simple index. In fact, in the private sector, its measurement is mostly straightforward. The total volume valuation of outputs for a firm or an industry can be derived by multiplying the numbers of the outputs (units of goods and services produced and successfully marketed to customers) by the prices for which each has been sold. Price here automatically controls for the variations in the value of different products within and across firms. This allows us to derive a price-weighted measure of overall output that is then divided by a measure of total inputs to obtain a productivity ratio.

The fundamental difficulty of measuring productivity in government services has been that we do not have anything equivalent to a price for (most of) the many different services and goods that government departments and agencies produce. Public service outputs are generally supplied to citizens, firms or other stakeholders for free, or at highly subsidized prices. In many cases (for instance, policing and law and order functions, or defence spending) the consumption of public sector outputs is often made mandatory or imposed on citizens (some of whom may be very reluctant 'clients' of the services). So the conventional wisdom for almost all of the last century held that it was not feasible to value the diversity of government outputs – and hence we could not achieve any effective measure of the volume of outputs at an organizational level for government departments and agencies.

Instead, the predominant way in which government outputs were counted for national statistics and other purposes was by valuing the inputs that went into producing them – that is, by simply entering the costs of the government staff employed, and the materials and procurements and capital used up in their production. A single baleful implication followed. The productivity of government services (i.e., 'outputs' divided by inputs) was always automatically one, because it reduced to total inputs divided by total inputs. In other words, the productivity of government services was represented as always completely flat, decade after decade.

Of course, in practical public management terms, both governments and economists knew full well that this practice was a myth, a simple equation-filler for national statistical purposes. But faced with the methodological difficulties posed by the absence of public sector prices, it also became politically convenient for governments to go along with this myth at the national statistics level, because counting the *input* costs of government as part of national outputs tended to inflate GDP numbers. What's more, if private sector outputs slipped, and government increased its spending counter-cyclically to offset the risk of recession, then by definition national output started to recover straightaway, because the government part of it (defined by input costs) was already rising.

In addition, we shall see below that it was especially hard for central or federal government departments and agencies to develop indices to measure their own organizational productivity, chiefly because each government tends to have only one agency of each type – for instance, one national tax collecting body, one customs regulating agency, one education ministry or one social security agency. So there was nothing else in the country to compare these unique and often giant departments with. Cross-national comparisons might have provided a way forward, but in fact international bodies like the UN and the OECD have performed very poorly in addressing government productivity analysis (Van de Walle, 2008). Some countries and international organizations that at first seemed to have accepted the Atkinson Review (2005b) approach also backed off when the onset of recession made it seem likely to adversely affect their perceived growth numbers (Van Dooren, 2010). In addition, different countries' tax systems, education systems and so on vary a lot, making comparison across their unique central departments additionally difficult.

However, the neglect implied by the assumption that government productivity is flat did not mean that internal efforts to improve what government agencies are doing went by the board, or were small scale – they were instead extensive, but quite differently focused. One key role of elected politicians in liberal democracies has been to inject periodic new guidance impulses, new values, different priorities and alternative policy prescriptions into an otherwise essentially rather static government apparatus. Even in one-party systems (like China), or in 'semi-democratic' authoritarian systems with not very meaningful elections (like Russia or Singapore), the same role is fulfilled by clan, faction and sometimes ideology battles within the essentially oligarchic power structure. However, politicians' efforts overwhelmingly focus on redesigning and redirecting public policy in order to improve what they see as the effectiveness of the government.

Effectiveness can be defined as the level of politically or socially desired outcomes achieved, divided by the level of inputs used to produce them. But this is inherently a much broader and deeper concept than productivity, for effectiveness is often largely in the eye of the beholder. What any of us will see as being effective public policy will depend heavily on the values and beliefs that we hold about the good society, about social organization and about human nature.

Inside the government machine itself, two groups of people have devoted effort to the narrower tasks of making policy-making and implementation better. Some politicians (but still only a large minority at best) have been seriously committed to improving how the machinery of governance operates, especially a series of more reflective or 'out of the ordinary' prime ministers and presidents and their supporting officials. Second, many senior service public managers and unelected officials (both at senior and more junior levels) have long recognized that how well things are done matters a lot, and that it varies a great deal over time and across different government organizations. Inside government systems, one more persistent impulse for improvements has tended to come from finance ministers or treasuries who are anxious to save money, conserve national resources for the most urgent tasks and stem annual increases in the relative price of government outputs. Less commonly, personnel or human resources departments at the central level have played a role. So while the national statistics have counted government productivity as permanently flat, some politicians and most senior civil servants have struggled hard to improve how public policies are delivered and how administrative tasks have been accomplished.

Undoubtedly too, many of these improvement efforts have borne fruit in cutting costs or introducing new ways of working. But again the primary internal vehicle has tended to be a separate concept of government *efficiency*, which is primarily defined in terms of minimizing the amount of resources used to produce a given set of outputs. Inherently 'efficiency' measurement is very 'case by case' and it does not produce the kind of over-time data for whole-organizational performance that productivity series do for industry sectors or for private firms.

Indeed, the three characteristic ways in which public sector agencies have tended to improve their methods of working are both little concerned with outputs or output measurement:

1. *Efficiency drives* are special purpose exercises, occurring irregularly, often undertaken by new governments or by a government facing more than usually acute immediate fiscal pressures. They involve reviewing one or all departments' ongoing activities to see which might be pruned or cut back, often concentrating on areas where needs or technologies have changed since the last review, but policy commitments and delivery methods have not yet adjusted. Efficiency drives now typically involve finance ministries setting out in a top-down way a set of reduction targets for departments to achieve. How the targeted reductions are achieved in practice tends not to bother the finance ministry, so long as the financial numbers come out right. In practice, some proclaimed 'efficiency' drives are only retrenchment exercises that just involve departments or agencies stopping doing some of their existing activities ('real cuts'), rather than improving the way in which they do them. Others may achieve genuine productivity improvements, typically in recent decades by stripping out staff from administrative processes that can either be streamlined or automated more completely using IT.

2. *Mandatory efficiency dividends* are automatic annual reductions in the amount of money that finance ministries give to spending departments, usually fixed at a level of around a 2 or 3 per cent reduction per year across all government sectors. Each department knows at the start of any given year that they must be able to shave 2 or 3 per cent off their costs by the year end, largely irrespective of their individual situations. The common justification of such dividends is that they help introduce into the public sector a new discipline, one where continuously increasing productivity improvements are always expected. Instead of the old 'cost plus inflation' assumptions of officials in

earlier times, a given parcel of activities is now always expected to get cheaper to administer over time – for instance, because IT costs have fallen, or because improvements in delivery and procedures have been achieved. This message may or may not apply in different policy areas.

But it is important to note that the dividends can in fact be met in many different ways, many of which have no connection with improving productivity or even efficiency. A department where efficiency and productivity are actually stagnant can normally still shave its costs by the finance ministry's required amount – for example, by simply reducing its service quality (e.g., not answering phone calls, or piling up more unresolved cases) or by stopping doing some valuable activities that it previously undertook. And because dividends are cross-government they are just a priori funding changes with minimal impact in affecting how any given organization is managed. Dividends are not based on any individual analysis of how productivity levels are in fact changing across different departments or agencies, so for some agencies they are easy to meet, while in others they are far harder to achieve.

3.   *'Value for money' (VFM) analyses* are the typical kind of 'performance audit' undertaken by public sector audit agencies like the USA's Government Accountability Office (GAO), the UK's National Audit Office (NAO), the French Cour des Comptes and the European Court of Auditors (ECA). Across the OECD countries most other 'Supreme Audit Institutions' (SAIs, as they call themselves) look like or follow one or other of these models. The Anglo-American auditors – that is, GAO, NAO and the Canadian, Australian and New Zealand equivalents of NAO – are clear leaders in the development of 'performance audit' and VFM work. At the LSE Public Policy Group we have worked closely with the NAO and ECA over many years on improving VFM studies, and we have also undertaken some analysis for auditor-generals' offices in other countries (including Canada, Ireland, New Zealand and Hong Kong).

None of these audit agencies systematically includes analyses of government sector productivity in either their regular VFM work, or in their financial audit analyses. The key reason why not is a turf issue – productivity is rather squarely seen as something that lies within the purview of *internal audit and control* units in finance ministries and within national departments. Internal audit has been very little studied (but see Buratti et al., 2012 for a pioneering analysis). These government staff work closely with SAIs, but they jealously guard their zone of influence (following codes of conduct developed by the Institute of Internal Auditors). Under their existing legislation, SAIs feel that they cannot legitimately take on a function that is associated with the regular, month-on-month and year-on-year improvement of government services. This restriction applies even when internal auditors and improvement teams are clearly not themselves studying productivity series and trends, and have little idea of how they could or should do so.

Some elements of productivity analysis are incorporated into how SAIs in the 'advanced' OECD countries do performance audit, however, but chiefly on a 'case by case' basis. VFM studies are typically quite long documents, mainly using qualitative methods, put together because somebody politically powerful (usually in the legislature) is unhappy with an aspect of performance. Often, perhaps government ministers, executives or managers are also unhappy, and sometimes they welcome an external audit report in order to help bring about an internal agency change. Hence public auditors doing VFM work will often try to put together either an effectiveness analysis of how a particular policy is being implemented, or a limited comparison of performance in the target area X with other look-alike areas Y and Z. The auditors almost invariably find that the data available on outcomes is of worse quality and less extensive than statistics for outputs or activities undertaken. And because auditors are conservative and evidence-based people they tend to follow the better data, and hence to produce a VFM study that is something quite like a productivity analysis in at least comparing output or activity levels with inputs. But it is a one-off exercise. It does not form part of a continuous series, and does not culminate in any lasting gains in knowledge. It is only rarely expressed in the explicit ratio of outputs/inputs that defines productivity. In short, VFM analyses usually employ ad hoc methodologies that cannot be replicated across different government agencies or sectors. Thus, they do not provide a framework for comparison across the public sector.

Typically, then, the systematic and evidence-based analysis of government productivity has been neglected behind a cloud of 'confuser' practitioner discourses, Table 1.1 summarizes the key differences between productivity and the range of other concepts often used instead of it, or confused with it, inside the government services sector.

Looking more broadly at whether or not the 'productivity' label appears in or is systematically omitted from public management discourse, there are often two apparently opposed, but actually quite congruent, tendencies – both of which marginalize genuine productivity analysis. Sometimes for short periods the word 'productivity' will feature

*Table 1.1   What productivity in government means, and how it differs
from alternative performance concepts*

Key Term	Defined As:	Used For:
Productivity	The ratio of outputs produced divided by inputs used	Assessing how a given organization is succeeding in progressively developing its performance of activities and accomplishing of outputs, either over time, or by comparison with other similar organizations
Economy	Using the minimum feasible inputs in sustaining the organization's activities and producing its outputs	Ensuring that an agency's activity mix does not contain 'waste' or other avoidable costs. For instance, an economy drive might terminate services that are no longer well used, or whose rationale has diminished, or which duplicate offerings by other government agencies
Efficiency	(a) *Technical efficiency* is about minimizing the resources used in producing a given level of output (b) *Allocative efficiency* is about choosing the right mix of inputs and outputs, given their prices	Both terms can be used to identify the minimal amount of inputs (technical efficiency) or the right mix of inputs (allocative efficiency) that an organization needs to use to produce services
Effectiveness	The ratio of socially desirable outcomes achieved by a department, divided by its inputs. Any worthwhile effectiveness analysis must try to separate out and control for the impacts of all other causal factors that influence policy outcomes – a stage that is rarely achieved in public management contexts	Evaluating how far government organization is going about trying to achieve the outcomes within its 'mission' in the socially optimal manner. For instance, an agency might be doing good, but in a way that is more old-fashioned or not as socially relevant as it could be

Table 1.1 (continued)

Key Term	Defined As:	Used For:
Value for money (VFM)	Given the range of activities that the agency is undertaking, and the policy objectives that it has been set by policy-makers, is the agency going about implementing its goals and targets in an appropriate and cost-effective manner? This is a general or over-arching criterion and it may incorporate some reference to elements including productivity, economy and effectiveness. VFM analysis is a form of 'performance audit' where the assessment is normally qualitative, although informed by some systematic evidence. Analyses may (or may not) culminate in a clear overall 'VFM judgement'. For example in the UK the National Audit Office defines VFM as the economy, efficiency and effectiveness with which departments and other bodies have used their resources to achieve given policy goals	A broader concept than productivity or effectiveness, VFM analysis is useful in providing a rich, overall picture of whether politically defined 'desirable' societal outcomes are being achieved through agency activities in a 'lean' or cost-effective manner. VFM studies may also assist public managers, ministers, legislators and other stakeholders in determining what corrective or improvement actions could help improve performance

prominently on the lips of government executives, especially those who have newly come in from the private sector. But normally this fashion occurs without triggering or being based on any systematic data assembly that actually relates government organizations' outputs to their inputs. Instead, some officials and agencies will refer to productivity in ways that greatly over-enlarge the concept's scope, so that it becomes equivalent in meaning to just 'everything conventionally seen as good or worthwhile about agency performance'. For instance, in 1970 President Nixon created a National Commission on Productivity, covering both the public and private sectors. It published early works on improving productivity in local governments (Hatry and Fisk, 1971), but the scope of its government-related activities quickly enlarged to encompass a huge range of potentially efficiency-related matters. In fact it collected no systematic data at all on government sector productivity and was abolished in 1979.

Often the tendency to over-inflate a 'productivity' label is closely linked with the recurring 'management myth' that somehow better 'leadership' by top managers is always an essential or easily implemented answer to problems of poorly performing organizations. For instance, a 2010 online guide by the UK's official Local Government Improvement and Development body entitled *Productivity: Getting the Best Out of Your People* argues that:

> In an organisation that delivers many different services, it can be difficult to measure the impact of individual people or processes on complex, multidimensional outcomes. In recent years, local government performance monitoring has focused on inputs and outputs. As the regulatory regime moves towards a focus on outcomes, the measurement of productivity will become even more challenging. A number of approaches and tools are available to leaders and managers to improve the productivity of their organisation. This is not simply about making employees work harder. It's about:
>
> – the people you employ
> – the skills they have
> – the goals they are set
> – the systems and processes they use
> – how motivated they are.

Although initial lip service is paid to something called 'productivity' here, it quickly becomes apparent that it actually denotes no more than 'good organizational performance, in all its aspects'. Little or nothing relevant to any aspect of organizational performance is missing from the list above. In 2011 another UK think-tank broadened the concept even further, proclaiming that local councils should maximize what it termed 'social productivity' – a concept so apparently inclusive that it means only 'everything good' (Kippin and Lucas, 2011).

Alternatively, and far more often, the restrictive 'outputs divided by inputs' view of productivity is often rejected by public managers and politicians. Historically this stance has been strongly supported by most academics in 'public administration', who regard it as an inappropriate, 'economistic' concept to apply in the public services. A vehement denunciation of productivity analyses as reductionist and inadequate has especially predominated in US academic public administration, where a strong tradition runs from political scientist Dwight Waldo (1948) (who saw productivity analyses as 'anti-individual') to Mark Moore's (1995) defence of 'public service value'. These scholars argue that both the democratic governance and the impartial, egalitarian administration of public services require a qualitatively different style of services management to be adopted from those in the private sector. In this view how public services are delivered – in fair, democratically accountable and citizen-responsive ways – is every bit as politically and operationally important as the efficiency or efficacy of its implementation.

US federal agencies' personnel have often claimed a double uniqueness, not only pursuing 'public values' without private sector counterparts, but also being the only such organization in a country, having no worthwhile comparator organizations, except for overseas counterparts (Kelman, 2010). US public administration is also strongly ethno-centric, often making no reference to other countries' experiences, or treating them strictly as marginal phenomena (see, for instance, Wilson, 1989). Hence the use of productivity analyses has seemed both inapplicable and rather threatening (especially at the federal macro-level) – even though comparisons across the USA's 50 states have spawned far more systematic and quantitative academic analyses than anywhere else in the world. A similar hostile stance found a more limited endorsement amongst public administration conservatives in the UK and Europe. In addition, few analyses have covered technological change as a key dynamic in public administration (Pollitt, 2011). But in some countries (such as the Netherlands and Scandinavian countries) a more multi-disciplinary concept of public administration assigned economics more of a role in understanding government, and hence did not see productivity analyses as inapplicable (Van Dooren and Van de Walle, 2008).

Public services are also commonly seen by civil servants and other officials, and by their many allies in academic life, as inherently much more 'complex' to administer than those delivered in the private sector. Officials in government agencies must answer to many more 'principals' than private sector managers, and take account of many more (and often contested) public values. And government organizations cannot exclude 'difficult' or costly-to-serve groups from their client base, unlike private sector firms that can tailor whom they serve so as to attract profitable or low-cost customers and to repel unattractive business. For the many thousands of politicians, officials and academics who have adopted such unquestioned beliefs as articles of faith, it has been an easy step to reject any relevance for productivity analysis (outputs divided by inputs) within the public sector.

Such a restrictive focus on only one narrow aspect of organizational performance is instead seen as mechanistic and objectionable in a multi-factor government context. Looking at outputs/inputs offers only a ridiculously impoverished, 'bean-counting' view of public management – one that ignores all the democratic and citizen-responsive process benefits that make the sphere of government production and public services so separate and distinctive. Only a small minority of public management work has questioned whether public and private organizations are not in fact quite comparable in the range of pressures acting upon them (Bozeman, 2004). After all, many private firms and industries also operate in intensely regulated environments that are politically sensitive and subject to strong scrutiny by shareholders, competitors, market analysts, consumer groups, media commentators, trade unions and a wide range of campaign groups and charities espousing green and social causes.

Our approach here rejects both the tendency to inflate productivity so that the concept becomes vacuous, and the effort to declare it irrelevant *tout court* to the government sector. In our view neither strategy is at all helpful. Public sector productivity is (and must remain) a single, deliberately limited measure, focusing solely on how many outputs are produced for a given level of inputs (see Figure 1.1). It especially needs to be carefully separated from the quite distinct concept of policy *effectiveness*, which is much more broadly concerned with how the outputs produced translate (or not) into desired policy outcomes. It also needs to be kept largely separate from discussions about efficiency or value for money, which are distinct concepts unlinked to the systematic accumulation of data on organizational performance that is our focus here.

Figure 1.1 also brings out one of the most important and distinctive aspects of a focus on organizational productivity in the government sector, namely the close connection between it and the adoption of innovations inside government organizations. Just as technological change has been a strong and vital driver of productivity improvements in private corporations and industries, so we should expect that innovations will play key roles in government sector productivity changes in several ways:

- improving the conversion of inputs into outputs for established activities, for example, by reducing the staff numbers needed to accomplish a task;
- introducing new inputs into the production of established outputs, as with the successive waves of back-office computer automation of record-keeping;
- improving productivity using qualitatively new inputs, for instance, pervasively deploying networked automatic cameras on roads to catch speeding motorists; and
- introducing new outputs, for instance, creating electronic tax forms that are simpler and quicker for people or firms to submit.

Yet against 'maximalist' views, Figure 1.1 also makes clear that many macro-innovation or political or policy-level factors in the public sector

Figure 1.1   How innovation influences productivity improvement via the introduction of new inputs, outputs and outcomes in government organizations, and why the analysis of productivity improvements need to be clearly separated from the analysis of effectiveness

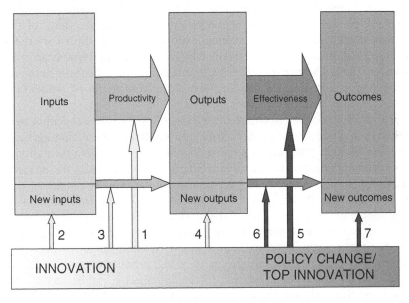

Types of innovation impacts: included in productivity analysis
1 improving the productivity of existing inputs;
2 introducing new inputs;
3 improving productivity using new inputs;
4 introducing new outputs.

Effectiveness analysis, excluded from productivity analysis
5 improving the effectiveness of existing outputs;
6 increasing policy effectiveness via new outputs;
7 introducing new outcomes.

cannot be incorporated into the study of productivity. So productivity analysis does not address at all the effectiveness changes labelled, 5, 6 and 7 in Figure 1.1, concerning improving the effectiveness of outcomes or devising new outcomes. Critically important though they may be for how the government sector performs, the politically driven changes in effectiveness fall outside the scope of our analysis.

It might be argued by critics here that some policy changes should be recognized as top-level innovations, and hence appropriately incorporated into any analysis of productivity. But which should these be? No clear methods exist for distinguishing genuine innovations from the many top-level changes that only represent a 'churning' of policy solutions, often because of the alternation of one political party in power followed by another. Similarly, many policy changes just 'recycle' earlier approaches that cannot be usefully seen as innovative. (For example, think of the domestic and international strategies of supporting birth control or urging teenagers to sexual abstinence pursued by Democrat and Republican presidents in the USA since the 1980s.) This difficulty strengthens the rationale for focusing narrowly on productivity as the conversion of inputs into outputs within departments and agencies.

The next objections to counter are those of officials or academics who argue that productivity analyses are inapplicable in government agencies because services generate intangible 'public value'; or because national government departments are unique – or, if not unique, they are far more 'complex' to administer than private sector processes. Advocates of this view argue that these factors must somehow be taken into account in calculating any valid measure of the productivity of government services. Yet, the counter view might be that government organizations that opt for complex-to-administer and hence high-cost alternatives when simpler alternatives exist have simply chosen to be less productive, and such decisions should not be compensated for in determining public sector productivity. Similarly the objections of uniqueness or lack of comparators, and of government sector complexity, can all be simply met by studying government productivity changes in more sophisticated ways that are fully adapted to the public services context. In Chapter 2 we outline the key considerations here and show how new developments in the field in the last decade have resolved or ameliorated many of the traditional objections to deploying rich organizational productivity analyses in the public sector. Productivity analyses always need to be informed by an in-depth understanding of what public agencies do, what their policy goals and missions are, and what counts as service quality in their sphere of operations.

1.2   KEY FACTORS SHAPING PRODUCTIVITY CHANGES IN THE PRIVATE SECTOR

The concept of productivity has developed a great deal, from its initial origins in the engineering analysis of particular machines, to its economic conception and wide application at the firm and industry sector level. A common thread running through these different stages is a strong linkage between productivity and the analysis of technological change, which is now consensually seen as one of the primary drivers of modern economic and social advances.

The engineering concept of productivity is:

$$\frac{\text{Volume of total output}}{\text{Volume of total inputs}}$$

where volume is denoted in terms of units of output (for example, widgets produced by a machine tool in a time period) and in terms of units of input (for instance, hours of labour involved, units of material consumed, or power used etc.). The engineering approach assumes that at the level of an individual machine (say) the outputs all have a pretty homogeneous quality – for instance, because any given machine (set up in a particular way) produces a largely undifferentiated stream of products in the short term.

This simple engineering approach is then easily scaled up to the scientific study of the performance of the same firm or even the same industry over a long period of time, so long as the simple formula above is adjusted to take account of product differentiation, and of differentiation in the inputs used up in producing outputs. The formula now becomes:

$$\frac{\text{Total output * quality of output}}{\text{Total inputs * quality of inputs}}$$

The engineering concept as a fully specified idea has long been attractive to industry analysts (and to governments seeking to improve national technological performance) because it seems to get rather directly at technical change. It places central importance on technology innovations and reorganizations of production in expanding national economic performance.

In *the economic concept* of productivity, however, the focus shifts to outputs that can be sold to customers in a market and are competitive with other alternative products by offering consumers a welfare gain compared to other products (Tinbergen, 1942; Solow, 1957). The economic concept of productivity also has to recognize that the number, scope and variety of quality permutations in modern economies are all vast, while continuous quality changes in outputs are now pervasive to the point of being universal. The older engineering conception of homogeneous products measured in volumetric terms hence has almost no applicability, except on the most micro of scales. Economists solve this apparently huge extra difficulty in a characteristically simple fashion, by letting the price at which outputs are sold become the key indicator of how complex and high quality these products are. In the same way, the non-comparabilities of inputs (such as labour, material costs and capital equipment usage) can be simply dealt with by multiplying input volumes by their prices. As a result the productivity formula shifts again, to become:

$$\frac{\text{Outputs volume * output prices}}{\text{Inputs volume * input prices}} = \frac{\text{Total value of outputs}}{\text{Total value of inputs}}$$

This approach is not quite as simple as it may appear. A range of assumptions need to be made to allow these 'price-weighted' measures of outputs to be used, about the relatively uniform production mode across a given industry and about the strength and effectiveness of market competition.

In a perfectly competitive market all firms are 'price-takers' in a single, well-integrated system of exchanges, so that a firm will only be able to charge a higher price for its product if in fact its goods embody extra value for its customers compared to the products of rival companies. In pure economic theory terms, the benefits of our knowledge gain here are tremendous, because we can be certain that if a firm upgrades its products at a constant price then social welfare has unambiguously increased. However, if markets are oligopolistic or monopolistic, or consumers are not autonomous and discriminating, then firms may have the power to fix prices and to load their products with unwanted features at higher cost to consumers that in fact have little value for them, but allow prices to be raised (Galbraith, 1969). Here the linkage between higher prices and increased value to customers is no longer necessarily applicable, and the social welfare implications of technological changes and product 'improvements' may become more problematic to assess.

In the private sector *the key drivers* that make productivity grow over time operate at two levels – first, at the level of the industry taken as a whole, and second, at the organizational level in response to technological, logistic and structural changes within firms themselves. Given competitive capital markets and competitive product markets, the more efficient producers can expand their outputs. Accordingly they should sell more of their goods by drawing away the market share of less efficient, less technically dynamic or slower-moving competitors. Hence over time, production shifts from inefficient to more efficient producers. In study after study, across a wide range of industries, around half of all industry productivity growth can be attributed to this changing market share effect.

The remaining part of productivity change (which we may think of as around half in the private sector) is due to technical changes and improved organization, management practices and logistics inside firms and their delivery chains. In manufacturing firms, where the outputs are goods, technology changes often reflect research and development investment in new (or newly adopted) applications of science-based or engineering-based knowledge, as well as improved design and product development processes. Traditionally much of the literature on innovation led by R&D has concentrated on manufacturing, where changes can be tracked by such well-developed metrics of innovation as the numbers of patents and trade-marks, or the incidence of initial public offerings (IPOs) by technology start-up companies. Improvements in the storage and use of information within firms have been very important in IT (information technology)-intensive industries, especially since the mid-1990s. Information and communication technologies (ICTs) have been the catalysts for some of the most important developments, including the advent of flatter hierar-chies in large corporations, so-called 'disintermediation' (or 'cutting out the middle man') processes in e-commerce, and the development of new methods of marketing and identifying and reaching customers in the per-vasively digital, post-internet modern era.

A strong feature of modern ICT-led productivity growth is that it has extended strongly from manufacturing into major private sector services industries, such as banking, insurance, accounting, retailing and the com-mercial delivery of a wide range of professional services. Yet services, defined in contrast to goods by *The Economist* as 'anything sold in trade that could not be dropped on your foot' (Quinn, 1992, p. 6) are harder to study than goods manufacture. Some key modern services (such as mobile phones and computing, low-cost aviation and healthcare) are strongly technology based and driven, often with new products acting as keys for consumers to access a flow of continuing services. Some observers have even noted a tendency for many more, perhaps almost all, goods to be packaged and redefined as flows of services.

Yet across the service sector many productivity-enhancing changes are at root organizational or procedural innovations, and they can be only very poorly tracked by conventional innovation metrics. In areas such as banking or insurance, new products rarely involve physical goods changes that can be patented, but instead work by finding new combinations of 'characteristics' that appeal to customers at feasible costs. Similarly, quality factors are much more integrally and yet intangibly or diffusely bound up in the development of services than they are with goods, espe-cially in complex services that depend strongly on personal interactions between providers and customers.

For all these reasons it is often much harder to identify product improve-ments in services except by noticing shifts in the observed pattern of cus-tomers' demands – often in response to what some observers term 'hidden innovations' (Harris and Halkett, 2007). Similarly, quality improvements or deteriorations are often harder to track in service industries – for instance, the extent to which the growth of low-cost airlines has been achieved by substituting lower-quality standards in civil aviation services for previous formats. Yet still the prices paid by customers allow us to index (however imperfectly) the quality of private sector services, a key saving grace in an otherwise much fuzzier area.

In an influential analysis of 'relative price effects', William Baumol (1967) and others (Baumol et al., 1989) argued that the economic importance of low productivity sectors would tend to grow over time. This effect reflects the tendency of goods prices to fall fastest in high productivity sectors, where capital intensity increases, organizational improvements are most rapid and physical technological changes are concentrated (Jorgenson et al., 2007) – as in the Moore's Law prediction that the cost of handling a given amount of information in IT processor chips would halve every two years (Moore, 2006). By contrast in low productivity sectors, factor prices (especially the wages for staff) will tend to rise at least at the overall rate of inflation in the economy as a whole, but without delivering comparable levels of productivity increases – so that these services become relatively more expensive to produce over time. The strong implication is that the share of the economy absorbed by low productivity sectors will tend to expand, unless there are strong countervailing developments.

Amongst countervailing factors possible here, major technology changes may unlock a revolution where whole new areas of higher-tech production start up, as in the 1930s with electric goods. Here then high productivity industries may either grow or at least maintain their overall share of the economy. Alternatively, efficiency may also rise strongly in formerly low productivity sectors, as some observers claim happened in many US service industries through modern e-commerce disintermediation effects – so much so that 'Baumol's disease' was declared 'cured' by Bosworth and Triplett (2003). Nonetheless, the Baumol effect tends to reassert itself ineluctably over time. For instance, Baumol pointed out that the number of orchestra players needed for a Beethoven symphony performance cannot change over time, so that concert tickets will tend to rise in relative price over time. Similar barriers may apply quite widely. So IT-led productivity surges in services can reduce the imbalances for a time, but they may not redress the long-term growth in the services sector's share of GDP, generally seen as partly reflecting productivity lagging changes in manufacturing.

Looking in more detail at what specific factors drive modern productivity changes, private corporations have invested heavily in improving their

ICT and management practices. Yet, how these two factors specifically interplay has often been subject to some controversy. The largest literature analyses the role of ICT in the private sector. Here scholars have usually followed an approach where they estimate a production function in which ICT capital is considered as a separate input (the 'parametric' approach discussed in Chapter 2). Using regression analysis, these works then attempt to test whether ICT expenditure is statistically related to output. Early analyses following this approach found no clear evidence that ICT investment was significantly and positively related to output, coining the idea of an 'IT paradox' – where 'You can see the computer age everywhere but in the productivity statistics' (Solow, 1987, p. 36; Bailey and Gordon, 1988).

However, later research since the 1990s has reversed the position, finding strong evidence of a statistically positive relationship from ICT on productivity at the firm level (Lichtenberg, 1995; Brynjolfsson and Hitt, 1996). Earlier studies may not have found a significant relationship due to measurement problems caused by relying on very aggregated data. So the modern consensus largely attributes the 'IT paradox' problem to this approach (Lichtenberg, 1995; Lehr and Lichtenberg, 1998; Bloom et al., 2005; Aral et al., 2007). European studies were slower to find the same positive IT effects, but a recent compilation of relevant evidence shows similar patterns (O'Mahoney et al., 2010).

Also transcending the apparent 'IT paradox' of the 1980s and early 1990s, Brynjolfsson and Hitt (2003) found that computerization makes a contribution to measured productivity and output growth in the short term (using one-year time lags for new technology to have an effect). This is consistent with normal commercial expectations of quick returns to computer investments. However, they also found that the productivity and output contributions associated with computerization were up to five times greater over long periods (using five-year to seven-year time lags to look for impacts). Thus, investment in ICT may pay off most significantly after a certain 'adaptation period', an insight also successfully tested by Bartel et al. (2007) in their analysis of firms in the valve manufacturing industry.

A partly alternative explanation holds that a dialectic of ICT advances in recent years in networking (which foster organizational centralization, especially of control functions) and in databases (which support decentralized work processes) may have substantially improved the contribution that ICTs can make to productivity, when allied with other organizational and business process changes (Bloom et al., 2009b). Following a production approach, Bresnahan et al. (2002) analysed a sample of 300 large US firms and they found that ICT investment contributed strongly to increased output and productivity. The study also employed survey data on organizational changes and management practices and was one of the first to demonstrate that ICT investment *combined with* changes in management practices leads to increased productivity. This key contribution is often referred to as the 'organizational complementarity' hypothesis. A similar approach has been followed by Caroli and Van Reenen (2001) and Bloom et al. (2005) in their analysis of manufacturing firms, who also find support for the complementarity hypothesis about ICT and management practices.

More recently, in an analysis with panel data from 680 small and medium-sized (SME) Italian manufacturing firms, Giuri et al. (2008) found that ICT positively affects output and productivity. However, they did not find that ICT and organizational changes are related to increased productivity, contrary to the organizational complementarity hypothesis. The authors explain their finding on the grounds that compared with large firms, SMEs face greater difficulties in managing different inventions at the same time – especially in finding and retaining highly skilled personnel and re-engineering their business processes to fully integrate ICT into their organization. Accordingly, they argue that the interaction between ICT and management may be more complex than perhaps analysts initially thought.

Most private sector studies have traditionally relied chiefly on measures of ICT expenditure to gauge organizational commitment to new computerization, automation or internet-based technologies. Yet while a firm may spend significantly on buying new IT equipment, the specific impact of ICT infrastructure will depend on how much it is used by the firm's employees for productivity-enhancing activities. Especially since the advent of the internet and web era, the most advanced technologies are no longer necessarily the most expensive ones in equipment or staffing terms. The costs of web applications are generally far more modest than earlier mainframe computers or complex organizational networks. So the primary barriers to adopting web-based technologies may now be cultural and organizational conservatism, lack of appropriate expertise amongst staff, and perhaps similar gaps amongst customers or key stakeholders also. Accordingly, more recent studies have increasingly sought to employ more direct measures of ICT use. For example, in a study of a large recruiting firm, Aral et al. (2007) rely on innovative measures of actual ICT use, rather than on expenditure, to gain a much clearer picture of the impact of information technologies. They found that ICT use positively affects revenue and productivity in their detailed case study. Other studies in the private sector have adopted a similar approach (for instance, Bhansali and Brynjolfsson, 2008).

1.3 FACTORS SHAPING PRODUCTIVITY CHANGES IN THE GOVERNMENT SECTOR

There are two fundamental and well-founded reasons to believe that productivity advances in the public sector are inherently likely to be slower or of lesser scale than in the private sector. The first is simply that organizations rarely perform well in achieving goals to which they pay little or no attention. So over the last 80 years the widespread neglect of productivity analyses across the government sector itself makes it very unlikely that productivity growth there can possibly parallel those achieved in private sector firms and industries, where enhancing productivity has been the focus of sustained attention, careful analysis and multiple improvement efforts. We shall see in Chapter 2 that in at least some large national government agencies in some countries this position began to be rectified from the late 1980s. More recently, national statisticians have also sought to measure productivity across very large sectors within the public services (such as all of education, or all of healthcare as national systems). Recent academic work has also made considerable headway in analyses of performance across networks of decentralized public service agencies (Jones and Thompson, 2007). But these newer developments still do not even begin to compare with the huge weight of managerial expertise and academic attention devoted to improving the organizational performance of private sector firms and industries. So the probability seems high that the unexamined productivity of government organizations is not increasing as fast.

Second, in the absence of strong and vigorous industrial competition within the government sector, the transfer of outputs from unproductive to more productive firms (which accounts for around half of all productivity advances in private sector industries over any given time period) either may not happen at all in the government sector, or will happen only in very weak ways. Public services have traditionally been delivered in the form of comprehensive national, regional or local monopolies. Thus OECD countries at national level generally have one tax collection agency, one social security agency, one defence department, and so on. At regional level, each state or regional government again provides its range of services within its territory without any competitors or alternatives. Finally, urban or local governments or local-level quasi-governmental agencies are also local monopolists within their area, in supplying environmental or planning services, providing local policing, or running local schools and hospitals.

Many past administrative reforms have been devoted to removing any 'duplication' or 'overlaps' of government services, and to pruning out any 'slack' capacity within them – although slack is exactly what is needed for any competition between providers to flourish. At best then there can be 'competition by comparison' between decentralized agencies in large public service networks at local level, but not even this is feasible at central or regional level. Government practices also usually encompass only modest rewards for those agencies performing well, and few penalties for those that are lagging in performance – whose clientele are largely locked into a single dominant supplier. Hence the 'ecological' or 'stay fit to survive' pressures on government sector organizations are likely to be very weak.

The root of the problem here was well captured by the US political scientist Herbert Kaufman in a 1976 book that asked *Are Government Organizations Immortal?* – to which his answer was 'Sort of'. Normally it takes a considerable amount of societal effort and political lobbying to get a new function inscribed on the restricted list of 'essentially governmental' functions that must be provided as public services, not least because of the strong initial 'gates' erected by finance ministries or treasuries. So once established, public services tend already to draw on strong support from beneficiary groups and stakeholders. New departments and agencies also prudentially tend to build out their political support amongst legislators and allied interest groups, typically by adding in protective layers through accreting extra functions to their original missions. Consequently, so long as agencies can survive the perilous first years after their initial creation, most established government departments and agencies are very long-lived organizations indeed, with relatively few complete organizational 'deaths' occurring.

Of course, depending on their institutional status, organizations in the public sector can be re-branded, de-merged from their current 'parent' department, or merged with neighbouring agencies. In 'Westminster system' polities such as the UK, this 'making and breaking of Whitehall departments' is an exceptionally frequent occurrence (White and Dunleavy, 2010). Also in the UK at the sub-Whitehall level the degree of organizational churn is (if anything) even greater, both in terms of the numbers of organizations affected and the costs of rearrangements. The National Audit Office (2010a) counted over 90 significant reorganizations in just five years 2005–09, at a minimum cost to UK taxpayers of £780 million. Other 'Westminster' systems (such as Canada, Australia and New Zealand) also reorganize more than the OECD norm, but not as much as the UK. At the other end of the spectrum, the US federal government has almost always maintained a relatively static structure of departments in the post-Hoover reorganization period from 1952 to now. The one giant exception was the creation of a new Department of Homeland Security (a new mega-unit integrating 28 previous departments and agencies) in 2002 after the 9/11 attacks (Bullock et al., 2006). However, even in Washington there have been more frequent alterations at the sub-departmental (or 'Office') level.

The key sources of reorganizations and churning within the government sector are political, chiefly the advent of new governing parties, prime ministers, presidents or governors – who must seek to impose new priorities upon the administrations they inherit as soon as they gain office (DiIulio et al., 1993; White and Dunleavy, 2010). There are also longer-term or more 'cumulated' pressures on government systems to change their structures in response to new pressures in their wider organizational environments. Key factors here are new issues and political priorities creating 'acute' pressures; the onset of repeated crises in particular areas of social life needing highly focused political and administrative attention; or more drawn-out malaise ('incubated' problems) in how a set of public policies are operating (Polsby, 1985). These pressures for change mean that the more recent academic debate about Kaufman's 'immortality' proposition has tended to qualify further his picture of extraordinary stasis in public sector organizational arrangements (Peters and Hogwood, 1982; Lewis, 2002).

Some public choice theorists have even developed accounts of a 'governmental market' where bureaucracies tussle ceaselessly for budget and turf gains (Breton, 1998), where most contracts are strongly contested and old-style public monopolies are a thing of the past. Additional components argue for the efficacy of democratic control processes (Wittman, 1995) – for instance, the interest group process ensures that policy responds sensitively to the balance of costs and benefits in different policy technologies and proposals for subsidizing services provision (Becker, 2003, 2005).

The growth of governmental contracting may also have had some countervailing impacts, by enlarging the scope of government services that are at some level competed for. Famously the 'new public management' (NPM) period from the mid-1980s to the mid-2000s placed a premium on separating out within government the 'purchaser' roles of defining contracts and commissioning procurements from the 'producer' role of delivering services or undertaking contract supply (Dunleavy et al., 2006b; Christensen and Lægreid, 2011; Halligan, 2011). Over nearly two decades the strong NPM countries (like the UK, Australia and New Zealand) brought in more and more mandatory competitive contracts. A substantial 'para-state' of government contractors developed in the private sector on a grand scale, accounting for 6.1 per cent of GDP in Britain by 2008 (BIS, 2008; Oxford Economics, 2008a and 2008b; CBI, 2009). The para-state chiefly has involved giant companies in areas like government IT

(Dunleavy et al., 2008), and in the much-extended zone of defence contracting. Some firms now operate on a transnational or globalized scale and claim 'best in world' expertise (Dunleavy, 1994). On a much smaller scale the para-state also began to involve many third sector organizations in areas like the delivery of social policy, but their overall share remained small. By 2007–08 total UK public spending on procured services reached £79 billion and on goods topped £67 billion. Taken together these areas almost matched public sector spending on wages and salaries, which was £159 billion (Oxford Economics, 2008a, Figure 2.1).

In a few countries, quasi-market systems inside major public services have also been pursued as a way of further enlarging the capacity for public services production to shift to more efficient suppliers (LeGrand, 2007). For instance, the Australian schools system sees public and private schools competing for children (customers) and associated public funding. In the UK National Health Service, and in Britain's locally managed schools system, hundreds of local providers are bound together into an integrated public service delivery system. Here there is some capacity for 'customers' (and hence associated tax-financed budget parcels) to migrate from inefficient or poor-quality providers to other providers nearby with better services on offer. Adding in new rights for citizens to choose where they have a hospital operation carried out, or for groups of parents dissatisfied with current choices to set up their own 'free schools' and get public subsidy (as in Sweden and since 2010 in the UK) adds an additional element to internal competition in the government sector.

But historically even such quasi-market changes have normally only operated in a limited way, especially at the margins of neighbouring public authority areas in more densely populated urban areas. Typically also, competition processes must be incremental – they cannot go far without jeopardizing the organizational and financial stability of the overall system and the state's ability to guarantee that services are universally available to citizens in a convenient and locally accessible manner. In particular, changes to run down or close poor providers or to expand good providers are usually quite slow and carefully regulated – because Western electorates will not normally tolerate structures for delivering public services that risk becoming chaotic or ineffective.

So the enhanced use of contracting, quasi-markets and intra-governmental competition between policy sectors, taken together with competition between alternative priorities and policy technologies, may have somewhat speeded up how the government sector moves the production of public services across from less efficient or productive providers towards better ones. But such moves have little of the *automatic and rapid reaction* to be expected in private sector industries. NPM changes have at best put in place some very slow-operating analogies to the strong and quick-acting ecological competition (Hannan and Freeman, 1993) that occurs in the most dynamic private industry sectors, like the restaurant sector where many thousand new start-ups and closures of existing outlets occur every year. The scale of any demand shifts from less productive to more productive organizations and policy spheres within the government sector will be at best a tiny fraction of that in competitive private industries.

Hence it follows that across the government sector, we are normally (and probably inherently) far more reliant on within-organization factors to drive through productivity improvements and to generate innovations. In this regard a large literature on the virtues of profit-maximizing firms as innovators (such as almost all writing by property rights economists) already takes a deeply pessimistic view of the incentives for individual officials to promote innovation, compared to those in the private sector:

> Government organizations do not benefit from the service of wealth-seeking entrepreneurs. Even if entrepreneurs were successful in initiating or restructuring government organizations for maximal productivity, there is no mechanism by which the entrepreneurs benefit more than other taxpayers, and there is no guarantee that taxes will be reduced as a result of increased efficiency. (Bozeman, 2004, p. 53)

Especially lacking are the strong incentive mechanisms – such as large 'prize money' salaries for chief executives, the lure of 'initial public offerings' (IPOs), or bonus schemes that capture any equivalent of improvements in 'shareholder value' for top executives' pay. On the other hand, Bozeman (ibid., p. 107) notes that: 'Research organizations of immense importance to national productivity, innovation and security are found in both government and industry'. And in recent times one of the effects of new public management reforms was to increase senior government officials' pay (for a time, before austerity conditions returned), and to link it via 'performance pay' to the achievement of wider organizational goals, and of cost reductions in particular.

Especially important influences on innovation rates are likely to be differing organizational or bureaucratic 'cultures', formed by formal and informal rules, mores and long-term values, which can determine and reflect members' values, beliefs and attitudes (Kerr and Slocum, 1987):

> Virtually all organizational changes involve changes in the behavior of organizational members. Employees must learn and routinize these behaviors in the short term, and leaders must institutionalize them over the long haul so that new patterns of behavior displace old ones. (Fernandez and Rainey, 2006, p. 172)

Organizational cultures are often expressed most starkly and completely in the production of artefacts (Schein, 2010, Ch. 2), including the internal organizational architecture of a department or agency, and (crucially for our current analysis) the codification of its business processes inscribed in its IT systems. In what Mintzberg (1983) calls 'machine bureaucracy' task areas (like social security, taxation and the control of immigration) the centrality of ICT investments for administrative change and policy capabilities has been strongly manifest since the later 1960s (Margetts, 1998). Here 'legacy' IT systems built up over decades created immensely cumbersome 'artefacts' whose internal complexity and accumulated characteristics then severely constrained both policy change and organizational performance (Dunleavy et al., 2008).

Yet, it is also possible to change public sector organizations through at least three different mechanisms:

1. *'Political' or top-down reorganizations* are important, as discussed above. In centralized countries, like the UK, one of the most typical consequences has been that waves of 'inorganic' change occur in agencies and departments – grounded in and responding to the ideology of newly elected governing party and their allied interest groups, and not in the 'organic' development of innovations in each agency and department separately.

2. *Changes in purely managerial ideologies and policy 'fashions'* have a great deal of influence within the public sector, partly because there the external control of professions is typically far less than in the private sector, and the level of professional autonomy far greater (Dunleavy, 1982). Cycles of public management change – such as the transition from post-war 'progressive public administration' models to NPM models – can thus have speedy and wide reverberations in many disparate organizations. Organizations' performance is so poorly monitored that executives rely on agencies performing 'rituals of modernization' to gauge which are well managed and which are hidebound (Meyer and Scott, 1992). Under NPM, many impulses for reorganization reflected belated responses to waves of fashionable management practices in the private sector.

3. *Technological impulses from the private sector and more recently from civil society* can also have strong effects, as in the development of business computing since the advent of personal computers from around 1976, and the development of the internet and online services since 1995. Often public sector organizations respond after substantial time lags in 'catch up' mode to private sector changes that they initially resisted or stood aloof from (Dunleavy et al., 2008, Chs 2, 6–8). But

perhaps these adoption delays have tended to reduce in duration. In a period of rapid technological change it may be unavoidable that both government internal architectures and complex IT systems will need to be comparable to those operating in private sector organizations. Indeed the IT development of some parts of the public sector has seemed to even up with those of comparable business sectors at some periods, especially in the largest-scale government organizations, before relapsing again, as since the advent of social media (Dunleavy and Margetts, 2010; Margetts and Dunleavy, 2012).

In many professionalized service delivery areas it appears reasonable to assume that productivity changes occurring in the private sector will tend to be generalized quite quickly to public sector counterpart activities. For instance, it seems deeply unlikely that productivity should increase consistently in private sector hospitals, but not in analogous public sector ones, carrying out very similar tasks with similar technologies and common professional staff. Similarly, we might expect improvements in office IT to positively affect productivity in file-moving public sector occupations (van der Torre et al., 2007). The multiplier expectations in (1) and (2) above also provide some grounds for expecting public sector changes to be particularly rapid and blanket, if 'critical mass' in adopting new innovations can only be achieved.

UK government especially shows a strong track record of responding to external pressures for modernization, especially to long-run changes in how private sector business operates, and to multiple short-term political impulses. However, if the leaders of government departments and agencies have long operated within (and hence internalized) a conservative culture resistant to change, then even if top political decisions impose major organizational reforms the detailed ways in which changes are implemented may have little impact on organizational performance and rather minimal change in productivity over time.

A significant management literature supports this expectation. Schein (2010) has argued that the reason so many change efforts run into resistance or outright failure is traceable to the inability of senior managers and leaders to effectively unfreeze resistances and create readiness for change before attempting a change induction. In a similar vein, Cooper (1994) earlier argued that an inertial conservative culture often strongly affects the implementation of new IT systems across different organizations. More recently, Ashworth et al. (2009) have shown that formal and informal institutional arrangements within an organization may mediate, and thus deviate from, the original objectives of performance-enhancing change measures. The phenomenon of 'permanently failing organizations' that survive for long periods in protected private sector niches adds weight here (Meyer and Zucker, 1989).

In the specific field of public management, Dunleavy et al. (2008, Ch. 9; Margetts and Dunleavy, 2012) have noted how public managers whose approaches were shaped during the heyday of the NPM may resist the implementation of significant organizational changes aiming to simplify procedures and move services online, which they describe as part of a new 'quasi-paradigm' style of public management change, called digital era governance (DEG).

How do these rather broad-gauge or top-level considerations come into specific focus on government productivity here? Thirty years ago, Jackson (1982, p. 196) asked 'What do the studies that have been conducted reveal about public sector productivity?' and responded cautiously: 'This is not an easy question to answer. Many of the studies are of varying quality, and of those which have been conducted in a careful and scientific manner, the majority conclude with the warning that their results are tentative and highly qualified by the assumptions made'. The early difficulties of measuring government outputs created barriers to measuring productivity change for many decades (Jackson, 1982, pp. 192–4), which were slowly overcome first in decentralized policy systems where comparative analysis became more feasible with improving output measures (Jackson, 1995 and 1997; Simpson, 2006).

Subsequently, however, an improved literature has grown up that employs similar approaches to those used in the private sector to measure productivity and its determinants in specific government agencies. As output measurement in the public sector became better developed in the 1990s, partly as a result of new public management and partly reflecting earlier progress in cost accounting and budgeting systems, so it became apparent that organizational productivity within government could be measured by weighting an agency's different outputs by the costs of producing them. In this sense, it could be possible to control for the varying values and significance of diverse public sector outputs. This cost-weighted output measure could then be divided by a measure of total inputs to obtain a productivity ratio. In the UK, this approach was first developed by the ONS from 1998 and it was then endorsed by the Atkinson Review (2005b). In other words, the public sector counterpart of price-weighted outputs (volume of units ∗ unit price) could be cost-weighted outputs. In Chapter 2 we explore in detail how the cost-weighting of outputs can be accomplished. We need only note here that this was the critical breakthrough that allowed interest in measuring how far government productivity does grow, first amongst scholars and later national statistics agencies, and later at the organizational level amongst some public managers.

By this stage the increased focus on IT investments in large national organizations in private sector firms elicited efforts to replicate similar studies in the government sector. For example, Lehr and Lichtenberg (1998) found a positive relationship between IT capital and output in their study of a number of US government agencies from 1987 to 1992. Likewise, Mukhopadhyay et al. (1997) also found a positive impact between IT capital and productivity in the US Post Service.

As in the private sector, recent scholars have also focused on the role of organizational changes, which have always been best studied in decentralized agencies carrying out common functions, where both regression analyses and data envelopment approaches can be applied (see Carrera et al., 2009, Ch. 1). For instance, Garicano and Heaton (2010) applied measures of organizational changes to a large panel of US police departments and found that management changes were positively related to partial productivity and output estimates. They especially noted that increasing IT investments on its own had little effect. Only when IT investments were accompanied by managerial and business process changes did positive performance improvements result.

Conclusions

Transposed to the public sector, productivity has been seen as valuable in indicating how efficiently public resources are employed in providing government sector services. The measurement of productivity has been seen as an important way in which elected politicians can hold government sector organizations accountable for their performance (Van de Walle, 2008). It can additionally provide managers with some key data they need to improve performance. Charting productivity changes also helps citizens and customers judge the value that government creates for them (Behn, 2003).

Yet for a very long period the study of government productivity at the organizational level has been neglected, attracting very little attention compared with that expended on private sector industries and firms. Most managers in the public services have little experience with productivity analysis, even though they may have some extensive efficiency-orientated or effectiveness-orientated datasets. This difference has persisted amongst academic analysts and public managers although in the modern period the public and private sectors often provide similar services. For example, if we expect private sector healthcare to grow its productivity each year, should we not expect at least somewhat similar processes to be occurring in public hospitals doing the self-same tasks? The business processes of government bureaucracies have also been extensively reviewed and transformed on private sector lines – at least, as understood by many advocates of new public management and many academics, both those for and against such changes.

From the 1990s onwards, and especially since the early 2000s, efforts to study government sector productivity have become more substantial in some countries. They utilize the fundamental innovation of cost-weighted measures of agency and department overall outputs, a development strongly advanced in the UK by the Atkinson Review (2005b) and some subsequent work by the ONS. In the next chapter we turn to examine in more detail the methodological debates about which concepts of productivity are most useful in the analysis of national, central or federal government agencies, which have no direct comparators. We show there how over-time productivity series are the most useful approach at this level. We also consider what qualitative and quantitative analysis methods can best help us to understand and enrich the analysis of patterns in the productivity series at an organizational level.

PART I

Nationally provided government services

2. Studying national agencies' productivity

The essential step involved in any organizational-level analysis of government sector productivity is to allow for the costs of different kinds of activities and services that a department or agency delivers. We use variations to ensure that the relative importance and the difficulties of producing different services can be taken account of when constructing a single output measure for the government organization for a given time period. The same approach also applies in comparing multiple providers across a larger services sub-sector (discussed in Part II). The process is called cost-weighting, and it forms the focus of our first section here. A debate has also taken place about whether effective analysis also requires us to measure the *quality* of public services, either over time or when looking across different comparable agencies in an overall public services network. Section 2.2 considers this thorny issue. Finally there are three very different ways in which we might approach the analysis of government organizations' productivity, depending on the level of data that is available. We review how these techniques (index-based, parametric and non-parametric approaches) might be applied to analysing national agencies' productivity in section 2.3.

2.1 USING COST-WEIGHTED OUTPUTS

For a private sector company or industry, the measurement of productivity is rather straightforward because its total outputs are simply defined as the volumes of goods and services produced and sold, each multiplied by the price involved. Dividing this volumes * prices amount by the firm's or industry's total input costs of producing the outputs yields *total factor productivity* (TFP), the most general measure of productivity. Since labour costs often account for a large portion of total costs, an additional measure is often calculated, dividing the volumes * prices amount by the total number or costs of staff employed in the firm or industry to yield labour (or staff) productivity.

We can generally expect that private firms in competitive industries will try to be as productive as they can be (within their organizational

33

capacities), since this will tend to improve their profits and to protect their market position. We can also legitimately expect that firms or industries becoming more productive will enhance social welfare. Where outputs are sold in competitive markets, we can safely assume that consumers buy what they find most worthwhile, and thus that genuine product innovations will (most often) be reflected in increasing market share or sales volumes. Competition helps to ensure that firms and industries with better products achieve more sales, and hence that over time the proportion of outputs shifts towards the most efficient and innovative producers. So the social benefits of innovations are already integrally incorporated in increased private sector productivity. Successful quality improvements to goods and services, those that enhance their value to consumers, will also help innovative firms to maintain a competitive edge.

The same analysis and assumptions cannot be easily extended to the public sector. Until recently the overall measurement of a department's or a government agency's mostly unpriced outputs was often difficult. So well-developed and consistent data streams on outputs produced over time have either only recently been developed or are still in process. In the UK, following earlier work (Pritchard, 2003), the Atkinson Review (2005b) made a major step forward by recommending that to measure outputs we should take into account the total number of each of the activities performed by a given organization (Iorwerth, 2006; Office for National Statistics, 2009; Rowlinson and Wild, 2009; Phelps et al., 2010) – a suggestion later taken up internationally. As Figure 2.1 shows, Atkinson recommended that these activities should then be weighted against each other according to the unit costs involved in producing them. In this step, the unit costs are used as proxies for the value of each of the different outputs produced, given that these are non-market outputs and thus do not have a price. For national statistics purposes, where the level of analysis is often highly aggregated, Atkinson also recommended that output volumes should be adjusted by quality factors – a controversial and difficult to implement suggestion, to which we return below.

Cost measures for the organization as a whole should then be assembled to cover the period for which the total volume of outputs measure has been produced. The volume of inputs can be composed from the three different types: labour costs, intermediate administration (or outsourcing and procurement) costs and capital consumption. For over-time analyses, costs should then be deflated using specific pay and price deflators. Dividing the chosen volume of output measure by this volume of input measure will provide a total factor productivity measure. By contrast, dividing the volume of output by a volume of input based on the number of total FTE (full-time equivalent) staff will provide an FTE productivity measure.

Figure 2.1   The Atkinson Review's suggested methodology for measuring
government productivity

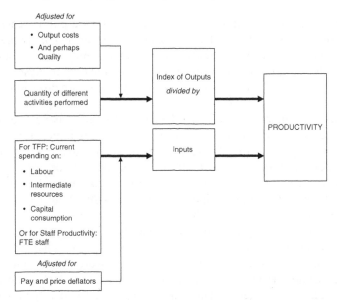

$$Total factor productivity\ (TFP) = Volume\ of\ output/Volume\ of\ total\ inputs$$

$$FTE\ productivity = Volume\ of\ output/Volume\ of\ FTE\ staff$$

Some significant practical problems commonly occur in measuring outputs within government sector organizations, in cost-weighting outputs so as to arrive at an overall index of an organization's performance, and in measuring inputs, which we discuss in turn.

Issues in Defining and Measuring Outputs

The Atkinson Review included three generally agreed principles for studying government sector productivity:

- Analysis should consider *the full range* of activities performed by a public sector organization.
- Unit costs should be used to adjust for the different costs of producing different activities. Ideally, in over-time analyses, these costs should be updated on at least a yearly basis to reflect the fact that the mix of resources employed by an organization in producing activities changes over time.

- Analysis should clearly identify the different inputs involved in producing the outputs analysed.

In order to correctly estimate a measure of total output volume it is
important to choose activity data covering the *full range of activities* performed by an agency, or the analysis may underestimate its productivity
figures. Choosing the right output measure requires the analyst to fully
understand the goals and tasks of the government organization being
studied.

At the same time, there are good reasons for not having too many
output measures. At the national statistics level it is important for the
number of activity or output measures that are created to cover only a few,
very fundamental and aggregated measures of the activities undertaken.
And studies seeking to implement the Atkinson recommendations have
typically focused on no more than several (one to three) output measures
for most agencies. Of course, there are some exceptions here, chief of
which are analyses of very large agencies handling huge policy areas, such
as social security and the collection of taxes (covered in Chapters 4 and
5). Here a large number of activities (up to 15, instead of three) may need
to be aggregated. However, it is important for analysts to bear in mind
that officials in each agency being studied often suggest overly numerous
measures of what their organization does, which if adopted could easily
make the analysis too complex. So, relatively parsimonious coverage of
key organization outputs should remain the goal.

Cost-attribution techniques in the government sector still tend to be
fairly rudimentary, and as a result broad gauge measures focusing on a
small number of outputs are also generally preferable. A key question to
ask about a government organization is what its broad mission is, and
what few main outputs capture that mission and can be cost-weighted in
a reasonably accurate manner. Main outputs tend to imply other secondary activities – for instance, running a schools system might be measured
in terms of the number of lessons delivered and the numbers of school
students taught, with these main outputs also tending to denote a whole
range of lesser activities (such as teachers marking children's homework,
talking to parents or liaising with other public agencies about students in
difficulties).

Table 2.1 shows the main elements of activities that could be covered
for the seven largest civilian central government service delivery agencies
in UK central government. For instance, looking in more detail at the
social security system, the processing of new claims and the payment of
the full range of social security benefits should be considered as outputs.
In the case of tax collection, the total number of tax returns processed for

*Table 2.1   Suitable output measures for productivity analyses in public
services operated by national government departments or
agencies*

Public Service	Activities to be Considered	Cost Weights	Quality Weights
Social security	Major different social security benefits. The numbers of new benefits claims processed should be separately distinguished from the payment of existing ones (because new claims are much more expensive)	Unit costs for each benefit, and for new claims and existing cases	Service administration here typically uses highly standardized procedures, so quality measurement should not be necessary. Normal technological advances should not be viewed as quality improvements. Applying a 'quality control' approach instead, analysts might weight for particularly poor service years in particular activities (usually limited to service crises)
Tax collection	Tax returns processed for the main types of taxes handled by the national tax agency, such as income tax, VAT or goods and services tax, business taxes, inheritance, capital gains etc.	Share of administration costs published by the tax agency for each type of tax	Same as above
Customs	Total number of import and export declarations	Share of administration costs for processing exports and imports	Same as above
Prison service (not covered here)	Number of total prison population and the numbers of new prisoners admitted	Unit costs per prisoner, or if not available then the share of administration costs. Admitting new prisoners is often more costly	This is a complex service so some simple quality indicators would be useful. Perhaps prisoners' escapes or access to drugs, and indicators of what life is like for inmates (such as cell overcrowding and prisoners'

Table 2.1   (continued)

Public Service	Activities to be Considered	Cost Weights	Quality Weights
		than looking after existing prisoners, so an appropriate cost weight for both would be useful	safety) could be taken as proxies of quality
Passport issuing	Number of passports issued	Unit costs for different types of passport services	This is not a complex service, so a quality control approach only is needed. But waiting times could perhaps be used as a proxy of service quality
Border protection (not covered here)	Total number of activities in border control, border enforcement, asylum and after-entry managed migration tasks	Unit costs or the share of administration costs for each kind of activity	This is a more complex service, with often volatile demand conditions. So it could be useful to have quality measures, e.g., the proportion of cases appealed for each activity area
Driving and vehicle licensing (centrally run in UK)	Total number of vehicle and driver transactions	Unit costs, or a proxy for costs (such as the average time taken per transaction)	A routine service where there should be little variation in service quality over time. The accuracy or up-to-dateness of records databases might be a useful proxy for service quality

the full range of taxes should be considered as outputs. Given the limited availability of cost data inside government, there is no point in over-elaborating a large number of different outputs to be considered unless cost-per-output weights are available – or useful proxies for such costs, such as the average time taken to process different tasks. Many 'public value' activities of government emphasized by Moore (1995) can be considered as operating in a pretty constant fashion across a whole tier of government, or as being an inherent part of any public service operation. Here again secondary activities – such as operating public information systems, providing democratic accountability or offering citizens redress processes (such as appeals against decisions) – do not normally need to be separately distinguished as department or agency outputs.

Issues in Cost-weighting Outputs

Once main outputs have been selected, as in Table 2.1, we still need to be able to add up the different activities in order to compose a single output measure. We noted already that the Atkinson Review argues that activities should be weighted according to the costs associated with producing them, a view with which other specialized guidelines such as the UN System of National Accounts (SN 93) concur.

In the UK, statistics teams from key government departments and large agencies can now usually elaborate the unit costs of different activities on a yearly basis. Sometimes useful or reliable data on per unit total costs are not available to managers or analysts. Here, however, it is normally still feasible to compute *the share of total administration costs* involved for each type of activity, a substitution procedure recommended by Atkinson. Especially in organizations that are essentially administering things, this sub-set of administrative costs can often be taken as a good proxy of the total cost of each activity. In preparing this book we had some contact with all the 30 or more different departments and agencies in UK central government while undertaking work for the National Audit Office (NAO), and we found some variations in the availability of per unit total costs or of data on the shares of administration costs to be used to weight outputs. The next four chapters and the Appendix describe some issues for services covered here.

In the largest departments, with the most sophisticated data series, and where very large numbers of cases may be affected, it may matter quite a lot how information on unit costs (or the proxy administrative costs) is updated from one year to another. Cost increases often occur gradually within a year, but productivity analyses generally update only on an annual basis. Simply replacing one year's average costs by another that is then multiplied by the number of all outputs within a year is a little crude on a large scale. Some large agencies with skilled analysis staff have developed a more accurate process for 'chaining' from one year's costs to another's. We used this approach wherever the requisite information was available to us.

Issues in Measuring Inputs

Amongst possible input measures, staff numbers are generally easily available and government managers often want to use them in order to compute labour productivity numbers. In the UK public sector some £159 billion a year was spent by government on public employees in 2007–08, that is, around 11 per cent of GDP (Office for National Statistics, 2010a,

p. 178). So, estimating and improving labour productivity in the government sector is a highly salient issue. But a great deal of care needs to be taken here. In the current era, the production of many government services is extensively outsourced to external suppliers – in the UK ranging from multinational systems integrator corporations such as Hewlett Packard at one end of the spectrum, down to very local charities providing social welfare services to local authorities or public hospital or family health services at the other. The rapid development of outsourcing meant that a further £79 billion was spent by British government departments, agencies and local authorities on procurement of services, roughly half the directly employed wage bill (Oxford Economics, 2008a).

The level of outsourcing may vary from one agency to another, or it may change over time. The annual growth in outsourced services in the UK over the last decade has been 6 per cent. A key form of outsourcing is to start using external suppliers to undertake parts of the activities previously performed in-house, that is, to produce intermediate goods. For instance, a form-processing agency might get a contractor to scan in documents or to handle its ICT operations. A rather different kind of outsourcing occurs where the final delivery of a whole tranche of outputs is devolved to an external supplier – as with private prisons, or NHS trusts contracting with hospices to provide a given number of days of care for dying patients.

Whenever tasks are partially transferred from government workers to outsourced providers the labour productivity of the staff who remain may seem to increase (since the same final outputs occur but with fewer internal staff), when in fact the costs are still there but are counted under procurement instead. Hence the interpretation of labour productivity analyses in the public sector always needs to be rather carefully carried out at an organizational level. TFP measures (including all forms of input costs) are generally preferable. In particular, TFP will only improve with outsourcing to the extent that using contractors is cheaper than the previous in-house provision. Consequently, looking at TFP avoids completely the possibility of the 'artificial' increases that can occur with labour productivity where the boundary between in-house and outsourced services changes across time or varies between organizations.

Can anything be done to mitigate these problems and to get more accurate and well-based staff productivity numbers? If intermediate goods provision is outsourced, it may be difficult to separate out particular proportions of an agency or department's overall outputs that are attributable to an external supplier rather than to in-house staff. However, where a whole block of the final provision of outputs is outsourced to an external supplier it may be feasible to go beyond just separating out inputs and to also separate out the in-house outputs and the externally supplied outputs. This would allow the compilation of labour productivity trends for in-house outputs alone. If reliable staffing details can be obtained from contractors, labour productivity across in-house and externally provided outputs could also be compared. Inside single large organizations (such as national tax agencies) the extent of outsourcing may also vary across regions or localities: in this case, if some outputs can be linked to in-house staff, and others to contractors, it may be feasible to legitimately compare in-house labour productivity under different arrangements.

Some difficult issues arise where labour productivity data will tend to flatter government agencies that are outsourcers relative to organizations doing more functions in-house. In multivariate regression analysis (discussed in more detail below) it may be feasible to control for this effect if data on the proportion of outsourcing is available. Even using well-evidenced dummy variables that categorize government organizations as having 'high', 'medium' or 'low' levels of outsourcing could be useful. Alternatively it may be feasible to consider separate regression analyses for different, more internally consistent groups of organizations.

The increased use of part-time staff, or temporary staff supplied by employment agencies, in many modern organizations also raises some issues for calculating labour productivity. In general, staff inputs should either always be denominated in terms of FTE positions where part-time and agency staff are counted as fractions of FTEs, or better still in terms of a total staff costs number.

In some public sector organizations there may be 'core' staff, seen as particularly critical to the agency's mission and whose numbers are well counted and matter politically. By contrast, the numbers of other 'fringe' categories of staff may be less carefully counted, and attract far less attention in political controversy and discussions. Sometimes the tenor of political debate is such that such non-core staff are labelled as 'back-office bureaucrats' (or pejoratively characterized as 'desk jockeys' or 'bean counters'). Here the government organizations involved will often take special care to play down the numbers of such staff, to restrict their growth or benchmark their operations (Cabinet Office, 2009b). Thus, in any defence system the numbers of uniformed military personnel are often highly salient, whereas support staff are not. In police forces, again the full police officers with powers of arrest are seen as 'core' staff, whereas the numbers of civilian or ancillary staff (such as 'community support officers' in the UK) are less discussed. Similarly, in public healthcare hospital systems, doctors and nurses are often seen as the 'core' staff, whereas administrators and clerical staff are not. Often agencies like these may be accustomed to relating their output levels just to their numbers of 'core' staff, while ignoring other staff – and even comparisons across multiple decentralized agencies may take place in these terms. In measuring labour productivity, however, it is vitally important that the most inclusive staff numbers are used. Otherwise, where transfers of functions from expensive core to fringe staff take place (a process called 'civilianization' in the police and the armed forces, for instance) it is possible that mis-estimates of labour productivity may be made in over-time analysis or in comparing across different organizations.

Finally, on 'fringe' staff it may be important to recognize that public authorities may have staff counts that are either over- or under-inclusive for various reasons. An example of an over-inclusive count in the UK are the staff numbers declared for NHS hospital trusts, which in their published form often include research-only medical staff in teaching hospitals – who actually do not take part in medical care, or have only a small part-time involvement with patients. Two examples of a potentially under-inclusive count concern part-time special constables in police forces, or fifth-year medical students in NHS teaching hospitals, whose role is somewhat like that of a junior staff person but who are not counted in employee rolls. These issues on over- or under-counted staff rarely change and so may not matter in over-time analysis, but they could produce mis-estimates in comparative analyses (for instance, in comparing teaching with non-teaching hospitals).

Some authors have argued that if the analyst's main interest is in developing productivity measures that aim to show how productive different public sector organizations are in producing outputs, staff productivity based on FTE numbers should be preferred. For example, Sargent and Rodriguez (2000, p. 4) suggest that when confronting data from different departments or statistical bodies it is better to rely on labour productivity estimates, so as to avoid biases in TFP estimates that can be introduced by government organizations making different assumptions on capital depreciation. The OECD productivity handbook follows a similar recommendation and suggests that researchers may often have to choose a partial productivity measure such as labour (FTE) due to the lack of reliable data (Schreyer, 2001, p. 12). However, for the reasons discussed above, especially the contemporary importance of outsourcing, we would caution that labour productivity and TFP analyses should always be closely compared for divergences, and in general it will be preferable to put most emphasis upon TFP analyses. Marked divergences in trends between the TFP and labour productivity curves should consequently always be investigated for changes in the proportion of work that is outsourced.

A final inputs issue in most government sector contexts concerns how to measure *capital consumption*. To calculate total factor productivity it is vital to make a monetary estimate of how much of an organization's capital (such as its buildings, computers, etc.) has been used up over the course of a year in the production process. The UK's Office for National Statistics (ONS) uses a sophisticated technique called the Perpetual Inventory Method (PIM) to estimate capital consumption at the level of large public sector policy fields (such as education and healthcare), where this approach has substantial advantages. However, this method requires additional data on the life span of the capital employed (see McLaren et al., 2008 for a review of the method). At the level of analysing organizational productivity, the method is overly complex and can only rarely be followed given data availability. So we suggest that a good proxy of capital consumption is capital depreciation, which is published in most public organizations' annual reports.

2.2 SHOULD QUALITY ADJUSTMENTS ALSO BE MADE?

In an ambitious and controversial way, the Atkinson Review also argued that government productivity analyses should utilize some *quality adjustment* measures wherever it can be assumed that the quality of the services provided has varied over time. The same would apply also in comparing productivity across organizations where the quality of outputs varies. There are clear dangers here as well, however. One is that productivity measures focusing on concrete outputs may tend to be blurred towards encompassing effectiveness elements that are inherently harder to measure (see Figure 1.1 above and surrounding discussion). It is also essential in organizational productivity analysis that we should have agreement amongst all stakeholders about what level of outputs has actually been achieved by an agency or department. Yet interpretations of service quality are often strongly contested in public sector contexts, for example, between government and opposition parties; or between government, public service trade unions and interest groups representing beneficiaries of different policies. In the UK and most other liberal democracies policy changes are also rarely developed in consensual ways. So contested quality improvements may lead analysts into difficult terrain.

There are two different contexts where the issue of measuring quality arises in an acute form, shown in Table 2.2. The case for a fully fledged quality adjustment is strongest in the first row here, because not to do so could lead to perverse effects in the measurement of outputs. For instance, suppose that hospital A processes patients for operations carefully and gives them somewhat longer post-operative care, so that its overall success

Table 2.2   Two contexts for potential quality adjustments or checks

	Advantages	Drawbacks
1 *Quality measurement is key for estimating outputs*, and ignoring quality effects may affect the basic measurement of outputs in perverse ways	Quality adjustments produce greater over-time consistency in basic outputs series, and a fairer comparative picture when considering agencies with differing quality levels	Quality measurement is difficult, so quality data is rarely available and costly to obtain Policy-makers always claim that all policy changes are improvements in quality. But the worth of many changes is often contested – and others may just be 'policy churn', with unproven effectiveness implications
2 *Quality measurement does not affect outputs data significantly*	Hard to see	As above Quality data is even less likely to be available in this context. The costs and delays in gathering extra data are not justified by improving the analyst's fix on outputs Citizens legitimately expect public service standards to modernize and improve in line with private sector standards and with general progress in IT and organizational technologies

rate with operations is higher. Meanwhile hospital B processes the same kind of patients but in a more rushed fashion, skimping somewhat on its post-operative care, so that somewhat more of its patients are then readmitted and treated again. If we ignore the quality variation here then hospital A will clearly have lower productivity than B, because it takes longer to do the same things. And in fact because of its extra readmissions hospital B may well appear to have greater activity levels, even though some of its cases are the same people where mistakes are being rectified – a result that is clearly perverse. Similarly, Bevan and Hood (2006) noted that up to 1999 British family doctors (GPs) spent as little as five minutes per patient on average consultations with their patients. By 2005 an expansion of healthcare funding meant that GPs were now able to reduce workloads and spend more minutes per patient on average for consultations, so that patient satisfaction improved radically in consequence. But in stark productivity terms outputs per GP session appeared to have reduced sharply. Equally in policing, it could be perverse to rate forces with high crime levels per officer (and thus more prosecutions) as more productive than forces with better records in deterring or preempting crime from occurring in the first place.

Arguably, a suitable choice of activity measures may partially control for some kinds of perverse effect. For instance, in addition to coping with fire and other emergencies the local fire services in Britain allocate a lot of staff resources to preventing fires – by providing free advice visits and fire alarms to local residents and by checking on potential hazards in advance. The evidence suggests that prevention measures greatly reduce the incidence and severity of fire emergencies. So if the output measures used here do not cover and appropriately weight both emergency response and prevention aspects, then productivity analyses could suggest that highly effective fire services have low productivity, the reverse of the truth.

But even where output measures cover all aspects of an agency's work, some direct quality measurement may also be needed. This kind of situation arises particularly in professionalized and personalized services, organized in decentralized public service delivery chains, as with health, education, policing and law and order services. In general, quality adjustments will be needed (1) the more complex the service being provided (as in healthcare or policing) and (2) the greater the variations in quality across agencies, localities or time periods being compared.

However, the second row of Table 2.2 shows a different case, where either a single agency is producing very consistent outputs that change little over time, or where a set of agencies are producing very standardized-quality outputs, as in social security systems. Here, nonetheless, the EU statistic body Eurostat (2001) still follows the Atkinson approach and stipulates that in the case of social security systems the kind of quality aspects that should be taken into account include the speed at which claims for benefits and existing benefits' payments are dealt with, whether payments are made on time and the number of errors made. In the case of tax collection, the number of errors encountered in each type of tax return processed might also be used as a quality measure.

But are such quality variations at all likely to be large enough to affect output measurement in a significant way, either over time in index-based approaches or across a set of agencies? It seems pretty unlikely that any of the Atkinson or Eurostat variables for social security or taxation will show any variation large enough to affect the output levels charted. For instance, overall benefit fraud and error levels in UK social security have very gradually reduced over more than a decade (National Audit Office, 2008b) from 3 per cent initially in 2000 to slightly under 2 per cent in 2011. Even if this change was incorporated into a productivity analysis, with such a tiny amount of variation the quality variable would have to be weighted very heavily before it made any difference to final output numbers. So seeking to measure such quality of service standards directly for many government organizations may entail a lot of effort for little apparent return.

Officials and professional staff inside government agencies often think of 'quality variations' in a very expansive way. In our conversations, many officials apparently view *any improvements at all* in how services are delivered as being somehow unusual or commendable. For instance, suppose a tax agency no longer makes customers fill out paper forms and instead offers an online e-form that is easier to fill in. Is this a quality improvement? If this change merely parallels (or more commonly lags) general shifts going on elsewhere across the whole economy, responding to general improvements in information technology, then we would suggest that it is not a quality improvement. Similarly, routine or incremental changes and improvements in services over time should not be claimable by government departments and agencies as quality improvements. In the private sector the standards of quality in goods and services expected by customers tend to upgrade every year, so that 'a unit of output' really means 'a comparably modern unit of output'.

In market contexts, out of date outputs will be priced down so that these problems are easily avoided. But it seems reasonable that a similar process should apply in the government sector too, where similar quality-recognizing pricing effects normally will not operate, and definitely not in 'compulsory consumption' areas. For instance, in UK prisons for many decades prisoners were subjected to an ordeal known as 'slopping out' where chamber pots used at night had to be transported from their cells with no WCs to toilet blocks each morning, a practice that was only finally ended in 1993. Should this change be counted as a quality improvement, or just as a long overdue rectification of output levels that were anomalously (unacceptably) low for an advanced industrial society? In general, citizens (and politicians acting on their behalf) expect public service standards to improve in line with private sector standards and progress in technology, both in substantive terms and in 'point of service' standards, for example, e-transactions and web-based information. In our view, improvements in services that merely maintain public services' position vis-à-vis the private sector cannot be legitimately claimed as quality enhancements.

In many standardized public services we do not believe that full quality measurement is necessary. Instead analysts only need to apply a much slimmer test. If we are looking at one organization or sector over time, has quality been at least consistent (or better still improving) in the study period? That is, can we be sure that quality has not declined in the study period? And if we are looking across organizations, are quality stand-ards across agencies broadly comparable? In most highly standardized and centralized services run by national governments discussed in the rest of Part I, it seems realistic to assume that the quality of the service provided is approximately constant over time. Quality adjustments here should only be needed occasionally when there is some clear and recog-nized major quality decline or a where a 'service delivery disaster' occurs (Dunleavy et al., 2009). For instance, in the UK service provision by the passports agency at one point reached near collapse (NAO, 1999); in 2003–06 there were major problems with the administration of 'Working Tax Credits', a scheme run by the tax agency to provide income subsidies to working households with low incomes; and the 2002 introduction of a new aged-persons benefit (called Pension Credit) caused major adminis-tration glitches in its early years. In each of these severe cases it might be relevant to apply some kind of discount to recorded output numbers in order to reflect the fact that normal quality standards were not applying – for example, millions of phone calls were not answered, service delivery became severely delayed and millions of customers experienced acute and avoidable anxieties. However, the weighting to be given to such a discount would need to reflect citizens' or politicians' estimates of the severity of problems, which are hard to derive in reliable and replicable ways.

So, overall, we take a more conservative approach to quality adjust-ments than Atkinson recommended. Quality-weightings should be espe-cially considered in the case of decentralized and complex public services such as health or police, where there are reasons to suppose that the quality of the service provided can vary significantly from one unit to the other. In Part II of the book we show how this approach can be devel-oped. By contrast, elsewhere we apply a more restrictive 'quality control' approach. Essentially we assume that quality levels can be assumed to be more broadly constant in centralized public services such as the payment of social security benefits and tax collection. And here we mainly take note of failures of quality control in the ancillary qualitative discussion of productivity data, rather than by seeking to alter the output numbers themselves.

2.3 THREE BASIC APPROACHES TO PRODUCTIVITY: INDEX-BASED, PARAMETRIC AND NON-PARAMETRIC STUDIES

The economic theory of productivity measurement in the private sector goes back to the work of Jan Tinbergen (1942) and independently, to

Robert Solow (1957). Three different techniques are generally used in the private sector to obtain productivity measures: index-based, parametric and non-parametric techniques.

Index-based Techniques

This approach was initially developed for productivity measurement in the private sector but these techniques are currently the most preferred approach for the measurement of public sector productivity, because they do not rely on econometric estimation (Atkinson Review, 2005b; Simpson, 2009). Formally, we can consider an organization as producing multiple outputs y_i using multiple inputs x_i. The different types of inputs generally are labour costs, intermediate administration costs and capital consumption, which is an estimate of the amount of capital services delivered in each year from durable inputs such as computers and buildings. The price of each output is p_i and the price of each input is w_i. Each quantity and price is observed in two periods t and $t + 1$, and we use the sign Σ to indicate the sum of a variable in each period. Output and input volume indices can then be expressed in the following way:

$$\text{Output index } Q_0 \quad = \quad \Sigma\, p_i{}^t\, y_i^{t+1} / \Sigma\, p_i{}^t\, y_i^t \qquad\qquad (2.1)$$

$$\text{Input index } Q_1 \quad = \quad \Sigma\, w_i{}^t\, x_i^{t+1} / \Sigma\, w_i{}^t\, x_i^t \qquad\qquad (2.2)$$

An index measure of productivity (Y) over time is then given by the ratio of these two indices:

$$\text{Productivity } Y^{t,t+1} = Q_0 / Q_1 \qquad\qquad (2.3)$$

The advantage of this approach is that it allows us to calculate productivity ratios that show how organizations employ inputs to produce outputs over time. Many studies in the private sector have employed the index-based approach to measure the productivity of specific firms or sectors. For example, Brandt et al. (2008) use an index-based approach to measure productivity in the Chinese manufacturing sector from 1999 to 2006.

When applied in the public sector, we have seen that the key piece of information needed to calculate reliable productivity estimates is what value to use to weight the different components of output in place of the prices p_i in equation (2.1). We follow the methodology developed by the UK's ONS and backed by the Atkinson Review, which is to use the share of administration costs for each type of activity, as a proxy of the value of each type of activity. Since agencies must collect unit costs data for the inputs element of a productivity analysis, it is normally feasible to extract the share of administration costs attributable to different streams of activity that the organization undertakes. However, in the public sector where annual budgets and data returns are still very dominant, it can be difficult to get accurate cost-weighting data for time periods that are shorter than a year.

Each type of input in the equations above must be deflated in order to account for the effect of inflation and to make yearly numbers comparable. *Labour costs* cover all the costs incurred in wages and other benefits (pensions, etc.) for maintaining the staff of a specific organization. Atkinson (2005b) recommends employing specific pay deflators, and in their respective analysis of social protection and Department for Work and Pensions (DWP) productivity both ONS (2008b) and DWP (2008) use specific pay deflators. DWP uses a civil service volume index while ONS used the Average Earnings Index (AEI) for the public sector (until 2010, when AEI was discontinued). Both indices have a high correlation with the GDP deflator for the whole economy. Where available, productivity analyses should clearly aim to use a specific pay deflator. However, if this is not possible, using the general GDP deflator will not bias results significantly. In over-time index studies it is key to identify any changes in the proportion of tasks that are contracted out or outsourced across the study period because this may bias labour productivity results. In this sense, if an organization has a number of activities that are contracted out, these should be included as part of the volume of outputs *only if* there is input data on the costs of such activities. This is in order to maintain consistency between the volume of outputs and the volume of inputs that are used to produce the productivity ratio. If the volume of output of an organization included outsourced activities for which there is no information on costs, the resulting analysis would tend to overestimate the productivity of the given organization.

Turning to *intermediate administration costs* (often labelled just as 'other administration costs' in public sector bodies' annual reports) one option for deflating these elements is to use the general Retail Price Index (RPI) in the economy, a strategy generally adopted by the ONS in Britain. However, some large departments (such as DWP analysts) have used the GDP deflator. Both indexes tend to be highly correlated and we normally use the GDP deflator. On *capital consumption* we noted above that ONS uses the Perpetual Inventory Method to estimate capital consumption. However, we could not operationalize this more complex method at an organizational level. Given the complexity of this method, we suggest that a good proxy of capital consumption is capital depreciation, which is published in public organizations' annual reports. The GDP deflator can also be used to deflate this input.

Once the different types of outputs have been cost-weighted and the different input costs have been deflated as explained above, they can be added to obtain total volume measures of outputs and inputs. This measure can be transformed into a 100-point index by using one year as the base, of course choosing the same base year for the index of outputs and of inputs. Dividing these two indexes will provide a total factor productivity (TFP) measure.

In the same way, staff productivity can be calculated by dividing the output index by an index of full-time equivalent (FTE) employees indexed to 100 and using the same base year. Another valid way to get a measure of labour productivity is to divide the output volume by an index based on the deflated labour costs of a given organization. Both are valid approaches for obtaining a reliable estimate of staff productivity and an analyst could decide on which measure to use depending on the availability and reliability of an organization's labour data.

As we noted above, most national or federal government organizations in liberal democracies are stand-alone – they have no direct comparators or competitors. Often, in addition, they deliver highly standardized services in a country-wide fashion, such as collecting taxes or paying social security benefits. These organizations can be massive in scale when compared with those in the private sector, and tend to be configured in what Mintzberg (1983) terms a 'machine bureaucracy' pattern, with strong internal standardization of tasks and processes. Here an index-based approach is often the only feasible method of examining such agencies' productivity records. There may also be other large national bodies that deliver somewhat more differentiated but still centrally governed services, such as the prison service in the UK or the federal prison system in the USA. Taken together these two sets of departments and agencies account for the vast bulk of central government staff and running costs. Index-based productivity analyses are highly applicable in centralized and standardized services and we devote the whole of Part I to them, partly because they have been rather a neglected area of study.

A key feature of the index-based approach is that it does not require a large amount of observations to produce meaningful productivity estimates, and the data needed for estimates to be made are generally available (or can be constructed) on at least an annual basis. After undertaking a systematic survey for the National Audit Office across different UK central government departments and agencies running centralized services, we found in 2009 that relevant output data are generally available for periods covering the last 13 to 15 years – beginning in around 1997. The availability of good-quality data is also the main reason why the Atkinson Review (2005b) and more recent publications in other OECD countries have also recommended index-based techniques for the measurement of productivity in centralized government departments and agencies (see, for example, Statistics New Zealand, 2010).

Parametric Techniques

A more sophisticated economic approach suitable for applying to whole sets of organizations consists of parametric analysis. This is based on estimating a production function for a firm or an industry in which the volume of output (Y) in a given period is the dependent variable and the volume of inputs for labour (L), intermediate consumption (M) and capital (K) are the independent variables. The function also includes a constant term A (technically known as a Hicks-neutral productivity shift parameter). The equation for a typical Cobb-Douglas production function is thus the following:

$$\ln(Y_{it}) = \ln(A) + \beta_1 \ln(S_{it}) + \beta_2 \ln(M_{it}) + \beta_3 \ln(K_{it}) + \varepsilon_{it} \qquad (2.4)$$

where

Y	=	output;
A	=	productivity;
S	=	staff spending;
M	=	intermediate goods spending;
K	=	capital spending;
β_1 etc.	=	coefficients;
ε	=	error term;

ln denotes 'natural log'.

This equation may look complicated, but this is chiefly because of the repetition of ln, which means only the natural log of whatever it is attached to, while the beta terms (β_1, β_2 etc.) are just numerical coefficients that weight each variable. This equation can be estimated by using data on a set of organizations i over time t. Fitting an ordinary least squares (OLS) regression model (the most common approach), it is then possible to estimate the contribution of each input to the output. For example, a positive and significant β_1 coefficient will indicate that staff spending positively contributes to output. Furthermore, in this model relative TFP is a possible measure of the managerial and organizational culture of the organization that is obtained from the residuals term ε_{it} in equation (2.4) above.

An extension of the parametric approach has frequently been employed in the private sector, which 'augments' the terms in the regression model in order to gauge how specific factors are associated with higher output and productivity. Many studies in the private sector have assessed how modern information and communication technologies (ICTs) are related to output and productivity by employing a parametric model as in equation (2.4) – here ICT capital is included as an additional input, and consequently the K term now only includes non-ICT capital such as buildings. For example, Caroli and Van Reenen (2001) employ a parametric technique with a production function in which management style and ICT capital are used as separate inputs. Bloom et al. (2005) also use a production function in which management is included as a separate input. In the private sector, the use of parametric techniques to assess the contribution of specific factors to output and productivity has developed a long way, because it is generally easy to build comparable panel datasets in which a large number of firms are observed over quite long periods of time.

In the public sector, creating or accessing such large N datasets has typically not been feasible for centralized departments, because all parts of even the largest government organizations generally follow homogeneous policies. For instance, tax agencies or social security agencies always implement standard policies nationwide. So parametric methods can only be used for looking at regional or state government agencies, or local agencies. Data series over time on output measures also tend to be available only recently in the government sector, and hence cover a relatively short number of years, insufficient to generate the numbers of data points needed for regression analysis.

However, in most decentralized and professionalized public services such as education or health, output observations and input data can be collected for individual schools or hospitals per year. And the spreading use of 'league tables' to give 'customers' (such as patients, or the parents of school children) information to support their choices of hospital or school has radically improved the availability and quality of data in recent years. Even in small countries the numbers of service delivery organizations is large enough to sustain extended analysis using parametric approaches. And in a medium-sized country like the UK the numbers of cases can be very substantial indeed, with 23 000 secondary schools for instance, while the 550 local authorities and around 200 hospital trusts in the UK provide smaller but still substantial numbers. Krueger (1999) and Street (2003) use parametric approaches to assess the contribution of specific inputs to output and productivity. In decentralized services such as acute healthcare trusts, even if data is available for only one year, it would be possible to estimate a regression. Ideally multiple N observations can be collated over a run of years to create a panel dataset.

Non-parametric Approaches

This approach also relies on accessing large volumes of data for the different inputs that an organization employs and outputs that it produces. However, unlike the parametric approach, these techniques aim to model the efficiency or production possibility frontier of a particular organization. One of the most common non-parametric approaches is data envelopment analysis (DEA). This relatively new approach is based on mathematical modelling and it is used when data on the different outputs and inputs of a given organization cannot be aggregated into a single output or input volume measure (thus preventing any use of the index approach described above).

DEA analyses take information on organizations' inputs and outputs and measure the efficiency of a particular organization by its distance from the 'outer envelope' of the data. The 'outer envelope' is assumed to measure the combination of outputs that a fully efficient organization could deliver given a specific set of inputs, and hence all deviations from the frontier are classed as inefficiency. Since the original DEA study by Charnes et al. (1978) there has been rapid and continuous growth in the field. As a result, a considerable amount of published research has appeared, with a significant portion focused on DEA applications of efficiency and productivity, covering both public and private sector activities.

In its most simple form, we can think of a set of organizations (say, eight bodies labelled from A to H) with each producing one single type of output and employing one single type of input, with their performance shown in Table 2.3. It is simple to see that organization A will be taken as the most effective and all the other ones will be considered as somewhat inefficient compared to this benchmark.

Suppose we now draw a simple graph as shown in Figure 2.2. Here the line that connects from the origin of the axis to the point represented by A is the 'outer envelope' or 'frontier of production' line, because A is the most productive organization, generating most outputs for its input level. This line will be significantly different from the regression line obtained

Table 2.3 Hypothetical information on eight organizations for a data envelopment analysis (DEA)

Organization	A	B	C	D	E	F	G	H
Input	3	5	4	3	8	6	2	5
Output	3	4	3	2	5	3	1	2
Productivity (%)	100	80	75	66.7	62.5	50	50	40

Figure 2.2   Graph of hypothetical information on eight organizations for a data envelopment analysis (DEA)

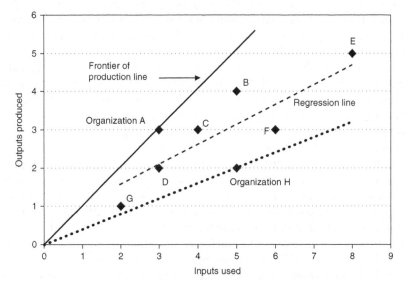

Note: This figure shows the same hypothetical data as in the first two rows of Table 2.3 above. The points show the input/output combinations for each organization.

by conventional parametric approaches (the line that minimizes the deviations of all observations from the line). In the DEA approach the 'inefficiency' of the other organizations with respect to A can be measured according to the angle of separation of those points from A. Thus, Figure 2.2 shows that H is the worst performing organization, attaining only 40 per cent of B's level of efficiency.

Data envelopment techniques rely on the use of extreme observations to determine the position of the production frontier and the top individual unit's efficiency score – by identifying the organization that achieves the maximum output for a given set of inputs. On the one hand this has advantages, since we know that the production frontier can be feasibly achieved. However, this approach may be very sensitive to any mis-measurement of the key data points, and DEA studies should only be performed in a research design that includes a large number of observations and well-measured data. Analysts could cope with this problem by comparing performance not against the best-performing organization (which may be untypical in many respects) but against another standard, say an organization on the 95th or 90th percentile line. Another approach is to aggregate together organizational performance on several different dimensions, ideally chosen to cover a wide range of stakeholder priorities and measures of organization efficiency and effectiveness, an approach applied to UK large firms across many different sectors by Yip et al. (2008).

A major attraction of the data envelopment technique is that when organizations produce multiple outputs, the method does not require information on how to weight these outputs for different organizations. It basically allows the data to determine the weights so that an organization's productivity is represented in the best possible light (Simpson, 2009, p. 266). This approach may be useful for productivity studies in the public sector because information on cost-weighting across organizations is often not widely available. In the private sector, different studies have employed DEA non-parametric techniques to measure the efficiency of firms. Among different analyses, Barros and Dieke (2007) use DEA to measure the efficiency of airports, while Agarwal and Mehrotra (2009) also use the approach to measure the efficiency of Indian retail companies.

Conclusions

Over several decades many advances have been made in understanding how to attribute costs to the different outputs that government sector organizations produce. The systems for doing this now in place in departments and agencies generally remain crude and far less detailed than those in the private sector. But they do now make it widely feasible to undertake productivity analysis in most reasonably large government organizations. At the national statistics level efforts to measure the productivity of whole sub-sectors of public services have also made progress. The essential step involved in both types of analysis is to cost weight different outputs, so that they can be aggregated effectively into a single output measure per organization (or per services sector) for a given time period (which will normally be at best per year).

At national government level it then becomes feasible to aggregate output measures for agencies and to develop productivity indices over time. For decentralized policy systems whole sets of similar delivery agencies can also be compared. Index-based studies are relatively straightforward to develop for large national agencies, and because comparison is across time, the uniqueness of the agency (its lack of comparators elsewhere) is not a major problem. Only if the agency radically changes its mission and activities, creating a disjuncture in the data series, are there major problems, although a whole sequence of smaller adjustments in activities may also create some difficulties of interpretation. Hence, index-based studies are best undertaken alongside detailed qualitative analysis of disjunctures that place activity changes in clear view. Even here, however, comparing productivity series across departments and agencies within the same tier of government can generate additional insights. For instance, it may help show whether some very strong government-wide events or policies (such as wage settlements with national trades unions or waves of administrative reform) have had more general impacts on multiple agencies' trend lines.

By contrast, the information requirements for more sophisticated parametric and DEA approaches can rarely be met in centralized services – the selection of index-based versus parametric or non-parametric approaches is almost always determined by issues of data availability (Simpson, 2009). Parametric approaches require a relatively large number of observations because they are based on fitting a regression model to a production function. Non-parametric approaches also need large N datasets, since they must identify the best-performing organization at a given time in order to compare how much less efficient the other organizations included in a given study are.

Even if we push through to the level of regional offices inside the bigger national government organizations, or even to the local offices level in the largest delivery organizations (such as tax or social security agencies in OECD countries), it is unlikely that parametric or non-parametric techniques can be usefully applied. In centralized services like these, regional and local offices are not autonomous centres of decision about the business model to be employed, but instead replicate standardized business processes. Hence, inter-office variations in productivity are likely to be constrained, although these may still be of great interest – especially perhaps in understanding labour productivity. However, the excellent levels of data needed here are also rarely available in this category of services. Hence, for the rest of Part I we focus on index-based approaches. We turn to a parametric approach only in Part II, covering decentralized services.

3. Rapid productivity growth – customs regulation

There is no inevitable law that means public sector organizations have to be characterized by lagging or flat productivity. Our simple antidote to this widespread view is to consider an area where substantial productivity growth has been successfully achieved. We focus here on the customs regulation of exports and imports in the UK, an area of operation that is one of the oldest and most fundamental 'business-facing' activities of the modern nation state. From the earliest period of the transition from mediaeval feudalism to Renaissance era states, the ability of monarchs and republics to regulate international trade was a cornerstone of their ability to raise revenues and to encourage (or depress) national economic activity.

In the modern period, we first briefly discuss how the growth of international trade has produced greater economic and political pressures for the speedier and streamlined implementation of customs checks. The second section examines how in an exceptionally open economy the UK government moved at an early date to effectively automate its customs operations and to shift from volumetric to risk-based methods of controlling shipments in and out of the country. Section 3.3 then shows in detail how the UK customs agency achieved rapid productivity growth in the decade from 1999, and traces the influences involved.

3.1 CUSTOMS REGULATION IN AN ERA OF TRADE GLOBALIZATION

The ability to monitor and to control the shipment of economic goods into and out of a territory has historically been one of the oldest and most fundamental functions of the state. In Europe the function began with the regulation of local markets by feudal barons and overlords and then extended to cover international trade with the growth of the first nation states. By the sixteenth century early modern states (often pushing towards absolutist monarchical forms at this period) developed comprehensive systems for regulating trade through ports and policing illicit evasion of revenue payments (smuggling) through permanent navies and extensive administrative checks. The economic and fiscal salience of this administrative function increased markedly in the era of the mercantilist states. Even in the free trade era in the mid-nineteenth century, promoted by the UK as the first industrialized state, the importance of customs rules remained great. The subsequent outbreak of protectionism, first at imperial scale in the late nineteenth century, and later amongst inter-war nation states, greatly rebooted the policy salience of the trade regulation function.

In the modern period the control of shipments in and out of countries has declined as a source of revenue at the nation state level because duty levels on imports have generally fallen. The European Union countries created a single, pooled customs area, and for a time the EU drew some significant revenues from external tariffs, now greatly diminished. Other kinds of controls remain pretty important within the EU area, because of differing VAT tax rates and regulations across member countries, creating new risks (such as 'carousel fraud'). Increasing numbers of bilateral trade agreements, and the much wider general push back towards free trade under the World Trade Organization process, have both tended to lower tariffs further. But the security and legal regulation aspects of exports and imports have tended to increase because of the international movements of illegal drugs, human trafficking linked to trade transport, and concerns about the movements in or out of weapons and of sophisticated technologies and substances with weapons-related implications. Even just for statistical and economic policy purposes, effectively monitoring imports and exports remains a key government function.

The invention of 'the Box', that is, steel shipping containers, in the mid-1950s had enormous cumulative impacts by the late 1990s (Levinson, 2006). The previously high labour costs involved in shipping and transshipping goods were revolutionized through 'containerization' – a complex but swiftly implemented process that rapidly closed traditional docks around the world, and led to the opening of new container ports. Containerization produced entirely new classes of massive ships, designed to move hundreds of containers at very low cost between continents. Unloading container ships required massive automation of transshipments, hugely increased capital investment and sophisticated storage and IT systems to track every container individually. As a result, the transaction costs of shipping large amounts of goods from one country to another were greatly reduced. The time needed to offload or load up ships was cut dramatically, and average shipping times also fell.

The WTO tariff reductions, containerization and many other stimuli all meant that international trade volumes in major OECD countries grew dramatically since the late 1990s as Figure 3.1 demonstrates. The economic centrality of international trade (measured as its share of GDP

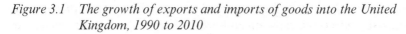

Figure 3.1   *The growth of exports and imports of goods into the United Kingdom, 1990 to 2010*

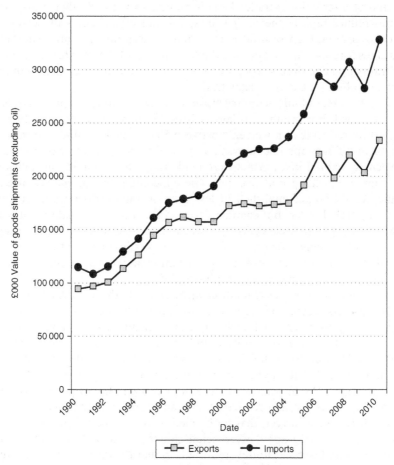

Note: The statistics shown are for goods imports and exports (excluding oil and all services, but including exceptional items, i.e., high-value deliveries, such as complete ships or sets of aircraft, sometimes separated out from monthly data).

Source: Office for National Statistics (2011), 'Value of UK trade in goods and services' dataset, downloaded 16 June 2011.

totals) increased rapidly in the same period, even for previously rather 'closed' (domestically focused) economies, such as that of the United States.

These startlingly swift changes in the commercial sector all piled considerable new pressures on customs regulators, who faced strong demands from exporters, importers and transport interests that regulatory checks should be radically streamlined to keep pace with the increased tempo of international trade. Time is money, so with all other transport times falling rapidly the resilience, speed and effectiveness of customs services around the world faced more intense scrutiny. The problem that business foresaw was that despite the speeding up of the private sector side of transshipment, the control processes run by government agencies would still introduce long lags to delay trade.

In other areas of inter-country movements, such fears have proven to be well justified. For instance, as late as 2010 a European Court of Auditors report on rail freight movements between EU countries found that many problems of incompatible railway gauges had been successfully combated. Expensive capital investments were made to enable the axles on railway wagons to be changed at frontiers where incompatible rail gauges meet, which could be accomplished in less than 30 minutes per train on the Austria–Italy border. But changing around the train lights, safety notices and other regulatory elements to meet different national laws (often also involving changing train crew who knew the specifics of regulatory rules in the destination country) took as long or longer than replacing all the axles on a train (European Court of Auditors, 2010a).

Traditionally, customs regulation agencies across the world have always been business-facing and claimed to recognize the need to help importers and exporters conduct their business expeditiously. Yet regulation arrangements were also long-lived and primarily focused on 'volumetric' controls. Here customs staff looked at what was declared on paper documentation needed for both imports and exports and proceeded chiefly by opening up or inspecting at random a certain (small) percentage of trade shipments. Containers and other loads were checked to see that the goods listed were correct; that no banned or controlled substances (such as drugs or pornography) were being shipped; and that any values of goods declared were accurately reported, so that the tariffs or taxes being paid were also correct. On average, volumetric controls in the UK and USA meant that between 2 and 5 per cent of shipments were physically inspected (varying with shipment types), with responsibility mainly localized with senior staff in each main port. Inspection rates were much higher in some European countries. Inherently, most purely random volumetric checks draw a blank. So to improve their hit rate, experienced customs inspectors developed over long periods of service their own sense of shipments or shipping companies that looked unusual. As a result, random checks would often be informally guided or supplemented by more focused attention on firms or types of shipments seen as problematic.

These routine primary checks normally absorbed the time and efforts of the large bulk of customs personnel.

In addition, customs agencies maintained small intelligence and investigative branches, which focused on major sources of tariff or tax frauds and of breaches in reporting requirements for exports or imports. They also liaised with overseas customs services, and with the police and security services, to counter organized crime involving imports and exports. Intelligence would be used to alert port inspectors about leads on particular shipments, or to help them focus their non-random volumetric checks somewhat better, on potentially more fertile areas for finding breaches of the law or regulations.

The speeding up and greater volumes of international trade flows have primarily been accommodated by customs services in two ways. First, there has been a growing internationalization of customs standards via multinational and bilateral agreements, originally focusing on removing tariffs on trade between the countries involved, so as to obviate the need for tariffs to be levied. In the post-containerization period, the increased importance of getting goods through docks and airports swiftly shifted the focus of international agreements towards pooled systems of registering and coding containers and cargoes. Changes here were designed to get rid of idiosyncratic or non-meshing information systems, help speed up processing at destination ports and improve information-sharing between different nations' customs services. International agreements now also contain undertakings on countries' inspection and approval times – for instance, to clear all containers through ports in 24 hours, unless there are serious grounds for investigation, in which case the time allowed increases to three days. Senior UK officials told us that signing up to such common standards also created a much stronger discipline on participating customs services. Mainstream exporters and importers often work closely with customs agencies to help curb problems, like pilfering, human trafficking and trade security. But they have also vigorously used their lobbying power to ensure that normal customs checks are as streamlined as possible.

3.2   THE 'AUTOMATION' OF CUSTOMS REGULATION IN THE UK

Until 2005 the responsible agency in the UK was Her Majesty's Customs and Excise (HMCE), a body that could trace its origins back in an unbroken line to the year 1203 (giving a real sense of how 'immortal' government agencies can be). Brigaded under the Treasury, HMCE was nonetheless set up as a non-ministerial department, partly to avoid any suspicion of ministerial or political interference in the impartial implementation of customs processes. The department still reported to the Chancellor of the Exchequer annually, and needed ministerial approval for major policy changes, business process reforms and new investments. But its day-to-day operations were controlled only by a historically ancient board, composed of its top officials, all of whom were senior career civil servants. In addition to operating customs regulation and collecting excise duties (essentially special goods taxes on particular classes of goods, like alcohol and tobacco), from 1973 onwards HMCE also collected value-added tax (VAT) on almost goods and services – a function whose financial signifi-cance rapidly dwarfed its customs work. (We consider the tax-collecting activities of HMCE in the next chapter, and so here focus solely on the customs regulation function.)

From the late 1980s onwards HMCE remained a non-ministerial department, but it was run increasingly on 'Next Steps' lines (see Chapter 4), like the new executive agencies. This change meant that the organiza-tion had more operational independence, so long as targets and goals set by its controlling department (the Treasury) were being satisfactorily met. Most requirements here related to revenue collection at low cost, but also in a timely fashion. An audit report in 2001 said that time delays for importers were short but could be made more 'challenging' for HMCE (National Audit Office, 2001a, paragraph 3.4). In the 1990s the depart-ment also came under pressure from ministers, central Whitehall depart-ments and industry stakeholders to contract out its IT operations in line with the Market Testing initiative. In 1999 most of its IT operations were transferred to ICL, a large UK company, once the UK's 'national cham-pion' for ICT. ICL was later taken over by the Japanese multinational Fujitsu, which in 2002 also signed a large Private Finance Initiative (PFI) contract with HMCE.

In 2005 HMCE was merged with the larger Inland Revenue (discussed in Chapter 4) to form Her Majesty's Revenue & Customs (HMRC). One of the key ideas here was to pursue greater integration of taxation collec-tion, especially between Customs and Excise's principally business-facing tax operations and those run by Inland Revenue (such as corporation tax). Customs became a much smaller function within a single, integrated tax agency. Three years later the detailed detection and small-scale prevention work of the customs function (such as anti-drugs smuggling measures against airline passengers) were moved out of HMRC and into the newly formed UK Border Agency, which also handled immigration at the border and illegal immigrants within the UK. However, the export/import func-tions and the regulation of trade movements remained with HMRC.

Government agencies dealing with businesses on a large scale were often the first to invest heavily in electronic communication with their private sector 'customers', even in the pre-internet period. In particular, many business-facing agencies developed electronic data interchange (EDI) systems early on, well before the advent of the internet. EDI systems are dedicated private networks facilitating large-scale electronic transactions, with their biggest business partners. In the mid-1990s Customs and Excise achieved a rapid take-off for computerized transactions by following a philosophy where the information they required should wherever possible form part of businesses' standard processes and information needs for importing and exporting. For import/export, HMCE first developed a computerized system to process export trade statistics in 1963 and an import cargo system in 1971. The department's EDI-based customs-declaration processing system, the Customs Handling of Import and Export Freight (CHIEF) was implemented in 1994, and was internationally influential. Solutions of the same type subsequently became widely used throughout the world. Even in 2012 the UK government's main business website claimed that CHIEF 'is one of the world's largest and most sophisticated electronic services for managing revenue and customs processes for the international movement of goods' (HMRC, no date).

The CHIEF system has controlled and recorded UK international trade movements (by land, sea and air). It linked customs offices around the country to ports, airports and thousands of businesses and was integrated with commercial processes to facilitate the movement of goods across national frontiers. CHIEF was provided free to all traders, with a choice of three routes for EDI input, either via third party agents, or by attachment to internet e-mail or to older standard messaging systems. Virtually all traders (99.8 per cent) used this system for import declarations by 2002, when we completed an NAO report on HMCE's progress (Dunleavy et al., 2002). A fifth of traders also used CHIEF for export transactions at the same date. The system handled the vast bulk of revenues collected at ports and airports, amounting to £14 billion of revenue each year via 16 million transactions by 2002. The CHIEF system was also used by HMCE to help collect international trade and transport statistics and to control the import and export of restricted goods. Other important EDI services included an Intrastat return service for collecting economic statistics, which by 2002 dealt with 40 per cent of traders. From June 2000, this system included an internet service for which some 3000 of the largest traders (10 per cent of the total) had registered by 2002.

Customs and Excise had significant early success with EDI in the import/export area by replicating pre-internet private networks already used by the largest private companies at the same time as making the original move from paper-based to electronic systems. Take up of the CHIEF import system was virtually universal because electronic declarations were standard for most imports at an early date. Smaller companies for whom it was not financially viable to purchase the necessary industry software used a registered agent, who submitted electronically on their behalf.

HMCE was also helped initially in doing business online by security of information considerations, which were of particular concern for its customers and for the agency itself. From the late 1990s onwards the UK government operated a version of an industry-led system for 'trust rating' material to be held electronically. It scored information on a scale that ran from 0 (the lowest security level) to 3 (the highest level). Most of Customs and Excise's information exchanges (such as the provision of trading statistics) were rated as level 1, which is why they could be easily computerized. As we will see in Chapter 4, information with significant financial implications such as the VAT return were rated as trust level 2, for which HMCE long held that the most appropriate method of authentication was digital certificates – a solution that most businesses were extremely reluctant to adopt. Hence VAT collection moving online was delayed by more than seven years after the import/export system was introduced.

Yet in government information technology, achieving early progress can also sometimes have a rather stifling effect upon making later changes, and so it turned out with customs. At first, as the internet took off, HMCE's clients were left largely unaffected. Larger export or import companies already had EDI accesses developed in many areas of their business processes and internal systems, which they were very reluctant to redo or change away from, producing a conservative lobby for getting by, rather than continuously upgrading systems. Small businesses and individuals were also always the most reluctant to adopt any electronic processes at all, and small firms in the UK have consistently been laggards in using internet-based systems for their dealings with government, creating major problems for HMCE in other areas. As late as 2007, for instance, the vast bulk (95 per cent) of VAT returns in the UK was made on paper forms, with payments by cheque. In import/export, however, the problems with small firms were less, because commercial agencies and the Community Systems Providers provided services (for a fee) to small firms and individuals in all the major ports and airports (Businesslink, 2011).

Second, having achieved administrative simplification and instant communication via EDI processes early on, top officials at Customs and Excise were for a long time reluctant to invest in new web-based technology, unless it could be done as part of normal business change processes. Customs first opened a website in 1998, but it was then left completely undeveloped until a new site launched in 2002, which still lagged far behind other UK revenue agencies in terms of the information or services available online (Dunleavy et al., 2002, pp. 23–5). The New Export System rolled out in 2002 provided internal and frontier export clearance services. It included a web-based front end (using standard XML schemas), and pushed take up of this electronic service above 20 per cent. Some additional costs were entailed for electronic messaging, but the electronic service was successfully marketed as faster and more streamlined than the paper-based version, which the department subsequently restricted. The system allowed small firms importing or exporting to notify customs directly as well, by e-mail or via the customs website over the internet, as well as retaining Community Service Providers (CSPs).

During the 1990s one of the benefits of the investments made was that the number of the agency's 22 000 staff working on information technology services stabilized at around 950 (many handling VAT systems, however). This number dropped significantly to 660 staff in 1999 following the PFI deal with ICL/Fujitsu to provide managed infrastructure services (excluding mainframes) to offices throughout the UK, involving the transfer of assets and over 300 staff under TUPE (the EU's 'transfer of public enterprises' provisions). The new infrastructure was to provide all HMCE staff with a desktop system. The contract was held up by financial and logistical issues. During our 2002 NAO study of the department we found that the agency's desktop system already appeared outdated. For instance, even at this late date a significant proportion of staff in the department were using PCs rolled out since the signing of the contract that did not have access to the internet (see Dunleavy et al., 2002, p. 70).

The much wider benefit of HMCE's success with early automation was that over two decades the department handled progressively greater workloads with falling overall personnel numbers. This was achieved primarily through the strong development of risk management approaches to customs regulation and duty collection, based around but going well beyond the development of more automated systems for processing data. Instead of trying to audit or inspect all transactions using volumetric checks, customs instead progressively concentrated their attention on traders and problems chosen on a risk assessment basis. This allowed increasing targeting of their administrative effort on risk management and assurance, rather than on 'unproductive' inspections of perfectly regular shipments.

Electronic delivery of services greatly extended this pattern of development, allowing faster and more complete acquisition of data in real time. The change helped in several ways. First, by providing much more accessible information online, traders wishing to be compliant could get accurate and more immediate help with their problems, reducing the incidence of unintentional breaches of law or regulations or under-declaring of goods' values. So 'error' cases reduced and became somewhat easier to distinguish from fraud and intentional non-compliance. Second, electronic information (and later fully digital systems) made feasible the development of more sophisticated programmes for spotting anomalies amongst huge numbers of containers. Where problems were turned up, finding similar cases or identifying other shipments likely to be involved also became easier. The strong development of greater cooperation between customs services at both ends of international trade links, especially after the 9/11 attacks on the USA, also greatly facilitated electronic methods of working and improved intelligence functions.

There were some early hopes, strongly held in the US Customs Service around 2000 for instance, that it would be possible to condense out the wisdom of experienced freight inspectors into a customs 'expert system' that would routinize the detection of anomalous containers. Yet in practice the US service found that inspectors relied greatly on (different) hunches, intuitions and processing of multiple bits of information – about which ports or airports containers originated from, sent by which companies to which customers (interview, 2000). All this was interpreted in the light of a huge amount of informal knowledge about really current developments, very little of which could be systematized out into intelligence systems that genuinely worked in time-relevant ways. At the end of the day, in the UK, USA and Australia top officials stressed to us in interviews in the mid-noughties that detecting imports and export wrong-doing still came down largely to the skills and experience of the inspectors scanning interminable lists of electronic information about shipments.

Nonetheless, by greatly expanding the information base underpinning risk assessment, the growth of ICT systems made feasible efficiency savings for HMCE amongst its staff undertaking customs regulatory and informational work more generally, as well as supporting compliance and improved service quality. A key result was that by 2007 HMCE conducted far fewer volumetric controls than the customs service in any other EU country, checking only one in every 1000 shipments (or 0.01 percent) according to HMRC's returns to the EU (National Audit Office, 2008e, paragraph 2.18). This was the smallest proportion of shipments anywhere within the 27 EU countries, according to a study by the European Commission, as Table 3.1 shows. Almost half of EU countries still used volumetric checks on more than 10 per cent of their imports – the mean rate of checks was 9.6 per cent and the median was 7.6 per cent – all many times the check rate in the UK.

After reviewing these imports numbers, the UK's National Audit Office (hereafter NAO) noted that:

Table 3.1   *The proportion of import shipments checked by customs departments in the 27 EU countries, in 2007*

Number of Import Shipments Checked, per 1000 Shipments	Number of EU Countries
100 to 400	12
80 to 99	1
60 to 79	4
40 to 59	1
20 to 39	2
10 to 19	5
2 to 9.9	1
1 (UK)	1
Total	27

Source: National Audit Office (2008e, Figure 9), drawing on the European Commission's unpublished EU Annual Measurement of Results Report for 2007.

[W]e recognise that direct comparison of data between EU countries is problematic due to different volumes of traffic, differences in remit and practice, and variations in reporting numbers of examinations and rates of irregularities. The EU has no standard for the level of inspections required by each member country or for what an inspection should entail. The Department [HMRC] considers that its risk targeting justifies lower levels of examination, but the fragmented nature of its risk and intelligence information makes it difficult to assess. (NAO, 2008e, paragraph 2.18)

3.3   THE EVOLUTION OF UK CUSTOMS' PRODUCTIVITY

To estimate productivity for the customs function, we used the evidence detailed in Table 3.2. In output terms, the two main activities are the registering and inspection of exports and imports. The key output activities that we considered for customs are the total number of import and export declarations processed per year. This data is not publicly available but it was kindly provided by HMRC statistics teams from internal databases, and we thank them for their assistance. Declarations for both import and export declarations were then re-weighted by the relative unit costs in each year to create a total outputs data series.

We considered the need for making quality adjustments of outputs, but decided not to do so. A wide range of interviewees in the department across the period, together with limited surveys of stakeholder views and

Table 3.2   Data and adjustments used for the measurement of productivity in UK customs, 1998 to 2008

Variable	Evidence Used, and Adjustments Made
Outputs for processing of import and export declarations	Number of import and export declarations, obtained from internal data provided by HMRC for 1997–98 onwards
Cost-weighting of outputs	Unit costs for imports and exports, estimated from HMRC and HMCE annual reports
Inputs, for total factor productivity	Deflated total labour and other administration costs, obtained from annual reports
Inputs for staff productivity	Number of full-time equivalent (FTE) staff allocated to customs processing, obtained from annual reports

a systematic review of media commentary for our study period, showed substantial evidence of neither quality fluctuations, nor of major improvements in service quality over time. Quality declines might be hypothesized from the low level of shipments being checked by the end of the period, but no clear pattern could be identified in other data on seizures of illegal goods, the street prices of drugs or other customs key performance indicators (KPIs), which generally showed trendless fluctuations.

In 2001 the NAO noted that only 3 per cent of import cargos not otherwise 'profiled' would be checked (NAO, 2001a, p. 13). Seven years later NAO warned that checks on imports were very low by EU standards. In addition, the department had a ministerial target of finding problems in a quarter of its imports searches. Senior officials interpreted attaining this target as an unambiguous sign of increased efficiency in Customs' risk assessment. However, this apparently greater success was actually achieved through the department reducing the overall volume of its searches (thereby improving the ratio of problems found), and not by finding more problem shipments in absolute terms. NAO (2008e) did not recommend that search numbers should be increased – nor even that HMRC should conduct an annual random sample survey, to compare how the rate of discovery of problem shipments in that data moved over time.

A European Court of Auditors (2010b) special report on customs checks covered very small samples of checks in the UK (in common with ECA's standard audit methods). It found extensive problems with HMCE's pre-clearance checks, indicated by lots of red 'traffic lights' in its report, but a somewhat more reassuring standard of HMRC post-audit checks. However, the sample cases and transaction numbers involved here were tiny, and ECA teams are seen by many EU states as being over-punctilious in marking cases as not meeting legal requirements. We therefore concluded that the quality-weighting of outputs data was not needed in this case, nor indeed were there data series available that could provide useful quality weights.

Turning to inputs, for total factor productivity (TFP) we used a cost of staffing measure plus costs for direct materials and other costs, procurement, outsourcing of services provision and capital investment, to yield total administration costs. For staff productivity the inputs metric used was the number of FTE staff in HMCE (and later HMRC) working on the departments' customs processing effort. In all cases the outputs and inputs measures were set to 100 for a common base year, the financial year (April to March) 2000–01, which lies in the middle of our period.

The change from HMCE to HMRC running customs in 2005 posed some challenges in identifying the correct share of labour and other administration costs. Special care was taken to identify the share of labour and other administration costs allocated to the customs effort from 1997–98 to 2004–05 within the former HMCE department and from 2005–06 onwards within HMRC. The same focus was adopted to identify the share of labour and administration costs for the tax collection area, as explained in Chapter 4. (For more details see the Appendix at the end of the book.) We could not elaborate what we would regard as a fully reliable capital consumption estimate, because of irregular reporting by the department over years. But given that it represents a small share of total costs, we are certain at least that our numbers here do not unduly underestimate productivity in this area.

On this basis then, Figure 3.2 shows the levels of inputs and outputs over the decade for which we have data, and in the thickest line the total factor productivity trend. Productivity in this area shows an almost continuous upwards trend since 1997–98. This is mostly explained by a continuous increase in the volume of outputs (based on the total import and export declarations processed) and in the resulting productivity trend. Even in the last year shown here (the 'end of the boom' year 2007–08) there was still some growth of outputs, but because it coincided with increasing labour and other costs, this was enough to cause the customs TFP series to move downwards for the last two years shown in Figure 3.2. Our data do not cover the subsequent period, but customs productivity is likely to have declined significantly from late 2008 onwards into 2009 and 2010, because the credit crunch followed by the wider global financial crisis produced a big fall in the UK's overseas trade (shown in Figure 3.1 above).

Figure 3.3 shows our estimates of labour (staff) productivity in this area. The trend here closely follows our TFP estimate, but the range is much

*Figure 3.2   Total factor productivity in the customs regulation of trade,
1997–2008*

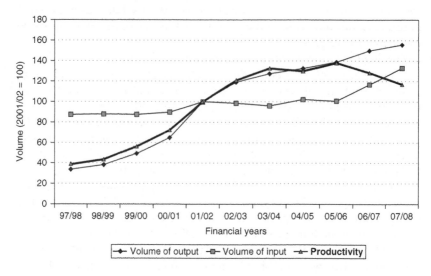

Figure 3.3   Staff productivity in customs regulation of trade, 1997–2008

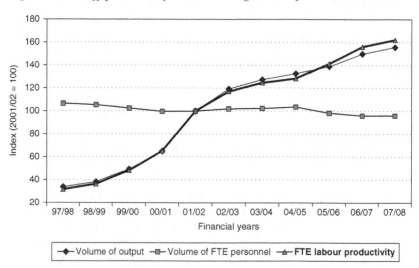

greater and the slope steeper. Unlike in the TFP curve, the line showing
staff productivity does not seem to decline with the onset of the economic
downturn. There is a continuous upwards trend in Figure 3.3, especially
in the late to early 2000s, which somewhat flattens off in the last years

shown. However, again the economic downturn since 2008 is likely to have dented staff productivity, since fall offs in international trade were very fast and deep, while HMRC cannot usually gear down its staff in customs regulation this quickly or extensively. (Traditionally HMCE had a lot of full-time staff and low proportions of fringe staff – no casual workers, for instance.) This is an interesting example of how some public services are very sensitive to demand changes (such as with customs and the issuing of passports), particularly if the government organization involved is not capable of quickly changing how it provides for and plans staff needs.

Conclusions

Over a long period Customs and Excise made a general shift in its administrative operations. It moved away from a reliance on staff-intensive volumetric processes and passive or uninformed checks. Instead the department shifted towards assessing risks proactively, a movement that affected the ways in which all its staff were deployed. The targeting of inspections and checks based on intelligence and expert judgement information then became feasible. The department was able to greatly reduce the time and resources spent on the routine checking of consignments that probably did not present any threat to revenue or security. Customs' early investment in proven (EDI) technologies for electronically interacting with importers and exporters allowed it to extensively replace paper-based administration systems. So far this commitment has largely paid off over more than a decade in use. The CHIEF system provided a critical underpinning of the reorientation to risk-based administration, greatly increasing the volume, systematization and 'real-time' qualities of all the department's regulatory information.

These twin shifts, in how work processes were organized and in how information flowed into the department, both meant that HMCE responded effectively to the post-containerization age. It met the demand for speedier clearances of shipments in and out of the country, and it was able to cope successfully with the strong growth of international trade volumes, especially from non-EU ports of origin and 'riskier' areas of the world. The increased workload was accommodated and quality of service maintained, while keeping Customs staff numbers relatively constant over a long period, and with relatively constrained increases in ICT outsourcing and other procurement costs.

As a result, staff productivity in the customs function of HMCE and later HMRC improved fivefold across the decade. However, a number of offsetting factors need to be considered. The increased outsourcing of IT functions and the transfer of some detection staff to the UK Border

Agency at the end of the period, both mean that this rate of change is somewhat deceptive. We also need to recognize that the general growth of international trade across the period provided a generally benign environment for Customs until 2008. Many organizations in the private and public sectors with constantly growing demands on them will tend to increase productivity, as existing assets are 'sweated' more, workflows are not disrupted by periods of slack demand and more consistent IT investments can be sustained.

Hence the increase in Customs' total factor productivity index is a better overall indicator of progress than staff productivity across the decade. It shows somewhat more than a threefold increase, after allowing for the effects of the 2008 trade downturn. This is still impressive and much of it can clearly be attributed directly to the department's own efforts – in changing management and administrative practices, making relatively forward-looking ICT investments, and encouraging importers and exporters to shift away from paper-based to electronic forms of information provision.

4. Growing productivity gradually – tax services

Tax-raising departments and agencies fulfil a unique role in any national or federal government by generating the inflow of financial resources upon which the work of every other department and policy sector depends (Osborne, 2002). So, maximizing the efficiency and effectiveness of tax-raising agencies has been a high priority for all liberal democratic governments for many decades. Yet taxation also essentially involves the state in directly requisitioning resources from firms, individuals and consumers, in what seems to most citizens and businesses to be an overtly coercive mode. Two key implications have followed for the operations of tax departments. On the one hand, requisitioning creates strong pressures for tax law to be absolutely clear-cut, and for its implementation to be comprehensive, strongly equitable (perhaps even rigid), and as exact (near flawless) in implementation as is achievable. On the other hand, there are also strong political and social limits upon exactly how vigorous or fine-grained the efforts made towards collecting tax can be, constraints that often shape tax departments' ability to develop their own productivity.

We begin with a short survey of the essential common characteristics of taxation systems in liberal democracies and advanced industrial states, showing how there are some fundamental principles that underlie both the strong and direct political control of tax policy, and the often distinctive organizational cultures of tax-raising departments. The second section shows in more detail how these imperatives and constraints have worked out in modern UK government, where a single tax-raising department has always been one of the largest administrative organizations across the country taken as a whole. Section 4.3 then shows in detail how the administration of UK taxes has been marked by moderate but significant productivity growth, especially in the decade from 1999. Finally, we give an interim review of which factors seem to have been most associated with Britain's improvements in tax system productivity.

4.1 TAXATION SYSTEMS AND THE MODERN STATE

Securing a tax base has foundational importance for any government if it is to function over any long period. The US political economist Mancur Olson (1993) tried to sum up this effect by characterizing any enduring state as a 'stationary bandit'. Historically, roving bandits (such as robber barons, raiding Mongol tribes from the steppes of Asia, or invading conquistadores) can have great success against less vigorous, less technologically advanced or just more settled people by sweeping in, breaking things (including the governance systems), looting and levying penal taxation, and then moving on, leaving an economic desert behind them. But any ruling elite that becomes stationary, fixed in one place, confronts the need to foster the economic development of its own domain. However much it adheres to a revenue-maximization aim, a now stationary government must confront the problem that immiserizing its population will over time starve their state of funding also, leaving it vulnerable in turn to takeover by its more prosperous, militarily advanced or technically advanced neighbours. So, longer-term revenue maximization turns on stimulating economic growth, by adjusting taxation to levels optimal for societal development.

In a somewhat similar vein, the political theorist Margaret Levi (1992) stressed that even a 'predatory' state interested in extracting the maximum taxation from its subjects confronts acute choices. Coercive tax collection is expensive and historically ineffective, often entailing the use of sanctions that are actively counterproductive for future revenue growth. For example, the British Empire used an ill-fated 'hut tax' for many decades in its African colonies – here the sanction for a family being unable to pay the tax was to burn down their hut, impoverishing the inhabitants further. Similarly, concentrating taxation on marketized (and monetized) transactions creates strong incentives for farmers to remain stuck in a subsistence agriculture mode, and for craftspeople to limit the scale of their activities to informal (or 'black market') exchanges, or payments in kind. This effect is a recipe for social stagnation, and one that some critics argue is still depressing growth across many developing countries, in the form of bureaucratic corruption (Shleifer and Vishny, 1998, Chs 4–5). Above all, Levi argues that coercively collecting taxes is administratively very costly, consuming relatively high proportions of revenues raised on the collection task itself, as with the 25 per cent share commonly assigned to 'tax farmers' in pre-industrial times. It is also ineffective, leading to the extensive suppression of information and evasion of payments by taxpayers.

By contrast, modern liberal democracies have developed much lower-cost taxation systems based on what Levi terms 'quasi-voluntary compliance' (Levi, 1992; Levi et al., 2008). Essentially the idea here is that the state maintains 'just enough' direct capacity to raise taxes to ensure that tax evasion is not a publicly sustainable option for individuals or companies due to pay tax. The role of government is not to directly compel the whole eligible population to pay taxes, but rather to 'hold the ring' so that the large majority who do pay taxes in a 'quasi-voluntary' mode can be confident that attempted evaders will be caught and punished. As a result most citizens and companies do not seek to evade payment of taxes, and will only follow legal options for tax minimization. This leaves the tax agency to focus concentrated attention on non-compliant individuals and firms, thereby providing assurance to compliant taxpayers that they are not 'suckers' bearing a disproportionate share of payments. Quasi-voluntary compliance would rapidly collapse if (most) tax evaders are not caught and controlled by the tax agency, since citizens at large would otherwise be encouraged to try free-riding – and once such a cycle gets started it is costly indeed to counteract.

In both liberal democracies and other forms of state, the extent of low-cost compliance and the resources needed to ensure it are both highly dependent upon the overall legitimacy of the government. Adopting visible taxes that are seen as unfair can quickly imperil the state's capacity to function, even in modern societies. For instance, the UK has seen two attempts to introduce a 'poll tax' levied at a flat rate per head of the population, separated by many hundreds of years. On both occasions it proved a deeply unpopular notion – because it meant that rich and poor citizens alike paid the same level of tax. The first occasion was in 1377–81 when monarchs introduced the original poll tax, eventually provoking opposition known as the 1381 Peasants Revolt that led an insurgent army to nearly topple the king. The revolt's leader was eventually killed and the uprising suppressed, but the tax was also withdrawn and not levied again for 300 years, and only then in a more graduated way. The second occasion was in the late 1980s when Margaret Thatcher's government introduced a flat rate 'community charge' to finance local governments, a device that almost everyone except government ministers identified as a poll tax. Within two years the numbers of people refusing to register or pay the tax mushroomed so fast that the payment burdens on the remaining compliant citizens grew rapidly. Tax protests spiralled, climaxing in a demonstration that became a riot in Trafalgar Square (Butler et al., 1994). In 1990 Margaret Thatcher was deposed as Prime Minister by the ruling Conservative Party's MPs, and her successor in office immediately abolished the poll tax in favour of a graduated 'council tax'.

Similarly, in spring 2000, a Labour government led by Tony Blair was caught by surprise after a protest against an 'escalator' arrangement for automatically increasing taxes on petrol and diesel led to lorry drivers and farmers blockading oil depots and endangering the country's fuel supplies. The escalator rises in fuel duty were slackened and the government had to take extensive new measures to prevent any future fuel blockade from becoming similarly effective.

Although tax resistance to unpopular or unfair taxes can still grow quickly, the more normal picture is that elected governments who are responsive to public opinion retain a high level of legitimacy. As a result, governments in well-established liberal democracies have been able to develop taxation systems that are remarkably efficient compared to earlier models, and that especially allow for a remarkable minimization of the scale and intrusiveness of tax-raising operations. Three key steps are needed here:

1. *Relying on tax bases that rise automatically with inflation*, so that a given tax rate will deliver rising money amounts of taxation without a need to increase the tax rate – because increasing tax *rates* is politically visible and unpopular. Income taxes and general taxes on consumption, such as value-added tax (VAT) or goods and services tax (GST), both have this key characteristic, which is why their importance as funding sources has tended to grow strongly in modern times. In acute contrast, most property taxes do not meet this criterion, because although property values do indeed rise with inflation (and often by more than inflation), complex revaluation exercises are normally required to record these increases. Such exercises are administratively expensive to conduct, and hence infrequent. They are also always politically controversial, because long-delayed revaluations of property values can often have drastic implications for what residents or businesses have to pay.

2. *Getting companies to administer tax payments* for the government, rather than asking final consumers or individuals to do so, hugely cuts government costs. Hence in most countries income taxes and social security contributions are collected through 'pay as you earn' (PAYE) systems, where employers dock the taxes due from salaries before they are paid to their staff. Requiring that government, the employer and employee are all notified, and making companies file detailed accounts of their tax payments, greatly reduces the risk of tax evasion by creating publicly visible information (Kleven et al., 2009). Similarly, flat rate consumption taxes like VAT, GST and excise taxes are paid automatically to government by (larger) businesses, again minimizing fraud or evasion levels. Companies and other 'interme-

diary' organizations can also far better insure against the risks and costs of tax administration than can individual citizens, making this a politically optimal choice for rational politicians (Horn, 1995). And unless tax rates are altered, citizens may not be clearly aware of how much 'invisible' taxes they are paying from year to year..

Some other flat rate or generally applicable business taxes (such as employment taxes levied per employee) also qualify under the heading of allocating tax payment obligations to companies wherever possible. Similarly a few substantial specific excise taxes are paid by just large businesses – such as the substantial petrol and diesel taxes in the UK, where an amount close to £27 billion was expected to be paid to Her Majesty's Revenue & Customs (HMRC) principally by just seven or eight major oil-retailing firms (Adam and Browne, 2011, p. 4).

But corporation taxes in many countries do not qualify here. These taxes are often littered with tax exemptions ('tax preferences' in US terminology), and they are dependent on companies' variable and distinctive performances and policies, which must be individually understood and established. As a result, business taxes of this kind can often prove relatively expensive to collect – for instance, because large companies can 'transfer price' assets between countries in hard-to-follow ways, and hire expensive lawyers to turn major disputes into protracted legal cases.

3. *Relying on general tax bases*, applied across the economy as a whole, is strongly recommended by public finance theory because it minimizes any subsequent distorting of the pattern of economic activity as people or firms seek to avoid paying tax. In administrative and political terms, the more general a tax is, and the earlier or more preemptively it is collected, the less visible it becomes, the less feasible it is for citizens to mobilize against paying it and the lower the transaction costs of collecting it. Hence PAYE income tax systems have tended over time to become flatter with fewer grades of tax due and an emphasis on reducing the number of tax exemptions or 'preferences' in the tax code – although progress here has been stuttering at best. Similarly, automatic sales taxes like VAT or GST have tended to grow at the expense of more economically distorting excise taxes levied on particular individual goods (such as petrol and diesel, luxury goods or imports). One or two small countries have moved towards a 'flat tax' levied at the same rate on everything (supposed to improve economic efficiency), but no large economies. However, it is nonetheless true that in the UK the basic rate of income tax and the VAT rate have tended to converge over the last two decades (Kelly, 2011).

These developments mean that in advanced industrial societies tax systems have become increasingly effective over time, but simultaneously less controversial to administer. The rather misleadingly labelled 'tax productivity' rate measures how much tax is collected as a percentage of the theoretical tax liability of businesses and individuals, and should normally be high for mature liberal democracies with long-lived tax systems (Becker and Mulligan, 1998). This is an acute contrast to countries with still developing tax competencies, where tax evasion levels can be very high, and to 'failing states' where government often collects only a minority of the theoretical taxes due. The efficiency of modern tax-raising systems is best dramatized in rapidly growing economies – such as those of South Korea, Malaysia and in recent years China (whose tax efficiency is underpinned by drastic punishments for evasion). Here if growth is X per cent, then it is common to see tax revenues growing annually by more than X per cent. For example, between 2001 and 2007 Malaysia's tax receipts grew by 70 per cent in six years (Taha and Loganathan, 2008, p. 65).

Three factors shape how tax departments operate at a detailed level: how information is managed, the distinctive bureaucratic culture of tax agencies and how compliance costs for citizens and firms are minimized. We discuss these in turn.

Acquiring and Acting on Information

This is critically important for most operations of government, but never more so than for taxation. Governments need two different kinds of tools here (Hood and Margetts, 2007): (1) *detectors*, for finding out information about society, in this case about incomes, sales of goods and services, company profits, inheritances, etc., and (2) *effectors*, for getting things done, for implementing actions in society.

We can cross-reference these categories against five main mechanisms at government's disposal:

- *Nodality*, the fact that (legitimate) governments occupy a central position within the information systems of their society, where other social actors tell them things for free (e.g., that someone is not paying taxes) and pay special attention to government messages (e.g., a notice that they must pay tax by the end of the financial year).
- *Authority*, the legal and regulatory basis that allows governments to compel citizens or firms to do things (e.g., file a tax return declaring their incomes or sales), and allows governments to take actions (e.g., raid a non-compliant firm for a tax investigation and seize its data and papers).

- *Treasure*, especially public expenditure, but also the state's owner-ship of other resources (like buildings or land, or sometimes the ability to conscript labour, as with compulsory service in the armed forces). Treasure allows governments to hire officials and to spend money (e.g., informing citizens of their tax liabilities and deadlines via TV or internet adverts).
- *Organization*, denotes the massing of officials into basic bureaucra-cies (such as a national government tax department) so as to process information from detectors (e.g., scrutinizing tax returns and issuing tax notices) and to concert action via effectors (e.g., pursuing non-payers or launching investigations of risky-looking taxpayers).
- *Expertise*, denotes going beyond basic 'machine bureaucracy' set-ups so as to develop highly specialized expertise and high-level arte-facts, such as sophisticated tax IT systems for auto-handling online submissions of tax forms, or data-mining to identify non-compliant or high-risk taxpayers.

Putting together the five first letters of the headings above, we get the acronym NATOE, which serves as a handy mnemonic of the range of tools at government's disposal.

It would be easy to conclude that the primary tool at the disposal of any tax agency is authority, specifically the tax code and the legal powers that it gives to the collecting department to compel the submis-sion of information and the payment of taxes assessed. The secondary tools would then be organization, especially the scale of personnel at the department's disposal, and treasure, its ability to spend to support that organization. Yet in an age of quasi-voluntary compliance, there is a strong case for arguing that it is the nodality of the tax agency that is crucial, its staff's ability to secure information from a wide range of soci-etal sources and to secure attention for department messages in return; plus the expertise embodied in its ICT systems for correctly identifying and monitoring taxpayers according to their risk status. Table 4.1 shows a listing of the key internal and outward-facing tasks confronting modern tax departments.

A McKinsey benchmarking study (Dohrmann and Pinshaw, 2009) found large variations in the percentage of total spending by functional area of tax administration spending across nine mainly OECD countries, shown in Table 4.2. The most consistently sized activities were the pro-portion of resources devoted to examinations and collections. Taxpayer service and tax submissions costs showed the greatest variations across countries, although this might also reflect variations in how these terms were understood across different departments. (As in other consultancy

Table 4.1   The key tasks of taxation departments

	Organizational and Managerial Tasks	Service Delivery and Operational Tasks
Internal-facing and corporate tasks	Planning, budgeting and resource allocation Monitoring and evaluation Coordination of department Financial management Personnel management (especially talent development and retention of skilled inspectors) ICT management Asset and property management Internal audit and control	Fiscal studies and research Policy development and liaison with stakeholders New tax legislation and tax code updating Monitoring tax liabilities and information levels Intelligence operations Collecting information from third parties
Outward-facing tasks	Risk management policies and settings Managing legal actions and debt recovery efforts Anti-corruption External relations	Registering new taxpayers Taxpayer services, especially activities building up voluntary compliance, including: – developing and operating easy-to-use online services; – management and design of the department website; – design of tax forms and customer communications; – taxpayer education; – assisting taxpayers in difficulties; – policies towards tax intermediaries Processing declarations and payments Monitoring of tax withholders and collection agents Risk analysis and 'customer segmentation', leading to: – targeting of investigations and audits; – search and seizure actions; – launching legal actions and prosecutions Debt management and recovery of arrears Handling of appeals and complaints

Source: Own research, plus Dunleavy et al. (2003); Gill (2003); Hasseldine (2010, Table 1, p.4).

Table 4.2   Shares of total administrative costs spent on four main functional areas by nine national tax departments

Function	Percentage of total administrative spending by tax departments			
	Median	Minimum	Maximum	Range
Examinations	36	28	46	18
Taxpayer service	24	13	52	39
Submissions	24	1	28	27
Collections	17	9	26	15

Source: Dohrmann and Pinshaw (2009).

reports, it is often hard to tell how precisely variable labels were defined to respondents here.)

Distinctive Bureaucratic Culture of Tax Agencies

The bureaucratic culture of tax departments and agencies is characteristically strongly shaped by their unique tasks within the government apparatus. Because they are essentially requisitioning resources from firms and citizens, tax departments always operate in a strongly legalistic way. Their every action has to be related to specific powers given by the legislation and the tax code, to which they must stick exactly. Tax departments are usually set up with a measure of bureaucratic independence in operational matters from direct control by the ministers or presidential cabinet running the government, so that they are in a position to defend (mostly) the integrity of existing systems and structures. But tax *rates* are directly set by top government leaders and legislation, while the tax department's internal operations are often closely supervised by the legislature. Hence officials themselves proclaim that there is much less delegation of discretion to professional staffs in tax bureaucracies than in other departments. Rule of law considerations are paramount.

However, tax departments may also operate a more professional or discretionary style when dealing with large companies and big players in income tax terms, partly because the taxpayers here deploy strong legal and tax expertise that is complex to manage and match, and the legal and enforcement costs can also rapidly mount up – placing more of a premium on negotiations. In the UK there were scandals in 2008–12 about top-level deals being cut between HMRC top officials and lawyers (Osborne, 2011). Campaigns about company non-payment of taxes by UK Uncut and other critical groups have called into question the reality of 'rigid' tax administration for at least some macro-negotiations between tax officials and major firms. One difficulty in assessing the real state of affairs is that in the UK and USA, tax bureaucracies are also deeply conservative (almost paranoid) about retaining data and information they have collected. Tax information about the incomes of individuals, company profits information and the tax compliance status of firms and people is highly sensitive in most Western countries – but not in Norway where tax returns are public documents.

In terms of their size, national tax departments are usually large or very large organizations when set against the landscape of other government agencies or even major firms in the country as a whole. Their essentially coercive role and large size both mean that they are characteristically organized as what Mintzberg (1983) terms a 'machine bureaucracy', with an emphasis upon the complete standardization of procedures, which are then comprehensively and impartially implemented. Of course, many subsections within tax departments function more on the lines of professional bureaucracies, especially the specialist staff (in ICT or legal services) and teams of elite tax investigators. But in both personnel and administrative cost terms the dominant 'operating core' of tax departments (in Mintzberg's terms) remains the field offices and services covering the whole country (usually in regions). Also included here are the ICT services supporting them – although IT functions are often outsourced to system integrator IT corporations in the modern period (Dunleavy et al., 2008, Ch. 6).

The decline of large manufacturing industries in many Western countries has tended to emphasize even more than before the large size of tax departments. In 1999 at the start of the main period we shall focus on here, Figure 4.1 shows that in advanced industrial countries around 1.5 to 2 people per 1000 population worked for national tax departments. In somewhat less industrialized countries with less of an effective mass taxation system, the numbers of staff were proportionately much lower. The USA is unusual amongst national agencies in having proportionately fewer staff – but many important taxation functions also reside at the level of the 50 states in the USA, which are not counted here.

One of the by-products of working in a large, secretive organization that is semi-detached from the rest of government, and having a job that is often unpopular with other citizens, is that tax department staff can often be rather inward-looking in their culture and attitudes. They typically join the department at a young age and maintain lifetime careers within it, in the UK with much less of the inward and outward movement of staff that increasingly characterizes other sections of government. In the USA, the

Figure 4.1   The number of tax staff per 1000 people in the national population, in the late 1990s

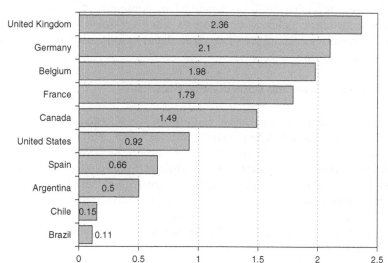

Source: Gallagher (2005, Table 8, p. 138).

Internal Revenue Service (IRS) is so unpopular with citizens at large that (possibly apocryphal) stories amongst federal officials suggest that its staff quite frequently marry each other, and rarely reveal to other people their precise jobs within government.

Historically, tax agencies developed a style of communicating with their grassroots 'customers' that is imperative, rigid and unresponsive, with infrequent contacts – often just once a year with self-assessing taxpayers and small firms. The emphasis upon impartial implementation characteristically produces dense, legalistic prose in letters and forms, inflexibility in applying payment deadlines and an enforcement style that can look unsympathetic to individuals' situations (Dunleavy et al., 2003). This can create particular problems where (as in Britain) the tax department is later assigned responsibility for paying out subsidies for working people (or families with children) via tax credits linked to low household incomes. Such subsidies can be quite critical for family living standards and often require much more frequent updating of reported incomes by tax credit recipients, and much more flexible and sensitive handling of cases by the tax department (Millar, 2008). This can demand a culture shift that is hard for a tax department's staff to adapt to.

In more routine ways tax departments also interact more frequently with businesses – for instance, dealing with monthly declarations of income taxes under PAYE and VAT returns. But here they deal mainly with more specialist staff or personnel in companies, or professional tax intermediaries (such as accountants filing for small businesses). So routine communications are often more fluent, cooperative and effective in problem-solving.

Cutting the Transactions Costs of Being Compliant

This is a relatively new emphasis within tax bureaucracies, and it is still often a rather controversial orientation for older staff and ingrained departmental traditions to come to terms with. In the USA there has been a strong emphasis throughout the post-war period on 'paperwork reduction' and keeping the size of forms and information demands to an absolute minimum for taxpayers – even while the tax code itself became longer and longer. But US tax practice also requires everyone over an income threshold to file a declaration of their incomes, which imposes considerable costs on millions of citizens. In other advanced countries there has been a main emphasis on taking low-income citizens and smaller businesses completely out of the income tax and VAT nets respectively. The development of PAYE systems also increases the automaticity of income tax payments for the vast majority of taxpayers, especially compared with the US universal filing approach – although the US does have pre-pay workplace withholding arrangements for lower-paid staff that mimic some PAYE effects. In most income tax systems higher-rate or non-PAYE taxpayers have to file returns, but simplified returns are sometimes feasible for smaller income levels.

Setting the thresholds at which citizens or companies have to file tax returns at all is one of the most critical decisions that policy-makers can make, since it determines how fine the regulatory mesh is and largely sets what the administrative burden is on the tax department. For instance, OECD data in 2001 showed that the levels set for firms to file VAT declarations ranged from a turnover of around £5000 a year in Italy (so that virtually all own account workers had to file), through £53000 in the UK (which many self-employed workers did not have to be concerned with) up to around £150000 a year in Japan (high enough not to pull in two- or three-person firms).

In the period since 1995 there has been far more emphasis on stimulating voluntary tax compliance through the greater simplification of tax filing processes and payments, especially via the better design of tax forms and greater 'segmentation' of customers into low-, medium- and high-risk categories. Often conservative tax agencies remained wedded to complex, multi-question forms in the income tax area, arguing that tax codes required very comprehensive responses (Dunleavy et al., 2003). But the development of online tax filing in the internet era has allowed tax information and forms to become much more closely tailored to different individuals' situations than previous paper-form technologies. The complexities can be retained, but they are no longer apparent to users with simple tax situations, since they never need to fill in complex sections. Similarly, tax departments have gradually come to fully accept that taxpayer education, maintaining an excellent website, and providing responsive assistance to taxpayers seeking to be compliant are all key aspects of their work – and increasingly important in minimizing subsequent administrative burdens.

4.2 TAX ADMINISTRATION IN THE UK

Historically, the collection of taxes in Britain was the responsibility of two departments of ancient origin, each with a strong and distinctive character. First, the Inland Revenue (hereafter Revenue) was in charge of collecting direct taxes on individuals, especially income tax deducted at source via PAYE by companies, and for self-employed people paid by individual self-assessment forms. In addition, the department collected inheritance tax, a social security tax (called National Insurance Contributions, in fact paid mostly via the PAYE system) from individuals, some taxes on companies, especially corporation tax (on companies' declared profits) and petroleum revenue duty on petrol and diesel. Second, Her Majesty's Customs and Excise (hereafter Customs, discussed in Chapter 3) was in charge of collecting indirect taxes, overwhelmingly from firms and small businesses, especially VAT on almost all goods sold, some particular excise duties on alcohol and tobacco (taxed at much higher rates) and import duties, as well as processing imports and exports. (The customs arrangements for its trade regulation work are covered in section 3.2, Chapter 3.)

The UK's system of taxation has evolved into the pattern shown in Table 4.3, where half of all receipts come from PAYE income taxes and National Insurance, plus another addition from self-assessment income tax. Indirect taxes (collected by Customs and Excise prior to 2005) account for a further 30 per cent of taxes. The last sixth of taxes come mainly from corporation tax and capital gains tax. The last column of the table also shows that 91 per cent of all taxes remitted to the central government are actually paid across by businesses. Most of the big taxes are wholly paid across by firms, and there are only a few taxes (like stamp duties) where both firms and individuals pay across substantial sums.

Table 4.3   The relative importance of taxes collected by HM Revenue &
*   Customs in 2005–06, and the proportion remitted to HMRC by*
*   businesses*

	Receipts in Billions (£000 m)	Percentage of all Central Taxes	Proportion (%) Remitted by Businesses
Income tax, PAYE	113.9	28.6	100
National Insurance (social security contribution)	85.7	21.5	97
VAT	*72.9*	*18.3*	*100*
Other Customs and Excise taxes/ duties/levies	*48.0*	*12.0*	*100*
Corporation tax (on profits)	42.0	10.5	100
Capital gains tax (on property and investments)	22.9	5.7	0
Income tax, self-assessment (net of repayments)	18.2	4.6	0
Stamp duties (on property and share transactions)	10.9	2.7	40
Other receipts	8.4	2.1	52
Tax credits (income support payments to low-income households in employment)	–4.7	–1.2	90
Other repayments	–5.0	–1.3	96
Inheritance tax	3.3	0.8	0
Petroleum revenue tax	2.0	0.5	100
Total	398.4	100.0	91

Note: The taxes collected by HM Customs and Excise before 2005 are in italic. All other
taxes were collected by Inland Revenue.

Source: HMRC (2006), *Annual Report, 2005–06.*

Individuals directly paid to HMRC only self-assessed income tax, capital
gains tax and inheritance tax.

We first review the organization and development of both departments
relevant for this chapter. (We start from the late 1980s, partly because
tax changes are slower moving than many other policy areas, and partly
because we have some data series on productivity that can be pushed
this far back.) We then look at what happened after the merger of the
two departments to form Her Majesty's Revenue & Customs (HMRC)
in 2005. To help in following this story, Figure 4.2 provides a summary
overview of the main changes that have taken place in the area of UK

Figure 4.2   Main changes in tax collection administration in the last 20 years

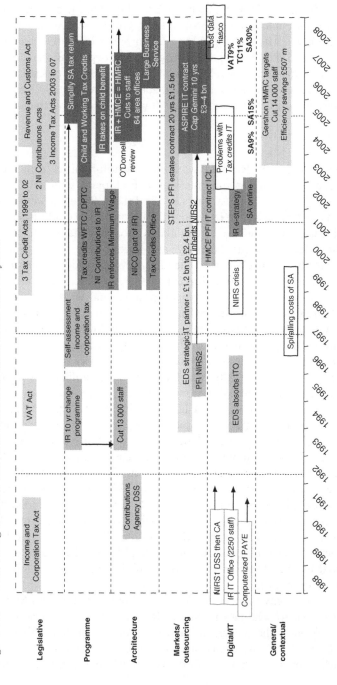

Note: In Figure 4.2, the abbreviations used are: ASPIRE consortium of computer firms; EDS and ICL major computer firms; HMCE Customs and Excise; IR Inland Revenue; ITO Information Technology Office (an agency within Inland Revenue); NI National Insurance; NICO National Insurance Contribution Office; NIRS National Insurance Register System; PFI Private Finance Initiative; SA Self-assessment Income Tax; STEPS acronym for property transfer consortium; TC Tax credit; VAT value-added tax; WFTC Working Families Tax Credit.

tax collection during the 20 years from 1988 to 2008. On the bottom axis, general elections are marked with broken lines. On the vertical axis there are six general areas where changes have taken place: legislative agenda; implementation and change of specific programmes; organizational architecture; market outsourcing developments; digital/IT developments; and general/contextual changes such as the impact of the influential Gershon Review (2004) on improving the efficiency of government departments.

Inland Revenue

Like Customs, the Inland Revenue was run as a non-ministerial department by a board of civil servants, making it the largest 'semi-detached' unit in Whitehall. The Commissioners of the Inland Revenue were first constituted as a department in 1849, and the organization could trace its history back before that under a different label (Board of Stamps) to 1665. Although brigaded under the Treasury, and accountable for its overall performance to the Chancellor of Exchequer, Revenue jealously guarded the operational conduct of tax enforcement from 'political' or partisan interference. Consequently tax administration has never been seen as politically or ministerially influenced in the UK, and corruption in the levying of incomes or corporation taxes is almost unknown. The department also always sought to maintain the 'integrity' of the tax code in its dealings with ministers, avoiding if possible changes away from previous law and precedent, and generally resisting new and unfamiliar tax ideas. To help in these tasks, by the 1990s it maintained a large policy staff.

In 1988 the Thatcher government launched its 'Next Steps' initiative to hive off the control of large-scale delivery operations by civil servants from being directly run by Whitehall departments and into newly created executive agencies. Both Inland Revenue and Customs were at first little affected, since they were already set up as non-ministerial departments in an 'executive' configuration. However, the longer Next Steps went on, the greater the stress placed by ministers on both departments formulating business plans on more private sector lines and accounting more explicitly to ministers for their performance within the same 'framework' used for executive agency reporting. Like Customs, Inland Revenue was also regularly reviewed by the House of Commons' Public Accounts Committee and Treasury Committee.

The Conservative governments of Margaret Thatcher and John Major were slow to push for changes in Inland Revenue, partly because their attention was fixed on the agencification drive elsewhere across Whitehall, and partly because they were anxious to maintain the inflow of public finances. However, at the height of efforts to curb Whitehall personnel numbers in 1992 the Treasury cut its staff by a quarter. The following year Treasury ministers announced a ten-year change programme for Inland Revenue, which aimed to reduce the department's staff numbers by 13 000, with an ultimate aim that by 2002 its total staff numbers should fall to 42 000.

As a key part of achieving this change, Revenue's top officials targeted the department's big in-house IT capacity (called the Information Technology Office), which had nearly 2250 staff. The Revenue's main IT operations were completely outsourced in 1994 to the US systems integrator company EDS, already the dominant corporate player in the UK. EDS's market share in civil government IT rose to 64 per cent after this deal. Under the ten-year Revenue contract, 1900 staff in the Revenue's data centres moved across to EDS under the normal TUPE ('transfer of public enterprises') provisions. The initial contract price was a low-looking £250 million over ten years, a hugely long contract. But in what became the normal 'six for one' arrangement for UK government information technology, the contract cost rose first to £1.2 billion, because the incumbent main contractor EDS could negotiate change contracts worth five or six times the initial competed-for value of the contract. When the EDS deal finally ran out in 2004, Inland Revenue had in fact paid EDS over £2.4 billion. However, from the start of the contract there were operational problems with Revenue computer systems, with officials complaining about downtime, delays in fixing problems and so on (see Dunleavy et al., 2006b, p. 142).

Another important aspect at the outsourcing level, was the award of a PFI (Private Finance Initiative) contract called STEPS to a firm called Mapeley for the administration and development of office accommodation for both Revenue and Her Majesty's Customs and Excise (HMCE) in 2001. While the contract was subject to some controversy regarding the financial situation of Mapeley, independent assessments judged that the contract had been beneficial for both departments (National Audit Office, 2009b).

The low initial cost of the IT outsourcing and its subsequent escalation reflected the fact that in other areas the Conservatives in the 1980s and 1990s were largely content to squeeze Inland Revenue for 'efficiency savings', while actually letting the modernity of its buildings, work processes and information technology gradually worsen, year on year, with no major new investments. The one big project in the department that was pushed ahead and launched in 1996 was a brand new and lengthy self-assessment form (on paper), which now legally had to be completed by around 9 million self-employed and higher-rate taxpayers. It 'represented one of the largest changes in tax administration for decades' according to the National Audit Office (NAO, 2001b). Spurred on by Conservative ministers who admired the leanness of the IRS's operations in the USA, some senior Revenue officials had pressed for all UK citizens to have to file a self-assessment form. However, from the outset, the assessment system was also much more expensive to administer than collecting taxes via PAYE, so that ministers in the end never agreed to the universal filing idea. Instead the vast bulk (92 per cent) of income tax continued to be collected via PAYE, and the remainder via self-assessment.

The declining numbers and sizes of major employers in the UK, plus the growth of 'portfolio careers' where people work for much briefer periods for many more employers, might have been expected to over time cause a drift of people out of the PAYE system and into self-assessment. The threshold for the higher-rate (40 per cent) tax band was also uplifted by less than inflation for many years, which brought more and more people into the higher-rate category. This might have meant that more people had to submit self-assessment forms over time. However, in the late 1990s and 2000s Inland Revenue counteracted many of these trends by periodically reviewing who was required to submit assessments, and how onerous the burden was on different types of taxpayers. By the mid-2000s the department had taken most older people with occupational pensions, and some higher-rate taxpayers with very simple tax affairs, out of the self-assessment net.

The paper form for self-assessment that Revenue produced was also controversial from the outset. It was intended to be comprehensive and so was extremely long and complex for non-accountants to fill in, with dozens of questions, most of which had little relevance to ordinary taxpayers. The main self-assessment paper tax form was widely criticized as completely inaccessible for ordinary individuals. A 2003 National Audit Office (NAO) study of *Difficult Forms* noted that it was still massively too complex for most people filling it in, and that Inland Revenue had taken years to design and introduce a shorter tax form (Dunleavy et al., 2003). The department ran a highly over-cautious 'pilot' of the shorter form that took five years, and involved 50 000 people using the new form, before very slowly rolling it out nationwide.

Far more significant changes in Revenue's structures and operations took place following the election of a modernizing Labour government led by Tony Blair in 1997. For their first two years in office Labour ministers stuck with the Conservative spending plans, which included no allowance for administrative improvements. But members of the new government were in fact taken aback by the degree to which civil service offices, IT and working methods had been allowed to decay under the Conservatives. They quickly resolved that when public spending could grow again many long overdue, modernizing improvements must be made. Collecting taxes more effectively was a priority here, since Labour's wider public spending plans depended on first bringing in resources.

By 1999 ministers were impressed by the level of IT service delivered by the outsourced Revenue arrangements, compared with the difficulties experienced at the Department of Social Security (DSS) that ran the welfare payments systems, and where a major reorganization was anyway in progress (see Chapter 5). Part of the DSS set up on 'Next Steps' lines, the Contributions Agency (CA), was responsible for collating information on individuals' liabilities for National Insurance (NI) contributions, monies that in fact the Revenue had collected on behalf of DSS for years. Now ministers decided to transfer the whole function to Revenue, renaming it the National Insurance Contribution Office. The shift increased Inland Revenue's staff in 2001 by roughly 10000 FTEs (full-time equivalent' staff), year on year. One factor that impelled ministers to change was acute controversy over a computer system used for NI, the National Insurance Recording System, which was set up as a PFI contract between the Department of Social Security and the management and technology consultancy firm Accenture. The company failed to deliver the new NISR2 system that it had promised in time for the switch off of the old system in 2000–01. This led to the underpayment of thousands of pensioners whose records could not be satisfactorily validated, and expensive manual rectifications.

A second accretion of Revenue's functions involved a major functional (and identity) change when it began to act as a transfer agency as well as a revenue collection agency. This shift followed from efforts by the Chancellor of the Exchequer, Gordon Brown, to expand the state's support for families in work, so as to create extra incentives for people to move off welfare rolls and into employment. In 1999 a system of 'Child Tax Credits' was introduced, where households with children and low incomes would be paid a monthly amount by Inland Revenue. Subsequently in 2003 the tax credits ceased to be solely linked to children and became general for low-income households with people in work. The new responsibility created many difficulties for Inland Revenue, which had to move from dealing with individual taxpayers only once a year to updating data on household incomes far more frequently. Acute problems arose where the department paid tax credits to households based on their last period incomes, but where someone was now earning more money than before. Essentially families would be over-paid credits and then subsequently Revenue would try to recover the monies after they had already been spent. Where households failed to notify Revenue promptly of increases in incomes, the amounts of over-payments could quickly mount up, creating serious debt liabilities for low-income households. Despite massive

*Figure 4.3   The numbers of FTE staff working on taxation and customs
trade regulation roles, 1994 to 2008*

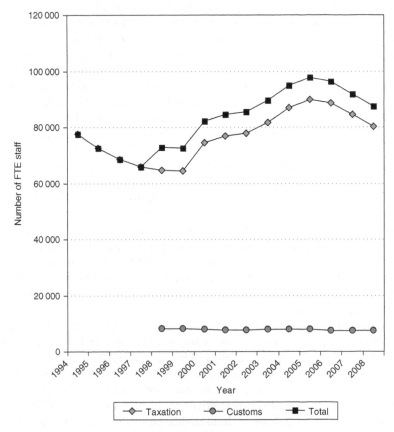

Source: Analysis of data in annual reports for Inland Revenue, Customs and Excise and
HMRC.

advertising campaigns designed to remind tax credit recipients to always
tell the department when their circumstances changed, the problems of
over-payments and recoveries mushroomed, deluging Revenue call centres
with angry customers and leading to a doubling of complaints in 2005–07.

The addition of new functions to Inland Revenue's responsibilities considerably increased the number of staff working on overall taxation issues,
as Figure 4.3 illustrates. From a low point in 1998 the two departments
covered here grew by more than a quarter to peak in 2006. This change
contrasted sharply with the stable numbers of staff working on Customs'
regulatory functions, discussed in Chapter 3.

Figure 4.4　The development of self-assessment tax returns online, 1997 to 2008

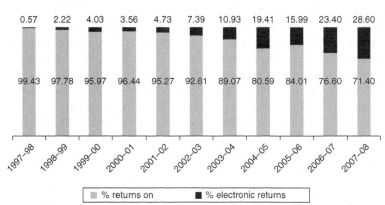

| 0.57 | 2.22 | 4.03 | 3.56 | 4.73 | 7.39 | 10.93 | 19.41 | 15.99 | 23.40 | 28.60 |

| 99.43 | 97.78 | 95.97 | 96.44 | 95.27 | 92.61 | 89.07 | 80.59 | 84.01 | 76.60 | 71.40 |

1997-98 1998-99 1999-00 2000-01 2001-02 2002-03 2003-04 2004-05 2005-06 2006-07 2007-08

▨ % returns on　　　■ % electronic returns

Source: Computed from HMRC data provided by the department's statistical teams.

Another area of change was more positive, but proved slow to develop, namely the introduction of online forms for self-assessment taxpayers and businesses dealing with Inland Revenue. In a 1997 speech to the Labour Party conference, the Prime Minister Tony Blair pledged that all public services would go online by 2008, a limit that a 1999 National Audit Office report demonstrated was so far away that no Whitehall department was taking it seriously (Dunleavy et al., 1999). The government responded to a resulting critical Public Accounts Committee report by bringing the online service deadline forward from 2008 to 2005. Additionally, they specified for both Inland Revenue and Customs and Excise that they must be achieving 50 per cent of their overall transactions with customers online by 2005. Immediately after Blair's speech, Revenue identified online submission of the self-assessment income tax form as one key change it needed to make a priority. By 1998 it had an early service in place and Figure 4.4 shows that the proportion of taxpayers submitting online very gradually expanded up to 2002. One of the key problems was how to uniquely identify taxpayers online, and the cumbersome solution that the civil service came up with (which persists to the present day) is called the Government Gateway. Its clunky operations meant that it was only from 2003 onwards that the numbers of taxpayers filing online really began to grow at all.

In 2002 another NAO report considered the slow take up and commissioned consultants to report on cultural barriers to e-government (Margetts and Dunleavy, 2002). Arising from this work and other criticisms Revenue commissioned a later paper on how to use incentives to induce businesses to switch over to digital submissions, which recommended a 'staircase' approach of strengthening incentives via gradually mandating online returns (Margetts et al., 2006). From 2009 the new department HMRC required self-assessment taxpayers wanting to file on paper to do so before the end of September, while those who delay to the last minute and submitted their forms later on would have to use the online service. Since most taxpayers hang on to near the final deadline, this change to partial mandation had an immediate effect, with the proportion of self-assessment forms sent in online growing very fast. The digital share reached more than three-quarters by the 2010–11 financial year and began to plateau off. The online service was also much easier to use than the paper forms and the answers that taxpayers gave dropped straight into HMRC tax databases.

However, the progress on growing individual taxpayers' responses disguised an underlying stagnation in Inland Revenue's and later HMRC's thinking (NAO, 2002a, 2002b and 2005). By the 2000s around 10 000 businesses in the UK accounted for two-thirds of PAYE income tax receipts, but the systems they were using (although computerized in some respects) were essentially static, dating back almost to the 1944 origins of the PAYE system itself. Businesses remitted amounts to the Revenue for their employees' total tax liabilities, monthly or quarterly depending on their size, and they provided wages and payslips to the workers involved, detailing how much tax had been paid. But firms did not tell Revenue monthly or quarterly how to split up the tax paid across the staff involved – because right through into the 2010s' decade the Revenue had no computer systems capable of accepting this 'real-time' information. Instead firms had to complete an annual return at the end of each tax year, which told Revenue on an annual basis how much each staff member had earned and how much tax they had paid. These annual statements had to be submitted by July (after the end of the tax year), but the information in them was often only really processed by Revenue by September in the year. Thus tax officials were never handling tax information about individuals that was less than six months out of date, and for data affecting the start of the year the information was 18 months out of date. All the real-time information that firms collected and remitted to employees monthly was never used by Revenue – because it could not be accepted or processed. Yet one of the first laws of taxation is that the more time elapses between a tax liability being incurred and tax officials learning about it, the greater the loss in revenues collected that can be expected. It was not until 2011 that ministers finally pressed for and agreed to implement a large contract to bring in 'real-time information'. Even here the pressure came in large part from the Secretary of State for the Department for Work and Pensions, who wanted to better integrate the payment of tax credits with payments for welfare benefits.

A key reason for the huge lapse of time in grasping the nettle of out of date information was ministers' and officials' aversion to launching the substantial IT contracts needed to modernize Revenue's huge and dated legacy IT systems. The department's relationship with its original IT supplier (EDS) proved to be reasonably problematic, as the company negotiated hard over any changes in what it was contracted to do, progressively raising the prices that the department had to pay for any alterations and new provisions insufficiently anticipated in the original contract – a process that most IT contractors with government thoroughly understood and relied on in their initial contract pricing. In 2004 the problems of tax credits being overpaid to low-income households exploded, with complaints against Revenue spiking sharply upwards, and ministers and MPs being sharply critical of the department. Revenue blamed EDS for many of the problems and launched a legal case against the company to recover hundreds of millions of pounds overpaid to families who later had problems repaying the amounts that they had inadvertently accumulated. Eventually the case was settled out of court at a cost of £95 million to the company.

The souring of relations with EDS meant that Revenue was resolved to re-compete its ICT contracts in a rigorous fashion, and not to become 'locked in' to depending on the company. In 2004–05 the department's top management rejected an EDS renewal tender in favour of a rival bid that was seen as more cost-effective, from a consortium called ASPIRE, within which the leading company was Capgemini. The new HMRC contract for 14 years was costed at more than £4.5 billion. Subsequently it too was renegotiated within a few years to give average 'price-point' reductions of around 10 per cent in costs, in return for which Capgemini gained a further four years on the deal, taking the contract length to 18 years. This was an enormous slice of time, especially in IT terms, where technology generations change wholesale every two to three years.

Customs and Excise

The main taxes collected by Customs at the start of our period were VAT, a flat rate sales tax paid by all businesses with a turnover above £50 000 a year (excluding only very small own-account worker businesses) and excise taxes. VAT required traders to file very simple monthly or quarterly returns of the VAT amounts that the firm had collected on its sales, to log and deduct from this sum the amount of VAT that the firm had itself paid, and to make payments of the resulting net amount due. Excise taxes required mostly similar filing by businesses selling particular commodities, especially tobacco and alcohol, both taxed very heavily. Almost all Customs tax transactions were carried out with businesses rather than with individuals. The main exception was individuals paying import duties, far and away the most expensive of all the taxes to collect, but of very minor significance in the department's overall tax activities.

Because of the success of the CHIEF system for imports and exports (described in Chapter 3), Customs was not immediately worried by the prime minister's requirement that 50 per cent of their transactions should be online by 2005 – when we interviewed them in 1999 they felt that the statistical returns here would cover much of their 'electronic' total. We looked at Customs' computer systems for registering VAT and excise liabilities and payments in detailed work for the NAO, and at that time they closely resembled those in Revenue. Customs ran a jungle of over 90 different legacy, mainframe systems that were complex to coordinate. We have commented on Customs' relations with its IT supplier, ICL/Fujitsu in Chapter 3. The company ran mainframe systems and networks effectively enough, but it was very slow to develop any level of web expertise.

The department very slowly set about introducing VAT returns online, but its initial approach (in 1998–2002) was a dismal failure because it required companies to pay a substantial cost for a digital certificate that they could use for no other purpose. The VAT return was also easy to fill in manually (consisting of only seven pieces of information), and small companies especially liked sending in a paper form and paying by cheque to best protect their cash flow. Paradoxically the return's very simplicity meant that the department found it difficult to bring VAT returns online in a way that would save much money, especially while they were running paper and online systems together. At one point the Customs Board thought about creating a new IT-based unit to develop VAT returns online in competition with its existing main line of business, but in the end did nothing. It stuck with its clunky system and neglected the Customs website, on which much of the information by 2002 was partial or incorrect.

A 2002 NAO report expressed deep scepticism about the department's online strategy and doubted whether the department would have 50 per cent of its transactions online by 2005 (Dunleavy et al., 2002). The Chief Executive assured the Public Accounts Committee that it would meet that commitment, but he subsequently left the department within the year to return to the private sector, as did his IT director. Figure 4.5 shows that in fact Customs made much slower progress than Revenue in getting its customers to file VAT returns online, which only began to grow appreciably after Customs was merged to form HMRC in 2005. Online VAT

Figure 4.5   Online and paper-based VAT

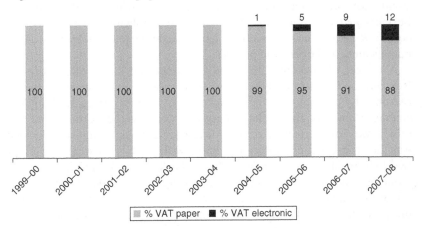

Source: Computed from data provided by HMRC statistical teams.

transactions remained a small minority of the total by the end of our study period in 2008.

The Merged Department

In 2005 the Labour government led by Tony Blair decided to take a decision shunned by previous cabinets and to merge Customs into the Revenue, creating a new super-department, Her Majesty's Revenue & Customs (hereafter HMRC). The move was made partly at the urgings of the Treasury's top official, its permanent secretary Gus O'Donnell, who was persuaded that staff and cost economies would flow from pushing Revenue and Customs operations together. In particular, the O'Donnell Review (2004) concluded that the merger would allow staff savings – and would mean that businesses would no longer have to deal with two Whitehall tax departments, each with different cultures, IT systems and methods of working. O'Donnell was also frustrated that so many policy staff worked for Revenue and so few for the Treasury on tax issues, so in the reorganization a substantial transfer of top tax policy expertise into the Treasury took place (Treasury Select Committee, 2004).

A new HMRC board was created to maintain a degree of collegial overview of both direct and indirect taxes collection, but a Chief Executive (rather than just a board chair) was appointed to produce stronger accountability for change. A number of non-executive directors, all from business, were created to sit alongside the top officials. In 2008 a new role

of Chairman of HMRC was also created on business lines to take responsibility for providing strategic leadership, approving the department's
business plans, monitoring performance and policing the standards of
corporate governance. This left the Chief Executive to focus on day-to-day
management and operation policies.

A merger of two such historically distinct and large-scale bodies as
Revenue and Customs was bound to be costly and disruptive, a key
reason why previous British governments held off from making the
change, even though by the twenty-first century the norm across the
OECD was for national governments to have a single tax agency. (France
was the other main exception here along with the UK. Historically it had
two long-lived tax departments, dating back to the French Revolution
– one of which was responsible for assessing tax liabilities and the other
for collecting taxes. The French government also finally decided to merge
these two in 2005.) The costly creation of HMRC was to be paid for by
tactics familiar from 'mergers and acquisitions' strategies in the corporate
sector – namely rationalizing areas of overlap, pooling the two departments' staff, integrating their links with taxpayers (especially with businesses who collect the vast bulk of taxes for government), and cutting out
duplications in office networks, staffing and ICT systems (O'Donnell,
2004).

A huge 'transformational change' programme was also created in
Inland Revenue in 2000, long before the merger took place, representing
a substantial drive to modernize its procedures, update its ICT systems
and exploit the increased use of ICTs and online filing systems to try to
reduce staff numbers. Upon its formation HMRC promulgated a similar
plan, with the same ambitious (hence almost bound to be disappointed)
'transformational change' title. It initially had no fewer than 21 'high priority' objectives, marrying long-term modernization projects with efforts
to exploit merger 'synergies', later reduced to 'just' 13 main programmes
(NAO, 2008d).

At the same time as these difficulties some senior officials and 'insider'
observers claimed that strong improvements in performance followed
from the application since 2005 of another management initiative, the
PaceSetter programme. Implemented with the McKinsey management
consultancy and focusing on the department's field services the programme aimed to:

- Redesign service delivery processes so as to eliminate waste and variability and maximize flexibility. HMRC senior management argued
that this would improve productivity and service quality, as well as
reducing lead time on innovations.

- Change the department's current management processes so as to create appropriate management infrastructure to sustain improvements.
- Change the mindsets and behaviours of leaders and frontline staff to support the new lean business systems and to deliver continuous improvement.

HMRC implemented the PaceSetter programme in ten of its major processing sites. There were three main components: lean implementation (following private sector initiatives, originally led by the Toyota car manufacturer), operational management (OM) and senior leadership (SL). Bottom-up approaches to improving performance through lean implementation were supposed to be closely connected to the more top-down OM and SL elements, driven by the strong commitment of the leadership team down into the wider organization. Official reports from HMRC claimed that the PaceSetter programme received strong acceptance from managers and frontline staff (HMRC, 2007). However, its concrete impacts on tax collection productivity have been closely bound up with the programme of staff reductions, and so the National Audit Office (2011b, p. 10) found only 'a small positive impact on staff engagement'.

In terms of departmental IT systems, under the merger, the Revenue's systems and staff became the dominant ones. The National Audit Office pointed out how the HMRC could not only save costs but also develop a strategic relationship co-partnering with a single supplier and having a better overall accountability for IT delivery (NAO, 2006). The previous Customs contract with ICL/Fujitsu was now absorbed within the ASPIRE contract. Independent evaluations highlighted the utility of re-centralizing the formerly separated Revenue and Customs IT contracts. One of the benign changes occurred in VAT payments, where Figure 4.5 shows that some slow progress at last began to be achieved in getting processes online. The Revenue adopted a strategy of first incentivizing companies to go online, and later mandating the largest firms to do so in tranches, and this began to make slow headway.

However, Capgemini and the ASPIRE consortium continued to have great problems in getting the administration of tax credits improved. The introduction of a New Payments System (NPS) was also billed by HMRC as a radical modernization and integration of its complex legacy computer systems. But in fact the system rapidly ran into massive difficulties in the period 2008 to 2010, and had great difficulty in coping with people receiving incomes from multiple sources. It especially lost track of many pensioners' receipts from the Department for Work and Pensions in working out millions of PAYE taxes, meaning that elderly people were suddenly confronted with 'overdue' tax bills of thousand of pounds (Dunleavy, 2011b).

The attempted implementation of the myriad 'transformational programmes' and the NPS also overlapped strongly with the pushing through of a government-wide efficiency effort (launched by Tony Blair in the run up to the 2005 general election), called the Gershon Review. This was supposed to 'free up resources for the frontline' by cutting 'back-office' staff, removing waste and improving overall efficiency. Since HMRC in 2005 accounted for 91 000 staff (a fifth of the Home Civil Service), and was now more closely accountable to the Treasury (responsible for ensuring that the Gershon Review succeeded), it was inevitable that the new merged HMRC had to offer up large-scale staffing reductions – eventually reaching 34 000 jobs in total.

The combination of large-scale job cutbacks occurring at the same time as a Herculean effort to force together the historically entrenched bureaucratic cultures of Revenue and Customs was not a happy one. Staff morale and confidence in the HMRC senior management fell precipitously from 2007 onwards, reaching a nadir in December 2010 after the scale of the NPS fiasco emerged. An internal survey of 51 000 staff showed that just one in nine employees were then confident in their senior management, and just one in seven felt motivated to deliver the best service to customers (UHY Hacker Young, 2010). Unsurprisingly a Cabinet Office 'capability review' (2009a) of HMRC leadership sketched a large agenda for improvement.

4.3   PRODUCTIVITY IN UK TAX ADMINISTRATION

Since HMRC is now an integrated department, we measure productivity for its two predecessor departments combined. As Table 4.4 shows, we thereby cover all direct and indirect taxes for ten years forward from 1997–08. (We exclude some small aspects of Revenue activities here, such as petroleum revenue tax, where the number of returns from major oil companies is very small, and stamps on property transactions. Including these tiny constant elements would make no remotely visible addition to the department's activities or output data.)

The key data series used here for outputs is the numbers of tax returns for the major tax categories above, the indicator that was also recommended in the influential Atkinson Review (2005b). The logic of using the returns is that almost all other elements of HMRC tax activity (such as taxpayer education, investigations and audit work, or debt recovery) are closely related to returns, usually by ratios that are broadly stable

Table 4.4   Data and adjustments used for the measurement of productivity in UK taxation, 1998 to 2008

Variable	Evidence Used, and Adjustments Made
Outputs for processing of taxes	Number of tax returns processed for: income tax; corporation tax; capital gains tax; inheritance tax; VAT; excise duties; other indirect taxes. Internal data were provided by HMRC covering 1997–2008 onwards
Cost-weighting of outputs	Unit costs for each tax above, estimated from HMRC and Inland Revenue/HMCE annual reports
Inputs, for total factor productivity	Deflated total labour and other administration costs obtained from HMRC and Inland Revenue/ Customs and Excise annual reports. However, it was not possible to reconstruct a reliable series for capital consumption because it is inconsistently covered in annual reports
Inputs for staff productivity	Number of full-time equivalent (FTE) staff allocated to tax processing, obtained from annual reports (our data excludes Customs and Excise/HMRC staff working on import/export and regulatory work, covered in Chapter 3)

and endure across time. Indeed, the annual reports for HMRC and its predecessors show a strong fixation with maintaining as far as possible constant unit costs and stable levels of indicators of performance. Top officials seemed to place a premium on maintaining ratios, taking strong corrective measures if the costs of collection, evidence of non-compliance or any other key indicator seemed to be veering off course or off trend. However, at the end of this section we do briefly consider an alternative approach to HMRC and predecessor departments' outputs, one focusing on the amounts of taxation collected. In terms of cost weights to get to an overall activity number we used the share of administration costs for the different taxes collected to weight the different tax volumes. The weighted tax volumes were then added and a total index of tax output was set up, using 2001–02 as the base year.

All the tax departments provide good over-time information on the costs of collecting different kinds of taxes. Figure 4.6 shows how the overall pattern of costs per £1000 collected moved over time. The dominant trait here is for tax costs to stay rather stable over time, although there are noticeable declines in the costs of collecting capital gains, corporation and inheritance taxes. The costs of collecting income taxes fall

Figure 4.6   The costs of collecting the major UK taxes, from 2001 to 2008

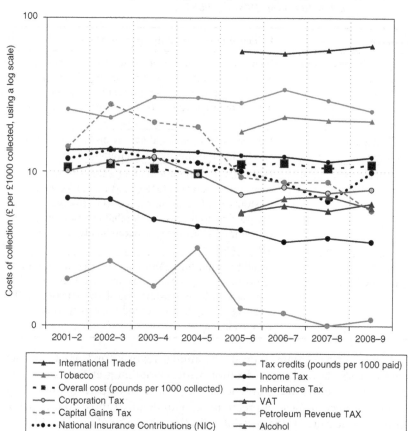

Source: Recalculated from HMRC (2006, Annex C, p. 69; 2009).

slightly. Excise taxes if anything became more expensive over time, and tax credit costs remained consistently high. The most cost-effective tax was petroleum revenue tax, paid in large instalments by the few major oil companies. Nevertheless, cost-weighting does make important differences across the years, and is essential to capture an appropriate overall measure of taxation outputs as a whole. However, in the figures below we use a rather different series for our cost weights, namely internal department cost weights per return processed.

Should quality-weighting be applied to the tax outputs series as consti-tuted above? Most of the operations carried out by HMRC and predeces-

Figure 4.7   Complaints against HMRC and its two predecessor departments, 2001–08

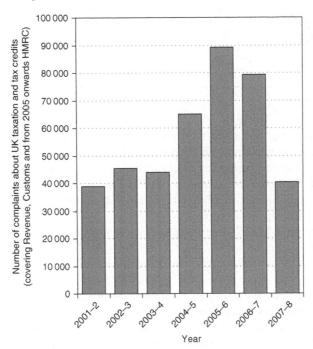

sor departments have remained relatively unchanged. This is true not only across the more recent ten-year period 1998–2008 on which we mainly focus here, but also in a longer-term perspective covering two decades forward from 1988, for which we briefly consider some indicative evidence at the end of this section. At various times in the last ten or 20 years, there have been significant teething troubles with one or another aspects of the tax system – including the launching of self-assessment, the initial introduction of online assessment (where the Inland Revenue's website crashed at the busiest time), and the early years of tax credit and over-payments. (The NPS problems occurred after our study period.) Figure 4.7 shows that in 2004–07 complaints to HMRC virtually doubled, mostly because of tax credits problems.

Towards the end of the period cutbacks in HMRC staff numbers plus continuing high levels of customer enquiries resulted in many calls going unanswered. Only 57 per cent of the 103 million attempted phone calls to HMRC in 2008–09 were answered. This compares with 71 per cent in the year before (2007–08) and a call-centre industry benchmark standard of

Table 4.5   Two key forms of tax gap in UK taxation

Tax Gap as % of Total Theoretical Tax Liability in:	Financial Year (April to March) Beginning in:									
	1999	2000	2001	2002	2003	2004	2005	2006	2007	2008
Self-assessment	10	12	14	16	16	15				
VAT gaps				15.7	12.1	11.8	15.4	13.3	12.3	15.3

Source: HMRC (2009).

more than 90 per cent (NAO, 2010a). Performance worsened in 2009–11, when some estimates put the proportion of unanswered calls above half. This is a significant indicator of organizational stress, and an important breach of the taxpayer assistance role that is integral to modern quasi-voluntary compliance systems (see Table 4.1 above), but it reached a height outside our study period.

On the other hand, there have also been some indications of service quality increasing in some aspects – notably the development of online self-assessment for income tax, which users generally rate as much easier to use than the paper forms; the new short form for self-assessment; a range of online forms in HMRC and Revenue dealings with business; and the slower progress on electronic VAT filing after 2005.

The most fundamental index of quality that HMRC officials closely monitor concerns the extent of the 'tax gap' in income tax self-assessment and in VAT, between what should be theoretically collectable at prevailing tax rates and the amounts that are in fact being collected. Table 4.5 shows that the VAT gap has tended to wobble up and down between 12 and 15 per cent, with no clear trend. The self-assessment gap seemed to increase from 2000 to 2002 and to stay high for three years, but HMRC stopped publishing this data thereafter, so that more recent movements are not known. The National Audit Office and Parliament's Public Accounts Committee also maintain a close watch on tax system operations. Their numerous quality assurance reports in this period are generally consistent with the maintenance of a stable quality standard over time and across different tax services (albeit with wobbles, fluctuations and even crises in different areas and aspects). We conclude from these data that the overall quality of service has been basically consistent across the broad range of direct and indirect taxes, and hence that quality-weightings are not needed for the outputs of HMRC and its predecessors in our study period.

In terms of inputs, we reiterate that the change from Customs and Inland Revenue to HMRC posed a few problems in identifying the correct share of labour and other administration costs, since Customs' systems

Figure 4.8   Labour and intermediate inputs productivity in UK taxation, 1997 to 2008

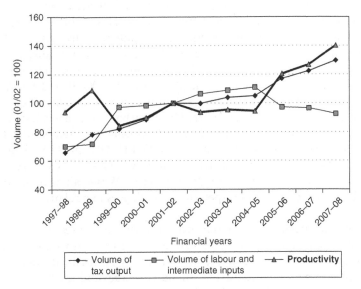

Source: Computed by the authors, from data supplied by HMCE, IR, HMRC.

were different. For total factor productivity (TFP) analysis we seek to consider all administration costs, divided across labour, procurement and capital consumption. However, there is a problem for the present study in calculating a measure similar to TFP, because data on HMRC's and its predecessors' capital stock and its estimated lifespan and depreciation (necessary for the calculation of capital consumption) are not available from public sources in a way that could be related to the tax collection effort. On the other hand good-quality data are available on labour and intermediate input costs, especially on the costs of the outsourced ICT services and procurement.

Accordingly, in Figure 4.8 we have estimated productivity ratios by dividing our cost-weighted output measure by an index based on the department's deflated labour and intermediate costs. We acknowledge that this measure is not the same as a TFP measure, but given the limitations of the available official data it nonetheless provides a good overall picture that gets closer to the idea of measuring TFP for the taxation departments. We use 2001–02 as the base year in calculating indices of outputs, inputs and productivity.

The pattern in Figure 4.8 is rather clear-cut. For most of the period covered there was no apparent pattern of overall growth in productivity, no upward trend similar to that found in Customs in Chapter 3. Instead there were relatively small fluctuations, with productivity above or close to the starting level only for a couple of years. This is chiefly because the costs volume for labour and intermediate inputs rose strongly (by almost five-sixths) from 1997–2008 to 2004–05, more than offsetting a three-quarters increase in the number of outputs in the same period. It is especially noticeable that in the middle period (from 2000–01 to 2004–05) the productivity trend was either flat or slightly downwards. This reflected the expenses of Inland Revenue incurred by absorbing other agencies; making significant investments in new ICT; introducing tax credits; and lastly the reorganization costs of creating a unified HMRC in 2005. Wage and salary settlements with the HMRC's unions were also relatively generous at this time, in common with a pattern across Whitehall as departments sought to attract and retain specialized employees in a relatively tight job market.

However, from 2005–06 onwards, for the last three years of our period, productivity growth was strong. This coincided with two related changes – the post-merger implementation of the intensified 'transformation' programme inherited from Inland Revenue; and the key period of implementation of the Gershon Review measures, targeted at reducing back-office costs and moving budgets to frontline services (NAO, 2007a). NAO concluded that the claimed headcount reductions for HMRC were clear-cut.

We turn next to labour productivity, with the inputs measure here defined in simple volume terms as the number of FTE staff collecting and processing taxes in HMRC and its predecessor departments, on which high-quality information is available across the period. Again, this provides an important specific productivity measure for comparing across different public services, because it employs a common 'denominator', and might be thought to link more closely to innovation. However, it is important to recognize that the extensive ICT outsourcing in HMRC and its predecessors influences labour productivity, and that over the period considered here there was a considerable business process outsourcing trend that transferred some functions from department staff to contractors and consultants over time. Again we use the financial year 2001–02 as our base year.

Figure 4.9 shows a pattern that is similar to but shows more pronounced patterns than Figure 4.8. We can roughly identify three periods. Up to 2001–02 labour productivity fluctuated as FTE inputs grew strongly while outputs also expanded. Staff numbers continued to grow for a further three years, but output volumes more or less stagnated, so that labour

*Figure 4.9   Labour productivity for central government taxation, 1997 to
2008*

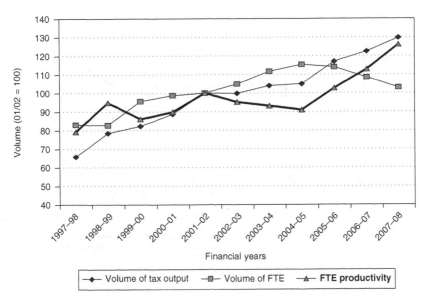

Source: Computed by the authors from public data collated from HMCE, IR and HMRC
departmental reports.

productivity dipped markedly downwards from 2001–02 to 2004–05. In
the final three years, staff numbers were first curbed and then markedly
reduced back towards 2001–02 levels, at the same time as outputs grew
markedly. As a result there was a strong growth of labour productivity
through to 2007–08. We estimate that FTE in tax collection fell by almost
10 000 staff from 2005 to 2008. However, we note again that the consequent apparent productivity increase may have reflected quality shading
of previous service standards. The National Audit Office (NAO, 2010d)
noted that in 2007–08 tens of millions of attempted phone calls were not
answered. The Treasury Select Committee (2010, p. 33) also noted exceptionally low levels of staff morale and trust in senior management at a later
stage (see page 100).

Before leaving the analysis of tax productivity, it is worth giving some
attention to an alternative way of trying to measure outputs in the tax
collection area, using an appropriately deflated measure of the amount
of tax collected as the output measure. This approach was rejected by

Figure 4.10   *The ratio of the deflated amount of tax collected to labour and intermediate inputs, for HMRC and predecessor departments, 1997–2008*

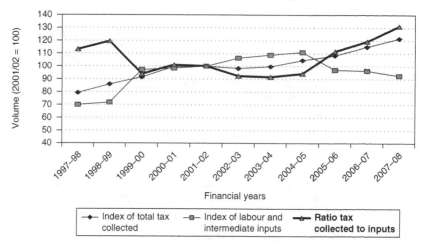

Note: We considered the same taxes as in the rest of the chapter. Data was deflated using 1997–98 as the base year and it was then adjusted using the same cost weights employed in the rest of the chapter.

the Atkinson Review in favour of the activity measure considered above. A receipts-based measure might be criticized as 'gifting' HMRC and its predecessors with the credit for increased tax receipts in boom periods, when receipts are often especially buoyant as a result of no extra effort or achievement by the tax collectors themselves. But the approach is one that is worth considering, because it chimes with the concerns of top politicians and the Treasury to keep on investing in tax departments so long as they are effective in bringing in resources. Accordingly, Figure 4.10 reruns the TFP-like analysis of labour plus intermediate administration costs productivity using deflated taxes collected as the output measure. This output measure was also cost-weighted using the share of administration costs for each type of tax as the weight.

One visible major effect in Figure 4.10 is to somewhat smooth out the output curve on this new basis, which now grows fairly markedly across seven financial years, the exceptions being 2001–02 and the next two years. With the same labour and intermediate costs as in Figure 4.9, the result is to produce a much longer slump in taxation productivity, which peaked in 1998–99 at a level that was then not consistently matched again until 2006–07, eight years later. Only in the two years at the end of our series did productivity clearly pass above the previous earlier peak.

A Longer-term Picture

A key advantage of an index-based approach to analysing organizational productivity is that the length of the available series increases inexorably, year on year, while (hopefully) the organization's essential identity and the consistency of its statistics remain intact. Because the statistical background to tax collection is reasonably sophisticated in Britain, we are also able to look back in time as far as 1988, albeit on a limited basis that must be hedged around with significant caveats (explained in more detail in the Appendix at the end of the book).

First, we can only go back using a 'taxes collected' measure of Revenue and Customs outputs, so that the caveats made for Figure 4.10 apply here also. The cost-weighting of outputs is especially 'rough and ready' the further back in time that we go, although we believe that it is still usefully indicative of the scale of the two departments' tax activities. Second, our measures of inputs differ here because we must use only aggregate published data for the 1988–98 period, and the same (for consistency) in the period thereafter. For the TFP-like analysis, we use the total staff pay bill and other expenditure costs as our measure of input. These measures are deflated, added and then converted into an index of input. For the staff productivity analysis, we use the deflated staff pay bill expenditure as our measure of inputs.

Bearing these words of caution strongly in mind therefore, Figure 4.11a shows a long-run total factor productivity pattern marked by four periods. From 1988 to 1995 overall productivity in central government tax services was broadly flat or lower. It then grew especially sharply in the 1997–99 period under Labour's initial tight spending constraints, combined with strong economic growth. From 2001 to 2005, the impact of departmental reorganization, new investment and tax credits sent productivity lower. But in the final two years productivity recovered to match that in 1998 (but not quite the unsustainable 1999 peak year). Across the whole period, productivity grew by a third, but the adverse impacts of significant productivity slumps in 1991–2004 and very markedly in 2000 to 2004 (neither fitting closely to economic recessions or downturns) is strongly apparent.

Turning to longer-term labour productivity, Figure 4.11b shows the same four periods, with no growth at all from 1988 to 1995. This was followed by strong growth to 1999–2000: labour productivity increased by well over a third in these few years. Again there was a marked dip downwards in 2000–01, not recovered in the next two years, and with a further

Figure 4.11a   *Longer-term total factor productivity patterns in UK central
                  taxation, using a 'taxes collected' measure of outputs, 1988
                  to 2008*

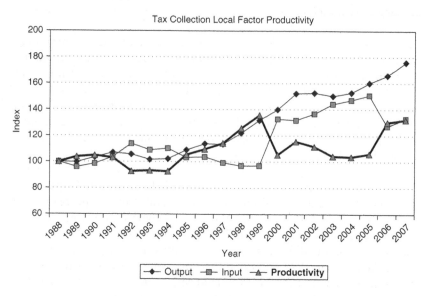

downwards dip in 2002–05. Strong growth followed after the 2005 departmental merger, coinciding with the Gershon Review and extensive staff
cuts. These combined influences helped to achieve a further improvement
of around a fifth in labour productivity by the end of our study period,
when compared to 1999–2000 levels.

The *overall picture of productivity change* that emerges from this
analysis is of some significant growth at the start and the end of our
main study period 1998 to 2008, with a period of either 'marking time'
or declining productivity in the middle, whose length varies somewhat
depending on the measures being considered. Both our longer-term
figures above are consistent with this pattern, confirming that productivity has grown significantly, but in quite short bursts of good years,
interspersed with long periods of stagnation or even (in the early 2000s)
significant declines.

An interesting corroboration of this picture is given in Figure 4.6
(page 102), which shows amongst other things that the overall costs
of collecting taxation in the UK stayed almost exactly the same across
the period from 2001 to 2008, neither increasing nor decreasing by any
noticeable amount. Most of the biggest taxes (in terms of administrative
burdens and revenues brought in) also show little change, with income

Figure 4.11b   *Longer-term labour productivity pattern in UK central taxation, using a 'taxes collected' measure of outputs, 1988 to 2008*

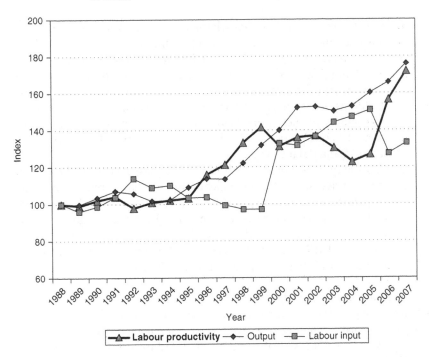

tax costs falling but almost imperceptibly, and collection costs for VAT and excise taxes showing trendless fluctuation. The costs of collecting tobacco increased for external reasons to do with the smuggling in of large amounts from other EU countries for VAT evasion reasons, a development not directly within the administrative control of Customs and HMRC.

4.4   KEY INFLUENCES ON PRODUCTIVITY CHANGE

Our productivity series for taxation is still a short one, and hence the possibilities for further data analysis are limited. However, the Inland Revenue, Customs and Excise and HMRC are all very substantial departments, and their tax collection activities are large. So over time they have produced for Parliament a useful amount of information on a number of factors that Chapters 1 and 2 highlighted as likely to be strongly associated in the modern era with changes in productivity. In particular, we have been able to assemble useful data series covering:

- *Expenditure on ICT*, which Chapter 1 showed was a key factor in modern business firms' productivity changes.
- *Outsourcing* via Private Finance Initiative projects, almost all of which in this period concerns major construction projects. Perhaps especially in the UK civil service, we know that moving into new buildings is strongly associated with organizations' substantial redesigning of their work teams and business processes. Hence we take PFI construction expenditure as a good proxy for the extent of major managerial change.
- *The use of consultants*, which is especially associated in the British civil service with the implementation of major reorganizations. Departments bring in consultants chiefly when they do not have enough staff to manage at the same time both their ongoing operations and the reorganization of activities or planning of major new projects. HMRC and its predecessors often used consultants to help implement IT-enabled business process changes.

Our data assembly task here was not without its complications, because before 2005 the two departments were not generally consistent in reporting this information over time, with some unexplained gaps or problems in the way that data were reported. For Customs and Excise (and later HMRC) we also needed to separate out the proportion of these data that was absorbed on collecting taxes (excluding the trade and customs regulation work). We estimated the size of the share to be assigned to non-tax work by using percentage weights based on total administration costs for each Customs activity.

With these caveats, Table 4.6 shows the data on spending on ICT, construction projects (PFI ones) and the use of consultants, denominated in terms of their share of the total administrative expenditure for HMRC and its predecessor departments. The total amount of administrative spending absorbed on these elements almost doubled between 2000–01 and 2007–08, reflecting the huge extent to which the Blair government prioritized the renewal and extension of the administrative capacities of the civil service at this time. We cannot get fully comparable data for the first year of our study period (1997–2008). But there are strong indications that expenditure at the end of the period on the three organizational change aspects considered here was between two and a half and three times more than in the start year for Table 4.6 – a very major change. Both ICT and PFI construction

Table 4.6 Expenditure on information and communication technology (ICT), PFI construction projects and consultancy as a percentage of total administration expenditure in central government taxation, 1997 to 2008

Year	97–98	98–99	99–00	00–01	01–02	02–03	03–04	04–05	05–06	06–07	07–08
ICT	8.1	na	na	9.1	10.2	9.2	10.5	13.0	13.6	16.3	17.0
Construction (non-ICT PFI projects)	0.1	0.3	0.4	2.8	5.6	5.4	5.3	5.5	7.7	7.3	7.4
Consulting	na	na	2.3	2.2	1.7	2.0	2.3	3.0	2.9	2.0	1.9
Total for these aspects	9.2	na	na	14.1	17.5	16.6	18.1	21.5	24.2	25.6	26.3

Source: Computed by the authors using data from Inland Revenue, HM Customs and Excise and HMRC Departmental Reports.

Figure 4.12a   Lagged ICT expenditure plotted against outputs for tax collection

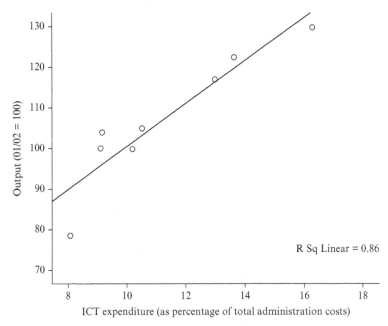

Source: Computed by authors based on data from HMRC and predecessors.

spending increased almost consistently across the years. Expenditure on consulting peaked in 2004–05 in the run up to the creation of HMRC.

To consider how the three possible explanatory factors are related to output levels, we lagged ICT, consulting and PFI (non-IT) expenditure by one year against the cost-weighted numbers of tax returns (our preferred total output measure). All three costs are investments that contribute to changing business processes, but they take some time to start to pay off. With this modification we then plotted each factor against the total output level and fitted a regression line across the plotted values. With so few observations, and with no controls applying for many other factors not included in the analysis here, it is inherently unlikely that there should be any close fit in these charts. And even where there appears to be an association, it can be taken as no more than a potentially interesting indication of some sort of association between the factor involved and output levels. Yet while we must be cautious on the interpretations of such results due to these two problems, the results can provide some initial evidence of the basic levels of association between the potential causal factors and output levels.

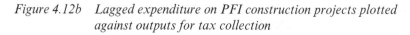

Figure 4.12b   Lagged expenditure on PFI construction projects plotted against outputs for tax collection

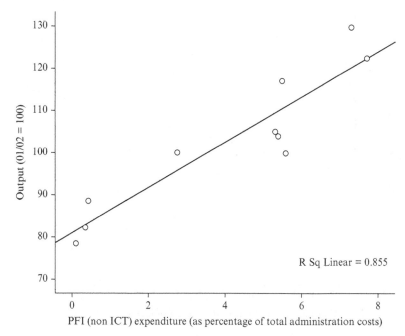

R Sq Linear = 0.855

Source: Computed by authors based on data from HMRC and predecessors.

Figures 4.12a to 4.12c show the resulting plots. There is a very close relationship between both ICT spending and PFI construction spending and the index of cost-weighted outputs levels. The raw regression score here suggests that up to five-sixths of the variation in outputs *might* be explained in terms of either of the two possible independent variables. By contrast, spending on consulting seems weakly related to the achievement of higher outputs. The raw regression score here suggests that only a seventh of the variation in outputs might be attributable to this factor. Expenditure on consultants may be more important during transitional times, but we also know from other work that periods of departmental and agency reorganizations in central government can often be associated with lowered output levels (NAO, 2010b; White and Dunleavy, 2010). With so few cases, these illustrations are only very lightly indicative, but the differences between the patterns for the first two factors and that for consulting are interesting and suggestive.

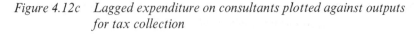

*Figure 4.12c   Lagged expenditure on consultants plotted against outputs
for tax collection*

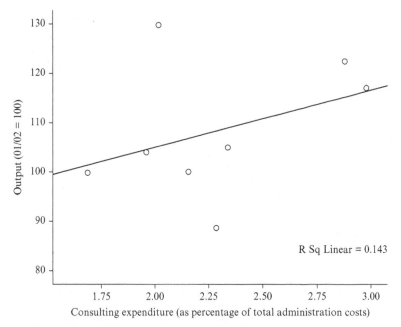

Source: Computed by authors based on data from HMRC and predecessors.

Conclusions

The development of productivity in tax services at British central government level is an interesting and complex story. The early productivity peak evident in our series was clearly in part an unsustainable spike. It may have reflected the postponing of overdue investments and absence of modernizing business changes under spending plans set by the Conservatives under Prime Minister John Major, influenced primarily by 'new public management' thinking. The New Labour government of Tony Blair set about a whole series of changes that effectively recentralized tax raising, first pulling in National Insurance to be wholly administered by Inland Revenue, and later merging that department with Customs and Excise to form the integrated HMRC.

The resulting mega-department absorbed for a time almost a quarter of the entire British civil service. It was (and remains) an overwhelmingly business-facing agency, principally relying on companies to remit taxes due. Nearly two-thirds of the huge PAYE income tax and National

Insurance receipts are received from the UK's 10 000 largest employers. Yet much of the department's workload also involved individuals or small firms. Large administrative efforts are still focused on individuals paying self-assessment income tax, capital gains and inheritance taxes; on small businesses whose compliance with PAYE and NI processes is weak or problematic; on a shifting canvas of major corporate and personal tax avoiders; and finally on a large numbers of small evaders threatening the viability of particular excise taxes (such as tobacco and alcohol duties in recent years).

The evidence reviewed here suggests that for much of the period from 1997 to 2008 progress in improving productivity in taxation was not conspicuously successful. There were some clear-cut achievements. Tax offices, some of the HMRC's major IT systems and the department's business processes were all extensively modernized. Yet the large-scale changes and capital intensification initiated by Labour only began to pay off clearly in the last three years of our study period. The growth achieved was most marked in terms of staff productivity, somewhat less clear-cut for a wide measure of productivity covering labour plus intermediate outputs, and almost not visible at all if we defined the key outputs measure to be the (inflation-adjusted) taxes collected per £ spent on administration. The overall cost of collecting £1000 in taxes (shown as the dashed line in Figure 4.6) was £10.60 in 1997–98 and £11.08 in 2007–08, a stasis that characterizes the whole series with minor wobbles. So on the one hand HMRC and its predecessor departments successfully counteracted the Baumol relative price effect by growing productivity enough to keep the costs of tax collection almost the same. But on the other hand, the departments' major investments in new ICT and business process reorganization were not enough to deliver sustainable reductions in costs of collection, even with the partial transition to online tax filing, on which many hopes for efficiency gains rested.

In addition, scholars of private sector service industries such as Grönroos (2007) have persuasively argued that improving productivity in services is not just about or primarily about saving costs (as it is in manufacturing). Instead, productivity change in services is often most closely associated with modernizing services and improving their quality, both of which are key for the sustainability of services firms. Unhappily the late growth in HMRC's productivity series also coincided with some significant indications of declining service quality, including not answering millions of phone calls by 2010, declining staff morale and other indicators of possible quality-shading. However, HMRC can at least point to success in overcoming the upwards jag in complaints around tax credits and the restoration of complaint levels that are consistent with previous experience.

Table 4.7   How the UK tax regime fared in international comparisons in 2000–01 (or other nearest year for which data was available)

Tax Collected per Tax Employee ($ millions)		Administrative Costs per Revenue Employee ($000)		Tax Declarations Processed per Employee (000s)	
USA	22.5	New Zealand	40	USA	2183
Australia	6.7	Ireland	48.0	New Zealand	1083
France	5.4	Australia	51.4	UK	725
Ireland	5.3	UK	57.2	Australia	610
UK	5.3	Canada	60.7	Canada	563
Canada	4.9	USA	87.5	Ireland	420
New Zealand	3.5			France	402

Raw Cost of Collecting $1000 (in $)		Cost of Collecting 0.01% of GDP in Tax Revenue ($000)	
USA	39	Ireland	108
Australia	77	Australia	319
Ireland	92	New Zealand	663
UK	108	Canada	889
New Zealand	114	UK	1689
Canada	128	USA	4021

Note: Strong performers in terms of cost efficiency of staff efficiency are at the top of the table, and weak performers are at the bottom.

Sources: Bastow et al. (2003, Table DII.iii 'Taxation and revenue'); data originally compiled from OECD tax data for 2000–01.

Finally, it is worth considering the scanty available evidence on how the UK appears to be faring in terms of international comparisons. In an analysis using 2000–01 data, Bastow et al. (2003) used OECD data to compare how Inland Revenue and Customs and Excise fared on some key indicators against other countries with some close characteristics, shown in Table 4.7.

Despite the UK departments' generally high international reputations, an interesting feature of these tables is that the UK did not top any of them, and instead often lingered in the middle or at the bottom. The best performance was in processing declarations per tax employee, where the USA and New Zealand with compulsory self-assessments come top but the UK ran third. In costs per employee terms, the USA and Canada paid higher salaries but minimized other costs, while the UK ran Canada close. In tax collected per employee, the USA was the runaway winner, with Australia a distant second, and the UK in a group of other countries. In terms of the nominal costs of collecting $1000 in taxes the USA was again clearly ahead of all other countries, with Australia running second and the UK lagging well behind. However, because different countries have radically different levels of GDP, nominal cost comparisons flatter high GDP countries (like the USA) and may well misrepresent the performance of low GDP countries (like New Zealand). A far better basis for comparison is the amount of administrative costs required to collect a small fraction of GDP, in this case one-tenth of 1 per cent. On this basis Ireland's extensive PAYE system and simplified corporation tax approach came top by a clear mile, while the USA's universal self-assessment regime came last by a long way, with the UK second from bottom. These comparisons suggest that in the early part of our study period, the UK was far from being an exceptional performer in international terms. The growth in productivity from 2006 on is still too recent to be evaluated in the international data, but the UK clearly had plenty of ground to make up.

5. How productivity can remain unchanged despite major investments – social security

Modern social security systems are the largest distributive counterpart of the government's capacity to raise taxes. Any welfare state is at root a system in which resources are requisitioned from those in work or on higher incomes, as well as from companies and from the well off, and then redistributed to the elderly, sick and disabled people, those unlucky in seeking work, and families or children in low-income households. Much of this redistribution is achieved through public services, supplied to all citizens by government agencies or by private organizations in ways that are funded, regulated and shaped by government. However, most social security transfer payments across the world are mediated in much less complex ways. Especially in simpler and more 'statist' welfare systems (such as that in the UK), monies are moved from the taxation department to a social security department, whose officials then allocate state benefits directly to eligible individuals or households. In more complex European welfare states such direct government transfer payments are often smaller because the state essentially supplements the social insurance that individuals have themselves taken out with other voluntary or quasi-private organizations, such as insurance funds, trade unions or social housing providers. But even here, the non-governmental providers are almost always organized in government-regulated schemes that are also underpinned in financial and risk-assurance terms by taxpayers. In the USA, welfare provision remains stubbornly partial and fragmented, dashing early post-war expectations of a 'positive service state' (Roberts, 2010).

We begin by considering how the direct delivery of social security benefits is characteristically managed in advanced industrial societies, in a distinctive administrative format that allows societies to pursue national conceptions of 'social justice' while still maintaining the rule of law. The second section looks at the particular set up for social security in the UK, especially three key changes made since 2000 – bringing together benefits administration with the provision of employment services; the rebuilding of services delivery around a phone-based model of communication with customers; and the transition to much more capital-intensive administrative processes. Section 5.3 examines the record of productivity change in UK social security, looking back two decades. We show that virtually no growth has been achieved, despite a belated but otherwise quite extensive modernization of services. Finally we seek to track down the factors underlying this (basically static) outcome, linking it to the main investment and managerial changes pursued in the recent period.

5.1   SOCIAL SECURITY ADMINISTRATION AND THE CONTEMPORARY WELFARE STATE

In *The Road to Serfdom* (1944) the economic philosopher Friedrich Hayek famously argued that vesting the ability to determine people's incomes and their feasible ways of life in a government bureaucracy must inherently undermine the rule of law. It would create a slippery slope leading to an over-powerful (even totalitarian) government, intrusively demanding full information about the life choices and behaviours of a state-dependent population. These people would have to be a compliant population, because their economic and social welfare would now be determined by the decisions (whims) of officials exercising power in discretionary ways. Hayek's (1944) conclusion was that any state attempt to operationalize a concept of 'social justice' must end in undermining autonomous citizenship and the rule of law, and with it any viable concept of democracy. In every advanced industrial country, this conviction has remained an influential but minority position through to the present day. But the Hayekian critique of administrative discretion has generally been rejected as exaggerated or over-fundamentalist. In most OECD countries convincing electoral majorities have been built by political parties (stretching from the political left through to the centre-right) committed to first construct and then maintain and defend an extended social security system. Each country has developed their own strong vision of the type of social justice and welfare state that government should pursue.

In every welfare state, however, the Hayekian critique has strongly shaped how social security administration has been designed, structured and regulated. To minimize or eliminate officials' discretionary power there has been a dominant emphasis upon establishing clear systems of rules governing legal entitlement to assistance, and on enforcing a highly egalitarian, impartial and non-discretionary pattern of implementation. National politicians have retained the powers to set benefit rates and eligibility rules directly through legislation, and social security departments are normally regular 'line' ministries under full political control.

But implementation has been extensively delegated to bureaucracies of various kinds.

There are partial variations around this pattern, especially where social security arrangements are set up as long-term 'trust funds', as with the US Social Security Administration (SSA) – its funds cannot be diverted or used for other purposes by the presidential executive. But at the same time, SSA operates under close congressional control. In some European systems too, where state funding inter-leaves with the funded models of voluntary sector social insurance providers, the social security apparatus may operate with a greater degree of independence. But most welfare states are still set up on a 'pay as you go' (PAYGO) basis, where the taxes of current workers and companies are used to fund the current outgoings – that is, the pension entitlements of previous generations of workers, and income maintenance for people who are currently unemployed, ill or disabled. If PAYGO commitments are allowed to rise then so must tax payments, and often on a literally massive scale – hence the general political centrality of social security decision-making.

At the same time the ideal of impartial rule of law administration under liberal democracy has meant that politicians are not allowed to intervene directly or individually in the administration of benefits, beyond the normal constituency role of legislators in assisting their voters. Instead a voluminous set of legislation and administrative regulation has been established that seeks to set out in precise detail how people are or are not eligible for benefit, and how much they should consequently be paid. Because social security systems aim to provide comprehensive support for people in need, whose circumstances are very varied, the accompanying rule books quickly mushroom in complexity, with many special conditions and exemptions seeking to cope with apparent anomalies in previous rules. But there is no social security counterpart to the enhanced occupational autonomy of doctors, teachers or even social workers. There is no legitimate space where the individual professional discretion of an official can displace the rule book's provisions. The embedding of complex rules in ICT systems increasingly fixes the complete legal specification of payments in machine code. Indeed numerous efforts have been made to construct 'expert systems' to administer benefits and to minimize the need for human judgement or intervention – so far without much success.

The push for impartiality creates a risk of creating a machine-like benefits system, one that operates in ways that treat often fragile people in considerable need without clear regard to their personal circumstances and situations. Yet officials seeking for information may make mistakes. And like anyone else, benefits agency employees may let their judgements of the claimants they encounter colour the ways in which they respond, with consequent scope for systemic biases to emerge in the treatment of different kinds of people.

Countries have pursued three basic strategies (that complement each other) in order to counter this effect:

1. *'Humanizing' strategies* for social security were established early on in the 1930s and 1940s. They focus on socializing agency staff into a strong 'public service' ethos, in which officials' values and internal reward systems centre in large part on doing a good job for the citizens they deal with. A strong management overview of how staff treat people, comprehensive training in treating claimants fairly and an organizational culture that stresses a degree of empathy for clients' needs are all characteristic of social security organizations. These elements serve to blur and soften the edges of their legal implementation culture. Compared with tax agencies, for instance, social security staff often interact with households frequently (instead of the tax agency annual interactions). And they also may have smaller individual caseloads to handle. Social security agencies all recognize that poor or disadvantaged households are highly dependent on their decisions for money if they are to survive from day to day: so they recognize an obligation to ensure that their services facilitate solutions instead of compounding clients' problems.

2. *Appeal, redress and legal challenge processes* give a second chance to claimants unhappy with the agency's decision on their case. They have a chance to ask for a second review by a manager, and after that if they are still unhappy to appeal what they believe to be wrong decisions to higher appeal bodies or to the law courts. In Europe the emphasis tends to be on administrative tribunals, which operate less formal independent review processes where ordinary citizens can present their own cases. In the USA the solutions embodied in the Administrative Procedure Act (1946) focused on providing internal review by higher-tier officials across federal government, including within the Social Security Administration. However, US practice has also rather quickly and strongly developed from the 1960s towards the pervasive legalization of social security disputes in more adversarial ways, with agencies facing suits or damages claims in the event of legal mistakes.

3. *Improving 'point-of-service' standards* to approximate those in private sector service organizations has been an important development of the public service ethos under the influence of the 'new public management' (NPM) approach that dominated changes in public administration in many OECD countries from the later 1980s to

the mid-2000s. The 'managerialist' focus here was on moving away from rundown buildings; getting rid of block bookings of face-to-face customers with long queues and wait times; radically modernizing old-fashioned phone-handling procedures; and minimizing the most expensive interactions (face-to-face interviews). Instead service premises could be modernized to private-sector-like standards; clients would be booked only to individual appointment times, with queuing kept to a minimum; modern, high-capacity and web-enabled call centres would be established to handle much larger volumes of phone traffic more efficiently; and the need for face-to-face interactions with 'clients' would be cut to a minimum.

5.2   ADMINISTERING SOCIAL SECURITY IN THE UK

In comparative public policy terms the British welfare state has long been something of a halfway house between the more laissez faire minimalism of the USA and the generous income-replacement levels provided by social security in the older EU member states. The traditional UK approach to social security is statist, integrated, universalistic and highly centralized (Dunleavy, 1989a, 1989b). It is also characteristically mean in comparison with the level of income replacement made by welfare benefits in other European countries. For many decades the UK old age pension has typically paid no more than a third of median weekly earnings, compared with levels around 60 per cent to two-thirds in Germany, France or Scandinavian countries. Similarly, the UK system provides newly unemployed people with a benefit rate that is just 13 per cent of the average weekly earnings, compared to replacement rates that are more than four times as generous in the same set of European countries.

On the other hand, the UK system still (just) retains the attempted comprehensiveness of the original Beveridge Report dating from 1944, with its aspiration of providing 'cradle to the grave' coverage against ill luck and the adverse contingencies of unemployment, illness, disability and old age. Thus the UK welfare state provides a far more multi-pronged system of social protection than the minimal insurance against unemployment, short illness and the basic State Pension that the Social Security Administration in the USA delivers. Table 5.1 shows that the British system is far more comprehensive than the US welfare state in recognizing an obligation on government to provide money benefits to prevent people from becoming homeless, going hungry or coping with illness, disability or disastrous personal life choices. As a result, Table 5.1 also shows that the annual

Table 5.1 *The main social security benefits in the UK welfare state*
  (and those covered for the productivity analysis in section 5.3)

Category	Annual Spending in 2008 (£ billions)	Proportion (%) of 2008 Benefit Spending	Specific Names of Related UK Benefits Involved Included in Productivity Analysis
Benefits for unemployed people with insurance contributions (i.e., National Insurance in UK)	1867	1.5	Unemployment Benefit to 1996, and contributory Jobseeker's Allowance (JSA)
Benefits for unemployed people without insurance	8759	6.8	Income Support for the unemployed (from 1988 to 1996), thereafter non-contributory Jobseeker's Allowance
Benefits for working age people who are long-term ill	6575	5.1	Incapacity Benefit (before 1995, data include Invalidity and Sickness Benefit)
Other benefits for working age people	932	0.7	Other benefits: Maternity Allowance and Widow Bereavement
Loans to assist working age people on welfare to purchase consumer durables etc.	2399	1.9	Social Fund Grants and Loans (introduced in 1993)
Sub-total: Payments for working age people not in work	*20 532*	*16.0*	
Old age pension based on contributions	57 366	44.7	Basic State Pension State Earnings Related Pension Scheme (SERPs) War Pensions (paid separately by the Ministry of Defence)
Assistance for elderly people with low household incomes	7227	5.6	From 1993 to 2000 Income Support for people aged 60 and over; Minimum Income Guarantee up to 2003; from 2003 onwards, Pension Credit

Table 5.1   (continued)

Category	Annual Spending in 2008 (£ billions)	Proportion (%) of 2008 Benefit Spending	Specific Names of Related UK Benefits Involved Included in Productivity Analysis
Additional assistance to elderly people needing help to get around or cope with daily living	4440	3.5	Attendance Allowance
Assistance for disabled elderly people	9809	7.6	Disability Living Allowance (from 1993)
Assistance for people looking after the elderly or disabled	2173	1.7	Invalid Carers' Allowance, later Carers' Allowance
International Pension Credit	200	0.2	Paid to UK citizens living overseas
Sub-total: Payments to elderly people and the disabled	81215	63.2	
Assistance with meeting local housing rents	15745	12.3	Housing Benefit (administered by local authorities, repaid from DWP budget)
Assistance with meeting council tax payments	4124	3.2	Council Tax Benefit
Sub-total: Payments for anyone eligible on welfare rolls	*19869*	*15.5*	
Future Pension Forecasts	*345*	*0.3*	*Future Pension Forecasts*
Tax-free payment for each child	*6508*	*5.1*	*Child Benefit (paid by HMRC)*
Sub-total: Benefits paid and services given to all eligible people, whether on welfare rolls or not	*6853*	*5.3*	
Total benefits spending	**128469**	**100.0**	

Note: The italicized benefits are not included in the analysis below.

value of all UK social benefits paid to claimants in 2008 amounted to £129 billion, and total government social security expenditure amounted to almost £137 billion, that is, 12 per cent of the country's gross domestic product (HM Treasury, 2009). The rows in italics towards the bottom of

Table 5.1 show that there has also been a recent growth of tax credits for working families and for children, adding to the substantial payment of universal Child Benefit, until 2012 paid to all households with children (whatever their income levels). All tax credit payments are undertaken by HM Revenue & Customs (HMRC), with credits especially closely linked to the tax system (see Chapter 4). But this still accounts for less than a fifth of UK welfare state spending. The remaining monies (more than four-fifths) route through another integrated large ministry at central government level, the Department for Work and Pensions (DWP). It is on these that this chapter concentrates.

The department is a classic 'transfer agency' in terms of the 'bureau-shaping' typology (Dunleavy, 1991, Ch. 7). The total administrative costs for social security in 2008 were £7.5 billion, making this the largest administrative cost borne by any government sector. (The tax department HMRC came second at £5 billion.) Personnel numbers in the DWP peaked at over 131 000 in 2002, more than a quarter of the whole central government civil service. They then fell back to a low of just over 105 000 staff by 2008 – before substantially expanding again in 2009, reflecting the impact of recession in raising unemployment levels and benefit claimant numbers (see page 145). Although this is a massive administrative undertaking, it is worth stressing that running costs in the DWP accounted for only 4.4 per cent of its total budget in 2008, closely in line with bureau-shaping expectations for a welfare state transfer agency.

The policy and organizational context for delivering social security has changed extensively in the period since 1988, when useful data begin to be available. The timeline in Figure 5.1 summarizes some key influences, including the following:

- A rapid succession of *legislative changes* (32 separate Acts in 20 years).
- A frequent turnover of *top ministers* (12 times in the period) despite one single change of government in 1997 from Conservative to Labour (even for the UK, this is an extreme case of short-termism).
- Main *policy programme changes* in this area always centred on the introduction of new benefits and the phasing out of old ones, usually by new ministers.
- *Changes in the macro-organizational architecture* for administering social security benefits, especially the merger of two previously separate networks of offices to form a single Department for Work and Pensions.
- *The extensive use of ICTs and contractors* formed a strong dynamic in the administrative development of social security, with a major outsourcing in 1992, renewed in more comprehensive ways in 1998.

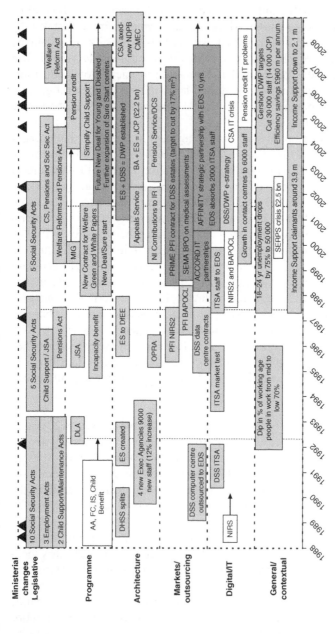

Figure 5.1   Main developments in the administration of UK social protection, 1988–2008

Note: In Figure 5.1, the abbreviations used are: ACCORD consortium of computer firms; AA Attendance Allowance; BA Benefits Agency; BAPOCL Benefits Agency/Post Office Counters Limited, joint programme; BPO business process outsourcing; CSA Child Support Agency; DfEE Department for Education and Employment; DHSS Department of Health and Social Security; DCS Disability and Carers' Service; DLA Disability Living Allowance; DSS Department of Social Security; EDS major computer firm; ES Employment Service; IS Income Support; ITSA Information Technology Services Agency (within DSS); JCP Job Centre Plus; JSA Job Seekers' Allowance; MIG Minimum Income Guarantee; NDPB non-departmental public body; NI National Insurance; NICO National Insurance Contribution Office; NIRS National Insurance Register System; OPRA Occupational Pensions Regulatory Authority PFI Private Finance Initiative; PRIME property sale and re-lease deal; Sema major computer firm; SERPs State Earnings Related Pension Scheme, a top-up pension; STEPS acronym for property transfer consortium.

128

- *Increased modernization spending* by Labour ministers on PFI new building contracts (around 5 to 7 per cent of administrative costs per year) and consultants (around 2 per cent of administrative costs per year), responding to the previous chronic under-investment under Conservative governments.
- *An attempted transition of DWP administrative processes* from paper-based forms and face-to-face contacts and towards phone-based customer contacts, all underpinned by a massive new investment in IT systems and in new buildings.

The Department of Work and Pensions was itself created in April 2002 by merging together two pre-existing large bureaucracies: the Department of Social Security, a cabinet ministry whose role consisted solely of assessing and paying out claims for welfare benefits; and the Employment Services Agency, a large but discrete part of a separate Whitehall department, covering education and employment policies. We discuss each of these 'parent' organizations in turn, before looking at how DWP itself developed after its creation.

The Department of Social Security

The Department of Social Security (or DSS) was formed in 1988 from the de-merger of a previous 'super-ministry' that had linked together Health and Social Security for two decades. Under the 'Next Steps' reorganization of Whitehall begun in 1988 (see Chapter 4), DSS was internally separated into four main agencies separated on functional lines:

- The largest component was the Benefits Agency, whose job was to pay out social security benefits payments, especially pensions, support for ill and disabled people and 'safety net' support for unemployed people not entitled to unemployment pay (run by a separate ministry, see below). Essentially the agency was the 'operating core' of DSS in Mintzberg's (1983) terms (i.e., the part of the organization that really set its identity and carries out its key mission functions). It maintained the department's local office network. At its peak size it employed nearly 70000 staff.
- The Contributions Agency had the job of monitoring National Insurance (NI) payments by employees (the UK version of a social security tax), and then passing the right information to Inland Revenue, who actually organized the collection of NI contributions. In 1999, after a series of embarrassing IT contract mistakes, and a

failure of service covering several months, the agency and its 10 000 staff were completely transferred away from DSS to Inland Revenue.

- The third main element of DSS was ITSA, the Information Technology Services Agency, which ran the large DSS computer centres and national IT systems. Most of its staff were transferred to private contractors when the department's IT functions were outsourced in 1999.

- Finally, the badly misnamed Child Support Agency (CSA) was created as an executive agency in 1993. It started life as a part of DSS in 1981 when Margaret Thatcher's government began chasing divorced fathers with obligations to make maintenance payments to dependent children. Operating very much as a semi-detached part of the department, from the outset its effectiveness was controversial, with administration costs commonly absorbing more than half of the sums recovered from fathers, and with repeated instances of IT and administrative crises. Efforts were made to refashion CSA's legislative basis and method of operating, and its IT systems were renewed, without much improvement. In 2008 the organization ceased to be an executive agency, converting into the delivery arm of a shortlived body (the Child Maintenance and Enforcement Commission), which was abolished in 2012 and its functions transferred to the Child Maintenance Group (CMG) within DWP itself. CSA lives on in a hollowed-out form (with no autonomy) as the body doing implementation for CMG.

Most of the early DSS period was taken up with the development of its 'Operational Strategy' to computerize social security records and office processes, moving away from a wholly manual set up with paper files and records, where the administration of income support for the unemployed and sickness/disability benefits was handled in hundreds of local offices (Margetts, 1991; Margetts, 1998, Ch. 3). More centralized structures were created for benefits administration, with computer records taking over from paper files. Local offices and paper forms were retained for interacting with customers, but the recording of decisions was moved onto computers. The Department chose as its contractor, EDS, the dominant system integrator firm in the UK at this period. Later the same company supplied the IT system installed for the Child Support Agency.

The strategy was planned to install computer networks and terminals and to last 15 years, but the whole idea of a 15-year computerization strategy was vitiated by the rapid development of IT, including the launch of PC-based systems (Margetts, 1998). Cost overruns also occurred and the efficacy of the new systems was queried by a number of Parliamentary select committee hearings and National Audit Office (NAO) reports. The Operational Strategy was more or less halted in 1999, after the expenditure of some £1.75 billion over 17 years. Its achievement was clearly to accomplish the long-delayed computerization of the benefits systems, but its legacy in terms of locking the department into outdated solutions and technologies (endorsed by both senior officials and their main contractors) is also hard to underestimate.

When we visited a series of Benefits Agency offices in 1999 on an NAO investigation, its 68 000 staff were equipped with just eight PCs capable of accessing the internet. None of its over 400 local offices had any access to PCs, or any knowledge of websites (Dunleavy et al., 1999, Part 2). The Department did have a small 'posterboard' website (of very low functionality), which was actually built by a couple of low-ranked officials from a Yorkshire office in their spare time. One of their main tasks in 1999 was to receive and collate the more than 200 e-mail queries a month that DSS received from UK pensioners overseas, print them out and then send them to the appropriate paper forms office. The relevant NAO report concluded that the department's websites 'have been relatively static and underdeveloped, cautiously funded and under-resourced, providing information within conservative and unimaginative designs' (Dunleavy et al., 1999, paragraph 2.31).

The working model of the department varied across its main benefits areas. The administration of pensions was generally a low-cost activity, costing on average around £0.5 to £0.6 per client per week in the late 1990s (Margetts, 1999). This was unsurprising since many pensioners were paid the same basic pension for many years, and rarely moved address. However, paying benefits to working age people who were unemployed, sick or disabled then cost around £5.50 per person per week. These clients had far more changes of circumstances, switches of address and a much higher incidence of new claims to continuing claims, all of which greatly raised costs. Maintaining a comprehensive network of local benefits offices to see clients in person was also costly, but DSS officials (and ministers) saw it as an essential check on who was receiving the higher-risk benefits, like Income Support.

Throughout its period of operation, under the Conservative governments of Margaret Thatcher and John Major, the political salience of the DSS was generally rising, albeit from a low ebb. Influenced by US developments, Tory ministers embraced a shift away from the automatic granting of benefits to unemployed people and towards more of a 'workfare' orientation, in which jobless people were expected to demonstrate that they were active in seeking work. Conceivably benefits could be withdrawn if jobless individuals refused to accept viable work that was offered to them. Initially this 'stricter benefits regime' stance was criticized by Labour and the trade unions. But in the later 1990s Labour too swung towards a strong endorsement of a humanized workfare look-alike approach – one that promised job seekers much stronger assistance and retraining in looking for work, in return for a responsibility on their part to move off benefits as soon as they could do so. The Blair government was influenced here by the active labour market policies of the Swedish welfare state. But the Labour vision also could not be achieved simply within the confines of the DSS brief, because the new vision was centrally linked to employment policies.

The Employment Services Agency

The Employment Services Agency (ESA) in 1988 formed a rather separate and discrete part of the Department of Employment. Its origins can be traced back to the 1909 decision to create Labour Exchanges where local jobs would be advertised by employers and the government would try to bring a degree of order to chaotic local labour markets. Labour exchanges helped jobless people to more quickly and easily find work by broadening their options and widening their job searches, with staff assistance. Later renamed Employment Exchanges and run by the Ministry of Labour, these local offices also took on the payment of unemployment benefits for jobless people looking for work and who had made the requisite contributions when in work to be entitled to receive benefits – called National Insurance.

Later on the parent department was renamed the Department of Employment, and in 1973 its network of local offices were renamed Job Centres. In 1988 the Employment Services Agency was created as part of the 'Next Steps' agencification process (see Chapter 4), where staff were moved out of main Whitehall ministries and into executive agencies. It was now run on more corporate lines, and operated Job Centres in most towns and cities. Finally in 1995, the Conservative government decided to merge the parent department of the Job Centre service with Education in a short-lived Department for Education and Employment (DfEE, which lasted in this form for just six years).

The Job Centre network was widely rated as a success until the advent of the 1981–85 recession, when it came under acute pressure because of the growth of mass unemployment. The department did succeed in somewhat updating its services and assisting job seekers more, but the linkage with DSS services was always problematic. Unemployment benefits (based on past National Insurance contributions) were paid for up to the first year that people were out of work. Thereafter a jobless person would need to move onto a different benefit (called Income Support) paid by DSS, transferring across from one local office to another, often several miles apart. Long-term unemployed people, or those who did not have the right National Insurance contributions, would not need to visit Job Centres to receive benefits, and so might not need any assistance with job seeking. Nor was it easy for DSS staff to check if job seekers were actively looking for work. Expertise in assisting with job searches and knowledge of local labour markets also lay with the ESA, and not with DSS staff.

In 1997 the Labour government under Tony Blair came to power pledged to introduce active labour market policies with a much stronger administrative push to get non-working people into employment (UK Government, 1998). Integrating service delivery across the DSS and DfEE boundary line became essential to the government's 'New Deal' programmes for young unemployed people, for lone parents, the long-term unemployed and the disabled – all of which stressed New Labour's 'rights and responsibilities' agenda. The 'stricter' Jobseeker's Allowance (JSA) regime of the Conservatives was now supplemented by 'guaranteed' intensive employment assistance after a particular duration of unemployment (Willetts et al., 2003).

There were two possible ways of resolving this conundrum, however: (1) to move the administration of all social security benefits for working age people across from the DSS and into the employment ministry DfEE, thereby downgrading DSS into something like the old Ministry of Pensions that existed in the 1960s; or (2) to move the Employment Services Agency across from DfEE into DSS, thereby creating a beefed up Job Centre operation that would now include not just Income Support for the jobless, but also all the job search assistance and administration of contributory Jobseeker's Allowance. Naturally enough ministers in DfEE fought hard for option 1, while DSS ministers argued strongly for option 2.

In 1999 the civil service began to trial joint workings between the two departments at the local level. Called the 'One' pilot, this experiment rapidly spread to more regions and localities and was quickly judged so successful that the pilot was never formally evaluated, but a decision was made to merge the operations of ESA and DSS for working people. A Whitehall inter-departmental committee spent two years comprehensively examining the whys and wherefores of creating a single new department bringing together all benefits and advice services for working age people in a service to be called Jobcentre Plus (JCP). The new agency would break away from the old, traditional images of 'labour exchanges' and provide a radically improved standard of customer service. A small working party was set up to create a blueprint for Jobcentre Plus, chaired by the Treasury second in command and including DSS and DfEE ministers and senior officials. Eventually it recommended that JCP should be created within DfEE (option 1 above). However, the Prime Minister deferred a final decision until after the 2001 general election (White and Dunleavy, 2010). After Labour won, the detailed dynamics of his cabinet-making led Blair to decide that option (2) should prevail. ESA would switch across from DfEE (which was now actually abolished in its old form) to DSS, so as to create a new Department for Work and Pensions.

The Department for Work and Pensions

The Department for Work and Pensions (DWP) formally began work in April 2002, but in fact it had already existed in proto-form for more than a year. It was perhaps the best prepared, longest incubated and most expensive departmental merger in UK central government, ever. The centrepiece of the reorganization was the creation of Jobcentre Plus (JCP) services offering unemployed, disabled and sick people of working age a more intensive regime of employment assistance. There were to be frequent checks to ensure that claimants were actively seeking work, or were using training opportunities, and that they were not simply languishing on benefits. Single JCP offices in town centres and accessible locations were created where all claimants had to register in person that they were seeking work and check in every two weeks for follow-on interviews, if they wanted to continue receiving benefits. Once jobless people reached six months and then a year out of work, more intensive interviews and assistance packages were mandated.

All the Job Centre buildings were remodelled nationwide from scratch, getting rid of queuing systems, screens and rundown premises. They were quite rapidly replaced with modern-looking, open plan offices where all claimants had to turn up for precisely timed interviews, and with security guards on hand to protect staff and to ensure that no one was admitted before their appointed time. The old-fashioned cards advertising vacancies were replaced by computerized 'kiosks' showing vacancies on screens and allowing some details to be printed. There were some dedicated phones for ringing up potential employers, but not a single PC was available for use by unemployed people across the 850 local offices, a situation that persisted until 2010 (Dunleavy et al., 2009).

The mature JCP model, which applied throughout the later 2000s, still had very complex processes to administer the benefit, described in detail in Dunleavy et al. (2009, Part 2). Jobless people claiming benefits had to ring up a DWP call centre for around 40 minutes and explain their situation and details to the contact person. They then ended up with a local JCP appointment, where they needed to show up at the Job Centre with their documentation to establish their identity, and be given advice by a JCP local worker on looking for work. However, the person seeing them face to face did not make a decision on their benefits – instead the JCP staff only completed a computerized form that was next sent on to one of 77 Benefit Decision Centres organized at (small) regional levels. Here the information relayed by the call centre and the local JCP officials was used to make a decision. Information was lost and had to be repeated at each of these stages, and the efficacy of the DWP computer systems and networks was so poor that 40 per cent of the time information did not transfer in a satisfactory or timely way from the call centre to the local JCP offices, or from JCP to the remote decision centres (Dunleavy et al., 2009, Part 2).

In addition, the computer kiosks that seemed such a good idea in 2002 were pretty much obsolescent by 2009. On our visits to Job Centres during late 2008 they were being little used. By contrast in the equivalent Australian service (called Centrelink) there were hundreds of proper PCs available to jobless people for them to search for jobs and e-mail applications. In the UK there were none at all: unemployed people had to be sent to local libraries or other online access centres to do such tasks, making it very unlikely that JCP officials could monitor whether they did or not. Similarly, in the Access Canada service set up in the later 2000s there was a strong emphasis on clients or customers sitting on the same side of the desk as those helping them and looking at the same information on computer screens. But in every JCP office we visited during 2008, staff sat on the other side of desks from claimants, and could not turn their screens to show clients what jobs were on offer or how to operate web-based applications. Yet by this time Britain's largest employer (the NHS) was only accepting e-mail applications for any of its positions.

A large part of the estimated direct costs of integrating the ESA employment services into the new department arose from pay differentials between the two departments, which cost a minimum of £143 million to equalize over the years after 2002 (White and Dunleavy, 2010). In addition, the convulsion of JCP services clearly produced a productivity dip, with staff and managers focusing some of their attention on protecting and enhancing their own positions in the complete reorganization of services for working age people. Using a metric derived from private sector mergers and acquisitions, White and Dunleavy estimate the short-term costs of lower productivity at £166 million. The separate and long-standing Employment Services Agency organizational culture was also imperfectly absorbed in the new hybrid DWP, causing some staff to leave, and others to retire early.

The other two sections of DWP covered pensions and services for the elderly and those for the disabled and carers. They were also affected by extensive change processes. A 2001 review of strategic options for the new department concluded that it badly needed to modernize its services, and that the key way to do so cost-effectively was to transition away from expensive face-to-face services for elderly and disabled customers, and also to move on from paper form applications. Instead, the DWP's whole ways of communicating with its elderly and disabled customers would be revolutionized, by using phone-based administrative processes. Huge, modern call centres would be built and phone-based applications brought in, especially for modernized benefits.

The new benefit, Pension Credit, was launched in 2003 to replace Income Support and supplementary provision for elderly people with poor National Insurance records and hence only small State Pensions. The new credit aimed to guarantee anyone aged over 60 a defined weekly income. To register, people phoned up a call centre and went through a long-ish conversation with an advisor who filled in a complex form on computer as they spoke. Staff aimed to give callers a decision on their entitlement more or less then and there, at the end of the conversation. Yet when we visited several Pension Credit call centres in 2008 we found that barely one in four of the lowest-income applicants for the new benefit could be given an immediate decision, called 'sunny day' cases by the staff (Dunleavy et al., 2009, Part 3). The vast bulk of cases involved applicants submitting paper documents and additional information about their housing, employment status or bank accounts, which always greatly extended the decision-making process, often for four to six weeks, and caused many applications to lapse and have to be restarted. This was mainly due to the supplementation characteristic of this benefit, which required that a claimant's earnings and savings were first assessed to determine how much extra income they should get. The DWP computer systems set up to optimize phone applications also worked in a very cumbersome way with conventional paper applications – yet a third of elderly people preferred to start their application off in this way, printing off forms from the internet or getting copies from charities. IT limitations also meant that paper forms were no quicker to process than the long call centre conversations. Experienced DWP grassroots staff often evaded the newer, screen-based IT systems that took so long to fill in, in order to complete applications more quickly directly on the older mainframe computers (dating from the Operational Strategy era).

Meanwhile in some other areas of DWP, our visits in 2009 found some administrative functions operating essentially unchanged from 1970s' processes. DWP paid an important benefit for sick or constrained elderly people who needed extra help with day-to-day household activities like washing, dressing, cooking and going to bed. This was called (misleadingly) Attendance Allowance (AA). In a 2003 study of 'difficult forms' for the NAO this form was by far the longest, most complex and most complained about government form (Dunleavy et al., 2003). As result of the NAO study, the AA form was eventually simplified and the number of questions greatly reduced, but our 2009 study (Dunleavy et al., 2009) found that it still took elderly people at least three hours to complete, and was almost impossible for them to fill in without extensive assistance from families, carers or case workers. All AA applications were on paper, even though very sensitive and hard-to-explain matters were involved, and processing and decisions took several weeks.

The DWP decision to remodel the department around phone-based processes was based on analysis of survey responses in 2001–02 that showed that far fewer DWP customers were using PCs or had internet access than in the population at large. As a result, throughout the noughties there were no developments at all undertaken to put core DWP transaction services online. There were two rather separate exceptions, a long way removed from benefits-based transactions. First, the old ESA labour market services had begun to move online in the late 1990s, before the formation of DWP, because there was already an evident demand from businesses and employers to have a web-based job vacancies service. This ESA-initiated project developed rapidly in the noughties. By 2007 the now JCP labour market systems were carrying details of 40 per cent of all job vacancies across the country. At first vying with private sector services, and often criticized by major private competitors at that time, the DWP provision was eventually guaranteed and stabilized against being outsourced by an EU ruling that all member states must deliver web-based employment services for their populations. Later the key JCP site developed fruitful information sharing of huge blocks of vacancies with its main private sector rivals, enhancing their mutual effectiveness (Dunleavy et al., 2007, p. 6).

Second, the DWP's provision of web-based information about benefits slowly improved, from its ineffectual 1999 beginnings (discussed above). A 2002 study by NAO following up on government departments' website provision found that DWP was still lagging behind in terms of its departmental website, with incomplete, inconsistent information presented in complex and inaccessible ways (Dunleavy et al., 2002). The 2003 study of 'difficult forms' followed up by demonstrating that DWP websites still offered a poor access route for citizens seeking information about their eligibility for benefits.

A cabinet sub-committee reviewed the cross-departmental picture of poor website development and in 2007 concluded that a new strategy was needed, focusing on creating two new government 'super-sites'. The ambition here was for the central government to replicate some of the BBC's (British

Broadcasting Corporation) success in building up a well-presented store of information, going beyond news and into information provision more generally. One super-site (called Directgov) would be citizen-facing, and the other (called Businesslink) would be company- and employer-facing. Initially established under the Cabinet Office, the two sites later moved to be sponsored by main departments, Directgov by DWP and Businesslink by HMRC (which Chapter 4 shows is extensively business-facing).

Directgov focused on copying and migrating information for citizen services across from departmental websites in a rewritten and re-presented form. It achieved early success when the Transport Department began using it for its forms for motor vehicles and driver licences (see Chapter 6). The rewriting and re-presenting of DWP's benefits materials proved much more complex and by 2009 was only partly accomplished, with partly inconsistent wording still appearing on the DWP's own websites and on Directgov (Dunleavy et al., 2009, p. 7). By this time, though, DWP assumed departmental responsibility for running Directgov, which subsequently somewhat speeded up the transfer across of information. With the migration of service-related information supposed to be completed in 2011, Directgov's salience as a source of government information had markedly increased over previous failed government portals. Experiments by the Oxford Internet Institute in 2009 found that by using Directgov, nearly seven in ten respondents (amongst internet users) could find out salient details about eligibility for different DWP benefits (Dunleavy et al., 2009).

However, the government super-sites plan had expected Directgov to develop portal-like 'synergies', where citizens looking for one piece of information would also learn about other services and complete online transactions. In fact, these behaviours did not grow much because the UK government had completely failed to anticipate the dominant development of Google and other search engines – where people go directly to the relevant information page for their specific needs, rather than navigating through the still crowded and complex Directgov opening screens (Dunleavy et al., 2007). In 2011 the government announced the supersession of Directgov by a more ambitious Government Digital Service. Instead of just providing passive information sheets (as all the DWP sites did), the new site aimed to actually help people to complete transactions online, something completely infeasible across the board in the DWP services until late 2009, and only slowly developed since then to the time of writing (mid-2012).

The development of DWP's means of communicating with its customers up to and beyond the end of our study period are summarized in Table 5.2, developed from material gathered for a 2009 NAO report on the department (Dunleavy et al., 2009). In the mid-noughties the department's

Table 5.2   The evolution of approaches to information exchange in the Department for Work and Pensions

Key Periods	Disseminating Information about Benefits to Potential Customers	Applying for Benefits	Contacts with Customers
Legacy approach before 1999	Paper leaflets Face-to-face explanations in local offices Media campaigns and advertising	Mailed in paper forms Paper forms completed face to face in local offices	Paper letters Face-to-face discussions
Major changes already made from 2000 to 2008	DWP websites developed and online information greatly increased Extensive redesign of leaflets and improved risk assurance on their information being up to date	Phone-based applications developed strongly for all customers Redesign of many paper forms Development of Carer's Allowance electronic claims Some claim forms available online	Phone-based contacts increased with all customers, especially those over 60 Local office access for customers over 60 removed
Immediate challenges from 2009 onwards	Consolidate and improve all online benefits information on Directgov (closing down DWP citizen-facing sites)	Develop the first two major online benefit applications for JSA and State Pension	Develop the first systems for online communications with customers via e-mails, web accounts etc. Develop 'Tell Us Once' procedures
Strategic long-run challenges (to 2017)	Further develop online advertising Develop Web 2.0 applications and facilities	Grow the proportion of online applications (to 40 per cent for JSA by 2011)	Grow the proportion of online communications Develop 'self-service' and online accounts

Source: Derived from materials gathered for Dunleavy et al. (2009).

expensive attempted transition to phone-based services was threatened by an avalanche of almost 195 million customer phone calls a year, many generated by the complexity of benefits rules and the opaque language in which they were communicated, and others reflecting payment delays and uncertainties. A quarter of phone calls were judged 'not value-adding' and DWP admitted to a Parliamentary select committee that its contact centres were so overwhelmed that 44 per cent of calls in 2005 were going unanswered. DWP's increasingly effective top management team took drastic action to try to cut the volume of calls – by making more use of postal forms; redesigning paper forms, contact centre phone scripts and web pages to try and get communication with customers right first time; and using intelligent voice recognition (IVR) systems to automate phone call handling (although IVR is much disliked in the UK). These radical efforts succeeded in cutting phone calls by 40 per cent by 2008.

But just as this battle seemed to being won, in late 2008 DWP top managers were shocked to discover from new research on benefits claimants that 51 per cent were already online with broadband internet access. This rate was substantially less than the UK population as a whole, but also a world away from the assumptions that had led the department to make its expensive transition to phone-based services. At the same time, the 2008 recession drastically increased the numbers of unemployed people registering for JSA, and also brought in a new wave of redundancies in sectors of business where people were used to doing things online.

Responding to numerous requests, DWP created a simple online form to pre-populate some parts of the form that call centres normally completed for applicants in a 40-minute phone call. This online facility was a cheap 'quick fix' that was expected to be of minor significance. Yet by December 2008 some 50 000 people a month were filling in and returning the form. The high level of demand led to top managers bringing forward to 2009 an online form designed to replace in full the initial contact centre phone call (Dunleavy et al., 2009, p. 5). Online pension registration was pushed back to later action in the UK – although it was successfully introduced in the USA and Canada in 2009 and expanded rapidly in both countries (Dunleavy and Rainford, 2011).

The DWP's startling conservatism in the face of online services, lagging more than a decade behind developments towards online transactions for UK tax paying, reflected a conflict of values within its organizational culture. The number one value for managers and most staff was maintaining the security, accuracy and integrity of the existing, complex benefits systems. The senior IT staff who were handling rules changes to DWP systems were especially conservative, with a change notification process that never took less than two years to implement any changes, small or large. Hundreds of minor system changes were under consultation or progressing towards implementation at any one time. This primary preoccupation with maintaining complex systems' basic stability was run close for top managers by a drive to minimize running costs, creating savings in staff numbers, improving efficiency and cutting fraud and error (NAO, 2008b and 2010c). These latter motivations were partially shared and partially rejected by staff, not anxious to see their job prospects worsened and workloads increased. Finally, a relatively strong 'public service ethos' was a core value amongst grassroots staff. At the top management level it focused on 'delivering the best feasible customer experience' (Dunleavy et al., 2009, p. 12). The huge modernization of DWP services, both in the smartened-up Job Centres and in the building and business processes used for the newer phone-based benefits like Pension Credit, testified to the strength of this third impulse. But improving the customer experience was throughout easily trumped by the drives to maintain benefits system integrity and keep costs to a minimum, reflecting strongly conservative influences.

5.3   THE STASIS IN SOCIAL SECURITY PRODUCTIVITY

The key past constraint on organizational learning about productivity in government has been the absence of reliable data on output measures. In the UK this information deficit in social security only began to be officially addressed in the mid-1990s. Our main analysis draws on valuable work by DWP's own analysts in cost-weighting outputs in sophisticated ways, and thus covers the period 1998–2008, which provides a useful perspective. But since ten years is still a relatively restricted perspective, we have also undertaken a longer-run 20-year analysis, covering the period 1988 to 2008, seeking to map productivity trends from somewhat cruder data series, assembled in a consistent way from publicly available data from the DWP and the ONS.

Table 5.3 shows that our analysis of the DWP and its predecessors' productivity is based on looking at data for the full range of its services. Because responsibility for the payment of some smaller 'social protection' benefits was transferred from the DSS/DWP to other government departments during the period under analysis, we excluded these benefits from our calculations, to keep our output measure fully comparable over time. Data were assembled on a financial year basis, starting in financial year 1997–98 and running forward for ten years. Again following the recommendations of the Atkinson Review (2005b), our key measures for 14 main areas are the number of applications for that benefit registered in

Table 5.3   Data and adjustments used for the measurement of productivity in UK social security, 1998 to 2008

Variable	Evidence Used, and Adjustments Made
Outputs for processing of benefits	Number of new claims, and number of ongoing payments, processed for: Jobseeker's Allowance and its predecessor; Incapacity Benefit; Maternity Allowance; Widow's Benefit'; Social Fund grants and loans'; State Pension; SERPS; Attendance Allowance; Disability Living Allowance; Carers' Allowance; International Pension Credit'. Internal data provided by DWP covering 1997–98 onwards For our longer time series (1988 to 2008) we use DWP published data on numbers receiving most of the same benefits. However, we exclude the smaller benefits marked ' above, but because we use a 'social protection' measure we must perforce include War Pensions (not administered by the DWP, but by the Ministry of Defence)
Cost-weighting of outputs	Unit costs for each benefit above, provided by DWP internal data
Inputs, for total factor productivity	Deflated total labour and other administration costs obtained from DWP statistical teams. Capital consumption was also provided by DWP staff
Inputs for staff productivity	Number of full-time equivalent (FTE) staff in social security and employment assistance, obtained from DWP annual reports and those of its predecessors. Longer-term data also include staff administering War Pensions

a year (claims), together with the total number of ongoing payments for that benefit per year (load). The logic here is that in terms of administrative costs, new benefits claims are far more expensive to process than ongoing load. Many of the transactions costs of administering benefits lie in judging people's eligibility, checking databases and documentation, coping with missing information and assuring against fraud or error. Especially once the DWP transitioned to using electronic payments to bank and Post Office accounts, the main costs of ongoing payments arose from processing changes of addresses and other altered circumstances.

To cost weight output volumes we again followed the methodology suggested by the Atkinson Review. Output volumes were weighted according to their share of total administrative costs for processing new applications for benefits (claims) and for the maintenance of existing benefit caseloads (loads). In this chapter we used weights calculated by the internal productivity unit at DWP, which are based on unit costs. The unit costs show how much was spent to produce each benefit payment as a share of total administrative expenditure. Again, in normal years the variations in costs are mostly quite small. However, costs are often higher in the first years of introducing a new benefit, because both the staff and claimants are unfamiliar with how it is supposed to work, and mistakes, operational failures and other 'teething problems' more often occur. As the benefit's operation become routinized, operating costs generally fall, unless an IT glitch develops, or a vulnerability in the benefit processing procedures becomes apparent (e.g., because of a new type of fraud spreading from one region to another). For our longer series covering two decades, we cost weight more crudely using an annual cost per 1000 benefit payments measure derived from the public annual reports of DWP and its predecessor departments.

Are quality controls needed for social security series, and if so what should they focus on? The Atkinson Review suggested that the extent of fraud and error in paying benefits was the most appropriate element to consider in quality-weighting. The National Audit Office has been qualifying the accounts for first the Benefits Agency and later the DWP since the end of the 1980s, on the grounds that the overall rate of fraud and error is too great to allow the accounts to be signed off. However, there has been consistent action by successive top civil servants at the department to counteract the problem. Rates of fraud have fallen by half in absolute number terms in the noughties, and declined from 2.1 per cent of benefits paid out in 2000 to less than 1 per cent by 2009 (Tinkler, 2010). Customer error has shown trendless fluctuation in the same period at between 0.6 and 0.9 per cent, and official error (mistakes made by staff) has grown slightly from 0.4 to 0.6 per cent (albeit with peaks of 0.8 per cent in 2004–05 and 2006–07, mainly around Pension Credit). These variations are so small that in our view they are well within the margin of error in the underlying statistical systems producing them. We would have to quality weight fraud and error very heavily for such variations to affect the over-time productivity trends in any visible way, although levels are much greater in some areas (such as Housing Benefit, not handled by DWP but delivered by local authorities). An NAO study (2008b) (and see World Bank, 2010) compared the fraud and error rates in the UK with those in other advanced industrial societies, and concluded that they are unexceptional in either direction – neither clearly better, nor worse.

A second dimension where quality-weighting could well be applied concerns the quality of DWP customer services. These certainly were clearly increasing in general modernity and point-of-service standards throughout

Table 5.4   The ratios of complaints to transactions for DWP agencies in 2006 compared with Centrelink, Australia

Name of Organization	Total Number of Transactions	Total Number of Complaints	Complaints per 1000 Transactions
Jobcentre Plus	48 202 000	40 000	0.83
Pensions Service	8 240 000	41 000	4.97
Disability and Carers' Service	na	8900	na
For comparison: Centrelink, Australia	9 870 000	39 300	3.98

Note: Transaction numbers in the first two columns are rounded to the nearest 1000. Centrelink transactions are those listed as individual entitlements in the Centrelink *Annual Report 2006–07* (Table 1, p. 11).

Source: LSE Public Policy Group (2008, p. 28).

the noughties, contrasting strongly with the very static and depressing condition of many DSS offices in the 1990s. Similarly, DWP call centre services generally improved, with the exception of some problems around the introduction of Pensions Credit (and to a lesser extent around earlier and later benefits changes). For instance, Table 5.4 shows that in 2006 DWP received nearly 60 times more complaints about its pensions services (mostly about Pension Credit) than it did about Jobcentre Plus. However, the overall DWP rate of complaints even in this peak year was less than two per 1000 customer transactions, lower than that of its Australian counterpart, Centrelink. Many other aspects of quality can only be guessed at – for instance, the peak of missed calls in 2005 did not generate as many complaints.

After reviewing a wide range of evidence we conclude that quality-weighting could enhance the accuracy of the main series below, but that the available data on complaints and problem incidence is not good enough to do this accurately or consistently. Equally, using the arguments made in Chapter 2, we do not believe that much of what the department's top managers regard as quality improvements (such as premises modernization and better point-of-service standards) can be accepted as such. DWP has no competitors and has a highly dependent customer base, making it a monopoly supplier par excellence. Hence, in line with the argument in Chapter 2, we regard the belated modernization of DWP premises and business systems in 2001–07 as largely a catch-up operation, bringing point-of-service standards up to touching distance of private sector service providers, but certainly doing no more than that. Important as these changes were for managers, staff and the continuing public support

Table 5.5   *Staff numbers in the Department for Work and Pensions, and before 2001 in the Department of Social Security, in thousands of FTEs (full-time equivalents)*

Year	1997– 98	1998– 99	1999– 00	2000– 01	2001– 02	2002– 03	2003– 04	2004– 05	2005– 06	2006– 07	2007– 08
FTE staff (000s)	115.8	118.5	114.6	116.1	124.1	131.4	130.8	126.9	118.3	112.7	105.9

Source: Authors' calculations assembled from data for DWP, DSS and relevant agencies.

for the service, it is hard to regard it as anything more than a late, forced accommodation to modern service organization standards, already well established elsewhere in the rest of the economy.

Turning to inputs, for the total factor productivity (TFP) series in the most recent decade we were able to obtain from DWP statisticians good-quality measures of 'total relevant expenditure', that is, the total annual costs of staff salaries, intermediate outputs and contracting, and good-quality numbers on capital stock depreciation. Despite the DSS to DWP transition, data are available on a consistent basis from financial year 1999–2000 (that is, for nine years). They also include one-off investment costs. All these costs were deflated according to specific and sophisticated pay and capital deflators, again provided to us for each year by DWP.

For the labour productivity series, the DSS and DWP staff numbers count is a well-established and reliable annual statistic in this policy area. At various times, this one department accounted for nearly a quarter of Home Civil Service numbers, so that its personnel numbers consequently attracted significant Treasury and parliamentary scrutiny. Table 5.5 shows that the numbers of FTE staff in DWP peaked in 2002–03, some 15 000 staff higher than the combined opening numbers of staff in the DSS and Employment Services Agency. They then fell by 25 000 by the end of our study period.

Turning then to the substantive analyses, we consider first the main study focus on the last decade, and then discuss the more tentative picture that we can draw for the longer period for two decades after 1988. Third, we compare the pictures offered by the two sets of productivity series.

Main Productivity Series for 1999 to 2008

The total factor productivity (TFP) series shown in Figure 5.2 was calcu-lated by dividing the output index by an index of inputs based upon all

Figure 5.2   Total factor productivity in UK social security, 1997 to 2008

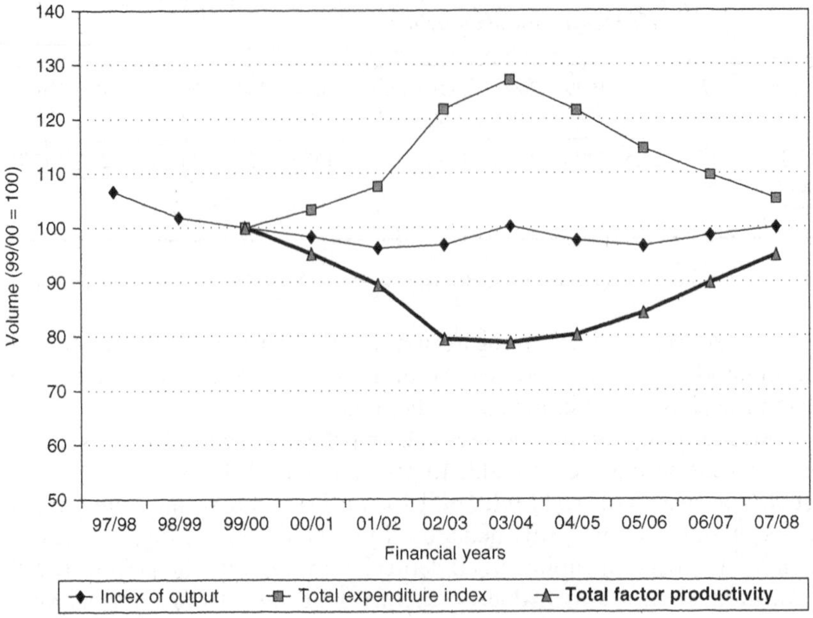

Source: Authors' calculations based on data provided by DWP.

staff salaries, other administration costs and capital depreciation costs, deflated as set out above. The overall outputs curve here declined slightly from 1999 to 2002, and then fluctuated around the new level for the rest of the period. The total inputs costs curve increased to 2003–04, especially sharply in the last two years with the DWP reorganization and launch of new benefits. There was also significant extra spending on consultancy and on new IT systems at this time: the combined expenditure for both headings more than tripled from £94 million in 2001–02 to £306 million in 2003–04 (see section 5.4 below for a fuller discussion). Input costs then fell at a fairly steady rate for the rest of the period, largely under the influence of the departmental merger being consolidated, and DWP offering up large staff reductions during the cross-government Gershon Review (see Chapter 4).

Consequently the overall TFP productivity trend for social security administration shows a decline from 1999 through to 2002, where it bottomed out for two years. There were then steady improvements in the last years of our period, with rises here responding to the decreases achieved in input costs. DWP maintained a consistent quality standard in its services,

Figure 5.3   Labour productivity in UK social security, 1997 to 2008

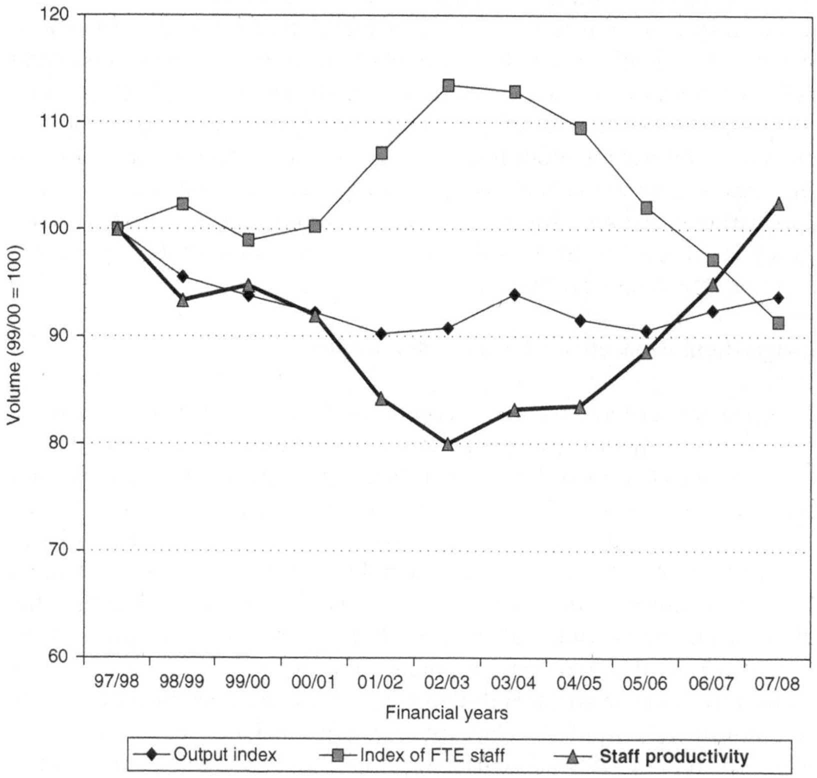

Source: Authors' calculations based on data from DWP.

so these gains are solid. Given that outputs remained almost stable during this later period, the increase in productivity was wholly attributable to the reduction of overall administrative spending for social security.

Looking at staff productivity, we divided the total cost-weighted outputs index for social security by an index of the number of FTE staff employed. Figure 5.3 shows that the key feature here is the large jump in staff in 2001–03, during and following the DWP merger. Given the static nature of the overall outputs curve, the result is inevitably a large apparent slump in staff productivity in the reorganization years, also evident in the DWP's own official analyses (DWP, 2008) and in a separate analysis by the Office for National Statistics (ONS, 2008b). However, a trend for falling productivity was evident before this acute downwards blip.

The 2002–03 nadir in productivity coincided with the troubled introduction of Pension Credit and a range of other new DWP initiatives, which reflected specific ministerial efforts to achieve greater policy effectiveness. We would normally expect the conjunction of all these reorganization and policy changes to have some significant negative impacts on staff productivity as new systems bedded in; benefits staff gained expertise in how to operate novel benefit procedures; and customers (plus their families and charities or care workers advising them) gained more experience of new application processes. However, a substantial recovery of staff productivity levels occurred from 2004–05 onwards, with a somewhat steeper curve than for total factor productivity.

Longer-term Productivity Trends, 1988 to 2008

To get a longer-term picture, we need to shift to data where far more caveats about quality apply. The essential move here is to compute our own cost weights for different main benefits outputs, and use them in a consistent way across the whole two decades period. They are derived from the data published annually by the Office for National Statistics in the Abstract of National Statistics and in DSS/DWP departmental Annual Reports. These estimates are clearly somewhat lower-quality data than the ones used in the previous calculations, because the cost-weighting of benefits activities is based on cruder annual allocations of costs across benefits derived from the departmental reports' costs attributions. In addition, the 'social security' outputs measure used here also includes some benefits not paid by DWP (or DSS before it), most importantly, a diminishing amount of veterans' pensions administered by the Ministry of Defence (specifically the Service Personnel and Veterans Agency within MOD). To maintain consistency we have included the relevant MOD administrative expenditure also in the inputs series used here.

Figure 5.4 shows an especially rapid (step) increase in output volumes in the period 1991 to 1992, a period of economic recession, with a gentle increase in other years before and after this up to 1995. After that date output volumes fell back gradually. Total input costs on this basis grew steadily from 1988 to 1995, increasing by more than 40 per cent in this period. Costs were then pruned sharply for two years, before starting a gradual rise in the run-up to the departmental reorganization. Trends in these series for the decade since 1999 are generally very close to the patterns discussed above.

The TFP curve thus shows two long-term and sizeable dips, plus two recoveries. At the nadir of the first dip, in 1991–92, productivity levels were down by more than a sixth. However, by the end of the first dip, in

*Figure 5.4   Longer-term estimates of changes in total factor productivity
for UK 'social protection' services, from 1987 to 2008*

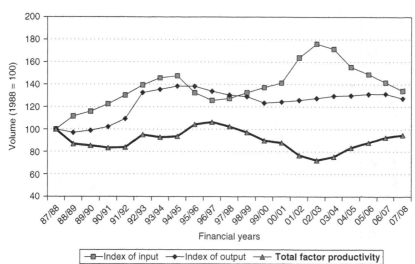

Source: Authors' calculations based on data from National Statistics and DWP/DSS
departmental reports.

1996–97, productivity levels were somewhat higher than they had started
from in 1988. During the second dip, productivity levels were down by
three-tenths in the worst year, 2002–03. By the end of our study period, in
2007–08, total factor productivity levels were still somewhat worse than
they had been in 1988. So the net effect of a series of massive organizational changes across 20 years was to leave social security TFP almost
unchanged, in fact slightly worse than it was at the start of the period. This
is disappointing enough for a period of such high hopes and such energetic
reorganization and reinvestment. However, in addition, the long duration and large amplitude of the two TFP dips implies a substantial loss of
social welfare caused by failing even to consistently maintain previously
achieved productivity levels.

Comparing Productivity Estimates

To assess the reliability of our 20-year TFP estimate with the ten-year one,
we compare both estimates in Figure 5.5. This also includes two other official UK government estimates of social security productivity for the last
decade, both using an Atkinson-derived methodology for cost-weighting
outputs. The first is from the Office for National Statistics (2008a) focused

*Figure 5.5   Comparing four estimates of total factor productivity in UK
             social security, 1988 to 2008*

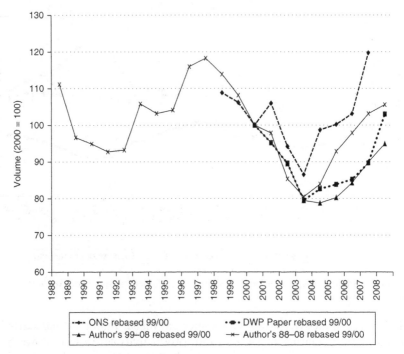

on all social security benefits (not only those paid by DWP). The second
comes from DWP's internal productivity unit (DWP, 2008). To make
comparison more straightforward, we have rebased all four productivity
series on the same base year, which is 1999–2000.

There is a striking level of broad agreement between the four data
series for their common period, 1997–2008. All four estimates show that
productivity levels fell appreciably, bottoming out in 2003–04. Taken
overall the ONS clearly offers the most benign interpretation of the last
ten years' data, identifying the gentlest decline in productivity to 2003
and the strongest recovery since. The other three projections are broadly
convergent. Our long-term view agrees closely with the DWP series on the
2008 endpoint, while our short-term series is somewhat more pessimistic
on the revival of productivity achieved. Overall, our estimates suggest
that total factor productivity in 2008 was no higher than in 1988. In the
next section we turn to consider the factors that may help account for this
relative stasis.

5.4 KEY INFLUENCES BEHIND THE LACK OF PRODUCTIVITY GROWTH

Three factors might help put the long-run lack of change in DWP's productivity into sharper focus:

1. *A high rate of exogenous political, policy and organizational change* can be expected to have adverse implications for organizational productivity in government. We have seen that DWP had a great deal of ministerial alternation in office, including 12 top ministers (Secretaries of State) in twenty two years, from 1988 to 2010, plus extensive changes of junior ministers – none of which is helpful for the long-range growth of productivity. Pursuing greater effectiveness, ministers extensively remodelled benefits rules and introduced new benefits (like Pension Credit), as well as requiring the DWP to undertake new tasks (like the active labour policies demanded from Jobcentre Plus). In addition, each new top minister and junior ministers tended to make a series of smaller initiatives to put their mark on services, especially under New Labour.

   Large changes of benefits always create a rise in unexpected implementation difficulties. In machine bureaucracies backlogs of cases can quickly build up. Redress cases (complaints, appeals and interactions related to them) can spiral in a short period. Customer behaviours can also be adversely affected, with many more people complaining more readily when service levels pass tolerable limits. These issues then take time to deal with and to renormalize, especially in an organization without much 'fat' or slack in it. Major policy launches and organizational restructuring tend also to distract senior managers from improving day-to-day operations, perhaps delaying incremental systemic improvements for several years, impeding training and causing other adjustments useful for driving up productivity to be put on hold. All of these factors clearly contributed to slower progress in DWP's productivity over time. There was a departmental and government commitment to 'benefits simplification', but little evidence that it was effective at this time (Work and Pensions Select Committee, 2006b). More useful was improved DWP communications with its customers (especially after 2005–06).

2. *Government-wide pressure for greater efficiency* was clearly important in the Gershon Review period, from 2005 to 2008, when all the DWP productivity series reviewed above bounced back (albeit with some significant differences in timing). The chief impact here was through staffing numbers being reduced by just under a fifth from their peak

levels (Work and Pensions Select Committee, 2006a). (Yet just outside our study period, in late 2008 the upsurge in unemployment claims led Jobcentre Plus to re-contact some 6000 staff who had just left the agency, in the hope of re-employing many of them to cope with the increase in demand.)

3. *Investing in new business processes, increased capital spending and organizational modernization* should also have paid off for DWP in terms of improving productivity. From 1999 onwards DWP spent a lot of money on new IT systems, new buildings and capital investments and new working methods. Each of the many changes made under this heading was necessarily supported by a strong Whitehall business case, in which cost reductions played a key part. All the key modernization changes were advocated partly on the grounds that they would lead to some demonstrable increases in productivity. From the literature reviewed in Chapter 1 we might expect that the use of more and better ICT, improvements in customers contact methods, the introduction of modern management practices, greater use of outsourcing and bringing in consultants to speed up reorganizations would all boost productivity growth. The mix of initiatives in DWP's case was in most respects quite comparable to that in other areas of UK central government. But in fields like tax collection and customs regulation we have seen that total factor and staff productivity trends moved upwards much more strongly over these decades. (The same mix of investments applied in prisons also, again with favourable results; see Bastow, 2012, Ch. 4, and 2010.)

To explore this last issue in more detail, we have again assembled data series for the 1998 to 2008 period, covering the same dimensions reviewed in Chapter 4:

- *Expenditure on ICT* strongly reflects the policy change factors noted above, none of which can be implemented without altering the underlying computer recording and payments systems. While compiling NAO reports in early 1999 and again in late 2008, we visited large DWP field offices in two northern regions and the transitions made in the department's ICT systems across this period were impressive. In 1999 all back offices operated 'dumb terminal' systems, no staff could look at the internet, and the operations were all conducted on mainframe systems from the Operational Strategy period that were slow and problematic. A decade later all staff were connected to high-powered departmental networks with modern PCs. They could look at the internet, and in the call centres they were using web-based programs to run through a call script using algorithms, and also calling up additional information. However, we did note that the newer IT systems were time consuming to operate, and that around four in ten of the staff preferred to enter information directly into the 'legacy' IT systems wherever they could do so. Experienced staff (the minority who were long-term DWP folk) found it quicker to enter data directly into the same 'OpStrat' computers of a decade earlier than to use the newer screen-based systems. Managers frowned on this gambit, because it reduced the possibilities of checking on benefits decisions. But they were also dependent upon their most competent staff to meet demanding workload targets, and so could not curtail the practice.

- *Outsourcing via Private Finance Initiative projects* in DWP again focused exclusively on major construction projects. Our two sets of visits to large DWP offices showed huge changes in the department's built environment. In 1999 thousands of the department's Newcastle staff still worked in rundown offices, many appearing to be in pre-fab buildings from the early post-war period. A decade later they had all moved into purpose-built, suburban call centres located on modern business parks. Some of the vast new buildings almost resembled 'Star Wars' sets in their scale and modernity. Again these substantial transitions were also strongly associated with DWP radically redesigning its work teams and business processes. So we take PFI expenditure as a proxy for the extent of major managerial change.

- *The use of consultants* was again closely bound up with DWP's major reorganizations. Firms and agency staff were brought in to create extra capacity to do much of the change management workload, while most in-house staff kept ongoing operations on track. Like HMRC, the Department of Work and Pensions also brought in consultants later in the noughties to help implement 'lean' approaches to redesigning service pathways.

Assembling relevant data for these factors was as difficult as for the taxation departments, described in Chapters 3 and 4, and following through the merger of DSS and the Employment Services Agency raised some similar issues. Hence a general caveat still applies to data on these three factors, that the information involved was assembled from a range of sources. (And see the Appendix for more details of sources.)

Table 5.6 shows spending on ICT, PFI construction projects and the use of consultants as shares of the total administrative expenditure for DWP and its predecessor departments. The total amount of administrative

Table 5.6   *Expenditure on information technology, PFI construction projects and consultancy as percentages of total administration expenditure in UK social security, 1997 to 2008*

Year	1997–98	1998–99	1999–2000	2000–01	2001–02	2002–03	2003–04	2004–05	2005–06	2006–07	2007–08
ICT	7.18	6.06	5.47	5.00	4.55	3.91	4.88	6.88	6.44	11.27	11.43
PFI (non-IT contracts)	na	5.11	4.73	4.49	4.50	4.18	4.85	6.64	7.15	6.94	6.88
Consulting	na	na	na	na	1.57	2.07	4.04	2.18	1.69	2.12	na
Total for these aspects	na	11.17	10.20	9.49	10.62	10.16	13.77	15.7	15.28	20.33	18.31

Note: Before the financial year 2001–02 data for ICT correspond to spending by the Information Technology Services Agency. From this point onwards ITSA activities were outsourced to EDS via a PFI contract. ICT values after 2001–02 are annual payments for all ICT-related PFI contracts; na = data not available.

spending absorbed on these elements doubled from a tenth of total administrative spending in 2001–02 to a fifth in 2006–07, a major increase in investment and capital intensification. However, in the intervening years this share was less, and it also fell back again slightly in 2007–08. The increases were greatest in ICT, but concentrated in the last two years of our period. PFI spending on building grew less but was more consistently up throughout 2004 to 2008. Consultancy spending showed a large upwards jag in 2003–04, and was slightly higher also in the two adjoining years.

We followed the same procedures here as those discussed in section 4.4 in Chapter 4, lagging ICT, consulting and PFI (construction) expenditure by one year against the cost-weighted output index level and fitting a basic regression line. Again with so few observations we cannot read much into the patterns obtained, but the tables obtained can still provide some insights into how our three factors appear to be associated (or not) with changing productivity levels.

Two of the charts below, Figures 5.6b and 5.6c, strongly suggest that there is no connection between either PFI construction spending or consultancy spending and the index of DWP outputs. Figure 5.6a at first sight seems somewhat different – perhaps an eighth of the variations in outputs might be attributable to IT spending as a proportion of administrative costs. However, the regression line here is strongly shaped by data from the last two years of our study period, when high levels of ICT investment coincided with rising DWP output levels, which were in fact principally

Figure 5.6a   *Lagged ICT expenditure plotted against outputs for social security*

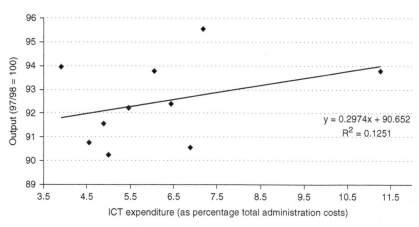

Source: Authors' elaboration based on data from DWP departmental reports.

Figure 5.6b   *Lagged expenditure on PFI construction projects plotted against outputs for social security*

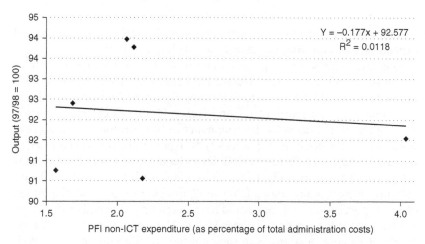

Source: Authors' elaboration based on data from DWP departmental reports.

due to the onset of economic recession. So overall, what is most interesting about the DWP explanatory factors is how much weaker they apparently were than was the case for HMRC and Customs. These factors critical to the administrative reorganization of social security seem to be hardly

Figure 5.6c   Lagged expenditure on consultancy plotted against outputs
for social security

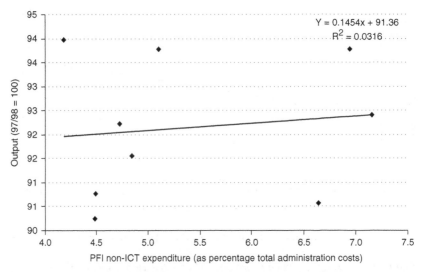

Source: Authors' elaboration based on data from DWP departmental reports.

correlated at all with improvements in outputs. Figure 5.6c plots lagged expenditure on consultancy against outputs for social security.

This result can be best explained in terms of the overall conservatism of the department's efforts at restructuring. From the outset, the DSS/DWP organizational culture was one that clung tightly to its past administrative practices using paper forms and legacy IT processes. This mindset, was hugely strengthened by the dominance of 'mainframe guys' (and they were all men for many years) in its key ICT positions. It was accentuated by outsourcing most IT responsibilities to large and conservative systems integrator firms, especially EDS. Thus many different intellectual and cultural barriers made senior DWP staff unable to grasp the magnitude of the opportunities that they could have taken up at the end of the 1990s to effect more far-ranging changes in how their new department would go about its core mission, as in their conservatism about using the Web (Dunleavy et al., 1999, paragraph 2.31). By 2002 the picture had not shifted much. In particular, at the same time that the almost equally conservative Inland Revenue hierarchy were (slowly) getting to grips with online self-assessment, and that Customs was trying and failing to move VAT transactions online, first DSS and later DWP top officials rejected any idea of developing online transactions. Instead, they persuaded min-

*Figure 5.7   The changing pattern of the DWP's customer contacts, 2005
to 2008*

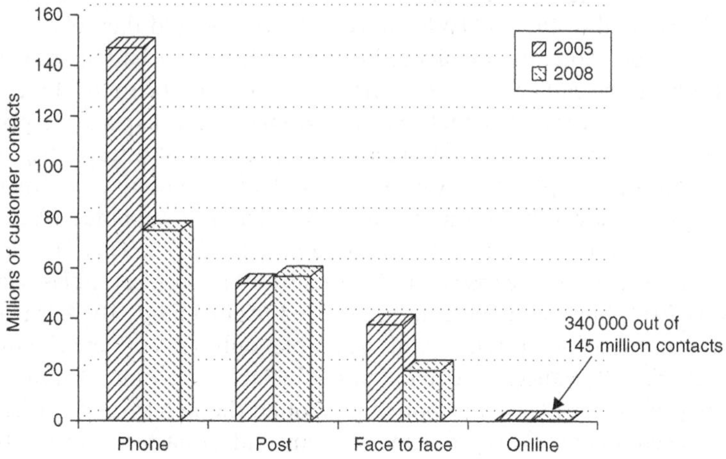

Source: Dunleavy et al. (2009, Figure 3, p. 13).

isters to move the department lock, stock and barrel into a phone-based
model of customer contacts, and they put on one side any developments at
all of online transactions models.

The consequences are rather dramatically captured in Figure 5.7, which
shows the mix of DWP communications with its customers in 2005, at
the height of the mushrooming growth of partly abortive phone calls to
the department unleashed by the initial business process transition. By
2008 the reimposition of tight management of phone calls had succeeded
in reducing their numbers by 40 per cent. And, of course, by this time
face-to-face contact had been further reduced, except for Jobcentre Plus's
surveillance of jobless working age people. But the net effect was chiefly
to *increase* once again the importance of paper forms and documentation
sent in by post. At the height of the internet boom, the department's online
communications accounted for no more than half of 1 per cent of transactions by 2005. By 2008 the online numbers had barely increased, and
before fieldwork began for the critical 2009 NAO report DWP still had no
benefits transactions being transacted in whole or in part online, nor any
publicly announced plans to do so.

The DWP's first hurried efforts to create some online capability, partly
in response to the critical NAO report on its customer communications
(Dunleavy et al., 2009), also misfired. During 2008 the facility to pre-
register an initial JSA application online was no sooner announced than

the take-up grew rapidly to 50 000 users a month. But all that happened to apparently e-applications then was that the details given were recorded in an Excel file, which was downloaded at the start of the next day's business and distributed to the 26 DWP call centres, who would then phone back the would-be claimants involved, but only when they had spare capacity. Because the call centres were often busy, it could be up to three days before people were called back. Since customers expect speedy responses to online submissions, by this stage many people had already begun to worry that their application was lost and so had rung up anyway, thereby starting duplicate applications running. When a more capable JSA online process was started in mid-2009, it had a patchy record. This first online DWP transaction was expected to be used by 40 per cent of jobless claimants by 2011, but its implementation proved problematic. 'By April 2011, 20 months after the option became available, only 17% of new claims for Jobseeker's Allowance were made online' (Public Accounts Committee, 2011b, p. 9). In early months many users found the JSA system crashed or experienced other serious problems, with around a quarter of applications started in this way failing to make it onto the DWP systems as they should.

Organizational conservatism also remained starkly evident in many other aspects of DWP operations. The JSA process with its three stages was estimated by some critics to be costing £450 million extra per year because claimants had to interact twice with JCP, and then a separate set of benefits decision-makers went over the paperwork for a third time (Clory, 2009). The electronic kiosks in Jobcentre Plus shut out job seekers from learning about electronic job search, instead of facilitating it. And as the numbers of jobless increased in 2009, Labour ministers still refused to allow JSA applicants to offer online proofs of looking for work (such as e-mail job application letters). They insisted on low-risk as well as high-risk claimants still showing up every two weeks at massively overcrowded Job Centres, for contact interviews whose length perforce fell from the previous ten minutes to two to three minutes each, arguably a waste of time for all concerned.

However, it is important to note in closing that departmental officials at first strongly contested this narrative and denied that opportunities to save administrative costs have been foregone. They argued that retaining the face-to-face interactions of its staff with working age people was essential for DWP to properly develop 'active labour market' policies. In their view the Jobcentre Plus model contributed to slowing the growth of unemployment in the 2008–10 recession considerably below previously forecast levels, and thus it helped to contain the much larger rise in unemployment payouts that could otherwise have occurred (Sharples, 2010). Moving to more online transactions, in this view, would have perhaps shaved administration costs, but at the risk of stimulating more jobless benefit claims because of relaxed 'disciplinary' effects on those seeking work. The plausibility of this counter-argument is hard to assess, but DWP's long lags in moving a whole range of transactions with customers (and not just job seekers) online are beyond doubt.

In mid 2010 under new Conservative ministers DWP also completely changed its stance on online applications for benefits, partly responding to new 'digital by default' expectations from the Cabinet Office. As part of the shift towards a single universal benefit, the department now announced that it was aiming to move 80 per cent of its JSA customer transactions online by September 2013. But MPs doubted that this represented realistic business planning, as opposed to a target driven by austerity pressures. A leading House of Commons committee noted that:

> The Department could not explain the basis of the 80% target at the hearing. Subsequent written evidence from the department stated that 86% of JSA customers already use the internet and 67% have access in their homes, while just over 40% are "ready, willing and able" to use online JSA services. (Public Accounts Committee, 2011b, p. 9)

Conclusions

Despite extensive efforts at transforming DWP's business processes, the rather depressing conclusion we have reached is that its productivity remained almost unchanged across 20 years. Even allowing for adverse effects on productivity from frequent policy shifts and organizational restructuring on DWP's efficiency, there is a clear performance gap. DWP was characterized by a conservative organizational culture, especially in envisioning its major business processes and in all aspects of its IT operations. As a result, its large-scale organizational changes after 2001 were exclusively directed towards an already outdated, phone-based administration model. The department almost completely neglected to develop the potential for 'digital era' changes to online transactions approaches.

The parallel here seems to be with those private sector industries in earlier periods where 'computers are everywhere except in the productivity numbers' (Solow, 1987). Private companies in the 1980s and early 1990s invested millions of dollars in automation and new IT investments that subsequently could not be traced through into increases in productivity or corporate profitability. Similarly in our study period DWP seems to have managed to modernize its business processes at huge expense but without realizing sufficiently strong benefits to boost its productivity levels. However, recent trends in productivity have been upwards, and the external impetus from the Gershon Review cut staff numbers appreciably.

After a Conservative and Liberal Democrat government took office in 2010 (outside our main study period) a leading Tory politician (the former party leader, Ian Duncan Smith) became the DWP Secretary of State. He had specialized in social security matters for many years while in opposition, and was clearly strongly committed to reforming welfare systems and operations. A key Conservative pledge was to introduce a single universal credit (or benefit for those not working) that is also integrated with the tax system. Implementing this pledge promises to inaugurate a new era of radical change in UK benefits administration from 2015 onwards, a shift in which radically new IT systems and business process capabilities will again be absolutely central. DWP contracts for the IT aspects of the universal benefit/universal credit transition were let in 2011, at initial costs of around £1 billion. Meanwhile, DWP has also planned large staff reductions, and is under intense austerity pressures to cut £2.7 billion from its running costs within a few years, by early 2015 (Public Accounts Committee, 2011b). The usual caveats apply about difficulties in shifting conservative organizational cultures, reorganizations normally depressing productivity, and the past poor record of major IT projects in UK government. Nonetheless, the conjunction of strong pressures suggests that some future productivity gains may still be realized in UK social security administration.

6. Broadening the picture – two national regulatory agencies

Many of the core (or inalienable) functions of government are regulatory ones, concerned with the establishment of the legal identities of citizens and with the registration of roles and granting of permissions. Constitutional and legal provisions cluster thickly in regulatory areas, normally requiring that government involvement is undertaken by civil servants or independent agencies, but still squarely within the government sector. In the two areas we examine here, the provision of passports and the government registration of drivers and motor vehicles, there is also a high potential for corruption and malversation. Hence, directly employing public officials to administer these services has historically been seen as important for assurance and effectiveness. In addition, other governments will only accept foreign citizens and vehicles entering their territory on an inter-state basis. So international treaties and protocols all require that passport provision and vehicle licensing remain government controlled.

Both these policy areas have many important points of continuity with the departments examined so far. They are old-style regulatory functions, requiring the 'case management' of millions of forms and applications. Passports and driver/vehicle licensing are relatively discrete and specific services, and hence were early candidates to be allocated to executive agencies in the UK in the late 1980s. In both cases the development of business process outsourcing has also reshaped how they are delivered to citizens. As in taxation, social security and customs, both functions are run by machine bureaucracies, where first computerization, then service automation and most recently online access to services have all had major impacts. Accordingly, we discuss the two functions in a comparative mode, beginning with passports and moving on to driver and vehicle licensing.

6.1   ISSUING PASSPORTS

In modern times we tend to take it for granted that the whole territory of the globe is carved up amongst nation states, and that to move legally from any one part of it to any other it is essential to have a passport, identifying you as a citizen of one country or another. Yet in fact this situation is a recent administrative construction. Only from the closing years of World War I onwards did it become the norm. The shift to our modern world, where governments collectively try to 'lock down' the citizenship of 7 billion people before allowing any of them to move across national borders, has required constructing a sizeable bureaucratic apparatus for certifying citizenship. We begin by examining the background growth in demand for travel and why passports are needed. Next we look in more detail at how this function has been organized in the UK. The final subsection here analyses passports productivity data, finding a complex overdetermination of the essentially static picture in the UK.

The Demand for Passports

In the eighteenth century a passport was a letter of government safe conduct, issued in varying forms to specific people, mostly for short times and specific purposes. They were often given by one state A to citizens of *another* state B, to allow them to visit A's territory. During the early French Revolution, its embattled republican regime launched the first efforts to enumerate the entire population of the state, mainly with a view to mobilizing larger armies via conscription. The innovation also allowed the French state for the first time to rigorously discriminate between its citizens and others, and hence to comprehensively close its own borders to outsiders (non-citizens) when needed.

These intensive bureaucratic efforts at identification were long denounced as the hallmark of tyrannical government by most sections of the British, US and similar societies. Only in 1857 did the UK begin to systematically limit the issuing of passports to its own citizens. And even then many millions of British people and of the subject races of the British Empire moved across the huge British global territories without much significant documentation – a pattern applicable too in much of the French overseas empire. Until well into the late nineteenth century, mass immigration into the United States especially (and some other rapidly growing countries) also involved huge waves of people acquiring their first state-issued identity documents only *after* they had landed in Ellis Island or thousands of other entry ports. So it was not until 1917 that a model of systematic passport issuing was generalized to cover most countries at a Geneva conference.

In a world of closed and comprehensive borders, a passport has become the sine qua non of foreign travel, a carefully controlled record of citizenship that also guarantees a right of readmittance and continued residence in your home country on returning back from overseas. The reciprocal nature of passport treaties and conventions means that a person has to be certain of being able to return to country A before countries B or C will admit them within their frontiers – for otherwise B or C might fear that if they admit someone they will get stuck with housing a 'stateless' person, who could not later be deported to a 'home country' if need be.

Countries still vary sharply in the extent to which their citizens hold passports. In the USA, the continent-spanning size of the country, plus the relatively small scale of overseas trade as a proportion of the domestic economy, meant that for much of the post-war period only a very low proportion of citizens had passports. In 1989 there were just 7.3 million US passport holders (Department of State, 2012), although by 2001 this had grown strongly to 51 million. In the tighter security regime following 9/11 the ability for US citizens to enter Canada and Mexico on an identity card was rescinded, and passport holders subsequently doubled to 110 million by 2011. Even now, though, this is still only 36 per cent of US citizens. Even inside the legislature, amongst US Senators who are key actors for setting foreign policy, the proportion of passport holders for many years was just over half – far less than might be expected for such elite decision-makers.

By contrast, in the modern period, the great bulk of UK citizens have held passports, which are still needed to travel to the country's nearest neighbours in continental Europe. With the removal of exchange controls on sterling in the 1970s there was a rapid expansion of cheaper overseas holidays, later further fuelled in the 1990s by the development of low-cost airlines in Europe. Figure 6.1 shows that before and during our study period overseas visits by people resident in the UK (including some overseas residents of course) grew by 180 per cent between 1986 and 2006. Greater household incomes and cheaper holidays and flights meant that more and more UK citizens visited, first, European countries bordering the Mediterranean, and later more far-flung destinations across the world. A 1989 change of the law also meant even the youngest children needed to have their own passport, complete with a photograph and biometric information before they could leave or re-enter the UK.

As a result, around five-sixths (84 per cent) of the UK population now hold passports and the context of passport operations in the UK has consistently been one of buoyant and rising demand. For the most recent ten years, Figure 6.1 demonstrates that the demand for new or reissued passports is closely linked to travel patterns. In addition, UK residents' overseas trips concentrate somewhat more in the summer months (27 per cent in the second quarter, and 36 per cent in the third). By contrast, fewer people travel overseas in the first quarter (17 per cent) and the last quarter (20 per cent) of each year. As overseas trips grew every year from 1991

164   *Growing the productivity of government services*

*Figure 6.1   The growth in the number of overseas visits made by people
living in the UK, 1986 to 2009, compared to passport
applications 1999 to 2008*

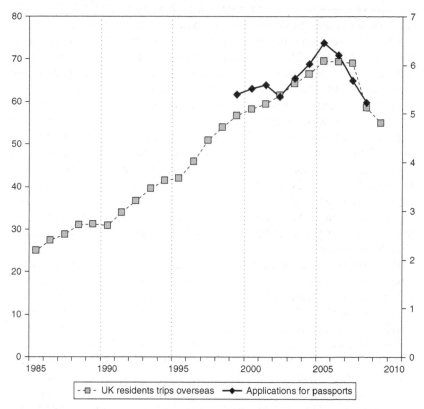

Sources: Overseas trips – Office for National Statistics (2000, Table 2, p. 4); and Office
for National Statistics (2010a, Table 2, p. 8). Passport applications – data from Identity and
Passport Service (2009).

to 2006, so the trend for UK passports issued was consistently upward.
Passport applications rose from just over 4.5 million a year in 1999–2000
to peak at just under 6.5 million in 2005–06, before falling back by a fifth
to 5.2 million in 2008–09. The number of UK passport holders reached a
peak at 50 million in 2006, falling back somewhat to 45 million in 2011.
In 2009 and 2010 the economic recession and the depreciation of sterling
relative to the euro and other currencies meant that many fewer British
people could afford to take foreign holidays. But this is the only decline
shown in the figure.

The Administration of UK Passports

Throughout the twentieth century the Home Office was the Whitehall department responsible for issuing passports and checking the identity of citizens at the point of issue and reissue. Its responsible division was called the Passport Office, and like the rest of the department it operated under full ministerial control. In 1988 the Conservative government of Margaret Thatcher launched the 'Next Steps' programme of moving operational elements out of main Whitehall departments and into executive agencies (James, 2003; Pollitt et al., 2004). The passport operation was transferred out of the main Home Office into a newly created agency with its own management team, the Passport Service, which was still of course staffed by civil servants and remained part of the wider Home Office departmental group.

This change greatly boosted the 'freedom to manage' of top officials in the service, and the agency negotiated its own pay and conditions arrangements with staff. The requirements for reporting to ministers were also radically reduced, and formalized. Henceforward the Passports Service principally accounted for its performance against a restricted set of ministerial operational targets governing the costs of passports, speed and regularity in normal passport issuing, security standards, and the speed and quality of customer service responses to users, as well as a key batch of aggregate financial requirements. Gradually over the next decade, as the Passport Service no longer functioned as part of an integrated department, the number of Home Office staff who knew how the passports operation worked in detail fell, and the ability of ministers or top civil servants to influence its operations insensibly reduced, year on year – a pattern apparent across Whitehall (James, 2003).

The ethos of Next Steps agencies (especially under the Conservative governments under Margaret Thatcher and John Major) was strongly shaped by 'new public management' (NPM) ideas. This approach had three main component themes (Dunleavy et al., 2006a):

- *disaggregation*, the splitting up of large, hierarchical organizations into smaller units, of which the Next Steps agencification process was a leading example;
- *competition*, especially promoted in central government via compulsory competitive tendering of blocks of work that could be taken over by private sector contractors; and
- *incentivization*, especially bringing in 'performance-related pay' for staff, and large bonuses for top managers paid for strong agency performance against its targets.

In its new agency format, the Passport Service closely followed all these elements, developing its own operational independence strongly. Many of its key business processes (such as the 'industrial' task of securely printing and despatching passports to citizens) were outsourced to private companies, in line with Conservative party doctrines. And the agency was run by top managers who paid strong attention to meeting ministerial targets, in order to maximize their own pay and bonuses.

Throughout the 1990s the agency was pressured by the Treasury and its parent department to expand its outsourcing further, to modernize its business systems and to minimize or even reduce the costs of passports to citizens. Under agencification the Passport Service was increasingly financed by the fees it charged to citizens for issuing passports. But Conservative ministers were at first wary of allowing fees to increase in a manner that could encourage lax administrative practice in the agency. Hence the service was expected to deliver more surplus within a pretty static level of fees. By 1999 under a Labour government the core passport fee was £21 for a standard passport. Cost-cutting and using new technologies were both very fashionable amongst NPM managers. The Passport Service top echelon became strongly committed to a scheme for using a private contractor to speed up and cheapen the 'ancillary' process of collating citizens' details from handwritten application forms onto the service's databases, preparatory to in-house civil servants deciding whether or not to issue a passport. At that time all passport applications were made by means of paper forms submitted by mail, or in some cases pre-checked (for an extra fee) at Post Offices.

The major IT contractor Siemens won the tender for converting written forms by using optical character readers (OCRs) to scan paper forms and produce electronic versions of each application. In summer 1998 the firm conducted pilots of machinery and software for accomplishing this. The pilots were strongly adverse, with many warning signs that the scanning process was working poorly. However, the agency hierarchy ignored these teething problems and committed 25 per cent of its passport-handling capacity to the new process (National Audit Office, 1999). Evidence quickly emerged that the Siemens process was hardly working at all. Nonetheless, in early autumn 1998 the agency top brass committed a further 25 per cent of their passport-handling capacity to the same process. At almost the same time, Labour ministers made a policy decision that henceforward all children would have to have their own UK passport, instead of being included on their parents' passports as was previously the normal practice until they were teenagers. At a stroke the demands on the agency mushroomed, while half of its capacity was bound up with a new IT function that was apparently not working at all. Fortunately though, demand for passports is lower in the winter and so for a time the service was able to cope.

However, it was apparent early on that in the run up to the next holiday season the agency could face problems. Yet the service's top management hoped all the time that the Siemens process could be made to work, and that the many teething difficulties in extracting complete data from hand-written forms could be ironed out. It became taboo to envisage any other eventuality, so top managers did amazingly little to prepare for the administrative storm that was looming. By Easter 1999 people applying began to notice that they had sent in applications and their old passports but had not got any renewals back. Maximum processing times stretched beyond the agency's ten-day target, to between 25 and 50 days (National Audit Office, 1999, p. 8). As rumours spread virally amongst customers that the service was overstretched, many people reacted by bringing forward the time when they applied for passport renewals, so as to offset against possible delays in time for their holidays. An avalanche of early applications built up, which progressively began to almost shut down the agency. One after another all of the Passports Service's English centres became swamped with millions of unopened sacks of mail containing a backlog of 565 000 applications (almost double the normal backlog). So many sacks were unopened that urgently needed documents were often unable to be found (ibid., p. 1).

As the peak holiday season came perilously close, so all the Passport Service's phone lines in England were swamped by enquiry and complaint calls, rapidly becoming permanently unobtainable. By early summer, long queues of emergency customers were waiting around several blocks to try to get a passport in person from the London office before losing their holiday. The volume of public complaints reached a crescendo. Even acquiring any information about how long passport renewals would take became almost impossible, since the phones rang unanswered. Tellingly, senior service officials left their website completely unaltered throughout the crisis. Eventually in July 1999 ministers stepped in to renew many passports for a further year until the service could get sorted out, and also continued for a year a short-term British Visitors' Passport that was previously intended to be phased out. Compensation for cancelled holidays was paid to thousands of customers, and the agency's Chief Executive resigned.

In late 1999 a National Audit Office report on the unprecedented crisis and virtual collapse of the agency's operation in England found that the primary motivation of the service's top officials had been to slightly reduce the £21 fee for the standard passport. Yet what customers wanted above all was a responsive and completely reliable service; most did not care about such a small price difference, compared with knowing that they could submit an application and reliably get a passport in a decent timescale. In response to the crisis, the Passport Service had to reorganize its services in a root and branch way, reverting for a time to manual processes until the OCR system could finally be debugged. The agency revised its staffing upwards, installed new, high-capacity call centres and at last transformed its previously 'desert' website into a more modern means of communication with all its customers. The service also greatly expanded the use of its higher-fee emergency service that provided passports after a face-to-face interview in a single day. All of this cost money and the passport fees were raised to pay for it, reaching £27 in 2000, and then £43 in 2003 (more than double the 1999 fee).

The 9/11 attack on the USA and the massacres of citizens and passengers involved occurred two years later. The aftershocks produced a worldwide strengthening of passport controls and security, strongly driven by the US authorities. International passports agreements were progressively revised to include new requirements for extra security checks on applicants and their family histories, and new provisions for 'biometric' passports incorporating much better photographs. New questions were introduced about the citizenship of applicants' parents and grandparents. There were teething difficulties. In mid-2006 the press reported that 10000 applications a week were being rejected for having the wrong kind of photograph (Jenkins, 2006). So-called 'e-passports' were brought in towards the end of the noughties. They looked almost the same as conventional passport documents but in fact incorporated a chip that allowed all the component information to be electronically readable by scanners used by immigration staff at border gates.

All of these changes, and normal levels of associated teething difficulties, also began to raise the Passport Service's staffing and costs by the middle of the decade. Later, at the very end of the noughties, came new international requirements for all new passport applicants to be interviewed in person by civil servants, which radically increased security and administration costs. Back-office processes also had to be greatly strengthened. By 2005 the 'standard' passport cost rose to £51, and then jumped to £72 in autumn 2007 and £77.50 in 2009, an increase of 270 per cent on its 1999 level.

The costs of running the agency also increased in several dimensions. Staffing levels progressively grew across this period, from 1800 employees in 1999 to 2400 by 2003, and then reaching 3600 in 2006, finally peaking at nearly 4000 staff in 2008–09 (a 230 per cent growth on 1999 levels), before falling slightly later. Partly these increases reflected the new security demands on the agency, but they also stemmed in part from the decisions to stick with mail applications, and to opt for OCR technology in 1999, followed by the commitment of huge resources to making it work. These steps locked the Passport Service into pre-digital modes of customer applications and into a long-term relationship with its main contractor Siemens. Applying OCR to handwritten paper forms (with their inevitable variability) was a very early form of automation, and one that almost inherently set the agency up for bad customer relations because OCR cannot tolerate spelling mistakes or corrections. Not surprisingly a 2003 NAO study of *Difficult Forms* found that the passport application was seen by the public as one of the most difficult government forms to complete (Dunleavy et al., 2003). Unclear questions (especially for the children's application) added to the perceived complexity caused by the agency's inability to accept a form with any kind of correction, deletion or ambiguous lettering. The new photograph requirements in 2006 later increased the rate at which forms were being rejected and sent back to customers to redo. Around 40 per cent of the agency's wealthier customers also paid the Post Office an extra fee (initially £3.50 in 1999, later £5) for counter staff to check that their applications were in a satisfactory condition for submitting, because of the service's extreme pickiness on how forms looked.

In fact the agency introduced OCR at just the moment when the growth of the internet made this technology very dated as a way of semi-automating customer transactions. The Blair Labour government requirement that all public services be available online by 2005 caught the Passport Service by surprise. Top officials saw e-submission as an unnecessary twiddle to their main technology (OCR from handwritten forms) of minor importance, since renewal applicants still had to send in their old passports and new applicants had to send in birth certificates and often other paper documents. UK government more generally also had no recognized electronic signature or identifier (Dunleavy et al., 2002). Hence Passport Service managers consequently implemented only a hard-to-use application passport form online, which applicants filled in electronically (thereby eliminating the handwriting problems) and submitted to the agency online. The forms were then subjected to some preliminary checks, printed off by the agency and mailed back for the applicant to sign the form and return with their required documents. This time-consuming 'double application' provision nominally met the letter of Prime Minister Blair's pledge to allow online services, but of course was far from being a complete electronic application. Because it took many days longer than going down to the Post Office and using paper forms sent in by snail-mail, very few customers initially took up this little publicized option.

In 2008 the Passport Service finally got out from under its long-term ICT contract with Siemens and constructed a new technology contract with a group of eight different IT providers, who all became recognized suppliers but had to compete or collaborate amongst themselves to win specific blocks of work. Signed at the peak of expectations that the service would be enlarging its wider government role in verifying identities (see below) the deal saw the agency at last increasing its use of background database checks in deciding whether to approve or further investigate passport applications. For most UK citizens, the information provided online for instant checks by government databases and private suppliers (such as credit rating agencies) had radically improved. In other countries, like the USA, this expansion of available online data (including facsimiles of documents online) underpinned maintaining a wholly remote passport applications system. However, the UK's Passport Service was initially reluctant to use credit rating agencies' information.

The expansion of online applications elsewhere in government, especially at Her Majesty's Customs & Excise (HMRC) for self-assessment income tax, and improvements made in the Government Gateway first stage of access, finally persuaded the top Passports officials to improve their online application offer. From 2007 onwards, access to the service was feasible via the super-site Directgov (see Dunleavy et al., 2007) and increasing numbers of applicants began to use electronic applications. Demand was later boosted by a guarantee that online applications would be posted back to people within 48 hours of receipt for them to sign. In fact, this online promise often got suspended in the summer because of high take up for the partly electronic service. The Service also discouraged people who were close to travelling overseas from using the online process. People with under three weeks to go had to show up in person with documents at service offices and so sign their forms then (for an extra fee).

A wider context for improvements in passports checking technologies, and for the agency's staffing growth, was a long-time preoccupation of the service's top managers and the Home Office with broadening the agency's mission beyond simple passport issuing – to become instead the preeminent central government centre of excellence in identity verification and management. There was a large potential 'market' for the agency here, since UK government lacked any central or definitive register of citizens, as well as any modern form of electronic identifier (LSE Identity Project, 2005). There were a number of rivals for the position as central register:

- The National Insurance (NI) number issued by the Department for Work and Pensions (DWP) and supposedly comprehensive for adults over 16. It suffered from there being many more numbers in use than the relevant population and did not cover children under 16.

- The National Health Service (NHS) number run by the health service, covering the whole population, but which also had a problem with duplicates.
- The driving licence, covering around five-sixths of the adult population, but again not children (see below).

Both the NI and NHS numbers were supposed to be 'lifetime' numbers, issued to people once only and held for many decades. In fact duplicate numbers arose because people lost or forgot their previous numbers, and the government computer systems and office files could not then unambiguously re-find their old numbers – for instance, if people changed their addresses or could not remember their address when their initial numbers were issued. Hence, the Home Office saw a potential for its departmental group to accrue revenue if a broadened passport number could become the basis for all government identification – because then they could charge other departments and new commercial users to access the new database.

In 1998 the Passport Service was temporarily renamed the United Kingdom Passport and Records Agency (PRA), when it took on the provision of a criminal records database, but after problems this extra function was then rapidly hived off again to a separate organization (the Criminal Records Bureau) in 2002. The short-lived PRA label was scrapped, but the passports agency was now renamed the Identity and Passport Service (IPS) to signify its widened remit and ambitions. By the mid-2000s the Home Office assigned IPS a central role in the administration of the new national identity card that the Blair government envisaged, backed by a huge database of more than 60 million UK citizens. It would include a mass of information held electronically on chip and a biometric photograph.

However, the proposal attracted a storm of criticism on cost and invasion of privacy grounds. Academics from the London School of Economics (LSE) ran into unprecedented flack from ministers when they independently estimated that the total costs for ID cards would be £11–18 billion, far more than the £5.5 billion admitted by the government (LSE Identity Project, 2005). The government numbers implied a cost of £36 for an ID card alone, but a combined cost of £96 for the five-sixths of people getting a card at the same time as renewing their passport. However, the LSE costs implied a combined fee of £110 (more than five times the £21 passport charge in 1999), so media and public criticisms of rising costs levels were strong, especially given the series of passports fee hikes across the decade.

As Labour Prime Minister, Gordon Brown was more sceptical about the ID cards project. He and the Treasury insisted on a fixed commitment of funding, which radically cut down the scale of the proposed new ID database. Yet still Labour ministers funded the Identity and Passports Service to do preparatory work for the electronic ID card's introduction. Following the 2010 general election, however, the new Conservative–Liberal Democrat government scrapped the whole ID cards plan and the associated database.

So, after many years of striving to go beyond passports the only extension of the Identity and Passport Service's role came from its 2008 takeover of the General Register Office. This was a small central agency setting policy, supervising and providing some central facilities for the nationwide network of local register offices run by English local authorities. These provide the UK's system of official registration for births, stillbirths, adoptions, civil partnerships, marriages and deaths. This limited area of central services for non-passport work only accounted for 5.1 per cent of the agency's revenues in 2009–10 (Identity and Passport Service, 2010, p. 41).

The Evolution of Productivity in UK Passport Services

One benefit of the agencification process is that some kinds of information provision improved. We focus attention solely on the passport-related work of the Identity and Passport Service and its predecessors (taking out of analysis the small non-passport activities present in a few years of the study period, from 1998–2002 and since 2008). Table 6.1 shows the evidence used to determine the Passport Service's productivity for our study period, the ten years following the crisis year of 1999. The key output activity is the supply of passports to UK citizens – all the rest of the agency's administrative work (such as customer service activities) is concerned with and funded by passport applications and their accompanying fees.

Because the agency's outputs are essentially similar across different 'products' (e.g., different types of passports and normal versus urgent service streams) we treat them in the aggregate. But we allow for cost-weighting variations across years to influence the estimate of output levels. Over time there has been more and more take up by customers of the agency's more expensive services, especially in-person applications close to travel dates; passports with more pages (needed by frequent overseas travellers); more secure and expensive forms of postage and delivery; Post Office checking and so on. Similarly the growth of children's passports (which are sold at a cheaper cross-subsidized price, but are actually no less costly to administer) affected the activity mix in some years. So we cost weight to reflect this activity mix over time.

Are quality adjustments of outputs needed? Since the short-lived crisis of 1999, the agency has met its ministerial targets for passport service quality

Table 6.1 Data availability and methodology for the measurement of productivity in passport issuing

Variable	Evidence Used, and Adjustments Made
Outputs for processing of import and export declarations	Total number of passports issued, obtained from annual reports for IPS and its predecessor
Cost-weighting of outputs	Unit costs for different passport types, obtained from IPS
Inputs, for total factor productivity	Deflated staffing, outsourcing, procurement and capital costs published in IPS and predecessor annual reports
Inputs for staff productivity	Number of full-time equivalent (FTE) staff allocated to passport sales and to general administration, obtained from annual reports

Note: We thank IPS staff for supplying us with details of application numbers for the period 1999 to 2008 – earlier data were not available.

in a scrupulous way, and there is no evidence of any major subsequent fluctuations in the efficacy of services. There have been recurrent media and public complaints about the high levels of cost increases in passport fees, which ranged from 20 to 27 per cent hikes at intervals of two or three years. However, on its website the agency has consistently defended its fees record in two ways: (1) IPS argues that the UK had to conform to the new, post 9/11 tightened security rules and associated requirements, and that worldwide agreements on the UK are binding and require that it implement exactly the same changes as other countries; (2) the agency publishes comparator information on how much standard passport fees are in other OECD countries. The UK's fees position has consistently been in the middle of similar countries, charging less than some high-fee countries (such as New Zealand, Belgium or the Netherlands), but somewhat more than other large countries (like the USA and France). Despite the near tripling of customer charges therefore, these arguments are fairly plausible. Accordingly we conclude that quality adjustments are not needed in assessing passport agency productivity during our study period.

Turning to inputs measures, the executive agency status of IPS (and its predecessors) means that its annual reports provide excellent quality information on the full range of costs. By comparison with the mainline Whitehall departments discussed so far, there is particularly good coverage of capital depreciation. Also well described are procurement and outsourcing costs; consumption of materials and external services (such as on passport printing and delivery); and subventions paid by IPS to the Foreign and Commonwealth Office (FCO) for consular services to help UK passport holders who lost or damaged their passports while overseas. FCO re-charged the cost of this last element and IPS picked up the bill because passport replacement is an essential part of any passport service. Accordingly, a soundly based total factor productivity estimate can be calculated.

For labour productivity purposes, IPS and its predecessors recorded their staffing costs in detail. The agency initially employed mainly full-time staff, but later began to employ more temporary staff to cope with peak flow variations. In particular years more numerous extra people were taken on to cope with backlogs accumulating, or with larger than normal clusters of renewals. Later still, IPS switched to using agency staff from private contractors, so that additional staffing now appeared in their accounts under the outsourcing costs heading, which otherwise is principally concerned with information technology and secure printing costs. There are some indications that IPS has at times 'lent out' its staff to other agencies over its lower-activity winter months (which are peak time for most other government departments), but we could get no over-time data on this practice. In default of better information we assume that the over-time incidence of any such practice is standard across years, and the staff segment involved is small for our study period. As in earlier chapters, in all cases the outputs and inputs measures were set to 100 for a common base year, the financial year (April to March) 1999–2000, in this case the beginning of our study period.

Figure 6.2 shows that from 1999–2000 to 2006–07 the volume of activity in IPS and its predecessors tripled, before falling back in the next two years. However, this impressive output growth was almost exactly tracked by the growth of the agency's inputs costs. This is unsurprising since the IPS remit meant that it could neither produce passports at less than their costs (plus a substantial amount for consular support overseas), nor could it make a profit (beyond its required surplus for reinvestment). Given ministers' willingness to agree substantial fees increases after the 1999 crisis, in order to restore capacity and regularity to key transactions, and later in response to the post-9/11 demands for increased passport security, it is scarcely surprising that inputs have risen so far and so fast. The result is that total factor productivity in passports has remained almost completely flat throughout our study period, despite the partial and slow (but still increased) use of ICT and the advent of online transactions capabilities elsewhere in government.

Turning to Figure 6.3, the outputs curve is the same as before. But because of the strong growth of outsourcing costs in ICT and secure printing operations, and later in securing the services of temporary staff, the inputs curve here is different. The numbers of FTE (full-time equivalent)

Figure 6.2   Total factor productivity in passport issuing

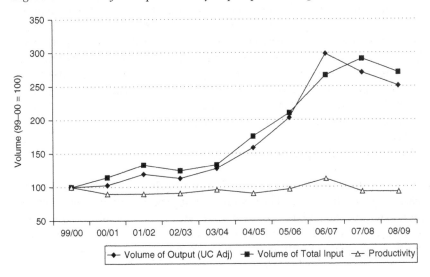

Source: Computed by authors from data supplied the Passport Service and successor
agencies.

Figure 6.3   Staff (labour) productivity in passport issuing

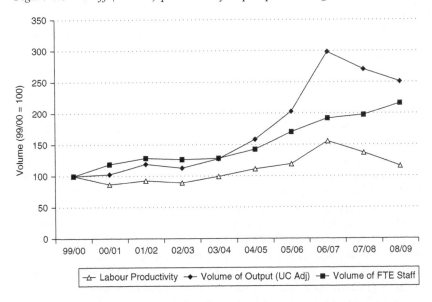

Source: Computed by authors from data supplied the Passport Service and successor
agencies.

civil service staff grew consistently across the period, largely because of the introduction of more documentation and face-to-face interview requirements for new passports and renewals in the latter part of the period. This growth was at a somewhat slower rate than total factor inputs. This growth continued into 2009–10 despite the downturn in passport applications. Consequently, labour productivity was stable for the first three years in the figure, but then grew to 150 per cent of the 2002–03 level by 2006–07. However, it then turned down in the closing years of our study period, to finish barely 15 per cent higher than in 1999–2000.

Conclusions on Passports

At first sight it might seem straightforward to chalk up the UK passports case as yet another area where assuming flat productivity in government is not (after all) such a bad approximation. But in fact the picture is considerably more complex than that. A nexus of three main factors more than accounts for the stagnation in passports productivity, in a fashion that is in many ways over-determined.

First, from 1988 onwards the governance arrangements around the passports function created strong incentives for the executive agency responsible to budget maximize (Dunleavy, 1991, Ch. 6). It was given the power to raise its own expenditures by levying fees from a completely 'captive' and dependent customer base, in a market where it was the monopoly supplier. This was a classic instance of the potential downsides of 'hypothecated taxation', because the agency could neither make a loss, nor accrue a super-profit (beyond its reinvestment needs) for its parent department, the Home Office. Little wonder then that the IPS's top management became preoccupied with constantly trying to expand and 'deepen' activities around passport security. They also sought (as it turns out, unavailingly) to increase the agency's 'turf' in the arena of establishing identity for government. The decision to vest the passport function in an executive agency pre-set many of these responses, which were further accentuated by the gradual loss of expertise about passports within the Home Office over time. So it is hardly surprising that the agency should end up by tripling its staff and almost tripling its administrative budget, on the back of sharply raised passport fees. Labour ministers' concerns to avoid any repeat of the 1999 passport crisis also ensured that in deepening its activities the agency was always pushing at an open door.

A second factor behind the productivity stasis was the agency's early (troubled) adoption of OCR technology from paper forms, followed by the trauma of sorting out the difficulties entailed by this highly conservative technology choice. The agency's reluctance to repeat its first bad experience of the risks with new technology, and similar ministerial concerns to stick to 'tried and tested' approaches, were given concrete form in the long-term contract with Siemens, the agency's main IT supplier. There was almost complete conservatism on the technology for handling all customer transactions for over a decade, despite the evident demand from customers to be able to apply online by the late noughties. As more and more applicants needed to be interviewed face to face anyway, the previous barriers to online applications over documentation and establishing identity could have been completely removed – but they were not. The agency's abortive effort to become a centre of excellence in identity management within government did at least mean that the Identity and Passports Service became much more adept at using other electronic sources of identity information in the course of its applications checks than it was at the start of the period. The re-contracting of IT services (at higher cost) to a more competitive group of contractors also marked a step forward. But the agency's progress in business process re-visioning and re-engineering customer transactions for the internet era was still feeble – especially compared to taxation and customs (discussed in Chapters 3 and 4), and in driver and vehicle licensing (see the next section). This contrasts with the agency's smoothly successful incorporation of new physical technology (such as chips and some biometric elements) into the passports themselves, and the ambitious plans made for the planned identity card and its databases, which came to nothing.

A third factor, of course, was the Passport Service's dependence on the international environment. After 9/11 there were strong environmental pressures led by the USA (and rapidly internationalized) for enhanced document security, and for the introduction of new checks into passports issuing processes. Labour ministers also became increasingly concerned in the noughties to be seen as 'tough' on admitting people into British citizenship. In defence of much higher fees, greatly expanded staffing and rising administrative budgets, the IPS top management attributed all cost growth and increased personnel to environmental changes and took refuge in the 'averageness' of the UK's passport fees. Yet the failure to grow productivity at all over a decade, in an area that was ripe for technological change, seems to underline the hollowness of this defence.

6.2   LICENSING DRIVERS AND VEHICLES

The development of new technologies, and their dissemination across society, often occasion strong demands for government to monitor and regulate the coming trends, and often to react in ways that are very different from what has gone before. Most innovations are disruptive and occasion alarm in some groups, and some are clearly dangerous. The development of cars, trucks and buses from their late nineteenth-century origins through to the 1960s clearly had huge implications for the speed at which travel could take place, and for the dangers faced by all road users. We begin by briefly considering growing motor vehicle numbers and the regulatory and taxing regimes that governments generally have created to cope with them. Next we describe the arrangements for administering driver and vehicle licensing (and associated taxation) in the UK, implemented by the Driver and Vehicle Licensing Agency. The last sub-section examines the organization's generally declining productivity in our study period.

The Growth of Motor Vehicles and their Regulation

The predecessors of 'horseless carriages', of course, were real (horsed) carriages, which in most countries were never regulated by the state. If you wanted to own a carriage, and could afford to do so, you could go ahead without obtaining any government permission, and drive around in it without any official certification of your skills as a driver. The normal civil law provided the main protection against reckless driving behaviours or other practices that damaged (or threatened to damage) the welfare of others.

From the outset, cars, trucks and buses have all been handled by legislatures and governments in very different ways, beginning with the famous early UK law that the first cars had to be preceded by a man carrying a red flag (and hence could only move at walking pace). The evident capacity for fast-moving motor vehicles to cause more damage to others (especially 'scaring the horses' or running down pedestrians), plus the enormous growth in their numbers over time, led to increasing numbers of accidents, especially before safety legislation and driver training belatedly caught up with traffic conditions and driving risks. The close and pervasive involvement of vehicles in many forms of crime, supplemented later still by their use by terrorists, have meant that all governments in advanced industrial states still closely regulate who owns and drives each motor vehicle, and monitor who in their populations is qualified to drive which type of vehicle.

In the 1880s when Daimler experimented with early automobiles there were less than 1000 cars in existence anywhere. By 1900 there were 8000 in the USA alone, and just under 4200 new cars were built in that year, to drive on the country's 144 miles of paved roads. There were at least as many cars in Europe. From there the numbers in use rapidly mushroomed in ways that were poorly documented at the time. By 1968 estimates suggested there were 170 million cars worldwide and nearly 47 million trucks and buses, a total of nearly 217 motor vehicles. These numbers

Figure 6.4   The growth of motor vehicles in the UK, 1990 to 2010

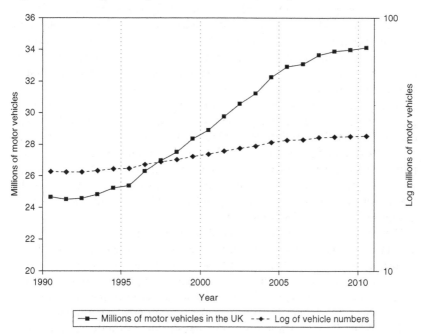

Source: Department of Transport (2011, Table VEH0103).

grew rapidly to 375 million cars and 109 million commercial vehicles (484 million vehicles in total) by 1985; and then again to 486 million cars and 185 million other vehicles by 1996, a global total of 671 million motor vehicles. By the end of the twentieth century there are at least 750 million motor vehicles worldwide, with China a new arrival in the major league.

More recently there have been some signs of stabilizing numbers of vehicles in advanced industrial states. Data from the USA show that the numbers of automobiles has remained almost static in the recent period, growing from just under 134 million in 1990 to 137 million in 2008, whereas the number of vehicles classed as 'trucks' doubled from 54 million in 1990 to 110 million in 2008 (Census Bureau, 2012). In part this reflected the growth of vehicle types like pick-ups and minivans, classed as trucks in US statistics. Total US vehicle numbers thus still expanded from 189 million to 248 million in the 1990 to 2008 period.

Figure 6.4 shows that total UK vehicles grew from 24.7 million to 34.1 million between 1990 and 2010. At the start of the period, the recession of 1989–92 produced the only substantial exception to the regular annual growth in new car numbers, which froze for six years, before something like normal growth resumed in 1996. Almost stasis returned in 2007, and was sustained by the recession that began in late 2008. Press reports in 2009 said that the number of cars on UK roads fell for the first time, but later official numbers still showed a small increase. The log value version of the same graph (scaled on the right-hand axis) demonstrates the static periods at the start and end of our study period, and the relatively slow growth in the middle. Looking in a bit more detail, the numbers of licensed cars grew from 19.7 million in 1990 to 27 million in 2010, with seven out of eight owned by private individuals and the remaining fraction by companies. All non-car vehicles grew from 4.8 million in 1990 to 7.1 million by 2010. Clearly then the vast mass of car-licensing transactions for the UK government were carried out by individual households and related to automobiles, and not by companies.

Driver licensing historically lagged behind vehicle licensing. The first US state to require drivers to register did so in 1903, while linking driver licensing with tests of drivers' skills began in 1908. For several decades, however, many US states only required drivers to pay a small fee to cover the cost of issuing their first licence, with no tests of driving proficiency in most areas, even when three-quarters of households owned a car by the end of the 1920s. It was not until 1959 that the last US state came into line and began testing drivers before issuing a licence – and the standard of the US test still varies somewhat across states.

Driver licensing differs from that for vehicles in a fundamental way, because once a driver has been registered they normally stay registered with no further questions asked until they reach an upper age limit, at which periodic checks or re-testing are introduced – in the UK at age 70. Most countries have imposed a legal obligation on drivers to keep their home address up to date, but the penalties for not doing so varied a good deal over time and across countries. Often the most important reason for someone to update the address on their long-held driving licence was to carry on using it as a form of personal identification in commercial transactions.

The driver licensing workload for governments is also influenced by the changing relationship between cars (especially) and households. For most of the post-war period the UK norm was that many poorer and older households, along with younger households in large cities like London, did not have cars. The vast majority of households with cars had only one, often with two or more drivers, while women historically drove less often than men. Households with two cars gradually expanded, and the proportion of women driving increased to parity with men, but only a few exceptional or larger households had three cars. However, Figure 6.5 shows that

Figure 6.5 *The proportions (%) of UK households owning different
numbers of cars, from 1971 to 2007*

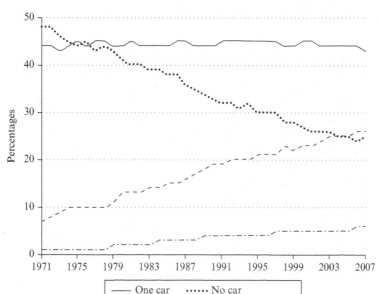

Source: Office for National Statistics (2010b).

in the period from the 1970s to the noughties the proportion of households
without a car fell sharply to around a third, and the number of households
with two cars rose above a quarter, while the proportion of single-car
households was static. Up to one in 16 households now have three or more
cars (reflecting mainly young adults living in larger households with their
parents, or people owning specialist cars as leisure interests).

The UK pool of drivers now stands at 42 million (an average of 1.56
per car) and comprises more than two-thirds of the total population.
However, more than a fifth of the population cannot legally be drivers,
because young people can only start driving at 17 at the earliest, while few
people over 85 are drivers for health or eyesight reasons. So the proportion
of the age-eligible population who are drivers is 83 per cent of adults in the
relevant age ranges, slightly more than for passport holding. Despite the
much smaller spatial scale and far more urban setting of the UK overall,
these numbers are not much different from the USA, where almost 69 per
cent of the population are drivers, or 87 per cent of adults in the legally
eligible age range (Bureau of Transport Statistics, 2008).

Western governments now impose five almost universal regulatory requirements on vehicles and drivers – covering vehicle registration, certifying roadworthiness, paying special vehicle taxes, driver registration and driver insurance:

1. *Vehicle registration*. All cars, trucks and buses must be licensed and uniquely identifiable by a number plate and ownership and address details must be kept up to date. In addition, registration details also include the vehicle's make and often engine block numbers to help safeguard against illegal vehicle sales and thefts. Normally vehicles must be re-licensed (for a substantial tax fee) at least once a year, or the registration lapses and the car cannot be driven on pubic roads.
2. *Certifying roadworthiness*. To be licensed, vehicles must normally be certified as safe to drive and roadworthy (established by regular testing), and operated within appropriate weight or usage limits. Annual checks on vehicles (in the UK called an 'MoT test' and covering cars three or more years from manufacture) are generally administered on the government's behalf by a list of registered and approved garages or service stations. They assess vehicles against a long list of government-set requirements and issue certificates, without which the car cannot be re-registered or driven.
3. *Paying vehicle taxes*. Vehicles must normally be taxed by the government before they can be licensed or driven, with tax revenues used either to supplement general state revenues, or to defray some or all of the costs of building and maintaining public roads.
4. *Driver registration*. Anyone in charge of a given type of vehicle must be certified as sufficiently proficient (and sufficiently healthy) to be driving. All governments now operate driving tests that new drivers or long-term residents from overseas must pass to be able to drive. These are sometimes organized by the same agency that does driver and vehicle licensing, and sometimes entrusted to a separate agency, (as in the UK where they are carried out by the Driver Standards Agency).
    At the other end of the age spectrum, driver licensing normally also requires getting older drivers to take periodic re-tests of their capacities at age 70 and above. The driver licensing agency also has to remove licences from people reported by their doctors as being chronically unfit to drive because of medical conditions (such as blindness, deteriorating eyesight, heart conditions or epilepsy). At the same time agencies must allow disabled people with the right capacities to drive appropriately adapted vehicles.
    Driver licensing also involves monitoring sentences given by the courts for speeding and dangerous driving, driving under the influ-

ence of drugs and alcohol, driving without insurance (see below), and traffic offences. Given people's dependence on cars for transport, a key penalty that the courts impose is deprivation of a licence or the adding of 'endorsements' to it. In the UK, drivers making smaller offences accumulate 'points' on their licence, which sit on their licence for three years. If their points total reaches a threshold during a given time period, drivers lose the freedom to drive for six months or a year – a system designed to make them drive carefully after having had one or two minor offences.

In most countries the police (or a specialist traffic police) are responsible for ensuring that the vast bulk of traffic and licensing laws are adhered to. In some countries the driver and vehicle licensing agency may take part more selectively in special sweeps or surveys, alongside the police, as happens to a small extent in the UK. For the police, driver and vehicle licensing is a key source of intelligence in tracking criminals and identifying people under suspicion. So cooperation between the police and the driver and vehicle licensing agency is of great importance for the effectiveness of the overall law and order function. This is especially true with the development of new technologies, such as automatic number plate recognition, where police forces can auto-access the data held on the vehicle-licensing database, using digital photographs of car number plates from roadside cameras.

All these elements mean that the driver licensing agency can hold a lot of sensitive personal information, and has to interact with a wide range of other public and professional actors to carry out its basic role. In the UK, the high proportion of foreign drivers from nearby continental Europe and Ireland also entails a great deal of extra work in tracking drivers and vehicles.

5. *Driver insurance.* One of the key roles of government is to regulate mainly private activities in such a way that the burdens of risk involved are allocated to those actors most appropriate or most able to bear the costs involved (Horn, 1995, Ch. 3). For road users, this means that they must have confidence that if someone else causes an accident they can recover the costs involved from the driver concerned, as well as being themselves covered for their own damage and their liabilities to others. Accordingly, Western governments require that all drivers must be insured against the 'third party' damage they may cause to others. Unless the owner can produce a certificate from an insurance company that his or her vehicle is currently insured then it cannot be re-registered. In theory then, people adversely affected in an accident can always secure adequate compensation for damage to their vehicles, property or health. But in practice, insurance is only

needed at the annual re-licensing date and it may well have run out
when an accident occurs. Police checks again play a key role in combating drivers being on the road without insurance.

Given the huge numbers of motor vehicles in the modern world, this
complete ensemble of requirements is a very tough task to undertake.
Substantial resources are needed to ensure that the full agenda of controls
is defined and systematized into administrative practices. Even in small
countries monitoring all these aspects is still relatively difficult. For large
countries (like the USA) or medium-sized ones (like Britain or France), it
requires major administrative organization.

In the USA, driver and vehicle licensing is a function carried out by the
51 states, and federal involvement is limited to linking up state databases
so that police in one state can trace cars or drivers from other regions,
and states and insurers can also track drivers' and vehicles' records over
time. One or two states have even delegated the function further so that
it is delivered to citizens by counties or cities. The DMV (Department
of Motor Vehicles) has long been a staple archetype of American public
sector bureaucracy, with attendance in person required and frequently
long queues to get or renew licences. A decentralized pattern is also followed in Italy, where cities and regions run most regulatory functions,
and the national government's role is limited to integrating the data thus
created. The great virtue of decentralized delivery in this fashion is that
face-to-face interviews and the establishment of the driver's identity in
person are still feasible. In addition, the scale of databases held at state or
city level is much less than for the country as a whole.

However, in Great Britain and some other large European countries
(like France) driver and vehicle licensing started off running in a decentralized manner, but has now been centralized and become a national government task. The registration function is run in a unitary way across the
country (in this case meaning England, Scotland and Wales, with a small
separate unit in the Northern Ireland Civil Service managing the function
in that province).

The Administration of Driver and Vehicle Licensing in the UK

Since 1974 driver and vehicle licensing has been a discrete part of the
Department of Transport, which has had various manifestations at
Whitehall level over the post-war decades (White and Dunleavy, 2010).[1]
However, these changing top-level architectures have not often (and not
deeply) affected the staff running the driver and vehicle licensing func-
tions. The car registration system in Britain began in 1903 with the intro-

duction of number plates for vehicles. Responsibility for issuing vehicle licences was assigned to the largest local authorities (called county boroughs in main cities and county councils elsewhere), and for many decades number plates included both year date and area identifiers. The set up was highly localized, with staff in each area accepting applications and checking documents face to face. Local authorities were then reimbursed their costs by the Ministry of Transport. Since police forces were also organized at county borough and county council level, cooperation between licensing offices and their local police force was also high.

The system grew rapidly after 1919 in line with the number of vehicles, creating some difficulties along the way in extending the old number plate system in a consistent way across local areas. There were many problems also in the 1960s with the slow and variable pace of computerization of local authorities. In addition, the extent to which cars, trucks and even buses moved outside their local area all greatly increased, making locally organized registration less and less of a fit with citizens' behaviour. Meanwhile, the separate driver registration function was undertaken at Post Offices and enforced by local police.

In 1974 both the driver registration and vehicle licensing functions were decisively centralized away from local government control entirely, with the creation of the Driver and Vehicle Licensing Centre (DVLC) under the Department of the Environment. DVLC pulled many of the former local authority staff into its network of 81 local offices. In addition, however, DVLC began using Post Offices to renew vehicle licences, to replace the more extensive local authority office network that was now lost. DVLC notified car owners every year (or six months) to renew their cars' registration, and owners took their documents (chiefly the 'MoT' test certificate and evidence that the vehicle was insured) to be checked by Post Office staff, who also accepted vehicle excise duty payments and issued tax discs for cars to display. This system grew progressively to eventually reach 3000 main Post Offices able to renew vehicle licences. People could also direct mail their renewals forms plus key documents to DVLC, but many were reluctant to risk valuable papers in the mail. DVLC responded by radically shrinking its own local office network, losing the last vestiges of the earlier face-to-face service. By 2011 there just a handful of local offices left. The core of DVLC's work shifted dramatically to the 'back-office' role of checking licence applications and vehicle registrations, and compiling and maintaining huge computerized databases for vehicles and drivers.

Like the Passports Service, DVLC was an early candidate in 1988 for executive agency status in the 'Next Steps' changes. Its operational tasks were substantial and specific, and there was no evident needed to keep driver and vehicle licensing functions integrated with the core Department

of Transport in Whitehall. Transport became a fairly small policy ministry after the change. Slightly relabelled and reformatted, the Driver and
Vehicle Licensing Agency (DVLA) was able to operate in a reasonably
self-contained way, little affected by which cabinet ministry's departmental group it fell into.

In functional terms, DVLA carried out all the five licensing, registering
and taxing functions set out above, that is, registering drivers, licensing
vehicles, checking that cars and trucks are safe and insured, and collecting
'vehicle excise duty' (VED) – a specific consumption tax levied on running
a motor vehicle on the roads, for which all cars must display a 'tax disc'.
The agency also records courts' rulings imposing loss of licences and more
latterly the imposition of points on drivers' licences, and their removal at
the end of the relevant time periods. To accomplish its tasks the agency
fields millions of enquiry phone calls a year from its customers, asking
about fees, forms and procedures. The 2003 NAO study of *Difficult Forms*
identified the registration for a photocard driving licence as one of the
most problematic of commonly used administrative forms across central
government, and so the level of calls was always great.

Financially, the agency's key activity is collecting the VED tax for the
government. The duty is levied at a rate that far outweighs the administrative costs of vehicle licensing, raising £5 billion in revenue in 2006
(when DVLA costs were £470 million), rising to £5.7 billion in 2010 (when
DVLA costs were £550 million). Vehicle excise duty contributes to the
general Exchequer funding. Once collected, it is passed over in whole to
the Treasury, while collection costs are assigned to the agency in return by
the Department of Transport. In UK budgetary structures, VED is not
hypothecated or tagged in any way to pay for roads building or improvements. In addition, the agency charged fees to cover its £250 million
costs for driver registration. DVLA also built up a lucrative business in
controlling the trade in high-value or desirable number plates, a side-line
strongly developed in a more commercial manner by top managers after
the organization moved to executive agency status. DVLA additionally
charges for breaches of its rules at a level sufficient to cover the costs of its
enforcement activities, debt collection and pursuit of legal cases.

The tripling of the numbers of vehicles from 1959 to 1970 was the
primary reason behind the centralizing of driver and vehicle licensing
in the DVLC in the mid-1970s to create a single automated database
for recording vast numbers of details. Since then a key function of the
organization has been to provide a continuously available computerized
data service (with a phone back up) to police forces tracking or tracing
any of the 34 million vehicles or 42 million drivers for which DVLA holds
records. However, the demands on this function have also continuously

increased over time. The police had a strong need for information that could be supplied in real time to officers in the field, checking misbehaving or suspicious vehicles or drivers. More recently the development of ANPR (automatic number plate recognition) technology for tracking vehicle movements via roadside cameras has many applications, both in real time for crime and terrorism prevention, and post hoc in criminal investigations. For a fee, DVLA also provides information on vehicles to local authorities and quite a wide range of private businesses that have a legitimate need to identify those cars that have been abandoned, mis-parked or are otherwise causing a problem.

There has been a substantial evolution in the development of the DVLA functions. The records inherited from local authorities in 1974 were in a relatively poor state of consistency and integration. Despite DVLC's efforts these legacy problems with its new databases persisted and proved hard to eradicate over many years. Drivers were legally supposed to update their licence details whenever they moved address, but many millions failed to do so. And unless they were stopped by the police for some reason, the incentives to comply were weak, with small fines and little enforcement.

Having a correct address would be more important for people if the driving licence was widely used for identification purposes, but historically the UK driving licence was not much used as a personal identifier because not everyone was a driver, and the licence itself long consisted just of a printed paper document, with no photograph. DVLA did not introduce an optional plastic card form of driving licence with an integral photograph of the driver until 1997, years behind US and European practice, and then primarily to facilitate UK drivers travelling to EU countries, where photo driving licences were already standard. Even at this late stage though the photocard alone did not constitute a licence for legal purposes, and the paper licence was retained (for instance, to show endorsements). (This situation continued to the time of writing, in 2012.) With this weak incentive for people to keep their DVLA details up to date, it was little wonder that the DVLA driver database was widely seen as out of date and full of holes into the early noughties. Some informal estimates put to us by senior government officials in central departments in the late noughties suggested that at any one time up to two-fifths of driver entries were out of date in some respect, usually the address details.

Vehicle licences are renewed every year, and owners are supposed to notify DVLA whenever they transfer ownership of a vehicle. As a result the vehicle databases were much more up to date than the drivers' register. Yet, they too had many holes and duplicate entries as a result of owners' failing to register transfers, or the systems failing to detect out-of-date addresses. Owners did not need to keep their vehicles continuously in registration, and so could easily say that a car had been taken off the road when skipping months out of insurance, or running other scams. In 2002 one in 25 vehicles stopped in random checks was unlicensed (and often uninsured), and loss through tax evasion was estimated at £193 million. Linking driver and vehicle databases effectively was also difficult given the prevalence of out-of-date driver address information. There were also reputedly large numbers of fake vehicle number plates and identities in the system, estimated at 100 000 as late as 2006 by the *Guardian* (Bowcott, 2008).

In the mid-noughties, Labour ministers launched a programme of legal and implementation changes, partly as an element of their drive to improve public services. But the government was also responding to police and intelligence service demands to strengthen counter-terrorism surveillance in the wake of the 9/11 attacks in the USA and the 7 July 2005 attacks in London. The changes made were designed to greatly improve the accuracy of both DVLA's driver and vehicle databases, and to strengthen their read-across capability. The subsequent introduction of compulsory photo driving licences in July 1998 was one element of the changes, plus the imposition of much stronger charges and fines for people failing to quickly update their address details. The rules governing when cars were regarded as 'taken off the road' and hence not liable for tax, and for how long, were also greatly tightened. Owners were now required by law to tell DVLA exactly when a car was back on the road before they could drive it again. The penalties for breaching the new tougher rules were also increased, with unregistered cars being liable to being taken away and crushed. To support this new regime, DVLA both employed more staff and increased the sophistication of its computer systems. Its top officials claimed that the quality and accuracy of its databases had radically improved as a result by the end of the noughties. The estimated levels of VED evasion fell to around a quarter of their 2002 level in cash terms, and under 1 per cent of vehicles were now estimated to be unlicensed, again radically lower.

Part of the agency's success in boosting citizen compliance with both driver and vehicle registration requirements lay in the development of its approach to transacting with its customers. The reliance on Post Office branches to process the vast majority of licence renewals on paper and face to face was a fairly expensive strategy for DVLA and its predecessors. The forms involved also made it difficult for customers to readily check if they had all the information, testing and insurance documentation and payment needed for renewing vehicle registrations. Nor was it easy for customers to ask Post Office staff questions because of long queues and shortages of time there. So DVLA was an early leader in developing contact centres where customers could phone up, overwhelmingly with enquiries. In the 1990s and early noughties the volumes of phone traffic and the numbers of call centres needed to handle them both grew considerably.

DVLA developed a basic website by 2002, initially using it as just a kind of online 'poster site' displaying the requirements for licensing, fees and other information. The Blair government requirement that all public services be electronically deliverable by 2008, later brought forward to 2005, was a strong stimulant for DVLA to try to get licence renewals online by the general government deadline. However, the agency initially interpreted the requirement as being met if they providing licence renewal forms online for customers to print off and fill in by hand, before taking them to a Post Office or DVLA local office for document checking. Only later on did better versions let customers fill in the forms online and print them, before taking them to the Post Office with their documents or mailing them in – so that they could sign the forms, still the key legal identity requirement.

However, the agency did later launch a much more ambitious and long-term effort to make the whole vehicle licensing process electronic, with people applying for licences online and the agency then checking online with garages that a valid MoT certificate was issued, and with insurance companies that vehicle insurance was in place. This entailed DVLA being able to recognize electronic identifiers, certificates and tokens from two very different kinds of organizations. Thousands of the UK garages conducting vehicle tests are small or medium-sized businesses, often with little formal organization. British private insurance companies, on the other hand, are mostly large or very large firms, with strong administrative capacities and operating in a basically oligopolistic market. Getting such a diverse range of actors to work together with government was a huge achievement, and the launch of the completely online vehicle registration process was very successful. In 2007 online registration was transferred from the DVLA website to the overall government 'super-site' Directgov. The transfer boosted the service, because its new web interface was simplified and improved – while the traffic generated also bucked up the fortunes of the super-site itself. Public recognition of the new service increased because customers could more quickly complete a previously complex transaction electronically, and without having to visit a Post Office in person.

The benefits of fully electronic transactions were substantial:

- DVLA no longer had to pay the Post Office a transactions fee for this business.
- The agency also did not have to handle millions of paper forms.

- Customers completing forms online had far more time to check that their responses to questions were correct. There were also no problems with handwriting and so on, hence error rates were less.
- The information from online applications dropped straight into the DVLA databases with no re-keying needed, speeding up the checking process.

However, the cost implications of the success in moving transactions online were limited by a range of factors. In 2010–11 nearly three-tenths (29 per cent) of driver registration was online, while for vehicles taxing the proportion reached two-fifths, up from only a quarter in 2007–08. However, there were indications that this proportion was tending to stick (DVLA, 2011, p. 3). It is much more expensive for government agencies to run two different systems in tandem, the paper forms and Post Office route versus the online route. Civil servants and contractors working in these areas have a rule of thumb that the largest cost savings only occur when the electronic route reaches 80 per cent or so of overall transaction volumes (as achieved, for instance, in HMRC's successful push for online income tax self-assessment). Yet this was difficult for DVLA to get to. It still lacked any agreed electronic identifier number that can be used across national government, so DVLA customers still had to register with the cumbersome Government Gateway before they could use the car tax/renewal facility. And not all forms of vehicles could be registered electronically. The result was that the agency achieved only a slightly stalled or halfway transition to electronic transactions.

The Development of Productivity Within DVLA Services

Again agency status is useful because a lot of relevant information is available for the analysis of productivity, but only for a shorter time than our normal study period, from 2002 to 2009. We show the evidence used to fix outputs and inputs in our usual format in Table 6.2. The agency's data on key output activities are finely granulated and so we cover six different main types of vehicle licensing and 11 kinds of driver licensing activities. In considering costs, the DVLA datasets unfortunately do not distinguish unit costs, nor tell us what proportion of total administrative costs can be assigned to different activities. This presents some difficulties in weighting outputs. However, DVLA activities are highly automated and hence the agency's finance and strategy team have adopted the practice of measuring the complexity of achieving outputs by the time taken to process a given transaction. There are three classifications – the output takes less than a minute to do; it takes one to three minutes; or it takes over three minutes.

Table 6.2   Data availability and methodology for the measurement of productivity in licence issuing

Variable	Evidence Used, and Adjustments Made
Outputs for vehicle and driver licensing	Total number of vehicles licensed per year, defined in terms of six activity streams: first registrations; changes of registration documentation; cherished transfer marks; duplicate registration documents issued; the number of police enquiries; and the number of customer enquiries
	Plus, total number of drivers licensed per year, defined in terms of 11 activity streams: renewals of driving licences; replacement driving licence issued; first applications processed; duplicate driver licences issued; exchange driver licences issued; vocational driving licences issued; medical renewals; Smart Tachos (for lorry drivers); ten-year renewals; the number of customer enquiries by drivers; and other driver transactions
Cost-weighting of outputs	Data provided by DVLA show outputs performed in under one minute; those lasting between one and three minutes; and those more than three minutes. We used this information as a proxy for costs. We weight adjusted transactions under one minute by 0.25; those taking one to three minutes by 0.35; and those over three minutes by 0.4 (thus a full transaction might involve four activities of less than one minute; or 2.5 activities lasting more than three minutes)
Inputs, for total factor productivity	Deflated staffing, outsourcing, procurement and capital costs published in DVLA annual reports
Inputs for staff productivity	Number of FTE staff in DVLA, obtained from annual reports

Note: The Atkinson Report (2005b) did not comment on DVLA activities.

This information is carefully measured, so weighting by time taken can serve as a reliable proxy for our more normal cost-weighting of outputs.

Turning to quality-weighting, the record of DVLA (and DVLC before it) was remarkably uniform, without any periods of administrative crises and without any marked changes in the apparent quality of the services provided. The introduction of the photocard driving licence was a substantial technical task for the agency, but it lagged years behind similar agencies in other countries shifting to this form of licence. It proved popular with

Figure 6.6   Total factor productivity in DVLA

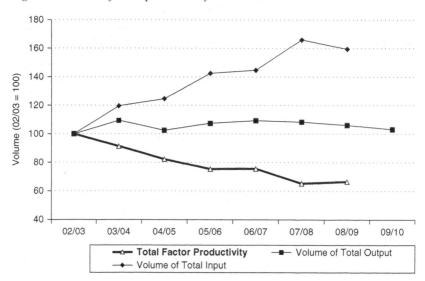

customers, but since it is now compulsorily consumed we can see no basis to treat it as a quality enhancement. The inauguration of online vehicle re-licensing was a genuine boost to quality for those customers using it, yet it seems entirely analogous to other e-commerce changes occurring across the economy at around the same time because of technological change. Clearly DVLA's estimates of vehicle tax evasion fell radically, which might imply a quality increase, but this was mainly due to stronger and more demanding regulatory powers given by Labour ministers in the mid-noughties. Claims that the quality of DVLA databases has improved could be a stronger basis for some re-weighting. But there is no quantitative evidence to back up this suggestion. And with increased computerization and more automatic enforcement by police there are several possible sources of improvements.

Turning to input costs, as with passports, for the total factor productivity analysis DVLA's agency status means that excellent information is provided in annual reports on staffing costs, the costs of outsourcing (mainly to the agency's main IT supplier, IBM) and capital costs. All costs were deflated to 2002 price levels. Finally, for the labour productivity analysis we obtained data on DVLA's staffing levels in terms of FTEs over our study period. Overall, we believe that these input data are of good quality.

Figure 6.6 shows our estimate of total factor productivity in DVLA over the recent decade. Despite the long-term growth of vehicle numbers (shown in Figure 6.4), from 2002 onwards our measure of total outputs in fact rose by slightly less than a tenth in the early years. It then bobbed

Figure 6.7   Staff productivity in DVLA

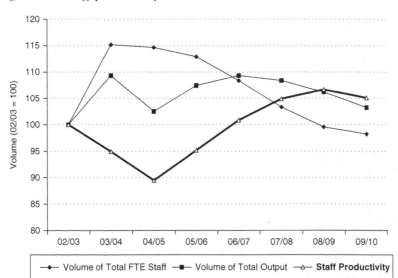

along at this level, eventually settling back at the original starting point in 2009–10 as the economic recession bit. Meanwhile total factor inputs rose much more strongly, by 60 per cent from 1999 to 2007. They ceased to grow as the Gershon Review savings on back-office costs began to have an effect (see also Chapter 4) in DVLA in 2008. Across the period, the combined effects of these two trends, however, was that total factor productivity in fact declined by nearly a fifth between 2002 and 2005, and then by a further tenth in 2007. Thus in 2009 productivity stood at less than two-thirds of DVLA's initial level eight years earlier.

Turning to staff productivity the total outputs curve is the same as before (although rescaled here). Figure 6.7 shows that in-house labour inputs climbed by 15 per cent in 2003, a steep increase. They then declined thereafter, and most steeply in the 2005–08 period. This also coincided with a crackdown on staff absences triggered by the critical NAO (2007b) report, perhaps suggesting that a general tightening up of internal agency management occurred here. As a result, staff productivity reached its lowest point in 2004 and then rebounded strongly to 2008, levelling off with the fall in outputs then. So there is a clear divergence in the evolution of the total costs of the agency and the number of FTE staff in DVLA. The stagnation in Figure 6.6 above apparently reflects the increasing costs of the agency's ICT function (run by IBM), plus other non-staff cost increases in the later part of the noughties.

Conclusions on Driver and Vehicle Licensing

Perhaps one of the key lessons of the DVLA case is that achieving productivity gains over time is not as straightforward as it may look. The
Baumol effect for relative prices in public services to rise over time is
not easy to counter or avoid. In our study period the agency was concerned to make step changes in the inclusiveness and accuracy of its
databases for both drivers and vehicles – to enhance their usefulness for
wider governmental purposes, including policing and anti-terrorism or
homeland security. In this last respect, completeness and accuracy are
especially important, since the intelligence task is appropriately thought
of as searching for a needle in a haystack. Some changes were introduced
in both areas, including the transition to a partly photocard licence for
drivers and the radical tightening up of the laws on continuously registering vehicles, transferring ownership and so on. Unfortunately, we do not
have information available on database quality that would allow us to
make appropriate quality adjustments over time, even assuming there was
a case for doing so.

In addition, the agency's lack of unit costs data means that we have
had to rely on weighting outputs only by the time taken to complete
them, which subdivides activities into only three time segments (less than
a minute, one to three minutes and over three minutes). So we probably
have less refined cost-weighting information here than in our other cases
examined so far. All of these costs- and quality-weighting issues mean that
we need to treat the current evidence of DVLA's falling productivity with
some caution.

However, there also seem to be some important substantive reasons
why the DVLA's productivity record shows a decline. Although the
organization has been an executive agency for a long time, there are
indications that it was not very tightly managed at periods. Its remote
location in Swansea restricts its labour pool, and the 2007 scandal over
sickness absence rates amongst staff (subsequently completely cured) suggests that internal management was poor up to then. It was only in the
Gershon period that staff numbers fell. These gains were more than offset
by cost increases in total factor inputs elsewhere. The organization also
has had high IT costs due to a very long-standing and apparently 'cosy'
relationship with one very large IT company. ICT costs rose very appreciably, and doubled in a new deal with IBM announced in 2009 (*Guardian
Professional*, 2009).

Finally, the agency has achieved an impressive transition to online
transactions for vehicle registration, but in a complex area where the share
of customers moving to electronic processes got stuck more or less in the

middle. While DVLA has shut down almost all of its original 81 local offices doing face-to-face transactions, the paper application and Post Office routes continue to predominate in how customers interact with the agency. This may be because of the poor Government Gateway interface, or because of customers' conservatism over the documentation requirements for vehicle registration, or because customers often still need to interact with a person in order to understand the agency's complex forms and requirements. A 2011 Cabinet Office resolve to promote 'digital by default' services may enable DVLA to restart the stalled progress towards electronic contacts becoming the norm (around 80 per cent of the total), and thus allow it to cut its cost base elsewhere. But in the past the agency has shown an inability to develop apparently straightforward innovations. For instance, it has no integrated household account to pool together its dealings with citizens at one address. It has not implemented direct debit forms of payment for vehicle excise duty especially. And more recently it has yet to develop apps to make licensing and re-licensing much simpler. These all suggest that at present (2011) DVLA still has a long way to go in its ICT and transactions modernization efforts.

Conclusions

Government regulatory agencies create their own demand, and coerce consumers into purchasing their products, putting them in an unusual position compared with firms. Yet they also mostly cover their administrative expenses through fees, putting them in a different position from tax-funded government departments and agencies. The different stories set out here reflect how regulatory agencies can resolve the tensions of their roles. In passports a signal disaster in core administration triggered a costly but successful effort to prevent recurrences, with administrative costs and (episodic) fees rising sharply. The agency additionally had to adapt to changing external demands for more 'homeland security' from politicians and external countries. In transport licensing the agency upgraded both its key licence 'product' and the quality of its databases, but was much more politically constrained in its ability to increase its revenue-raising and highly visible annual fees. Neither agency succeeded in increasing productivity, partly because the outsourcing of IT operations proved expensive, and partly because the inherent complexity of their forms and incomplete movement online kept internal costs high, as baffled customers rang up in huge numbers (and millions also paid Post Office staff for extra advice and checks).

NOTE

1. Throughout the early and mid-twentieth century it was called the Ministry of Transport, hence the famous 'MoT test' of the roadworthiness of Britain's older cars – a label that endures to this day. In 1970 Transport was absorbed into a merged 'super-ministry', the Department of the Environment, which lasted until 1976, before a Department of Transport split off again for a few years. In 1997 Prime Minister Tony Blair rolled up the transport function again into a wider ministry, called the Department of the Environment, Transport and Regions (DETR). His chief purpose was to provide a larger ministerial powerbase for John Prescott, the PM's key Labour Party ally against Gordon Brown. Yet DETR was as always too big and unwieldy to be successful, and Prescott proved ham-fisted as a minister. In 2001 Transport again once again became a cabinet department on its own.

PART II

Analysing decentralized government services

7. Methods and quality issues in analysing complex and localized services

Most public services are locally delivered, because they fundamentally require personal contact with customers or clients, or need to be provided in places that are spatially accessible by customers. Teachers normally have to be in the same room with a class of children in order to promote education. Health professionals currently cannot do much still to diagnose or treat patients in their absence. And police forces inherently have to deliver the protection of persons and property in the same spaces where people are living and working. Of course the development of second wave of 'digital era governance' is still extending very rapidly the boundaries of what public services are electronically (a-spatially) deliverable (Dunleavy and Margetts, 2010; Margetts and Dunleavy, 2012). Many public services that are currently locally provided may be de-spatialized in future, as has begun to happen with public libraries, given the growth of online information and e-books. But for the moment this is an exceptional case, and local provision still dominates the delivery of public services.

In Western countries the conventional organization of public services is to divide the whole territory of the state into discrete areas, each of which has a local monopoly provider for each service. This pattern always includes municipal councils covering most public services, but it may also involve two tiers of local councils, or higher sub-regional bodies for more specialized or high-cost services. There are often also separate boards or bodies covering hospitals and healthcare on the one hand, and police services on the other – the pattern followed in the UK. In the USA, school boards are also separate, and there are in total 86 000 local bodies, some very local indeed. In federal countries these local providers are brigaded under states or provinces, which originate much of the financial transfers involved, while in more unitary countries (like Japan or England) budgets flows directly from the national-level departments.

In any reasonably large nation, there are usually numerous local providers, most of them doing very similar things to each other under similar laws and budget provisions – thus apparently opening the way for effective comparisons of productivity rates across providers. With large N datasets, and with locally organized social and administrative data also being extensively available, it should be eminently feasible to undertake multivariate analyses that unpick the role of different causal influences on providers' productivity. So we should expect to see a very large and insightful literature on comparative productivity analyses across organizations and providers, plus the causal factors that influence them. Yet in fact, such a literature still exists only in small pieces. The number of insightful comparative studies has grown recently, but it is not large. Exploring the reasons for this situation structures the main sections of this chapter. The three key factors limiting the insights from existing comparisons have been as follows:

- The importance of quality variations across providers at the local level, given the key characteristics of complex, face-to-face public services, and some of the difficulties of tracking quality levels.
- The different ways in which quality-adjusted outputs are incorporated in parametric and non-parametric analyses.
- The problem that most previous studies have used very restricted sets of independent or explanatory variables. In particular the literature commonly does not cover key variables that bear directly on productivity levels, such as the quality of service management or an organization's level of use of modern ICTs.

7.1 DECENTRALIZED SERVICES AND QUALITY ADJUSTMENTS

Taking account of quality variation pulls productivity analysis towards looking at the *effectiveness* of government services, which is inherently much more difficult to measure. For this reason we argued in Chapter 1 that at central government level it was better to rely on comprehensively measuring agency outputs in all their key dimensions, so as to perfect output weights wherever feasible, rather than to feel impelled towards also bringing in quality weights. While we can get a high level of agreement on how to count basic outcome levels – like the numbers of patients admitted and treated in a hospital, how many children were taught in schools, or the numbers of crimes and arrests in a police area – it is far harder to get agreement on how many of these activities or treatments were effective, or which best indicate the quality of service provided. Ideally we need all stakeholders to agree on what output levels are, which becomes trickier if quality variations are factored in.

In practice, official standards are already extensively defined in health-care, education or policing, and these often have the effect of 'focusing' public discussions. While stakeholders often disagree about what is important, they are usually ready to accept officially set standards or bench-marks (despite their limitations), and then to focus mainly on comparisons over time (are we getting better or worse?) and across areas (are we doing as well as local areas that are 'need neighbours'?). Statistics useful for assessing overall quality standards are commonly collected, but often only for indicators bearing on particularly crucial activities at the core of that organization's 'mission'. For instance, fire or ambulance services often collect data on the time taken to respond to reach a fire, car accident or medical emergency – even though these urgent responses may comprise only a part of overall service activity. Pass rates in school public exams at standard grades can be compared across schools or school boards, but without controlling for the (probably dominant) influence of non-school institutions (like families, parental support and community values) on children's performance, raw success rates may not say much about the quality of school provision itself. Similarly 'deaths in hospital' rates can be compared, but it is much harder to assess the overall quality of medical care.

However, developments in public management, especially in the later 'new public management' (NPM) era, have tended to ease some of the problems of assessing local public services' quality. The growth of micro-local agencies (such as singly managed schools or hospitals) in quasi-market systems within the public sector has been premised on more comprehensive and regular official surveillance across providers. There are many more published objective indicators (pass rates in schools or morbidity rates in hospitals) useful for citizens in choosing between providers. Periodic standardized audits or evaluations by regulators also focus more directly on local service quality, sometimes producing mainly qualitative reports, but often also some form of summary or 'star' rating. In many ways a prerequisite for more effective quasi-markets is the impartial monitoring and re-regulation of services providers, which enhances comparisons.

Finally, public administration processes often result in the collation (but mostly not the publication) of statistics on 'citizen redress' that have a lot of bearing on quality provision (Dunleavy et al., 2005, 2010a). For instance, there are complaints against municipalities or other local agencies; upwards appeals or complaints from decisions to administrative courts, tribunals, ombudsmen or other appeal bodies; and legal cases and compensation payouts. Depending on your point of view these cases may be just 'the tip of the iceberg' of poor services (as people in the 'redress industry' tend to believe), or may reflect mainly serial complainers and litigants (as rank and file public officials often believe). Certainly these numbers incorporate some level of 'noise', but variations in citizen redress activity across similar organizations still do give useful indicators of the incidence of poor or unsatisfactory services being provided. We show in Chapter 8 that along with objective indicators they can be applied to try and quality weight service outputs, in this case relating to hospital treatments.

Service quality indicators are particularly indispensable in personalized services, those organized by professional staffs in decentralized delivery chains, especially if they involve elements of 'compulsory consumption' – as with health and social care, statutory education, environmental regulation, policing, social work and law and order services. In general, quality adjustments of outputs and productivity data will always be needed the more complex the service being provided (as in healthcare or policing); and the greater the variations in quality across agencies, localities or time periods being compared.

In three additional circumstances, trying to do without service quality data risks having especially perverse effects on the measurement of outcomes:

1. In many services, unmeasured (perhaps intangible) quality changes may trigger apparent falls in productivity. For instance, if doctors spend more time talking with each patient they see, there is a case for saying here that the quality of service provided improves – yet apparent productivity (if measured in a crude outputs/inputs measure) falls. At the least, the positive quality change means this decline is overstated. At the other extreme, unmeasured quality shading may allow apparent increases in productivity to be recorded, numbers that actually mask a worsening picture. For instance, the compulsory contracting out of hospital cleaning in the UK from the late 1980s onwards inaugurated a 'race to the bottom' in quality standards between cost-cutting contractors. By the mid-noughties this change was being blamed for part of a sharp growth in hospital-acquired infections (HIAs) in the NHS (NAO, 2004, 2009a). As part of the drive to reduce HIAs many hospitals took the cleaning function back in-house, or radically revised their contract specifications to stress quality instead of lowest costs, leading to the removal of more marginal or less reputable firms. Many other implementation changes were also made, and by 2011 the main infection rate (for an infection called MRSA) fell sharply (BBC News, 2011).

2. In many local services, exactly how and when a service is delivered, matters a great deal to what kind of output is being received. Going

into hospital for an acute procedure, but then also getting an infection that greatly extends and complicates your care is a good example of how seriously the nature of a complex service can be changed by poor implementation. In a related way, take the case of a patient who must queue on a waiting list for weeks or months before receiving treatment, during which time their medical condition can worsen dramatically, requiring much more difficult or serious interventions. Equally, getting a police response only long after a crime has finished being committed is a very different service from getting a response that is timely or more effective. *How* or *when* a service is delivered can fundamentally change the nature of *what* is being provided. Comparing across local providers where only outputs numbers are available, without employing useful quality-adjusted data, introduces inaccuracy and unfairness when comparing units with different quality profiles.

3. The strongest perverse effects introduced by a lack of quality information occur when providing a poor service actually directly *increases* apparent output levels, by boosting the demand for a service. For instance, police force X that is poor at detecting, arresting and trying criminals will let far more of them re-offend, and thus have higher crime rates and more emergency call-outs to crime scenes than another force Y, which does more effective preventative and detective work, nips criminal careers in the bud, or uses intelligence to forestall crimes being committed in the first place. Force X here will have the greater numbers of arrests and yet worse crime levels, while Y will have less activity being documented, although its crime level is also less. Similarly we noted in Chapter 2 that a hospital A delivering poorer quality care than a comparator B may have to readmit a lot of patients and redo the treatment, thereby boosting its apparent volume of outputs, whereas hospital B has a longer average hospital stay per patient and far fewer readmissions, so that its volume numbers take a double hit. In these and many other situations then a simple outputs/inputs measure could precisely misidentify the more effective providers.

These problems have been partly addressed in public policy systems that put a lot of emphasis upon targets and key performance indicators (KPIs), such as those in the UK under the Blair and Brown Labour governments (1997–2011). There are obvious incentives for top policy-makers to want to control 'games playing' around targets by local service administrators (Hood, 2006). For instance, on point (3) above the Department of Health introduced a new requirement for local hospital trusts to report hospital readmissions occurring within six weeks of an initial treatment or operation.

However, some commentators argue that any target-led or KPI-led system of controls *inherently* creates its own distortions in the behaviour of local providers who have to report defined performance. For instance, in the NHS, Hood and Bevan (no date) argue that there are always three different areas of performance: area (i) that is well covered by metrics, and where false positive or negative results do not occur; an intermediate area (ii) where metrics are only partially and inconsistently available, and where false-positive or false-negative readings of service quality abound; and an (always larger) area (iii) where no data is available. In this view, any performance indicator or target system for top-level policy control will necessarily fail because performance in area (i) will not look like (be synchronous with) performance in area (iii). In addition, false positives and negatives will mean that there are no error-free ways of understanding even performance in area (ii), let alone extrapolating to area (iii).

These counsels of caution can easily transfer over into counsels of despair, however. Hood and Bevan consider policy systems in the NHS that were extremely crude and elementary, and which were operated in a rather insensitive, 'command and control' way. Most KPI systems have shown increasing sophistication over time. An alternative 'intelligent centre/devolved delivery' model is conceivable – one where central administrators focus on acquiring a lot of high-quality information covering multiple output and output-quality indicators automatically. For instance, they might use the kind of digital reporting systems commonly used all over large-scale private service companies, like major retailers Tesco and Walmart. Local public service providers in such a system can be assigned more freedom to vary their service strategies and outputs mix, so long as their overall service quality and output levels are maintained within acceptable bounds. Top decision-makers here would have influence with local managers, but not exercise command and control over them on operational matters.

Whatever the balance of these arguments for policy-makers, in studying productivity researchers are usually looking at much more aggregated performance across local agencies. By ensuring that indicators of *all* an organization's main output categories are included in the cost-weighted overall output measure, many of the problems of biases towards 'core' services in indicators can be controlled. For instance, in a fire service it should be feasible to get at least some metrics of non-emergency or fire-prevention work, and in hospitals to control for case-mix effects. Researchers can also usually use administrative statistics on quality levels as part of a wider strategy for quality-weighting outputs. General 'quality of performance' weights can also help; for instance, looking at local public satisfaction with hospital, police or fire services. There may be problems here with local loyalism (citizens not wanting to run down their area); or alternatively low expectations problems (citizens inured to low-quality services not criticizing what they see as expected or inevitable). But it should not be out of the question to assemble baskets of measures that give a reasonable view of service quality variations across local providers.

7.2   INCORPORATING QUALITY MEASURES INTO PARAMETRIC AND DEA ANALYSES

With large numbers of comparable public service providers to analyse, it becomes feasible to deploy the two methods discussed in Chapter 1 but not realistically implementable at national government level – namely, parametric approaches using conventional regression techniques; and non-parametric approaches, where we focus on data envelopment analysis (DEA). We look more closely here at how quality-weighting of outputs can be incorporated in both approaches.

Parametric Approaches

Looking across a reasonably large set of local providers, this approach proceeds by seeking to estimate the influence of different explanatory variables (taken one by one) on productivity levels, treating each variable as a parameter for the influence of all other variables. Most commonly implemented via regression analysis, we can briefly give an intuitive and non-technical explanation of a parametric approach. Figure 7.1a shows the observed levels of police productivity (defined as the number of full-time equivalent [FTE] police per 1000 crimes in an area) plotted against a first explanatory variable, chosen here to be the percentage level of local unemployment. (The idea here is that as unemployment increases, so the seriousness of local crimes may increase, necessitating more police people per 1000 crimes.) A 'least squares' regression line is defined, one that minimizes the vertical differences between observed productivity levels for each agency, and the level that would be predicted for that agency given its placing along the horizontal axis showing the values for the local unemployment parameter (or variable). These vertical differences are called first-order deviations and the smaller the sum of deviations the more closely the points fit around the regression line, and more of the variance in productivity can be statistically explained by the X axis variable. Where the fit remains relatively poor (as is the case in Figure 7.1a), the next stage

Figure 7.1a–c   An intuitive view of ordinary least squares regression analyses of productivity variations across local providers

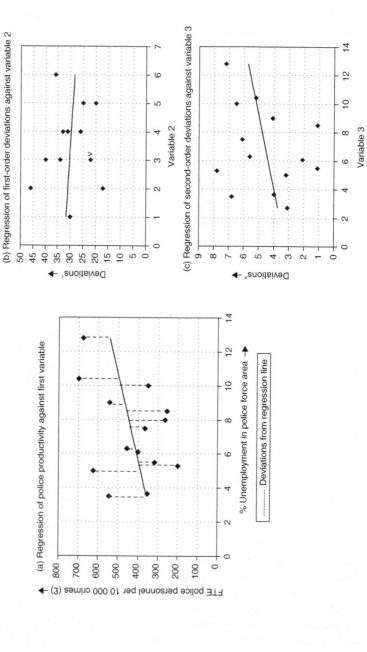

(a) Regression of police productivity against first variable

(b) Regression of first-order deviations against variable 2

(c) Regression of second-order deviations against variable 3

is to redo the analysis, this time matching the first-order deviations in Figure 7.1a against the values for a second parameter B, a step shown in an illustrative way in Figure 7.1b. Again we define a second regression line, measure the second-order deviations from that line and match these deviations in turn against scores for a third explanatory variable, as in Figure 7.1c. At each stage of this process the variance of the points for each local agency will broadly tend to reduce, and it will usually become harder and harder to find additional explanatory variables that make a difference.

In regression approaches, an important influence on the results can often be exerted by the ways in which explanatory variables are defined, how effectively data has been collected and by the order in which different variables enter the equation. Analysts can rely on statistical programmes to enter variables in an automatic way, in a sequence determined by their closeness of fit with the dependent variable (either the original productivity scores or the remaining, still-unexplained deviations calculated at each stage of the analysis). Alternatively, the analyst may define an order in which variables are to be entered, chosen on theoretical grounds to be a logically compelling sequence. Variables are then input in a fixed order, but the statistical package still determines whether any apparent influences found are statistically significant (that is, unlikely to have arisen simply by chance or sample fluctuations). It is common to finish up with quite a large number of alternative final models composed only of significant variables. Models can then be compared in terms of the overall proportion of the variance in the dependent variable that each model explains (the R^2 statistic). So long as the models basically agree in identifying the most theoretically and empirically important variables, we should normally choose the model with the highest R^2 statistic as the best. However, if models with different sets of explanatory variables emerge as almost equally significant, and particularly if the influence assigned to different variables seems to fluctuate from one model to another, then choosing between models becomes more complex.

How does quality adjustment influence the outcome of regression analyses? Essentially each local agency is still situated at the same point on the horizontal scales for the explanatory variables in Figure 7.1. But now the impact of the quality adjustment is to raise or lower the point where each local agency is located on the vertical axis productivity measure, as shown in Figure 7.2. Normally we should expect to see that quality adjustment alters the productivity levels at which scores sit, and incrementally reshapes the new distributions of local providers, without altering them radically, as shown in Figure 7.2a. However, the more that cost- and quality-adjusted productivity or output scores differ from the scores for

Figure 7.2a and b   Hypothetical impacts of quality adjustments on data patterns

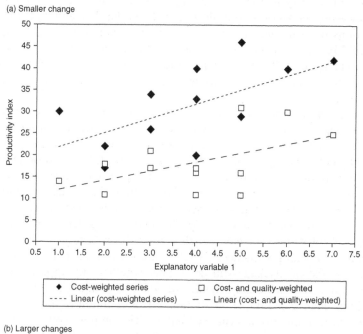

(a) Smaller change

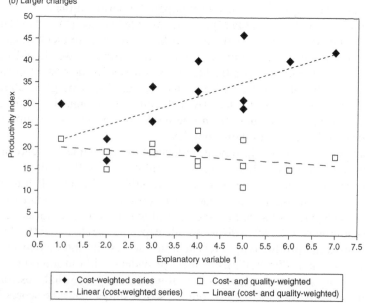

(b) Larger changes

cost-weighted outputs alone, the more likely it is that the cost- and quality-adjusted plot will have a different shape, including changing the signs of one or more of the explanatory variables from positive to negative or vice versa. Figure 7.2b shows a hypothetical illustrative example of one way this might happen.

To explore more about how parametric approaches work, readers should turn to Chapter 8, which sets out in detail a multivariate regression analysis of how productivity varies across English hospital trusts. The final things to note about this strand of work is that it makes some important assumptions, including (most fundamentally) that the same basic processes operate across the dataset as a whole, and that a 'tournament' of competing regression models is the best way to surface what these processes are. The more inclusive a study's variable set is by including all the factors theoretically linked to shaping productivity levels, the greater the confidence we can have that the analysis is not subject to missing variable bias. Getting stable and consistent scores for the influence of the same parameter on productivity levels across the different regression models tested is also reassuring.

There are a number of considerable advantages to parametric studies. First, they explicitly allow for unknown variables, and for the distribution of productivity levels to be influenced by random shocks – what matters is the location of regression lines and not particularly the locations of individual data points. Second, from regression analyses it is possible to compute 'elasticities', that is, an estimate of the extent to which a change in an explanatory variable can be expected to influence local productivity levels. Knowledge of elasticities is helpful for policy-makers in suggesting where to put resources or effort in trying to boost local productivity levels.

As usual, parametric approaches also have their limits on how far comparative studies can go in understanding which influences within local agencies or local social environments shape strong or weak productivity levels. First, *assembling large N datasets* is crucial. In general, the larger the number of agency data points included (the bigger the N), the more likely it becomes that there will be enough available information (enough degrees of freedom) to sustain an analysis of multiple variables. Now since the number of local providers per country is in fact fixed, this may seem a factor outside the analyst's control – as it certainly is for a single cross-section analysis, a snapshot at one point in time, such as our account in Chapter 8.

However, where it is possible to assemble good-quality data on local agencies' outputs, inputs and productivity scores across a run of years, along with data on explanatory variables for the same time period, then analysts can 'pool' the data for multiple years and use more sophisticated techniques (such as pooled regression analysis) to unpick the influences discovered. This approach can also check that the pattern of apparent causal influences on productivity remains stable over time, which it may well not do. It can also provide a direct analysis of the parameters most associated with improvements or declines in productivity over time. In practice, there have been fewer but quite important studies that use over-time panel data. In the private sector, Caroli and Van Reenen (2001) and Bloom et al. (2005) have used panel data to estimate the determinants of productivity across firms in different countries. In the public sector, Garicano and Heaton (2010) have used panel data for a set of police departments from 1987 to 2003 to estimate the determinants of productivity, which we discuss later in this chapter. We can expect that as data records and collection improves, it will be possible for scholars to do more comparative productivity studies using panel data.

Second, where *variations in service delivery are compressed* across local providers, this can inhibit the usefulness of regression approaches. The observed variance in local agencies' productivity levels may be extensively constrained by national governments (or state governments in federations) imposing standard laws, regulations and budgetary allocations onto local agencies. In addition, nationalized systems of professional controls may additionally restrict allowable 'good practice' (Dunleavy, 1982). Especially in centralized nations (like the UK and some other European and 'Westminster system' countries), these 'straitjacket' influences may constrain provider agencies into delivering standard services in standard ways, thus inhibiting the scope for local innovations, service variations, or the use of different technologies or business process models. Hence, the range of the dependent variable may be less than we would expect amongst (say) firms in competitive markets. However, in some previously centralized countries (such as the UK), some commentators have seen the creation of micro-local agencies (MLAs, such as individually managed or 'foundation trust' hospitals and local managed schools) as a countervailing tendency, arguing that MLAs have more scope to innovate and deliver services in less preordained, standard ways.

Third, the *widespread contracting out* of public services has produced in many countries (especially the UK) the development of large, oligopolistic firms that deliver the same services in many districts. Whether it is maintaining traffic lights, cooking school meals, collecting refuse, or providing hospital ancillary services, these companies use the same standard operating procedures nationwide. So the *apparent* diversity of local purchasers may actually be somewhat illusory in terms of the real number of providing organizations at work. A wide range of municipalities or hospital boards are signing contracts with an underlying and much smaller number of main corporate contractors, who implement services production. Comparing across localities in such a situation may say something about the choices made by the decision-makers within the provider bodies (the councils or hospital boards), and especially illuminate their commissioning or contract-negotiating skills, or perhaps just the dates when the contracts were signed. But the real organizational units undertaking actual production (and hence in an operational position to be able to improve productivity directly) are the smaller number of major firms in operational control of services. There are analytic approaches that might address such situations (such as hierarchical regression models), but so far they have not been applied in this area. The contractual data needed on who is actually delivering implementation where have also not generally been available.

Data Envelopment Analysis

One of the fundamental assumptions of parametric approaches is that there exists a production function that conforms to a particular probability distribution, which can be more successfully approximated by improving the available data, exploring more potentially important explanatory variables, and so on. By contrast, there are a set of analytic approaches that do not assume a given probability distribution. We focus here on one particular non-parametric approach, data envelopment analysis (hereafter DEA), which originated in operational research in the late 1970s, and was explicitly intended to help illuminate the assessment of performance of 'decision-making units' (DMUs) in non-market contexts (Charnes et al., 1978; Cooper et al., 2011). In particular, DEA seeks to cope with situations where production functions are not known, and to undertake comparisons based much more clearly on the best known data about what is possible for DMUs to achieve. We have already introduced (in Chapter 2) a simple (single-output) example of how DEA does this. It may be helpful to consider here a slightly more complex (two-dimensional) illustration of how the approach works.

Suppose that we have data for how a set of local fire services perform on two different kinds of outputs – the number of call-outs to fires or accidents that they have attended in a year, an indicator of their emergency services load; and the number of fire-prevention activities they have undertaken, such as inspecting premises for fire safety issues, or advising businesses and households on fitting fire alarms and taking other prevention measures. We also have data for the total costs of each fire service (or for the number of FTE personnel each employs, if we are examining only labour productivity). Even if we do not have accurate cost weights for outputs data, the DEA approach can be useful here in locating services

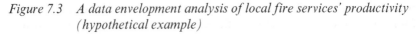

Figure 7.3   A data envelopment analysis of local fire services' productivity (hypothetical example)

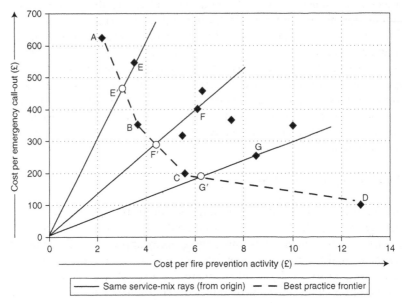

against each other, and in estimating how far performance might be improved – either by saving costs and personnel, or by expanding the demand for services (essentially applicable only for preventative work in the case of fire services). We compute separate ratios for each local agency of the costs per fire prevention activity, shown as the horizontal dimension in Figure 7.3, and for the costs per emergency call-out, shown on the vertical axis. We then graph the combined performances for a set of agencies on both dimensions. (To keep the diagram clear we show only a few data points, but a real analysis might have between 100 and 500 data points.)

The DEA approach argues that because the service mix between prevention and emergency responses varies widely, the best way to assess the relative efficiency of agencies is to compare their performance along same service-mix lines (shown as rays out from the origin). The best-performing agencies are those that in terms of their particular ray are as close to the origin (i.e., have the lowest combined costs of provision) as possible. A 'best practice' frontier is defined by joining up all those agencies closest to the origin as shown, with the requirement that the frontier must 'envelope' all other agencies' data points – in this case it is defined by four agencies, A, B, C and D. All the remaining agencies are higher cost and less productive. To see how much they are adrift from best practice, and what they could achieve if they could match best practice organizations, we look along the service-mix ray running through them, and extrapolate to where that particular ray cuts the best practice frontier. For instance, for agency E that point is E', and for agencies F and G it is F' and G' respectively.

The strength of DEA is that it draws on the available data to determine what is feasible. It does not try to identify the production possibility frontier (as parametric approaches do). The comparisons that DEA draws derive from known data about decision-making units, and its data demands are much more modest than for parametric studies. The approach can be extended to more than two dimensions of performance using linear programming statistical techniques to compare across multiple output/input ratios. These more complex models cannot be conveyed visually, but they are achievable using relatively simple software packages.

Critics of DEA argue that the approach is very vulnerable to the correct identification of the DMUs that are on the frontier. If the data for these particular agencies are not accurate, or if the frontier cases are very distinctive or unusual DMUs that are systematically unlike the main mass of agencies, then basing the whole frontier analysis on comparisons with them will not produce useful insights.

Crudely done DEA studies might even misinform policy-makers about what improvements are feasible. For instance, a study of Australian hospitals in the state of Victoria found that small, rural hospitals (using local generalist family doctors as part-time medical staff) were much cheaper than hospitals with a full-time staff of specialist doctors in towns and major cities. But that did not mean in any way that the bigger hospitals could or should try to match the lowest cost-base units, since their mission and case mixes were completely different (Steering Committee for the Review of Commonwealth/State Service Provision, 1997, pp. 51–67).

Yet DEA techniques have also been extended in recent years so that multivariate analyses can be conducted. In principle, different best-practice frontiers can be defined for different classes of agencies. Similarly the scope for feasible improvements does not necessarily have to be defined against the best-practice frontier for all agencies (which may often reflect special factors unique to different areas or organizations). Instead, just as with regression analyses, policy-makers can consider much more feasible kinds of comparative insight. For example, government executives, ministers or audit bodies can estimate how much input costs might be saved if DMUs in the lowest-performing three quartiles could improve their performance to match those agencies whose performance defines the 75 per cent frontier (where the second quartile starts). Alternatively it is possible to estimate how much output levels or services quality might be improved with the same change.

DEA approaches have become increasingly sophisticated in recent years. In fact, they have been extensively applied in private sector contexts for improving efficiency and productivity. Some useful applications to measuring local agencies' productivity have also been undertaken. The low data requirements for this approach mean that it can be deployed effectively even in circumstances where estimating cost-weighted outputs is difficult because the same staff or inputs are used to produce multiple activities or output streams.

The DEA techniques are especially helpful in conditions where the quality aspects of service provision are recognized as important, but where quality measures are partial or may not even be very tangible (as with services) – as in healthcare (Solà and Prior, 2001; Clement et al., 2008). This approach can help when it is not feasible to estimate the costs of providing better-quality services (or the savings that might be made from reducing service quality), given available information. Combining available quality indicators with data on multiple different outputs is a feasible application of DEA packages.

7.3   CAPTURING INDEPENDENT VARIABLES THAT ACTUALLY SHAPE PRODUCTIVITY

One of the most disappointing aspects of the literature on local service providers' productivity is that only a very restricted range of explanatory variables is considered, especially in analyses undertaken by economists and operational researchers. A large number of economic studies have focused on issues around economies of scale and scope, trying to produce definitive answers on what is the 'optimum' size of hospital or police force for maximizing outputs/inputs productivity (or less commonly for achieving maximum effectiveness in service delivery). Theoretically issues here have absorbed quantitative analysts. And if the cumulated studies could lead to especially clear or agreed conclusions then they might have high relevance for policy-makers – especially when governments periodically consider how to reorganize hospital care, or how to restructure the area structure of police forces.

However, the overwhelming conclusions of most studies in this vein has been that reliable evidence of scale economies peters out fairly quickly in the transition from small to medium-size facilities or local authorities. In most public services, scale economies are not readily apparent in the transition from medium-size to large facilities or municipalities – because big hospitals, big police forces and big city local authorities often confront higher-intensity problems, which are inherently more expensive to handle. In addition, most decision-makers facing operational choices are working with a fairly given set of facilities and production processes, and they are not remaking long-run service architectures. So their practical ability to change the existing scale and scope of services being provided is often small.

In the private sector the analysis of economies of scope has focused on how firms and organizations acquire additional capabilities from handling many different but related activities. For instance, with flexible manufacturing systems, modern firms have adapted their machinery, staff training and production processes so as to produce relatively short runs of many different products. Within the government sector there has not been any equivalent progress on economies of scope. Before the 1980s, in countries with highly modernized local governments and health authorities (like the UK), the issue of scale enlargement was chiefly discussed in terms of achieving a scale that would allow specialist facilities to be run by a single council or provider. But since then there has been a lot of progress in collaborative contracting and in constructing variably sized *coalitions* of public authorities to run expensive or specialist facilities. There are also now much better ICT and organizational networking arrangements for decentralized agencies involved in partnerships. Accordingly, groups of small or medium-sized local authorities or health bodies can often collaborate efficiently to provide specialist facilities that are collectively used and funded. The development of micro-local agencies in countries with previously centralized local authority provision (such as the UK and Sweden) has also undermined many previous claims for economies of scope, which proved not to be evidence-based.

In healthcare most comparisons have not been focused on overall productivity in hospitals or district heathcare providers, but on much more specific dependent variables, such as morbidity in hospitals for different kinds of treatments or operations. A large number of studies in a clinical audit vein have focused on just one kind of treatment, where the dependent variable is very consistently defined across hospitals. In the UK there have been some comparisons also of how hospitals or district health bodies have performed in terms of meeting specific or high-priority targets set by the central government (Cooper et al., 2010). But at any one time many things might be going right or going wrong in hospitals, only some of which relate specifically or solely to performance on a particular area of treatment. In any normal hospital, some medical teams will be performing well, while others are marking time, and still others are in a period of some decline in their activities or competences. So the performance of individual teams, in combating particular diseases or carrying out particular treatments will often look very different from an analysis of overall hospital productivity.

In particular, more segmented analyses do not usually capture well the importance of 'whole organization' elements arising from the general management of hospitals. For instance, a medical team that is performing well in terms of achieving high success rates with operations of type X at low cost may still be severely constrained in output or productivity terms if their hospital confronts a budgetary crisis that requires all units to cut back or to limit the scale of their operations. Similarly, where general patient care in a hospital is poorly managed in terms of prevention of infections, then large-scale outbreaks of hospital-acquired infections occur – as in the UK at the Maidstone and Tonbridge Wells Hospital Trust from April 2004 to September 2006 (Healthcare Commission, 2007). Here the otherwise good performance of many different medical teams across different wards may well take a general hit, because their patients become infected and have to stay in hospital longer with complications.

Perhaps surprisingly, there are only a smallish number of local productivity analyses that address issues of hospital-wide performance, and allow for administrative factors to shape performance. In particular, very few studies include variables covering overall organization factors bearing directly on productivity, such as the use of IT, or the quality of management and extent of modern management practices (but see West et al., 2006; Borzekowski, 2009). Far fewer studies cover such aspects because it is hard for analysts to specify and acquire data on these kinds of explanatory variables. In assessing management factors in particular, the problem is that we need independently specified indicators of the quality of managers or the modernity of management practices (separately measured from the organization's overall performance).

Of course, 'hybrid' data can be obtained on hospitals' or local agencies' overall performance that incorporate reference to their management, chiefly indices from external evaluators of how well a hospital or a local agency is being run. For instance, in the UK, hospital trusts were awarded 'star' ratings by NHS evaluators. Local authorities were given an assessment for managerial quality by a national body called the Audit Commission. From 2002 to 2008 this focused just on local councils' own services and activities, and was modestly called the Comprehensive Performance Assessment (Audit Commission, 2011). From 2008 to 2010 the evaluations also looked at how municipalities worked cooperatively with other local service providers (like the police force and health service); in this form it was called the Comprehensive Area Assessment. Locally managed schools in England have also been graded by an inspectorate, Ofsted.

The trouble with using any of these assessments, however, is that they were compound measures. Normally the evaluators made visits to each body assessed, and looked at a wide range of factors in making their judgements – such as the visible quality of service indicators, evidence of competence and good morale amongst staff, financial performance, the governance of the institutions and how effectively organizational leaders tackled problems. Nonetheless, at root the evaluations were also heavily based on units' objective performance. So instead of being genuinely independent measures of managerial quality, the evaluators' assessments largely incorporated and rested on the dependent variables that we are interested in analysing, namely the productivity, cost-effectiveness and output achievements of the unit being studied. As a result the correlations between such overall organizational management assessments and pro-ductivity performance may be so close that the overall assessments cannot be used as explanatory variables.

For information and communication technologies the problem has been quite different, namely that useful information on how far and in what ways ICTs are used in service delivery has been hard to find. In earlier periods, when IT was first being adopted and early automation processes were underway within local service providers, data on ICT costs and on the diffusion of particular styles of ICT use across local providers were more useful indicators than they are now. However, as we noted for private sector firms in Chapter 1, data on ICT spending levels no longer capture the actual use of modern ICTs very well. In the digital era a high relative spend on ICT does not necessarily signal an organization that is using a lot of up-to-the-minute technology, since web-based approaches are not as expensive as older ones. It may indeed indicate the reverse, an organization struggling along with older legacy systems and making little effective use of online transactions and internet-based services.

In the remainder of this section, we look at two recent and important studies that have innovatively addressed these problems. The first is an analysis by Van Reenen, Bloom and others that tries to unpick the influence of management practices on the performance of English NHS hospital trusts. The second is a large-scale, over-time analysis by Garicano and Heaton of how far the adoption of ICTs and related management practices by US police forces has helped to improve their performance across a long period. We also describe briefly an alternative approach that uses web-based research methods to assess management practices and ICT use, methods that we go on to apply in Chapter 8 to analyse productivity in English hospital trusts.

Analysis of Management Practices in Shaping Performance

A sophisticated interview-based approach to assess the quality of hospital managements in shaping performance was deployed by Nicholas Bloom, John Van Reenen and colleagues. The Bloom and Van Reenen (2010) method was developed for analyses of productivity and performance in private sector manufacturing firms, and it was later generalized to apply also to services firms and then to public sector organizations (see Bloom et al., 2005 and 2009a). It essentially involves the analysts drawing up a structured set of dimensions of management good practice (covering maybe 15 to 25 dimensions). These are derived from the previous literature and they are closely contextualized to fit the nature of the industry being covered. For each dimension the aim is to be able to score firms or agencies into one of three overall categories – not implementing that aspect of good practice, or partially implementing it, or fully implementing it.

To uncover this information the research team phoned an appropriate manager or member of professional staffs in 100 NHS hospital trusts and 21 comparator private hospitals, contacting either one or two persons per hospital (Bloom et al., 2009a). In a strongly evidence-based way, they sought to discuss with each interviewee 18 dimensions of hospital management, surfacing many different nuggets of information without using a fixed questionnaire. Instead, most questions were open-ended ones, and a more dialogic, 'elite interview' style of enquiry was undertaken on each dimension, until the interviewer could classify the organization's rating with some confidence. Interviewers were trained graduate students, 'double-blinded' by not being aware of a hospital's performance in any way. Each interviewer conducted around 46 interviews, so that they became experienced evaluators of responses. A key feature of this approach was that interviewees were also not told that they were being scored in any way.

Figure 7.4 shows examples of how questions were asked and ratings defined. In the hospitals study, the research team contacted 161 people, always including a senior hospital trust administrator in each case, and also reaching a senior doctor as well in some cases. At the end of the process, hospitals were assigned a composite score for their ratings for their management quality across all the dimensions.

The data for the management quality variable were then added into a dataset that included a large number of other possibly important independent variables, and were then regressed against a very useful and inclusive range of dependent variables. These included some specific indicators of hospitals' medical performance (covering the 28-day mortality rate for emergency admissions for acute myocardial infarction and the rate for

Figure 7.4   Two examples of how the Bloom et al. study of English hospitals assessed management quality on 18 different dimensions

(3) Continous improvement

Tests process for and attitudes to continuous improvement and whether things learned are captured/documented

a) How do problems typically get exposed and fixed?
b) Talk me through the process for a recent problem that you faced
c) How do the different staff groups get involved in this process? Can you give examples?

	Score 1	Score 3	Score 5
Scoring grid:	No, process improvements are made when problems occur, or only involve one staff group	Improvements are made in regular meetings involving all staff groups, to improve performance in their area of work (e.g., ward or theatre)	Exposing problems in a structured way is integral to individuals' responsibilities and resolution involves all staff groups, along the entire patient pathway as a part of regular business processes rather than by extraordinary effort/teams

(4) Performance tracking

Tests whether performance is tracked using meaningful metrics and with appropriate regularity

a) What kind of performance indicators would you use for performance tracking?
b) How frequently are these measured? Who gets to see data?
c) If I were to walk through your hospital wards and theatres, could I tell how you were doing against your performance goals?

	Score 1	Score 3	Score 5
Scoring grid:	Measures tracked do not indicate directly if overall objectives are being met, e.g., only government targets tracked. Tracking is an ad-hoc process (certain processes aren't tracked at all).	Most important performance indicators are tracked formally; tracking is overseen by senior staff.	Performance is continuously tracked and communicated against most critical measures, both formally and informally, to all staff using a range of visual management tools

Note: The dimensions shown here are those for 'continuous improvement' and 'performance tracking'.

Source: Bloom et al. (2009a, p. 28).

non-elective surgery), and two more general performance indicators (the size of the waiting list for all operations and the rates of MRSA infection, a particular 'superbug' on which a lot of public and NHS attention focused at the time of the study, in 2006). The study also looked at composite performance judgements made by a Department of Health body, the Healthcare Commission (HCC), which evaluated hospitals along two dimensions (on a scale from 1 to 4):

> The efficiency of resource use is measured [by HCC] by the number of spells per medical employee, bed occupancy rate and the average length of stay. Service quality is measured by clinical outcomes (readmission risk and infection rates), waiting times and a measure of patient satisfaction as well as job satisfaction of the staff. (Bloom et al., 2009a, pp. 6–7)

The basic distribution of the HCC rankings against the research team's scores for management quality is shown in Figure 7.5. This is a classic example of the kind of 'bait ball' pattern familiar across policy systems where decentralized agencies deliver services that are paid for from central government grants and are in turn subject to relatively intensive levels of central supervision. In 2006 the NHS in England was especially in the grip of a 'targetology' wave (described further in section 8.1, Chapter 8). Just as in nature, sardines or tuna form a 'bait ball' to maximize the chances of individual escape from predator attacks (such as sharks or dolphins), so this kind of pattern is functional for local agencies. So long as local managers can perform within the middle mass they effectively become invisible to national regulators and budget controllers. Hence few hospitals appear as excellent on even one dimension (in the top left or bottom right quadrants of the figure) because the effort to achieve excellence in one area could imperil performance and attract criticism if other areas lag or go wrong in the process. Only a few hospitals did well on both dimensions, at the top right. Similarly, there are few hospitals that are poor on both measures (in the bottom left quadrant) – because if their organization gets into this sub-target zone, hospital managers have strong incentives to focus attention on and fix the areas of conspicuously lagging performance. Managers hence rationally assign extra resources not to try to be excellent, but just to get themselves back safely hidden within the main mass of the 'bait ball'. It is clear in Figure 7.5 that there is no close fit between management quality and overall performance, although the average HCC scores did rise from 2.29 in hospitals scored lowest on management, to 2.58 for those with middling scores, and to 2.81 for those scored highest on management quality (all on a possible numerical range running from 1 to 4).

This initial basis for analysis looks unpromising. But a great advantage

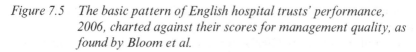

Figure 7.5   *The basic pattern of English hospital trusts' performance,*
2006, charted against their scores for management quality, as
found by Bloom et al.

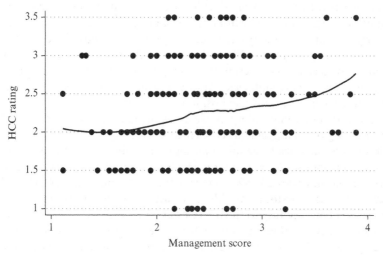

Note: Each point represents a survey response. The vertical axis shows the average
hospital care score (on a range from 1 to 4) in 2005–06. The horizontal axis shows the
average management score assigned by Bloom et al. (2009a) across their 18 questions. The
line is the local linear regression line.

of multiple regression techniques is that the picture can change greatly
when we take account of controls for other aspects of hospital trusts' situations. After controlling for hospitals' differing case mixes, and their size,
regional location, and whether they were speciality hospitals, Bloom et al.
found that better managed hospitals (on their scores) were significantly
associated with somewhat lower morbidity for emergency admissions,
lower waiting lists and with fewer hospital staff planning to leave. They
also found highly significant associations between hospitals being scored
better on their management measures and achieving high HCC performance ratings. The size of effects here was large, with management quality
accounting for around one-seventh of the variance in hospitals' average
HCC rankings.

The research team also found that the patterning of the management
quality scores showed that scores were higher in foundation trusts (a category of larger, better managed trusts to which in 2006 the central ministry
assigned more independence to set their own policies), and in hospitals
with more clinically qualified managers, and of larger size. Management
scores also seemed to be stronger in those parts of the country where

multiple hospitals were competing for patients (as in big cities) than in hospitals that were local monopolies.

Overall, Bloom et al. (2009a) concluded: 'Our measure of management quality was robustly associated with better hospital outcomes across mortality rates and other indicators of hospital performance' (p. 15). This is clearly an innovative approach and an impressive study. Its conclusions seem to offer rarely available and strong evidence to support the widely held 'managerialist' conviction that the quality of local management and organizational leadership clearly or obviously condition the performance of complex organizations like hospitals.

A key area of vulnerability, however, is the narrow informational basis for deriving the management scores themselves. Across most of the organizations characterized, the information basis is limited to the (admittedly detailed) responses from just one person, and in no case were more than two people interviewed. This seems a fragile foundation for grounding such a key explanatory variable. And although the study incorporates 'noise' controls relating to the interviewers for each case, it does not seem to include any variables that characterize the interviewees or could control in any way for their almost certainly variable perspectives. The famous Graeme Allison (1971) dictum that 'where you sit determines where you stand' applies in any organization. And without any real cross-checking of the management quality information from one respondent with other respondents, it is hard to know what reliance to place on them. The same criticism applies to this research approach in other contexts – for instance, to studying differing management practices across US, European and British manufacturing firms, where the same research team typically talked to one or two people only and drew similar, widely noticed conclusions about the importance of management practices (Bloom et al., 2005). Of course, the research team could legitimately respond to this criticism by asking: 'Well if not our approach, what alternative would you suggest for surfacing genuinely independent information on management practices?' This is an issue to which we return below in discussing web-based research methods, and where we implement an alternative approach in Chapter 8.

Analysing a Larger Over-time Dataset

Analysing a much larger, over-time dataset is the central innovation that allows a 2010 study by Luis Garicano and Paul Heaton to explore the role of IT investments in shaping the performance of US police departments. Using survey data completed every three years across the period 1965 to 2006 by many different US police departments, the authors built

Figure 7.6   The spread of ICT use across US police departments, 1965 to 2005

Source: Garicano and Heaton (2010, p.174).

up a dataset of police performance with 19 400 cases for many variables, around 13 000 to 16 000 for almost all others, and never less than 5000 cases. Their primary focus was on whether the huge take up of computers and other new IT by police forces across the USA produced any noticeable improvements in their performance, assessed not using productivity but measured in terms of arrest rates (an activity index) and crime rates (a measure of the problem environment). Figure 7.6 shows that larger police departments with over 100 employees were early users of ICTs, followed swiftly by medium-size departments, and at a much more gradual rate by the smallest (mainly rural) departments with less than ten employees. The authors' chosen IT use indicator was a compound measure of whether departments in a given year used computers for crime analysis, investigation and dispatch, and used data records for arrests, service calls, criminal histories, stolen property, traffic citations and warrants. The transition from mainframes to PCs to mobile computing was also covered.

To control for other variables the dataset also covered the size and complexity of departments (in terms of employee numbers, number of special units, number of organizational levels and total written directives); the make up of departments across uniformed officers, field operations staff and technical staff; the educational and training requirements for officers; and the demographic make up of the unit's local population (in terms of its size, the local racial make up, local poverty rates, mean household incomes and the education levels). The dependent variables for performance considered included the offence rates and clear up rates for overall crime (and those for sub-sections such as violent crime and property crime), and information about assaults on officers or deaths of police officers.

The authors' first and rather dismaying results were that they could not find any statistically significant effects demonstrating that the large-scale take up of IT by police departments was associated with any improvement in how they performed on the dependent variables. Rather than lowering clear up rates, increased IT use actually led to a growth in crimes being recorded, especially in relation to property crime. Detailed analysis showed that this negative association with crime amelioration was solely an information effect: 'Offense reports increase by 10% once computers are available for record keeping' (Garicano and Heaton, 2010, p. 184). Other than that, neither overall ICT use measures nor individual measures showed distinctive impacts on outputs or outcomes. The exceptions were that police forces making more use of computers and IT also subsequently upped their recruitment requirements to demand college education for all employees, and increased the amount of training they undertook. Careful checks were carried out for contaminating effects in the data, including the possibility that IT use may have only longer-lagged effects; that departments that were stressed, recently failing or mismanaged might be more likely to adopt IT as part of 'turnaround' reorganizations; that IT use responded chiefly to the level of contextual IT use in the local communities served; or that IT use responded only to the financial strength of the departments. After all these checks failed to shake the central finding, the authors conclude: 'It is surprising that IT appears to exert little effect on policing outcomes given the widespread use of IT in modern police departments' (Garicano and Heaton, 2010, p. 180). The authors explicitly link this central finding to the early wave of studies in private firms that found no boost from ICTs to firms' productivity or profitability.

They turn next, however, to exploring whether IT changes might have had effects but only *in combination* with shifts in management policies and in the organization of business processes to align them with the new technologies. Garicano and Heaton argue that a particular style of policing associated with the COMPSTAT approach introduced by New York Police Commissioner Bill Bratton was the most relevant change (see Bratton and Malinowski, 2008). They especially focused in their dataset on five aspects – the use of information technology for crime data collection and analysis; the adoption of a problem-solving paradigm to reduce crime rates; the use of feedback for priority-setting and evaluation; police forces using a geographic-based structure for deploying personnel to particular local areas; and stronger internal accountability. (Their data did not cover another key element of COMPSTAT, the empowerment of middle managers, and it only partly illuminated a final element, encouraging internal accountability for results.) The authors classed police departments that showed simultaneous elements of at least five of the seven COMPSTAT practices above in half the years covered as showing good management practices and then looked to see if this made a difference to police performance:

> The results are striking. Whereas the estimates on each of the individual management practices are of negligible magnitude and generally statistically indistinguishable from zero, the combination of practices into a COMPSTAT system yields positive and significant effects on clearance rates. The coefficient estimates of around 2% imply a roughly 10% gain relative to the average clearance rate of 22%. For violent crimes, which in many cases are an area of particular investigative emphasis, the point gains are even greater. (Garicano and Heaton, 2010, p. 193)

The authors further conclude that:

> One additional reason for the weak aggregate relationship between general IT and policing outcomes may be that while many agencies utilize some type of IT, relatively few have yet implemented all of the complementary management practices that allow IT to impact police effectiveness. (Ibid., p. 195)

Garicano and Heaton's overall conclusion is thus that:

> [W]hile the effects of general information technology on crime fighting and deterrence are statistically insignificant (in spite of our large samples), this effect becomes relatively large when IT adoption is undertaken as part of a whole package of organizational changes. That is, our results are a clear endorsement of what we have called here the complementarity hypothesis, and suggest that police departments, like firms, are likely to only enjoy the benefits of computerization when they identify the specific ways the new information and data availabilities interact with existing organizational practices and make adjustments accordingly. (Ibid., p. 196)

Overall, this is an impressive study that reaches carefully based conclusions, and takes issue with previous work (e.g., Levitt, 2004). There are two main issues. First, as is to be expected in a long-standing survey-based dataset, the information on ICT use in police departments is rather old-fashioned. It tracks well the onset of automation and the spread of initial computer use to new activity streams within police departments, especially in small departments. But the information seems of declining relevance for the assessment of practices in medium to large police forces, especially for the modern period with the bureaucratic development of websites, the primacy of online information, the use of online transactions and the adoption of social media in community-building.

Second, unlike Bloom et al., Garicano and Heaton do not have any directly accessed or purpose-designed information on management practices. By looking at survey questions included in their dataset that can be plausibly related to the COMPSTAT paradigm, they are able to partly overcome this barrier and to uncover a significant composite 'IT plus management change' effect – one that seems consistent with a great deal of research reaching similar conclusions for private sector firms. We carry over these key lessons to our own work in Chapter 8, which looks at hospital trusts in England. We seek to capture well-based information on trusts' use of modern ICT approaches, and their adoption of good practice management strategies.

Using New, Web-based Research Methods

Using new web-based research methods is the key step that allows us to avoid Bloom et al.'s dependence on responses from just one or two individuals per hospital trust, and to track more modern ICT use than that assessed by Garicano and Heaton. Across the social sciences, e-methods that exploit the availability of a great deal of new and different kinds of information in digital formats are only just beginning to develop. For instance, one can still scan most social science methods textbooks in vain for any guidance on these issues. Yet digital and web-based information sources are accessible, efficient, and at times offer major advances on previously available information. Websites provide new landscapes and sources for research. Especially given the transparency and accountability requirements that apply within the public sector, the websites of local government agencies and central government departments offer a uniquely objective picture of organization strategies and activity. Web-logs, listservs, e-mails, usage statistics and Twitter followers shed interesting light on where an organization's internal activities and external interactions are concentrated. Empirical sociologists recognize that both in business and in government the accumulation of massive amounts of transactional and administrative data has more or less made obsolescent the social sciences' previous primary reliance on survey data (Savage and Burrows, 2007 and 2009). In particular, the volume, comprehensive inclusiveness, objectivity and non-reactive qualities of transactional datasets have many advantages for analysts, decisively shifting the focus of research away from survey-

*Table 7.1   The four different ways that an organization's underlying
pattern of activities and their online presence can be related*

Organization Presents Itself Online as Doing	Organization is Actually Doing	
	A lot	Not much
A lot	1 Web census analysis correctly identifies high activity situation	2 Facade activity
Not much	4 Organizations with 'stealth' activities	3 Web census analysis correctly identifies low activity situation

based, small sample datasets to massive datasets that are transactional censuses, not sample studies (Dunleavy, 2010a).

The argument for this way of researching starts from the premises that in advanced industrial countries every salient public sector organization is now on the internet in some form, and so their websites, aspects of their transactional systems, and use of social media, along with forums, blogs and other elements are largely open for inspection. Their websites at least (but not intranets) can also be systematically crawled for information, although this needs to be done slowly because anti-virus software will otherwise repel attempts to fast-crawl a site (see Escher et al., 2006; Petricek et al., 2006). Sophisticated network techniques can then be used to analyse the 'graph structure' in the web data. Essentially, how the organization communicates with citizens, customers, businesses, civil society or other government or political bodies is fully open for analysis by political scientists.

Of course, what the organization *says online that it is doing*, and what the organization *actually is doing* may vary. Because of this problem, many social scientists have prematurely dismissed websites as useful sources of information, portraying them as simply public relations 'fronts' for organizations. There is a serious potential difficulty here, but in fact it is relatively easily managed in researching government sector organizations, as Table 7.1 shows. For online methods to work it is important that the vast bulk (say 95 per cent) of all organizational situations will be covered by cells 1 and 3, where an organization is either doing a lot or a little, and its web presence (when critically assessed using online research approaches) accurately reveals that situation.

The two other possibilities here would represent problems, if they are widespread and cannot be detected. 'Facade' activity (cell 2) occurs when a lively online presence masks low levels of underlying ('real') activity (or activity of a different kind) by the organization. This situation sounds plausible, yet it is actually much harder for an organization to sustain than might appear at first sight. Virtually all significant government organizations' web operations are now salient, complex and interlocked with their fundamental transactions systems and ways of working and doing business. All the chapters in Part I noted that essential business processes in government now operate via the internet – the time is long past when websites just held press releases aimed at creating a public relations gloss. Websites are too expensive to maintain properly simply for propaganda purposes. And facade content is anyway clearly visible for critical researchers using modern methods (see Table 7.2). Indeed, any intelligent citizen browsing a facade website can quickly detect it. The whole concept of 'digital era governance' stresses that, increasingly, government bureaucracies are *becoming* their websites, so that the organizational socio-technical system is increasingly manifest on the web. Indeed, it has to be completely manifest or else modern, pared-down systems of risk-adjusted administration will collapse (Dunleavy et al., 2008).

The second problem in Table 7.1 concerns covering organizations with large-scale 'stealth' activities (cell 4). They are delivering public services, or doing things politically, but they are not telling citizens or talking about what they do on the web. Again this sounds possible, yet who exactly are these bodies? Certainly this is irrational behaviour for any public service bureaucracy in an advanced industrial country that is citizen-facing or business-facing. It is also counterproductive for most interest groups, civil society organizations and parties, to be implementing activities yet masking this from the public and society. Cell 4 is far more typical of some kinds of companies, especially those providing commercially confidential services. Only a few special purpose government agencies (such as intelligence services and defence agencies), and their opponents in terrorist organizations, may actually have critically important classes of activity shielded from web revelation. Even police services and foreign affairs ministries must now increasingly operate on the internet, or risk being marginalized from society's key information networks (Escher et al., 2006; Hood and Margetts, 2007). Similarly, even many modern terrorist movements rely extensively on online sites to raise funds, maintain communications, distribute ideological memes and provide for decentred patterns of cell organization (Burke, 2007, p. 39).

Not only does web-based research use digital information as a new source of data, but it also entails adopting new methods for assembling and critically analysing information. There is a paradigm shift in research approaches, a switch away from 'reactive' and 'obtrusive' methods (such as sending out surveys where people are asked explicitly to give all the information collected, or to react to questions or propositions devised solely by the researchers). Instead, analysis moves towards 'non-reactive' and 'unobtrusive' measures, where information is collected without the interposition or even awareness of research subjects (the people or organizations being studied), and without the biases that can occur from researchers posing questions in ways that skew responses. The new *non-reactive measures* minimize the effect of question biases, peer influences, subjects giving 'improving' responses that conform to public or cultural norms, or delivering what they consider that higher tiers of government or the researchers themselves want to hear. Table 7.2 shows how the two broad approaches compare in several ways.

Non-reactive approaches relating to websites are also cheap to implement and facilitate comprehensive coverage of all agencies in a given category, rather than having to rely on sub-sets of data that cover only parts of the populations involved. Why sample when you can conduct a comprehensive census? Why worry about many aspects of conventional statistical significance if you can include the whole population in your datasets from the outset (also avoiding all missing case problems)? Why base analysis on a handful of cases (left largely unsituated in the wider field of all similar organizations) when you can cover them all, in detail? This basic shift of approach can be easily varied and extended in numerous ways – for example, using external or internal search engines and specialist media tracker sites to track the foci of memes in macro-content through their incidence in discourses; crawling websites for in-links and out-links to other websites and organizations (Escher et al., 2006); and using modern networking analysis to track influences (Cho and Fowler, 2007; Christakis and Fowler, 2008, 2010).

Our key approach in Chapter 8 relies on trawling systematically through the websites of organizations, and recording in great detail a large series of objectively recordable pieces of information that the website reveals about the organization. It is very important that the coding of items should be as objective as possible, and be as little open to misinterpretation as possible, otherwise researcher biases could creep in. This would vitiate some of the key advantages of using non-reactive methods, which include avoiding the need for personal judgements by respondents or researchers, and generating results that are completely replicable by other observers. Hence web-census methods need to focus on recording the answers to unambiguous questions that either require 'Yes/No' or 'Present/Not present' dichotomous codes, without the researcher needing to make complex, qualitative judgements. Examples of the single, unambiguous questions needed are:

Table 7.2   Comparing reactive surveys of organizations and non-reactive, web-census methods (WCM)

	Surveys of Organizations	Web-census Methods (WCM)
Coverage	A statistically representative sample, covering a fraction of the whole population of organizations	The whole population of organizations
Instrument defined by	Researchers define a strictly limited number of questions. Question wording effects extensively condition subjects' responses. Any incorrect or inappropriate single question wordings can contaminate significant sections of analysis and results	Researchers identify a large number (several dozen to hundreds) of discrete items to be coded as present or not. Items are structured and weighted to tap theoretically relevant dimensions. Any single incorrect item has a tiny impact on overall indices
Type of methods approach	*Reactive methods* (surveys, interviews) – those contacted may report erroneously, edit their responses or misrepresent situations	*Non-reactive methods* – items are coded as objectively present/ absent in the organizations' websites, using simple dichotomies
Researcher– subject interactions	Obtrusive – respondents know the study is underway and the precise content of its questions	Unobtrusive – organizations need not be alerted that a study of them is underway
Costs	Substantial	Low
Key 'meaning' problems	Responses may be artefacts of the questions asked. Responses are a poor guide to these people's actual behaviour. The effects of interviewer and coder judgements may be hard to spot or control for	Organizational behaviours are established, but the salience and meaning of items coded may be disputed (at both an individual and an aggregate level).
Key problems with interpreting the information gathered	Who exactly in the organization completes and returns surveys varies a lot, and may not be known. The 'authority' status of the actual respondents is typically unclear, along with how far they consulted others	1 Controlling for 'facade' activity – which shows up clearly in well-designed coding frames 2 'Stealth' activities that are not detectable on organizations' websites (not likely to be a problem with *normal* government or civil society organizations?)
Key technical problems with datasets	Small sample sizes. Extensive non-response. Extensive missing data problems in achieved responses. Mistakes cannot be post-corrected by researchers without going back to respondents	Complete returns are always achieved, without missing data or non-response problems. Mistakes and miscodings can be post-corrected by researchers

- Is a copy of the agency's Annual Report easily findable on the site?
- Does the agency website include a link to the national ombudsman?
- Does the agency website include a link to a next-tier-up appeals body?
- Does the agency provide information for prospective staff thinking of moving into the local area?
- Does the agency provide users with any online guidance on how to make a complaint?
- Does the agency website use pictures/videos/social media?
- Does the agency have a Twitter page? A Facebook page?

(Some terms here may need explicit standardization, for example, in the first question here, 'easily findable' means that an experienced web researcher having spent an hour on the agency website, could not find the Annual Report online.)

A necessary feature of a web-census approach is that questions are reductionist – they focus on small, precisely codable characteristics of the organization's online presence. Taken on their own, in themselves, no single one of these indicators ever means very much. However, the method is holistic. It works by covering dozens of these small characteristics, whose cumulative presence or absence clearly does build up a picture and have meaning. Hence researchers must choose multiple small indices that are well adapted to assessing deeper-lying agency characteristics, and which can be simply aggregated into overall scores for each agency. This is the approach we deploy in Chapter 8 for characterizing the management practices and extent of ICT use across English hospital trusts in a manner that is fully independent from considerations of their overall performance, or of how they are ranked by health service inspectors or regulators.

Conclusions

Because multiple local providers play key roles in delivering most major public services in welfare states, we can compare across providers and also deploy more sophisticated parametric and non-parametric methods. Yet so far the insights derived from doing so have not been particularly illuminating, partly because of the importance of quality adjustments in complex services and the greater difficulties of getting large-scale data on intangible quality variations. Too many analyses have also focused on easily quantifiable but relatively remote influences on the productivity performance of local providers (such as the sizes of agencies or area populations), while not covering factors that in theoretical terms are likely to have the most immediate consequences for productivity change. Modern, web-based and non-reactive methods can prove helpful in expanding the range of explanatory variables to include factors that seem likely to really matter for productivity – such as management practices and overall management quality, and how far local agencies make full use of modern ICT in delivering services

8. Hospital productivity in England's National Health Service

The National Health Service in England is one of the largest connected sets of public sector organizations in Europe, and on a par with the provincially run and more mixed health systems in large countries such as China and India. The vast bulk of NHS activivites (69 per cent of the output index in 2007–08) is made up of hospital and community health services (Peñaloza et al., 2010, p. 6). Most trusts operate just one or two hospitals, and hospital sizes vary from smaller 'district general hospitals' for a single city or area, through to large, multi-specialism hospitals in regional metropolitan areas and in Central London.

In this chapter we explore in detail what influences seem to shape the overall productivity of the acute hospital trusts in England. We begin by setting the scene, looking at successive governments' attempts to boost the efficiency of NHS hospitals by introducing elements of competition to attract patients between hospitals, interspersed with other periods where policy stressed more the integration of services and the stabilization of hospital budgets in a more predictable fashion. Our second section sets out the methods that we have adopted to compare productivity across the 154 acute hospital trusts. We use a parametric approach, and in addition to cost weights, we use a quality-weighting of trusts' overall outputs. As independent variables, we operationalize measures of management competence and innovativeness, and of the extent to which trusts make use of information and communication technologies (ICTs). The third section considers the results, which suggest that ICT use has a strong effect on productivity levels, and one that interacts with the influence of management practices.

8.1 THE SEARCH FOR GREATER EFFICIENCY IN NHS ACUTE HOSPITAL CARE

Successive governments have paid constant attention to how the hospital sector in the NHS was managed. There have been frequent reorganizations and new initiatives in almost every year of the last three decades. For most of the post-war period, budgets were allocated directly to hospitals by top-level and regional NHS bodies (guided top-down by the Department of Health). Each ordinary hospital was assigned a local area for which it was (by and large) the dominant provider. Specialist care saw more movements of patients out of the locality, especially to larger hospitals in regional centres or London. But this did not qualify the basic arrangement where each local population primarily looked to its local hospital for treatment. Hospitals were given a bed capacity, budget and staffing levels to go along with this local need.

In 1988 the Conservative government under Margaret Thatcher resolved to make a radical change in this set up. Ministers sought to introduce a 'quasi-market' in healthcare, where the budget for treatments would be allocated to local consortia of family doctors (called general practitioners, or GPs in the UK). These groupings would purchase hospital care on behalf of their patients and would be able to take their custom to whichever hospital they liked, paying attention specifically to how good the care was and how much each treatment cost. The idea was that hospitals would no longer get a budget 'as of right', but instead have to compete with each other to attract patients to fill their beds, thereby creating a dynamic that was 'sure to' increase efficiency and cut NHS costs.

In the event, the new arrangements proved an expensive thing to try to set up from scratch, and the number of hospital managers and accountants soared to try to make an overly complex system work. Even establishing a list of hospital operations that everyone could agree on cost millions of pounds. The scope of competition between hospitals also quickly proved to be strongly limited both by patients' and GPs' lack of information about hospitals' performance, and by repeated government interventions in order to keep hospital budgets stable and prevent disruption as demand patterns changed.

From 1997 the Labour government under Tony Blair pursued a different course, initially scrapping the quasi-market provisions altogether, and seeking to reintegrate services in a joined up way. More importantly from 2000 on Labour raised health budgets strongly to improve care levels. Both measures improved the effectiveness of provision and boosted public confidence in the NHS, but ministers became frustrated that large spending increases did not seem to have proportionate effects on improving hospitals' performance. Later on in its term Labour reintroduced more diversification of healthcare providers in a different and more incremental fashion, with Independent Treatment Centres competing with mainline hospitals to undertake simpler sets of operations, especially in areas previously under-supplied. Ministers also took steps to improve choice and 'personalization' by requiring that hospitals publish much more information on their performance.

However, in other ways the avenues of 'citizen redress' in the NHS were radically reduced (with the complete abolition of bodies called Community Health Councils) and made more 'businesslike' and NHS-dominated (Dunleavy et al., 2010a). There were though a few offsetting trends later in Labour's period of office. New information websites like NHS Choices were opened from 2005 on, where patients could post testimonials or comments on their hospital care. By 2009, in consultation with their GPs, prospective patients could also exercise a limited choice of which of four hospitals to choose to have their operation in.

Yet towards the end of Labour's term in office, the withering away of patient redress avenues, and the constant reorganization of hospital regulation arrangements, both came home to roost, with spectacular crises in care at two English acute hospital trusts. One at Maidstone and Tonbridge Wells resulted in the deaths of over 90 patients, and illnesses for 1000 more, in a single year, through failure to recognize or control the outbreak of a common hospital infection, *Clostridium difficile* (Healthcare Commission, 2007). The second in Mid Staffordshire caused the premature deaths of at least 400 patients over three years through very poor care standards in its accident and emergency department, despite repeated local protests about unexplained deaths (Healthcare Commission, 2009).

In mid-2010 a Conservative–Liberal Democrat government took office, and the Conservative Health Secretary, Andrew Lansley, introduced a third version of a healthcare quasi-market in a reform bill that the government admitted would cost £1.8 billion, and which informed critics estimated would cost twice as much (*British Medical Journal*, 2010). In Parliament the bill attracted strong criticism from Labour and Liberal Democrat MPs as measures that would 'privatize' the NHS, and because the Coalition government needed to retain its majority the bill's provisions were extensively watered down. Consortia of GPs would still once again 'commission' care and have more options for where their patients went for treatment, but they would have to do this in consultation with hospital consultants and other health professionals. So the government claimed that the 'integration' of the NHS would not be jeopardized. At the same time alternative providers from the private sector and from the third sector (e.g., hospices for looking after dying patients) would be better able to compete with hospitals, and hospitals would be able to compete more with each other. It remains to be seen how much change in effective patient choice or GP choice will be introduced by the new wave of reform, and whether it will have positive efficiency effects (as ministers claim) or negative effects (Dunleavy, 2012b) on how healthcare is provided.

It is clear from NAO assessment of central government reorganization costs (National Audit Office, 2010b) that the investments made in repeatedly reorganizing the architectural arrangements of the NHS have cumulatively cost billions of pounds over the last quarter century. There has also been a commitment of hundreds of millions of pounds in seeking to improve managerial practices and competencies, modernizing business processes, developing the leadership and managerial competencies of senior NHS administrators and trying to encourage the spread of what has been conventionally recognized as 'best practice' at different periods of time. Acute hospitals are very large and complex organizations, with an average of 4000 staff each, organized in strongly siloed professional/ medical specialisms. They have a complex set of governance arrangements covering budgets, professional practice, the exercise of medical judgement, the standards for patient care, responding to new medical technologies and treatment innovations, meeting government-set targets for performance and staying on the right side of many different sets of regulatory provisions (administered by different quasi-governmental and professional bodies). Guiding hospitals through this maze of management issues so that they can recruit and retain the right staff, keep up to date in their treatment approaches, meet patient needs safely and effectively and yet stay within budgets and meet demanding governance requirements is hence a difficult task.

The importance of improving the 'quality' of hospital managers has accordingly been regularly stressed throughout the recent period – not only in the professional discourse of NHS managers themselves, but also in the declarations of relevant government departments (especially the Department of Health) and many different health regulatory bodies. Given this emphasis, many healthcare trusts have tried adopting different organizational and management approaches in recent years to improve the provision of their services.

A report from the NHS Confederation looked at the causes of failure in five underperforming hospital trusts (Protopsaltis et al., 2002; NHS Confederation, 2002). They argued that in all five cases hospital failure occurred as a result of:

- poor leadership, including a reluctance to make decisions and an unwillingness to delegate;
- problems with the trusts' internal organizational culture and a lack of clinical engagement;
- distraction, large projects occupying the majority of senior management time caused less attention to be paid to monitoring regular healthcare implementation;
- poor operational management, including inefficiency in clinical or operational areas;

• strategic and external problems, including a failure to address longer-run issues, make fundamental changes to clinical services, and poor quality control.

Incoming managers brought in to turnaround the five failing NHS trusts typically focused their activities on four things – internal restructuring; improving the trust's performance against core targets such as waiting times and financial viability, training staff better and improving the trusts' communication with eternal stakeholders. In addition, the report emphasized:

– giving detailed consideration to failures, in order to avoid adopting over-simplified solutions;
– adapting new strategies to differing circumstances;
– giving greater priority to preventing problems from arising, rather than fire-fighting those that arise;
– major cultural change inside failing trusts, including changing the chief executive;
– realistic expectations about the time needed for recommended changes to take effect.

The Healthcare Commission (2007) report on the poor handling of two *Clostridium difficile* infection outbreaks at the Maidstone and Tonbridge Wells hospital trust showed that the failures there cost the lives of more than 90 patients with many more seriously ill. Many of the problems itemized above also occurred in this case (and in fact recurred two or three times). In particular, the trust's management board allowed their infection control consultant to leave without being replaced for a long while, and failed to act promptly to recognize or combat the hospital infections crisis – chiefly because they were so distracted by many other big decisions – including correcting a budget deficit, implementing a big new PFI building project and applying to the government for 'foundation trust' status.

Closely associated with improving NHS management practices have been major government efforts (partly aided by the professions) to redress a severe deficit in the use of information and communication technologies by the NHS acute hospitals. During the 1980s and early 1990s a couple of more ambitious hospital IT projects failed badly, with bad publicity and criticisms in Parliament. These experiences put chief executives off from making large ICT investments. Pressure on budgets until 2001 also pulled all available resources into direct patient care. By the time that resources grew again, the hospital sector was strongly set in a low-tech pathway by dominant professional practices – amongst doctors, nurses and managers.

Although family doctors computerized some of their administration using small PC-based systems, hospitals wards had very few PCs and little modern ICT in place. They were consequently very slow to adopt modern forms of patient records and to seek to digitize information. Up to the time of writing (mid-2012) paper files and folders remain the dominant medium by which NHS hospital doctors, nurses and other medical professions record and retain information. Over several decades acute hospitals conspicuously failed to transform their business processes using network and database ICTs. They also made few moves to engage with their patients and stakeholders using internet-based digital processes. Substantial barriers seem likely to remain in the hospital sector, leaving it as one of the most conspicuously digital-lagging major service industries in the UK for some time to come.

However, a major commitment was made under Tony Blair's premiership in 2002, following which the NHS did invest significant resources in a highly centralized 'big bang' programme for introducing modern systems and technologies, called the National Programme for IT (NPfIT, pronounced 'NP fit'). This plan sought to create a secure 'national spine' (network) for inter-hospital communications, and for links between hospitals and with GPs. Massive change programmes affected many different areas, especially the creation of fully digitized patient records (accessible in a short form at any hospital), and the digitizing of all X-ray records.

The NPfIT approach was to be financed by large amounts of central funding, and implemented by means of a tightly centralized set of nationwide contracts with a few of the largest ICT firms, especially British Telecom (BT), the UK's former nationalized phone company, and Accenture, one of the 'big 4' world management and technology consultancy firms. On some estimates, by April 2010 the NHS had spent around £6 billion in rolling it out (*Computer Weekly*, 2010) and the total costs that were supposed to be spent eventually have been put as high as £13 billion. Some NPfIT features, such as the electronic patient care records, proved very difficult to even pilot, and had not been fully implemented nationwide by the time the programme was halted in autumn 2011. But many of the supporting e-services and systems that form important parts of the national framework (such as online systems for storing and communicating digital X-ray pictures) became operational in 2009–11 to varying degrees at local and regional level.

Critics have argued that the NPfIT programme quickly followed a familiar UK template for large-scale government IT disasters (Public Administration Select Committee, 2011). Some key parts of the architecture, such as the provision of a fully digitized patient record, proved far more difficult to get right than was envisaged. As problems became evident,

Accenture pulled out of the whole programme, taking an estimated £200 million financial hit in the process. Critics argued by 2010–11 that the full delivery of some NPfIT features (such as the national 'spine' for inter-hospital and hospital-to-GP communications) and the partial implementation of most features at scale, should already have had some observable potential effects on efficiency or productivity levels. But evidence on these lines was actually very hard to come by, with the Department of Health unable to point to any study documenting realized benefits.

Early evaluations of NPfIT by the National Audit Office (NAO, 2008) seemed to bend over backwards to give the programme the benefit of the doubt, and NAO were criticized as vesting too much credence in Department of Health promises of future benefits. Later audit studies (NAO, 2011a) concluded that large parts of the spending undertaken represented poor value for money and that the scheme as a whole was not delivering benefits proportional to its costs. The Public Administration Select Committee (2011) recommended scrapping what remained of NPfIT and spending the remaining money on alternative schemes.

In response, ministers in the Conservative–Liberal Democrat government ceased completion of NPfIT as originally envisaged. They opted for a much lower-cost and more decentralized and voluntary approach, in which acute hospital trusts were no longer compelled to take on board the full set of NPfIT requirements. Trusts could now choose to buy into some more modest centrally promoted ICT initiatives, or not. How this new approach will work in combating the still evident under-use of ICTs within the acute hospital sector remains to be seen. The climate of very tight financial resources for the NHS inaugurated by Coalition ministers in 2010 seems unlikely to see hospitals committing substantial resources to ICT change. However, ICT initiatives that could directly and immediately foster cost or staffing reductions (for instance, automating patient records, or moving more booking systems for patient appointments online) may survive such financial pressures.

Given this political, management and ICT context, it is probably not surprising that the few research studies of the productivity of the NHS have tended to come to pessimistic conclusions. Most work looked at aggregate productivity trends in the health service at a meta-level. Castelli et al. (2007) examined a number of years from the late 1990s on, finding that productivity trends were generally negative over time. A similar pattern occurs in recent Office for National Statistics studies (ONS, 2008a), which argue that the productivity of healthcare provision as a whole in the UK fell consistently during the period of the greatest expansion of NHS funding in the noughties. The authors mention that such negative trends may be a consequence of the increased NHS spending that the

Labour government implemented from 1997. However, the quality adjustments that ONS makes to allow for improvements in NHS outputs are probably not enough to capture other key changes at this time, and critics have stressed that some perverse effects are incorporated here – as with the case of doctors spending more time with patients discussed already.

Amidst all the sound and fury over NHS reorganizations, it remains the case that information on how acute hospitals are operating remains scarce and patchy. Some management consultants claim large productivity gains remain to be made (McKinsey, 2010). Ministers still often seem to make decisions based on gut instincts, and perhaps the rapid generalization of something that seems to work well in pilot implementations. This pattern is not what might be expected if policy-making were genuinely evidence based.

8.2   METHODOLOGY AND VARIABLE SPECIFICATION

In the analysis below we seek to assess how far interconnecting management and increased ICT factors have begun to achieve trackable impacts on healthcare trusts' performance. Untangling the effects of these two variables within the NHS context should contribute to the wider literature on government productivity (reviewed in Chapters 1 and 7). And it should have significant interest for scholars in areas like health service management, e-health and perhaps health informatics. We focus only on acute hospital trusts because this sector absorbs a large portion of the healthcare budget, involves the biggest and most complex organizations, and handles the most difficult and expensive medical cases. We have seen above that government targets, advice and programmes designed to encourage the use of new ICTs and good management practices have all focused very heavily on acute trusts.

The Coverage of our Dataset

We assembled a dataset for the acute hospital trusts in England for the financial year 2007–08. We excluded hospitals in Scotland and Wales, because they were run under different policies set by the devolved governments of these two countries, and this would blur a focus on the roles that managerial modernization and ICTs played in shaping hospital productivity. All our cases operate within the framework of recent policy summarized in section 8.1 above.

Our dataset was constructed using data from the following sources:

- A database compiled by the Centre of Economic Performance (CEP) at the LSE on acute trusts across England based on publicly available sources. From this database we took the relevant information on each acute trust related to service quality, waiting times and patient satisfaction.
- Data from the NHS Information Centre on complaints management and medical workforce. These are two separate datasets available on the centre's website. The first one includes the total number of complaints, complaints handled within the target time (25 working days), complaints handled outside the target times and complaints that are still being pursued. The second one includes the total number of medical staff broken down by grade in each health organization.
- Hospital Episodes Statistics is a database of 'Hospital providers', from which we took information on the numbers of finished consultant episodes, numbers of outpatients appointments, mean waiting times and patients' age.
- The NHS Staff Satisfaction Survey 2008 provided a series of variables about staff commitment to their work, whether training has been provided in the last year and the amount of unpaid overtime.
- We generated data on key independent variables covering each hospital trust's visible use of modernizing management practices and use of ICTs and solutions using web-censuses. The approach uses web-census methods as discussed in Chapter 7, and we explain below in the third sub-section how we collated information on 59 variables to compose a management modernization index and an ICT index for acute trusts.

Our study sought to cover all Acute Health Care and Foundation trusts in England, that is, the 171 organizations who between them are responsible for the management of all 478 hospitals. In fact, our complete dataset includes slightly less than all English trusts, for several reasons (the Chapter Annex below gives a complete listing of those covered). While we were conducting the study, we found that 15 trusts had changed their name and eight trusts had merged into four new ones, while one trust had more of a primary care character (see notes to the Chapter Annex table). This brought the total number of trusts analysed down to 166. In the case of the trusts that merged, we did an average of the available data, so that our final measure of output and productivity reflected the work and resources of the hospitals included in the new trusts. For a further 13 trusts within this group we could not obtain a complete measure of output quality, and therefore, productivity. This is chiefly because there were no data available

*Figure 8.1   Our approach to measuring the labour productivity (of medical
               staff) in NHS acute trusts*

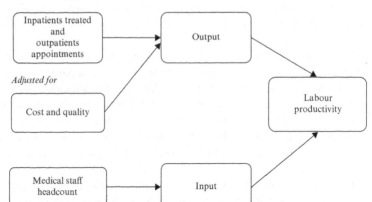

on complaints, patients' satisfaction levels or mean waiting times – the three
variables that we used to quality adjust outputs (see below). Therefore, we
ended up with a total dataset covering 153 acute trusts.

The key dependent variable for this analysis is labour productivity in
the NHS acute sector, and Figure 8.1 shows the way in which this measure
was constructed. We calculated this as the ratio of our measure of outputs
to the numbers of medical staff (that is, doctors and nursing staff) in each
trust. Labour productivity becomes a reliable comparable performance
measure when used across different units but with a common denominator. Our output measure is primarily based upon the number of outpatient
appointments and inpatient spells, but adjusted for cost relativities so as to
account for the different costs of 'producing' a unit of outpatient appointments and of inpatient treatments.

To measure initial *outputs* we used the total number of inpatient spells
(in 2007–08) at trust level, and the total number of outpatient appointments per trust in the same year in order to create a single output measure.
Information on inpatient spells and outpatient appointments were taken
from the Hospital Episode Statistics database on 'Hospital providers'.

Cost-weighting Outputs

Turning to cost-weighting outputs we followed the methodology discussed in Chapter 1 and suggested by the Atkinson Report (2005b) and
subsequent publications from the Office for National Statistics (ONS).
Outpatient appointment and hospital spells data were both weighted
according to the share of total administration costs involved in produc-

Figure 8.2   *The distribution of cost-weighted outputs across acute hospital*
                trusts

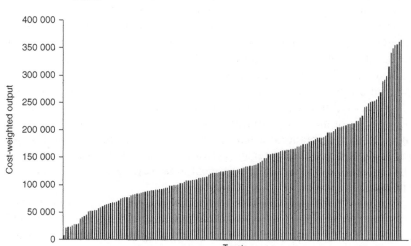

ing them. For this purpose, we used the data on administrative costs for inpatients and outpatients in the Kent University manual on NHS unit costs (PSSRU, 2007). From these data, we aggregated all the costs related to treating outpatients and those related to treating inpatient spells. The resulting unit costs were on average £479 for inpatients and £152 for outpatients, so that inpatient costs were somewhat more than three times more expensive that those for outpatients. This is consistent with other recent publications that also suggest a relationship of 3 to 1 in inpatient to outpatient costs (Castelli et al., 2007). Therefore, we multiplied the number of inpatients by 0.75 and the number of outpatient appointments by 0.25. Finally, we added the weighted inpatient and outpatient numbers to obtain a cost-weighted measure of output. Figure 8.2 shows the distribution of hospitals' cost-weighted outputs that resulted.

Our key methodological innovations in the analysis below focus on the development of means of further quality-weighting our cost-weighted output measures and on the specification of the independent variables relating to management practices and ICT use. We discuss each in turn.

Quality-weighting Outputs

Because quality variations across units may otherwise introduce the strong 'perverse' effects in productivity analyses discussed in Chapter 7, we also use quality weights to construct productivity measures, reflecting current best practice in the study of productivity among decentralized public services where quality variations may potentially play a significant role and cannot plausibly be assumed to be constant (ONS, 2007a, 2007b).

There is ample evidence that the quality of service may vary widely across acute hospitals. For example, an outpatient appointment obtained with a delay of only two weeks should not be considered similar to one gained only after a ten weeks' delay. Similarly, having a timely operation to head off problems is a much better outcome for a patient than having emergency treatment once a crisis has occurred. There are obviously many dimensions of medical treatment and surgery quality that are exceptionally difficult to obtain information on, let alone systematic data. But we are focusing here on aggregate performance across trusts, and not on the performance in particular treatment areas (the focus in most medical studies).

Because of our trust-level focus, we chose as quality indicators average patient waiting times, patient satisfaction and the ratio of complaints resolved in target times divided by the total complaints received per year. Clearly there are a large number of other quality measures that could be considered, and the three elements we have chosen are generic and non-medically specific ones. However, they do tap important aspects of patients' experience and represent relevant quality aspects, the data needed were widely available in the sources we consulted for this research and the use of three measures adds additional checks and balances. We took mean waiting times from the HES online 'Hospital providers' tables for 2007–08, the complaints ratio from the NHS Information Centre for 2008–07 and patient satisfaction from a number of different Patient Satisfaction Scores included in the CEP database.

We proceeded by creating five-point interval scales for each of the adjustment variables. Each interval was given a percentage adjustment that varied from 0 to 100 per cent. Then, we multiplied the output variable by the respective adjustment percentage for each of the three adjustment variables as follows:

For mean waiting time we developed a five-point percentage weight scale based on the limit of 18 weeks established by the NHS as the maximum time it should take for patients to be referred to treatment. We considered that any NHS trust with a mean waiting time exceeding 126 days (18 weeks) should be given a 0 per cent quality adjustment. Table 8.1 shows the whole interval breakdown and the percentage quality adjustments employed.

For mean patient satisfaction the data was compiled from information included in the CEP database on NHS trusts for five different patient satisfaction scores covering: overall experience; access and waiting; information and choice; relationships; and whether hospitals were clean, com-

Table 8.1   Mean waiting time adjustment

Mean Waiting Time (based on target)	Percentage (%) Quality Adjustment	Distribution of Trusts (%)
> 126	0	2
≤ 126 > 94.5	25	13
≤ 94.5 > 63	50	61
≤ 63 > 31.5	75	20
≤ 31.5	100	4

Table 8.2   Mean patient satisfaction adjustment

Mean Patient Satisfaction	Percentage (%) Quality Adjustment	Distribution of Trusts (%)
> 4	100	2
> 3 ≤ 4	75	84
> 2 ≤ 3	50	12
> 1 ≤ 2	25	2
≤ 1	0	–

Table 8.3   Complaints completion ratio adjustment

Mean Complaints Ratio	Percentage (%) Quality Adjustment	Distribution of Trusts (%)
> 0.85	100	35
≤ 0.85 > 0.7	75	41
≤ 0.7 > 0.55	50	15
≤ 0.55 > 0.4	25	6
≤ 0.4	0	3

fortable and friendly. These used a five-point scale from 1 to 5 ranging from 'very dissatisfied' to 'very satisfied'. To employ these data, we took the mean result of these five questions. Table 8.2 shows how this was implemented.

For the complaints completion ratio we used data from the NHS Information Centre on the percentage of complaints for each trust that were completed within the government target of 25 working days. We created the intervals shown in Table 8.3 and used the associated quality adjustment levels to adjust the measure of output for each trust.

Each trust's cost-weighted output was then multiplied by each of three corresponding quality adjustment percentages to obtain a cost- and quality-adjusted output measure in the following way:

$$CQWO = CWO * MWTA * MPSA * CCRA \qquad (8.1)$$

Where

$CQWO$	=	cost- and quality-weighted output;
CWO	=	cost-weighted output;
$MWTA$	=	mean waiting time adjustment;
PSA	=	mean patient satisfaction adjustment;
CCA	=	complaints completion ratio adjustment.

To give a concrete illustration of what this step means, Table 8.4 shows an illustrative set of five trusts whose cost-adjusted output measures are also adjusted for quality.

As laid out in equation (8.1), our quality-wighting procedure provides a 100 per cent quality adjustment. To account for some extra variation in such weighting procedure, we also estimated three extra scenarios in which the total adjustment was in between the full cost- and quality-weighting and the cost-weighting. To illustrate such scenarios it was necessary to calculate the difference between the cost-weighted output and the full cost- and quality-weighted output:

$$DIFF = CWO - CQWO \qquad (8.2)$$

We then calculated the intermediate weighting scenarios between a full cost- and quality-weighting and a cost-weighting at 75 per cent, 50 per cent and 25 per cent levels. A higher level indicates a value closer to the full cost- and quality-weighted figure:

$$CQWO\ 75\% = CWO - (DIFF * 0.75) \qquad (8.3)$$

$$CQWO\ 50\% = CWO - (DIFF * 0.5) \qquad (8.4)$$

$$CQWO\ 25\% = CWO - (DIFF * 0.25) \qquad (8.5)$$

We therefore calculated three additional productivity estimates. These estimates were included in our regression models. The impact of quality-weighting on outputs distribution across trusts is shown in Figure 8.3 (for $CQWO$).

Inputs were defined as the number of medical staff per acute trust

Table 8.4 Examples of adjusted measures

Trust Name	Total Cost-weighted Output	Overall Patient Satisfaction	Patient Satisfaction Adjustment Index	Complaints Ratio	Complaints Ratio Adjustment Index	Mean Waiting Time (days)	Mean Waiting Time Adjustment Index	Total Cost and Quality-adjusted Output
Oxford Radcliffe Hospital	269 875.28	3.00	0.75	0.89	1.00	44.00	0.75	151 804.85
Heatherwood and Wesham Park Hospitals	163 795.08	3.00	0.75	0.61	0.50	58.00	0.75	46 067.37
Royal Free Hampstead	172 705.36	2.80	0.50	0.18	0.75	55.00	0.75	48 573.38
South London Health Care Trust	289 615.08	2.67	0.50	0.77	0.75	66.00	0.50	54 302.83
West Hertfordshire Hospitals	134 272.92	2.80	0.50	0.49	0.25	82.00	0.50	8 392.06

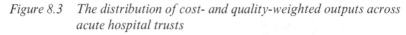

*Figure 8.3   The distribution of cost- and quality-weighted outputs across
            acute hospital trusts*

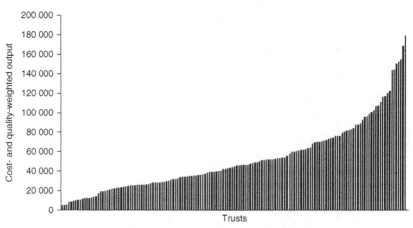

obtained from the NHS Information Centre (that is, covering doctors,
nursing and other medical staff). We take into account here only the
medical staff devoted to patient care, that is, the total number of medical
staff, but *excluding* staff members on honorary contracts. These contracts
are NHS appointments for senior academics in medical research (at the
level of senior lecturer or professor) to provide them with the opportunity to be affiliated with a hospital while still allowing them to focus on
their research work. In most published analyses this important issue has
not been picked up. However, we judged that these doctor-researchers
should be excluded from the total number of relevant medical staff,
because they are not directly responsible for the delivery of health service
outputs to patients. Our measure of inputs has most impact on improving
the productivity data for those historically important teaching hospitals
that are also major centres of medical research. Overall *labour productivity* was obtained by dividing the total cost- and quality-adjusted output
measure (as defined above) by the level of medical staff inputs for each
trust.

Specifying Independent Variables

There are a large number of possible influences upon the productivity of
hospital services. In light of the discussion in section 8.1, Box 8.1 itemizes
one potential set of influences. However, it is not easy to envisage being
able to easily operationalize variables for many of these influences. It

---

BOX 8.1   POSSIBLE MAIN INFLUENCES UPON
HOSPITALS' PRODUCTIVITY

Numbers of medical and non-medical staff
Training and morale of medical staff
Training and morale of non-medical staff
Quality of medical staff leadership and clinical audit
Professional culture of medical staff, especially awareness and adoption of
innovations
Research and development
Modernity and suitability of hospital built estate
Extent and modernity of medical equipment
Organization of patient work flows
Other aspects of quality of services
Top organizational leadership
Overall organizational culture
Quality of management
ICT use

---

should be apparent here that the potential influence of both the independent variables we focus on, namely management quality and innovativeness, and hospitals' ICT use, are not likely to have large effects on overall hospital productivity. So it is important to keep the limited maximum potential roles of management and ICTs in a clear perspective. The contributions that they make to shaping hospital productivity are likely to be small and perhaps rather subtle. We draw two implications.

First, it is important to control as far as possible for other influences that might affect trust-level productivity, such as most of those listed in Box 8.1. From extensive exploratory data analysis of bivariate relationships with cost- and quality-weighted hospital productivity, we constructed some key dummy variables that assume a value of one whenever a trust falls in any of these categories. These cover: specialist hospitals, those focusing on a limited range of patient conditions; teaching hospitals, which are the largest, most complex and most professionally important ones; and trusts located in London, where special historical conditions apply to many of the largest hospitals. This is also a region where the labour market conditions for securing full-time nurses are especially unfavourable and there is a strong dependence on agency and part-time nurses, with apparently strong adverse effects on hospital mortality rates, after controlling for many other factors (Hall et al., 2008).

Second, following on from Chapter 7, it is especially important to find indicators of the independent variables that we wish to focus on here that do not risk importing elements of other potential causal influences. In particular we are most interested in those aspects of management quality and innovativeness and ICT use that can be measured outside immediate medical treatment contexts, where professional influences are likely to prevail, and we need to control for staff training variables separately – which luckily is feasible to do from existing data.

To create a 'general training' variable, we chose a group of specific training-related variables from the NHS Staff Survey 2008. The 'general training' variable is therefore an average of the following variables' scores for the proportion (percentage) of staff responding:

- that they 'attended taught courses in the last 12 months provided or paid by the trust';
- that they had 'job training in the last 12 months provided or paid by the trust';
- that they 'had a mentor in the last 12 months'; and
- that they 'shadowed someone in the last 12 months'.

We transformed these data into scores from 1 to 6, according to the number of standard deviations from the mean of the originally measured variables. In this sense, we assigned 1 if the value fell more than 1 standard deviation below the mean, 2 if the value fell between 1 and 0.5 standard deviations below the mean, 3 if the value fell between 0.5 and 0 standard deviations below the mean, and we allocated scores 4 to 6 in the same manner for scores above the mean.

To measure both the quality and nature of management practices in hospitals, and how far hospitals used ICT, we utilized a web-census technique discussed in section 7.3 in Chapter 7. We surveyed each of the 153 trusts' websites for multiple indicators that were scored 1 when present or 0 when absent. Scores were then cumulated into aggregate indicators of management practices and of ICT use.

To measure management quality and innovativeness non-reactively we developed a large set of 41 indicators grouped into seven categories bearing on the generic management approach used by hospital trusts and measured via their websites. These covered essentially:

- the provision of information about transactions and treatment interactions to patients;
- patient empowerment features;
- outreach information for the local community;

- trust accountability and ethos;
- performance tracking and standard settings;
- managing and recruiting talent; and
- human resource development practices.

Table 8.5 provides a full list of the 41 indicators involved. We used such a large number of elements here because overall management quality and innovativeness is a complex construct, for which there are no simple or decisive online indications of good or bad practice. Hence a cumulative score across a large number of small and partial indicators provides the most feasible and robust solution.

Assessing ICT use in hospital trusts is somewhat easier, since there are better online indications of good or bad practice, and hence we needed a shorter list of 18 indicators. However, in addition we looked for indicators that are remote from the management list and are specific to the ICT area. They fall into four different dimensions covering:

- the provision of online information and documentation (which is a strong indicator of website development);
- good practice on website features;
- web usability; and
- ICT innovations.

Table 8.6 (on page 254) provides a complete list of these indicators.

8.3   ANALYSIS AND RESULTS

The descriptive statistics for the dependent and independent variables included are given in Table 8.7.

The results suggest a mostly unskewed pattern for the continuous variables. There is an understandably more skewed pattern for the dummy control variables but this is not a problem because we do not expect (or need) trusts to be normally distributed across these control covariates.

We estimated ordinary least squares (OLS) regression models using labour productivity as the dependent variable. To show the goodness of fit of our cost and quality productivity measure, we estimated one model first using only the cost-adjusted labour productivity as the dependent variable (Model 1). Then we estimated four additional models (Models 2 to 5) in which we also incorporated a quality adjustment to our output measure and hence to our labour productivity measure. As explained before, we

Table 8.5 *The composition of the management practices index*

Dimension	Indicator	Management Practices
Patient interaction information	1	Hospital site links to NHS Direct website
	2	Information on how to cancel appointments is provided
	3	Accessibility maps/plans are available
	4	Information about visiting hours is provided
	5	Links to individual hospitals are provided
	6	Links are given to local Primary Care Trusts (PCTs) in the area
Patient empowerment features	7	A Freedom of Information link is present on the home page
	8	Patient Relationship Management is explained online
	9	A name or picture is available for the Caldicott Guardian[a]
	10	Trust phone lists are provided
Outreach information for local community	11	There is a link to at least one local hospital charity
	12	The background and history of the trust is described
	13	Links are given to open events organized by the trust
	14	Links are given to hospitals' services
	15	Links are given to the communications team
	16	News on each hospital in the trust is available on the site
	17	Information is given on trust's new building projects
	18	Links to trust press releases are available
Trust accountability and ethos	19	An organogram or another indication of the trust's structure is provided
	20	Details of past and future trust meetings are provided
	21	The agenda for the next trust meeting is provided
	22	Biographies of trust directors provided
	23	Information is given on the trust's overall goals
	24	Information is given on the trust's values
Performance tracking/ standards	25	Links to standards or to performance documents/ information are present
	26	The trust's annual audit letter is available
	27	The Hygiene Code inspection report is available
	28	Recent developments at the trust are shown
	29	Information about the Care Quality Commission is given

Table 8.5   (continued)

Dimension	Indicator	Management Practices
	30	Infection rates are available
	31	Link to Annual Health Check is present
	32	Link to Care Quality Commission summary statistics on the trust is given
Managing and recruiting talent	33	Information is available online on pay scales in the trust
	34	Information on the benefits of working in the trust is given
	35	Programmes or placements for medical students are available online
	36	Advice for staff moving to the area is given
	37	Volunteering possibilities are present and explained
	38	The trust says that it has a flexible approach to part-time working
Human resource development	39	Links to learning possibilities for non-medical staff (nurses, carers, etc.) are provided
	40	There is a dedicated research and development section or link
	41	A Centre for Postgraduate Professional Education exists in the trust

Note: a.   Senior persons responsible for protecting the confidentiality of patient and service-user information and enabling appropriate information-sharing.

intended to estimate models in which the quality adjustment for the output and labour productivity measure was at 25, 50 and 75 per cent levels in between a full cost and a full cost and quality adjustment (Models 2 to 4). Model 5 uses our full cost- and quality-adjusted labour productivity model. The models also include an interaction term between our indices for ICT use and management practices. This helps to check in particular on the expectation in the literature that the effect of each of these variables on productivity is conditional on the values assumed by the other variable in the interaction term.

Table 8.8 shows the results of our models. The goodness of fit of the regression model improves gradually as the cost- and quality-weighting increases (as shown in the results for the different intermediate scenarios). The data for Model 1 demonstrate that amongst our control variables only that for hospitals' location becomes significant – trusts outside London show an increase of more than 71 points in the cost-weighted productivity measure, compared to those in the capital. Overall, Model

Table 8.6   The composition of the ICT use index

Dimension	Indicator	IT Measures
Online information/ documentation	1	Information on IT expenditure for the current (or past) years provided
	2	IT strategy documentation is available online
	3	Document reading software is available online
	4	Annual Report and Trust Accounts are available online
Good practice on website features	5	Website readability features are present
	6	Site map is provided
	7	Website comment box is available
	8	Web pages are dated
	9	Web pages are recently updated
	10	Web accessibility link is provided
Web usability	11	Less than seven items in each section's menu
	12	There are not more than 15 items in each section's menu
	13	Website search engine works effectively to find materials
	14	Pop-up web survey is provided
IT innovations	15	Web 2.0 features (videos, podcasts, etc.) are present
	16	A system for patients to manage their appointments is available or promised
	17	Information on waiting times is provided online
	18	Online donations to hospital charity are possible

Table 8.7   Descriptive statistics for the variables employed in the analysis

Variable	N	Mean	SD	Min.	Max.
Cost-weighted productivity	166	318.7	144.4	105	1456.7
Cost- and quality-weighted productivity	153	124.9	108.2	13.9	818.4
Cost- and quality-weighted productivity 75%	153	174.5	112.9	41.1	978.6
Cost- and quality-weighted productivity 50%	153	224.3	121.8	62.3	1138.8
Cost- and quality-weighted productivity 25%	153	274.1	133.8	83.7	1297.4
Management practices	166	23.8	4.6	13	36
IT use	166	8.8	2.4	4	16
Interaction term (IT × management practices)	166	237.2	82.8	78	504
General training	160	3.5	0.9	1	6
London	166	0.17	0.38	0	1
Teaching	166	0.04	0.21	0	1
Specialist	166	0.09	0.29	0	1

Table 8.8   OLS estimates on labour productivity

Independent Variable	Model 1 Cost-adjusted Labour Productivity	Model 2 Cost- and Quality-adjusted Productivity (quality at 25%)	Model 3 Cost- and Quality-adjusted Productivity (quality at 50%)	Model 4 Cost and Quality-adjusted Productivity (quality at 75%)	Model 5 Full Cost-and Quality-adjusted Labour Productivity
ICT use	27.15	32.51	33.57*	34.64*	35.709**
	(24.9)	(23.51)	(21.25)	(18.51)	(18.414)
Management	11.10	13.03	12.97	12.92*	12.867*
practices	(10.45)	(8.91)	(8.96)	(8.23)	(7.767)
ICT ×	−1.33	−1.54*	−1.55*	−1.56**	−1.58**
management	(1.03)	(0.97)	(0.88)	(0.811)	(0.766)
General	6.62	11.07	11.44	11.81	12.187
training	(11.63)	(11.32)	(10.23)	(8.39)	(8.869)
Specialist	−6.57	42.44	64.84*	87.23**	108.634***
	(38.8)	(41.07)	(37.15)	(34.11)	(32.184)
Teaching	−53.57	−18.13	4.28	26.75	48.229
	(65.19)	(64.71)	(58.54)	(53.73)	(50.709)
London	−71.86**	−78.82**	−78.98**	−80.13***	−80.287***
	(35.3)	(34.11)	(30.86)	(28.33)	(26.733)
R^2	0.09	0.10	0.11	0.13	0.16
N	160	147	147	147	147

Note: Standard errors in parentheses. * Significant at 10%; ** significant at 5%; *** significant at 1% (two-tailed).

1 explains just 9 per cent of the variation in the dependent variable, while Model 5, with a full cost and quality adjustment, explains around 15 per cent of the variation in the dependent variable. The results for Models 2 to 5 confirm that they fit the data better, with increasing R^2 levels compared to Model 1. It is also worth noting that as the cost- and quality-weighting increases, more coefficients become significant. These results also confirm the previous finding in Model 1 that London trusts are significantly less productive than those located outside the capital, while specialist trusts are also significantly more productive than generalist ones.

Three key explanations seem feasible here and will need further research to unpick. First, many Inner London or specialist hospitals are generally regarded by patients and GPs as the best in the country. Accordingly they may attract significantly more complex cases, whose treatment requires longer interventions – reducing the London hospitals' productivity performance on our measures. In other words there may be a substantial and unmeasured quality difference between London and non-London trusts in the nature of the treatments involved. Second, London trusts' productivity may be adversely affected by an inability to attract nursing staff, given the capitals' higher costs of living and property prices, which previous research has linked to a greater use of agency nurses and temporary staff, with apparently adverse consequences for patient mortality and other factors (Hall et al., 2008).

Across Models 2 to 5 the different coefficients become more significant as the cost- and quality-weighting increases. For the best fitting model, Model 5, the coefficients for the interaction term and its components are all significant. However, an important issue that arises when utilizing interaction terms in regression analysis is that the interpretation of the interaction term and its components cannot be made individually – because the effect of one component of the interaction term on the outcome is conditional on the value of the other component. As Brambor et al. (2006) clearly explain, when the results are listed for the coefficients of an interaction term like ICT and management here, they represent the effect of each variable when the other one is set to zero. In this sense, looking at Model 5 in Table 8.8, we can say that a unit increase in ICT use leads to an increase in productivity of 35.7 points, but only when the management index is zero. Likewise, an increase of one unit in our measure of management index leads to a productivity increase of 12 points, but only when our ICT index is zero. In real life, none of our trusts received a score of zero for either the ICT or management indices – so that neither of these effects is likely to be observable in our data.

So the results in Models 2 to 5 for the interaction term only tell us that when our ICT and management practices indices increase at the same time, then there is a negative and statistically significant effect on productivity. However, what these results still do not tell us is how ICT affects productivity given the specific and real values observed for the management index and, vice versa, how the management index affects productivity given the specific and real values of ICT. These are much more important and realistic situations for which a clear answer is needed. Graphical interpretation can help us to elucidate such interpretations. Figure 8.4 below shows the conditional effects of IT on productivity given the full range of values for our management index. These illustrations were created upon the results with our cost- and quality-adjustments fully implemented (i.e., at the 100 per cent level), as in Model 5.

Figure 8.4 clearly shows that the positive effect of ICT on productivity decreases as our management practices index increases. Thus, for trusts with management scores of more than 17 (that is, nine-tenths of all trusts), the effect of ICT on productivity becomes indistinguishable from zero.

Figure 8.4   The conditional effects of hospital trust IT given management practices

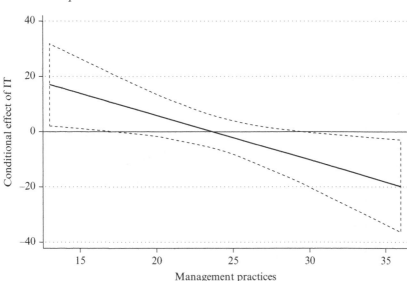

Note: The dashed line area represents limits the upper and lower 90% confidence intervals. The marginal effects and standard errors used for this figure were calculated according to results from Model 2.

Putting this another way, the results seem to indicate that in trusts with low to medium-low scores on our management index (comprising 11 per cent in our dataset) good ICT use can significantly help to increase productivity. However, our results also seem to suggest that as trusts become better managed so the pay-offs from using better ICT practices diminish. In fact, Figure 8.4 shows that in trusts with a management index score of 28 or more (comprising a sixth of the whole dataset) greater or more improved ICT use *negatively* affects productivity levels.

As mentioned before, it is also possible to model how management affects productivity given specific values of IT. Figure 8.5 shows the conditional effect of our management practices index on productivity given the full range of values of IT. The results here show that the effect of management on productivity is indistinguishable from zero for trusts with low and medium-low levels of ICT use. However, for trusts with an ICT use score equal to or higher than 11 (a condition affecting 23 per cent of the trusts) the effect of increasing scores on the management practices index on productivity is negative. We can interpret this result as suggesting that good management practices (as captured by our index) may not help to boost

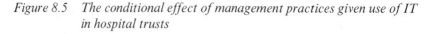

Figure 8.5   The conditional effect of management practices given use of IT in hospital trusts

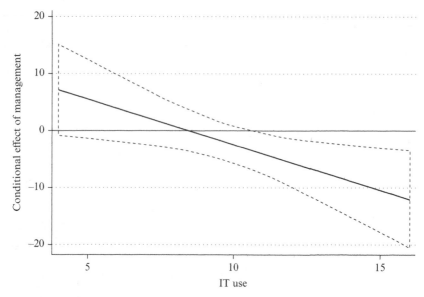

Note: The dashed line area limits the upper and lower 90% confidence intervals. The marginal effects and standard errors used for this figure were calculated according to results from Model 2.

productivity once trusts already have a well-developed focus on employing modern ICTs productively

Comparative Discussion

Our core analysis was undertaken using data available in mid-2009 and revised in 2010. In considering the results above, we are fortunate to be able to compare them to a closely parallel analysis of hospital productivity in England carried out by an in-house economist at the National Audit Office, and discussed with the Department of Health (NAO, 2010d, 2010e and 2010f). This analysis used a large but different set of independent variables, dominated by multiple financial performance indicators, some patient-mix data, extensive data on hospital estates and the numbers of different staff, plus other official statistics. The dependent variable was also different, namely a 'reference cost index' showing how much it cost hospital X to treat its patients, divided by the average cost of all English hospitals for the same case mix of patients. (There were also some adjustments for additional 'market forces factors', to allow for some regions of England being more expensive than others.) The dependent variable used by NAO was not quality-weighted. Nor did the dataset include anything resembling our staff training variables or indices for hospital management or ICT use. However, the NAO analysis was repeated using data from three different financial years, which is an improvement on our dataset.

The proportion of variance explained in the NAO analysis ranged from 27 to 36 per cent in a series of step-wise models (once specialist trusts were excluded, which previously raised the variance explained to higher levels). But the results here showed great variability in the variables that were assigned significance from one year to the next – strongly suggesting that the model was rather arbitrarily including variables for mathematical but not substantive reasons. (Step-wise regression enters variables in the order of their mathematical effects, and not a theoretically defined order.) Only two variables were present in all three year-models – namely the percentage of hospital floor area occupied (capturing trusts with surplus accommodation, often old premises of less functionality), and the operating surplus or deficit of trusts as a percentage of their total income (capturing how strong their financial management was). Trusts performing well here also had higher productivity. Three variables were present in two of the models – the trust's percentage bed occupancy (a measure of either effective management or perhaps levels of demand), and a dummy variable for large acute hospitals were both associated with higher productivity. The proportion of emergency to non-emergency admissions (i.e the rate of non-planned treatments) was negatively associated with productivity (in two models). Other variables assigned significance in one of the year-models included different staffing number and staffing ratio variables, more indicators of hospital size and type, and raw waiting lists times.

The NAO analysis then tried using alternative hierarchical models, where a more restricted set of explanatory variables were entered in the following order, said to be based on theory reasons: financial management; percentage of space occupied; percentage of emergency admissions (the main case-mix variable); total staff per bed; the turnover rate of doctors in the hospital; the percentage bed occupancy; and measures of hospital size and type. With this approach the three year-models here explained from 28 to 33 per cent of the variance and only three variables appeared in all of them – two being indicators of hospitals in a better financial state, and the last being the proportion of beds occupied. Three variables were present in two of the models – a dummy for acute teaching trusts was positively associated with productivity levels; meanwhile the total staff per bed ratio and the proportion of emergency admissions were negatively associated

*Table 8.9   NAO estimates of the savings that would be achieved if all
hospitals in England performed as well as the top 25 per cent of
hospitals, across four main variables*

Variable	2006–07	2007–08	2008–09	Average Values Included in the Main Report
Bed occupancy	760	1067	386	633
Total staff per bed	832		896	510
Emergency admissions	472	668		259
Occupied floor space	525			175
Total variables above	2589	1735	1282	1577

Note: £000s per year.

Source: NAO (2010d, p. 21).

with productivity. The percentage of space occupied was present in one
model. None of the other variables made the cut.

Based on these last regression results, the NAO analysis estimated that
if all the hospitals performed at the level of the top 25 per cent of hospitals,
the NHS could save an average of £1.6 billion a year. However, the actual
numbers involved varied strongly from one year to the next, as Table 8.9
demonstrates (in addition, the 95 per cent confidence intervals for each
variable were very wide in every year).

There are evident problems here in moving from the regression analysis
to policy implications because of a more general difficulty arising from the
changing presence of variables in different year-models in the NAO analysis. When this phenomenon occurs in regression analysis it is normally a
symptom either of problems in the variable specification, or of an incomplete variable set being present that omits some important causal factors.
In such situations regression models can rather randomly tend to include
and assign significance to whichever variable happens to do most work in
capturing part of the explanatory effect of the omitted variables.

Nonetheless it seems likely on both theoretical and intuitive grounds
that these four variables are indeed associated with productivity variations. The NAO main report points out some reasons why their chosen
variables may influence productivity in a direct way:

- Higher bed occupancy lowers costs by using staffed facilities more
  intensively.
- Managing hospital care as effectively with fewer total staff per bed
  will also be cheaper.

- Reducing the share of emergency admissions implies more planned care happens, and less really acute care, which is much more expensive to undertake. Planned care is also likely to be better organized, with less risk of unintentional resource waste than emergency care.
- Those trusts using more of the building floor space that they occupy will pay less in rents.

But different interpretations are clearly feasible. A general 'managerialist' argument might well legitimately argue that each of the variables above should actually be interpreted as a different indication of the same underlying phenomenon, namely that better managed trusts have higher productivity. Specific alternate interpretations of some of the variables are also feasible, for example, that the emergency admissions variable responds to other care-mix variations not captured by the analysis.

Conclusions

This research has sought to develop an organizationally focused approach to productivity analysis. We undertook a relatively ambitious test of how the adoption of modernized management good practice and improved use of ICT affect productivity across NHS acute trusts. This area is certain to generate more research over the next few years, given its salience in political, service delivery and financial terms. Our approach is innovative in employing unobtrusive and non-reactive measures for gauging ICT and management practices, drawn from a comprehensive web-census of all acute healthcare trusts in England. To our knowledge, this is the first time that such measures have been used in an empirical productivity study and the approach yields interesting insights. The results are broadly consistent with previous survey-based analysis of management influences reviewed in Chapter 7 but they differ in detail and specificity. We would argue this is because using non-reactive measures removes the 'public relations' and 'spin' effects that are inherent in survey-based and other forms of 'reactive' approaches.

Our research also innovated in implementing an extended version of quality measurement at the trust level, to safeguard against the risks of perverse effects when comparing across decentralized units where large variations in quality are known to exist, and following current best practice in public sector productivity measurement. The results of our quantitative analysis yielded interesting results. On the one hand, in common with earlier work, we found that trusts in the London area are consistently less productive than those in the rest of the country. Initially, we believe that this may reflect an adverse selection of more serious patient cases (from the point of view of London trusts), reflecting patients' and GPs' view that trusts in the London area generally are more expert and have better resources to manage complex interventions that require longer periods of care. In addition, Primary Care Trusts may only have been willing to pay the higher costs of London hospitals for a case mix that is on average less favourable for speedy completion of treatment. These effects may make London hospitals appear less productive, but chiefly because we have an untapped case-complexity dimension. Alternatively, or as well, the London results may show more difficulty in securing high-quality nursing and other staff in the region, due to higher housing and living costs and so on. In addition, our results also show that specialist trusts are more productive than the rest, which may reflect these trusts' advantage over general hospitals that stems from dealing only with specific (mainly planned) kinds of interventions, for which their staff are well trained and prepared, and adequate in numbers.

More substantively, our quantitative analysis sheds new light on the effects of management practices and ICT on productivity. Modelling the conditional effects of IT on productivity for the full range of values of our management index we found that the effect of more or better ICT on hospital productivity is positive and significant – but only for trusts with a low and medium-low levels scores on the management index. The pay-offs of good ICT use on productivity levels appear to be higher for poorly managed trusts. However, the same result also shows that the effect of more extensive ICT development on productivity may actually be negative for trusts with medium-high or high levels of management. This may suggest that as trusts become more complex, it is possible for managements to develop an over-focus on using ICTs that may not be beneficial for yielding high productivity levels.

Finally, modelling the conditional effects of management practices on productivity for the full range of values of our ICT variable shows that the effect of our management index is negative on productivity for trusts with medium-high and high levels of ICT use. This result confirms our previous interpretation that once trusts are reasonably well managed an excessive focus on ICT use may not be a good strategy for seeking to achieve sustained productivity levels.

All the results presented here are preliminary and it is important to bear in mind both that there are many other possible influences on trusts' productivity performances that have not yet been explored and that quality-adjusted productivity itself is just one of the areas to look at when evaluating how NHS trusts employ resources efficiently and innovate. Much work remains to be done on the further development of control variables in this analysis, and on the specification of quality-weighting and

of our management practices and ICT development indicators and aggregate indices. Nonetheless, this work already provides some useful insights
for practitioners in the health area and contributes by providing new and
fresh evidence for the recent public sector productivity literature that has
highlighted the interactive effects of new technologies and management
on productivity (Garicano and Heaton, 2010). In addition, by employing non-obtrusive measures to capture the role of ICT and management
practices, this research shows the potential of applying such an approach
to other areas in the public sector.

CHAPTER ANNEX ACUTE HEALTHCARE TRUSTS INCLUDED IN OUR DATABASE, AND SOME DATA CONSTRAINTS

Acute Trust Name	Number of Hospitals
Aintree University Hospitals NHS Foundation Trust	2
Airedale NHS Trust	1
Alder Hey Children's NHS Foundation Trust	2
Ashford and St Peter's Hospitals NHS Trust	2
Barking, Havering and Redbridge University Hospitals NHS Trust	2
Barnet and Chase Farm Hospitals NHS Trust	3
Barnsley Hospital NHS Foundation Trust	1
Barts and the London NHS Trust	3
Basildon and Thurrock University Hospitals NHS Foundation Trust	3
Basingstoke and North Hampshire NHS Foundation Trust	1
Bedford Hospital NHS Trust	2
Birmingham Children's Hospital NHS Foundation Trust	1
Birmingham Women's NHS Foundation Trust	1
Blackpool, Fylde and Wyre Hospitals NHS Foundation Trust	5
Bradford Teaching Hospitals NHS Foundation Trust	2
Brighton and Sussex University Hospitals NHS Trust	5
Bromley Hospitals NHS Trust	4
Buckinghamshire Hospitals NHS Trust	3
Burton Hospitals NHS Foundation Trust	1
Calderdale and Huddersfield NHS Foundation Trust	3
Cambridge University Hospitals NHS Foundation Trust	5
Central Manchester University Hospitals NHS Foundation Trust	5
Chelsea and Westminster Hospital NHS Foundation Trust	1
Chesterfield Royal Hospital NHS Foundation Trust	2
City Hospitals Sunderland NHS Foundation Trust	3
Clatterbridge Centre for Oncology NHS Foundation Trust	1
Colchester Hospital University NHS Foundation Trust	4
Countess of Chester Hospital NHS Foundation Trust	2
County Durham and Darlington NHS Foundation Trust	6
Dartford and Gravesham NHS Trust	2
Derby Hospitals NHS Foundation Trust	4
Doncaster and Bassetlaw Hospitals NHS Foundation Trust	5
Dorset County Hospital NHS Foundation Trust	2
Ealing Hospital NHS Trust	1
East and North Hertfordshire NHS Trust	4
East Cheshire NHS Trust	4
East Kent Hospitals University NHS Foundation Trust	8

Acute Trust Name	Number of Hospitals
East Lancashire Hospitals NHS Trust	4
East Sussex Hospitals NHS Trust	4
Epsom and St Helier University Hospitals NHS Trust	5
Frimley Park Hospital NHS Foundation Trust	2
Gateshead Health NHS Foundation Trust	3
George Eliot Hospital NHS Trust	1
Gloucestershire Hospitals NHS Foundation Trust	6
Great Ormond Street Hospital for Children NHS Trust	1
Great Western Hospitals NHS Foundation Trust	5
Guy's and St Thomas' NHS Foundation Trust	2
Harrogate and District NHS Foundation Trust	3
Heart of England NHS Foundation Trust	3
Heatherwood and Wexham Park Hospitals NHS Foundation Trust	5
Hereford Hospitals NHS Trust	1
Hinchingbrooke Health Care NHS Trust	2
Homerton University Hospital NHS Foundation Trust	2
Hull and East Yorkshire Hospitals NHS Trust	4
Imperial College Healthcare NHS Trust	5
Ipswich Hospital NHS Trust	2
Isle of Wight NHS PCT	1
James Paget University Hospitals NHS Foundation Trust	3
Kettering General Hospital NHS Foundation Trust	2
King's College Hospital NHS Foundation Trust	1
Kingston Hospital NHS Trust	1
Lancashire Teaching Hospitals NHS Foundation Trust	2
Leeds Teaching Hospitals NHS Trust	5
Liverpool Heart and Chest Hospital NHS Trust	1
Liverpool Women's NHS Foundation Trust	1
Luton and Dunstable Hospital NHS Foundation Trust	1
Maidstone and Tunbridge Wells NHS Trust	7
Mayday Healthcare NHS Trust	2
Medway NHS Foundation Trust	5
Mid Cheshire Hospitals NHS Foundation Trust	2
Mid Essex Hospital Services NHS Trust	6
Mid Staffordshire NHS Foundation Trust	2
Mid Yorkshire Hospitals NHS Trust	4
Milton Keynes Hospital NHS Foundation Trust	1
Moorfields Eye Hospital NHS Foundation Trust	1
Newham University Hospital NHS Trust	2
Norfolk and Norwich University Hospitals NHS Foundation Trust	2
North Bristol NHS Trust	5
North Cumbria University Hospitals NHS Trust	6
North Middlesex University Hospital NHS Trust	1

Acute Trust Name	Number of Hospitals
North Tees and Hartlepool NHS Foundation Trust	3
North West London Hospitals NHS Trust	4
Northampton General Hospital NHS Trust	1
Northern Devon Healthcare NHS Trust	5
Northern Lincolnshire and Goole Hospitals NHS Foundation Trust	5
Northumbria Healthcare NHS Foundation Trust	7
Nottingham University Hospitals NHS Trust	2
Nuffield Orthopaedic Centre NHS Trust	1
Oxford Radcliffe Hospitals NHS Trust	5
Papworth Hospital NHS Foundation Trust	1
Pennine Acute Hospitals NHS Trust	5
Peterborough and Stamford Hospitals NHS Foundation Trust	4
Plymouth Hospitals NHS Trust	5
Poole Hospital NHS Foundation Trust	1
Portsmouth Hospitals NHS Trust	4
Queen Elizabeth Hospital NHS Trust	1
Queen Mary's Sidcup NHS Trust	2
Queen Victoria Hospital NHS Foundation Trust	2
Robert Jones and Agnes Hunt Orthopaedic and District Hospital NHS Trust	1
Royal Berkshire NHS Foundation Trust	4
Royal Bolton Hospital NHS Foundation Trust	1
Royal Brompton and Harefield NHS Trust	2
Royal Cornwall Hospitals NHS Trust	3
Royal Devon and Exeter NHS Foundation Trust	5
Royal Free Hampstead NHS Trust	5
Royal Liverpool and Broadgreen University Hospitals NHS Trust	5
Royal National Hospital For Rheumatic Diseases NHS Foundation Trust	5
Royal National Orthopaedic Hospital NHS Trust	2
Royal Surrey County Hospital NHS Trust	3
Royal United Hospital Bath NHS Trust	5
Royal West Sussex NHS Trust	5
Salford Royal NHS Foundation Trust	1
Salisbury NHS Foundation Trust	1
Sandwell and West Birmingham Hospitals NHS Trust	5
Scarborough and North East Yorkshire Health Care NHS Trust	4
Sheffield Children's NHS Foundation Trust	2
Sheffield Teaching Hospitals NHS Foundation Trust	4
Sherwood Forest Hospitals NHS Foundation Trust	4
Shrewsbury and Telford Hospital NHS Trust	4
South Devon Healthcare NHS Foundation Trust	1

Acute Trust Name	Number of Hospitals
South Downs Health NHS Trust	1
South Tees Hospitals NHS Trust	2
South Tyneside NHS Foundation Trust	3
South Warwickshire General Hospitals NHS Trust	2
Southampton University Hospitals NHS Trust	2
Southend University Hospital NHS Foundation Trust	1
Southport and Ormskirk Hospital NHS Trust	2
St George's Healthcare NHS Trust	3
St Helens and Knowsley Hospitals NHS Trust	2
Stockport NHS Foundation Trust	2
Surrey and Sussex Healthcare NHS Trust	4
Tameside Hospital NHS Foundation Trust	1
Taunton and Somerset NHS Foundation Trust	1
The Christie NHS Foundation Trust	1
The Dudley Group of Hospitals NHS Foundation Trust	3
The Hillingdon Hospital NHS Trust	2
The Lewisham Hospital NHS Trust	1
The Newcastle Upon Tyne Hospitals NHS Foundation Trust	5
The Princess Alexandra Hospital NHS Trust	3
The Queen Elizabeth Hospital King's Lynn NHS Trust	1
The Rotherham NHS Foundation Trust	1
The Royal Bournemouth and Christchurch Hospitals NHS Foundation Trust	3
The Royal Marsden NHS Foundation Trust	2
The Royal Orthopaedic Hospital NHS Foundation Trust	1
The Royal Wolverhampton Hospitals NHS Trust	1
The Whittington Hospital NHS Trust	1
Trafford Healthcare NHS Trust	3
United Lincolnshire Hospitals NHS Trust	5
University College London Hospitals NHS Foundation Trust	5
University Hospital Birmingham NHS Foundation Trust	2
University Hospital of North Staffordshire NHS Trust	1
University Hospital of South Manchester NHS Foundation Trust	2
University Hospitals Bristol NHS Foundation Trust	5
University Hospitals Coventry and Warwickshire NHS Trust	2
University Hospitals of Leicester NHS Trust	3
University Hospitals of Morecambe Bay NHS Trust	4
Walsall Hospitals NHS Trust	1
Walton Centre For Neurology and Neurosurgery NHS Trust	1
Warrington and Halton Hospitals NHS Foundation Trust	2
West Hertfordshire Hospitals NHS Trust	3
West Middlesex University Hospital NHS Trust	1
West Suffolk Hospitals NHS Trust	1

Acute Trust Name	Number of Hospitals
Weston Area Health NHS Trust	2
Whipps Cross University Hospital NHS Trust	2
Winchester and Eastleigh Healthcare NHS Trust	3
Wirral University Teaching Hospital NHS Foundation Trust	3
Worcestershire Acute Hospitals NHS Trust	4
Worthing and Southlands Hospitals NHS Trust	3
Wrightington, Wigan and Leigh NHS Foundation Trust	4
Yeovil District Hospital NHS Foundation Trust	1
York Hospitals NHS Foundation Trust	4

Other Data Constraints

We originally collected data on 171 trusts, but eight trusts merged within our study period to form four new trusts, bringing the overall number down to 167. Good Hope Hospital NHS Trust and Birmingham Heartlands and Solihull NHS Trust merged into the new Heart of England NHS Foundation Trust; Hammersmith Hospitals NHS Trust and St Mary's NHS Trust merged into the new Imperial NHS Trust; Bromley Hospitals NHS Trust, Queen Elizabeth Hospital NHS Trust and Queen Mary's Sidcup NHS Trust merged into the new South London Healthcare Trust; Worthing and Southlands Hospitals NHS Trust and Royal West Sussex NHS Trust merged into the new Western Sussex Hospitals NHS Trust.

Fifteen trusts changed their names in our study period: Cardiothoracic Centre – Liverpool NHS Trust is now called Liverpool Heart and Chest Hospital NHS Trust; North Cheshire Hospitals NHS Trust is now called Warrington and Halton Hospitals NHS Foundation Trust; Royal Liverpool Children's NHS Trust is now called Alder Hey Children's NHS Foundation Trust; South Manchester University Hospitals NHS Trust is now called University Hospital of South Manchester NHS Foundation Trust; Chesterfield and North Derbyshire Royal Hospital NHS Trust is now called Chesterfield Royal Hospitals NHS Trust; Nottingham City Hospital NHS Trust is now called Nottingham University Hospitals NHS Trust; Southern Derbyshire Acute Hospitals NHS Trust is now called Derby Hospitals NHS Foundation Trust; Mid Staffordshire General Hospitals NHS Trust is now called Mid Staffordshire NHS Foundation Trust; North Staffordshire Hospital NHS Trust is now called University Hospital of North Staffordshire NHS Trust; North Hampshire Hospitals NHS Trust is now called Basingstoke and North Hampshire NHS Foundation Trust; Royal Berkshire and Battle Hospitals NHS Trust is now called Royal Berkshire NHS Foundation Trust; Royal National Hospital for Rheumatic Diseases NHS Trust is now called Bath Royal National Hospital for Rheumatic Diseases; Swindon and Marlborough NHS Trust is now called Great Western Hospitals NHS Trust; East Somerset NHS Trust is now called Yeovil District Hospital NHS Foundation Trust; Taunton and Somerset NHS Trust is now called Musgrove Park Hospital. One more body, the Isle of Wight Trust, was removed from the study because it is a mixed body that is primarily a Primary Care Trust.

For 13 further trusts we could not obtain appropriate data on output quality. These trusts are: Plymouth Hospital NHS Trust, Weston Area Health NHS Trust, Princess Alexandra Hospital NHS Trust and United Lincolnshire Hospital NHS Trust for which the 'Complaints Index' is 0. Then, Robert Jones and Agnes Hunt Orthopaedic and District Hospital and Birmingham Children's Hospital NHS Trust for which 'Mean Waiting Time' is 0. Finally for Royal Bournemouth and Christchurch Hospital, Poole Hospital NHS Trust, Bath Royal National Hospital for Rheumatic Disease, Royal Berkshire NHS Foundation Trust, King's College NHS Trust, Homerton University Hospital NHS Trust and Sheffield Children's NHS Foundation Trust no quality-adjusted output measure could be developed because there are no data available about complaints handling.

PART III

Sustainable increases in productivity

9. Embracing digital change and enhancing organizational learning

Improving productivity in government services is like dieting. (Almost) all of us agree that it would be a good thing to do. But there are a baffling range of theoretically (yet vaguely) plausible suggestions for changes, none of which are proven to work and few of which are as easy to implement as their proponents proclaim (McKinsey, 2011a). In the short term dramatic results can sometimes be achieved, but often in temporary ways that cannot be maintained so that performance quickly slips back into the old mould. Making an approach work for long enough to achieve worthwhile results is far harder than it looks. And shifting government organizations onto a new and sustainable pathway of continuous productivity improvements is the hardest task of all.

Yet there are also many factors that work in favour of improvement, of which we review two of the most fundamental in this chapter – digital changes and the push for organizational learning. First, we begin by clarifying the strong modern links between productivity and 'digital era governance', especially the factors involved in countering a prevalent bureaucratic conservatism about adopting or using new technologies. The challenge of rapid and disruptive changes towards using digital technologies has most dramatically worked out in the IT, media and cultural industries in the period since 1995, with radical consequences for once giant companies (like Kodak) and the recording industry. Yet up to now the digital wave has only lapped at the edges of government bureaucracies and their business processes, in forms like e-government initiatives (Kim et al., 2007; Dunleavy et al., 2008, pp. 105–9; Margetts et al., 2008). Even so we review how the analyses in Chapters 3 to 6 especially show that responses to contemporary technology shifts have already become central to productivity advances or stagnation across most areas of big government.

Second, public sector organizations are especially dependent upon their collective capabilities for analysing what they do and working out ways to do it better. Inherently in the government sector these processes of 'organizational learning' and innovation drive the bulk of productivity change in public agencies, and they will continue to do so for the foreseeable future. Speeding up and accentuating organizational learning is thus uniquely important within the government sector, far more so than in private business where intra-industry shifts of demand provide much of the motor of productivity advance. The strongly professionalized bureaucracies that dominate many public agencies have important capacities for recognizing failings and analysing through to solutions. But these capabilities work best in evolving professional services in incremental ways, and often become barriers to disruptive changes. There is no automatic assumption that government agencies will stay modern or efficient. The efficacy of organizational learning in departments and agencies is conditioned by a wide range of drivers for change, but also must overcome substantial barriers to innovation in these exceptionally long-lived organizations.

9.1   DIGITAL ERA CHANGE AND GOVERNMENT PRODUCTIVITY

The detailed analysis of UK central departments' over-time productivity profiles (in Chapters 3 to 6) strongly suggests that one of the most general and dominant problems in growing the productivity of government services has been countering bureaucratic conservatism about digital era changes. This difficulty does not just involve technical changes in IT, or even wider technology shifts, which, as we have seen in Chapters 7 and 8 may have little impact on their own on productivity levels.

Instead, the most pervasive and important digital era changes are normally full-spectrum alterations of whole organizations, considered as 'socio-technical systems'. Such shifts do not just involve the coordinated replacement or enhancement of computerized storage, networking and communications between agencies, customers and agency partners. For at least the last three decades they also essentially involve shifting from volumetric to risk-based administrative processes, and from the solo production of simple services by government agencies for passive consumers towards the *co*-production of more complex services with customers, users and citizens strongly involved (OECD, 2010). A large repertoire of organizational restructurings and developments are also entailed, especially in moving from government agencies that are relatively static, or at best show punctuated equilibrium patterns of change, towards more flexibly and continuously evolving organizations.

The significance of digital era changes is apparent from our contrasting case studies in the previous chapters, notably:

- The early adoption of digital working in a 'core mission' area of HM Customs and Excise (see Chapter 3), which sustained rapidly rising productivity in customs regulation alone (matched by an almost equivalent stagnation in shifting VAT administration into electronic pathways).

- The slow, initially uneven but later sustained push in parts of the income tax system (Chapter 4) towards modernizing databases and growing online transactions. Slow implementation meant that positive effects here were long delayed. But in tandem with later staff cuts, they did help produce some moderate productivity advances in Inland Revenue/HM Revenue & Customs (HMRC) over the long term.

- The short-sighted and partly tragic decision by the Department for Work and Pensions (DWP) to remodel itself in 2001 around phone-based processes, and then to do next to nothing about developing online transactions. DWP held off deciding to fundamentally simplify or adapt its complex business processes for the digital era for nearly a decade (see Chapter 5). The huge costs of reorganization around an already 'dead' model, combined with unhelpful political interferences and short-sightedness, produced an absolutely static productivity picture over more than two decades.

We can illuminate a little further the important role of digital era changes across these three detailed stories by combining our data on the role of ICT (information and communication technologies) spending changes, PFI (Private Finance Initiative) construction spending and the use of consultancies across the cases considered in Chapters 3 to 5. Again we interpret the PFI construction data here as indicative primarily of the large-scale business process modernizations that typically occur when new offices are opened or other facilities are relocated. New buildings can synergize strongly with the bringing in of new ICT systems to create the kind of complementarities discussed also in Chapters 7 and 8. Consultancy spending too might rise for some similar reasons. Alternatively, bringing in consultants may primarily be indicative of situations where normal civil service administration and planning cannot cope with a rush of new demands, especially new substantive policies being introduced for political or 'effectiveness' motivations at the same time that managers have to keep existing services running, which may lead to a drop in productivity. Consultants are also often brought in when 'inorganic' major reorganizations are undertaken – such as the government equivalents of 'mergers and acquisitions' in the private sector (White and Dunleavy, 2010). Again these shake-ups are often associated with productivity declines, perhaps for between two and four years afterwards.

The association between high levels of ICT spending and productivity

Growing the productivity of government services

*Figure 9.1   Productivity versus lagged ICT spending across DWP,
HMRC (tax) and Customs for 1999–2008*

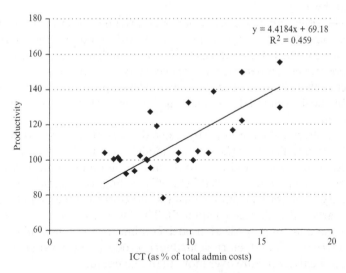

Note: The values for ICT, PFI and consulting expenditures have all been lagged for one
year, to reflect the fact that expenditure in these areas will have an effect on productivity in
the next year at the earliest.

increases taken across our three departments is shown in Figure 9.1. The
pattern here is first of all positive and, second, a relatively close association. Taken on its own, the trend line here suggests that increased ICT
spending alone could account for over half of the observed variance in
productivity increases. The association between PFI construction, construed as indicative of major administrative reorganizations and increases
in capital intensity, and productivity levels is shown in Figure 9.2. It is
again positive and shows a reasonably close fit around the trend line, sufficient to explain on its own around 38 per cent of the observed variance in
productivity increases. (Of course, these successive bivariable comparisons
are not additive. It is very likely that the effects of ICT investments and
of construction-as-indicating-reorganization charted here account for the
same portion of productivity change, not for different segments of the
overall effect.)

   Finally, the association between increased consultancy spending
and productivity increases in our three main departments is shown in
Figure 9.3. The relationship is clearly much weaker and not positive,
with a much wider scatter of points around the basically flat (indeed very
slightly negative) trend line. So no significant proportion of the variance in

Figure 9.2   *Productivity versus lagged PFI spending across DWP, HMRC (tax) and Customs for 1999–2008*

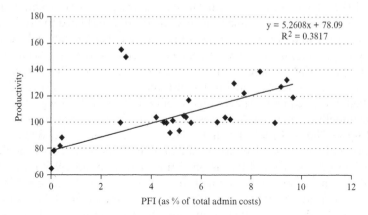

Figure 9.3   *Productivity versus lagged consulting spending across DWP, HMRC (tax) and Customs for 1999–2008*

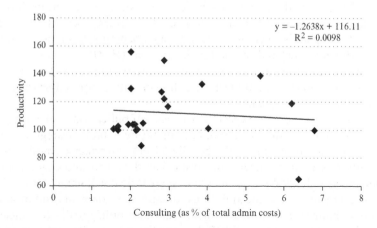

productivity levels could be ascribed to raising consultancy spending. This differing result suggests that, primitive though this plotting exercise must be with the paucity of available data, there clearly are differences between the influence of the three independent variables here.

Looking Ahead

Looking ahead to the next two decades, it seems clear that there remains a very substantial potential for digital changes to fuel productivity increases in public services. Such changes are likely to remain as fundamentally important to new business processes as they have proved to be since the mid-1990s. There is every indication also that the patterns of technological change are likely to continue to be fast, disruptive and hard to predict. So planning for and correctly anticipating future developments will remain every bit as difficult for government bureaucracies as it has been in the recent past. For instance, Chapter 5 showed that the Department for Work and Pensions 'listened to its customers' in an unsophisticated way in 2000. It consequently spent millions of pounds on a short-sighted policy of remodelling its business processes around telephone services – only to end up in 2008–09 realizing that a large majority of its customers were online with broadband internet and that the department was handling only half of 1 per cent of its customer transactions online. With the onset of recession and an unprecedented squeeze on its operational costs in the 2011–15 period, DWP has now altered course dramatically. It has adopted a 'digital by default' strategy that looks forward to no less than 80 per cent of its customer transactions being handled online by 2015. Under the guidance of its new Conservative minister, Ian Duncan Smith, in 2010 the DWP also finally launched a radical programme to integrate all of its previously fragmented benefits into a single 'universal benefit'. The next stage of this plan is to connect this reformed benefit system also with the tax credits administered by the tax department (HMRC), so as to create a 'universal credit' system of state transfers, spanning across benefits and tax credits, with the aim of always creating incentives for people to go out to work wherever they can.

The strong synergies expected between simplification and reintegration of benefits on the one hand, and digital by default strategies on the other, are clearly in line with the 'digital era governance' model, with its emphasis upon reintegration, needs-based holism and digitalization (Dunleavy et al., 2008). But, of course, a great deal will hang on the effective implementation of the ambitious software developments and business process changes in both departments that are anticipated. Nonetheless, the substantial *volte face* in DWP thinking fits closely with some emerging indications elsewhere in UK government that fully digital strategies do offer prospects for radically improving the productivity of large machine bureaucracies. In the integrated HMRC, staff numbers by 2011 had fallen to 68 000 from the 2005 merger peak of 105 000, thanks in large part to the transition to the major (if long-delayed) online submission of taxes (National Audit Office, 2011b). Perhaps staff numbers have been over-cut, since significant problems of quality-shading services (like answering telephone queries) have also emerged. But most of this reduction looks sustainable still.

None of this should be taken to suggest that digital changes are easily managed or guaranteed to work, however. A 'big bang' planning approach still prevails in UK government, despite the Coalition government push since 2010 for more modular IT contracts. A lack of flexibility in departments and agencies and an inability to do organizational learning well are also evident, e.g. in the lagging take-up of social media in central government (Dunleavy, 2012a). These factors clearly hampered the first wave of public management responses to the growth of the internet and the web (Public Administration Select Committee, 2011). Yet in a very similar way, we can reasonably expect that the next two or three waves of disruptive changes in information technology and networking (such as the growth of social media) are likely to still confront many similar barriers to change within government.

These problem traits are greatly strengthened in the government ICT area, where private sector markets for supplying IT services to government have often not been competitive or not functioned well, most notably in the UK and in Japan. Comparing these two countries with other nations with more balanced government–IT-industry relations (such as the Netherlands, Canada and the USA), Dunleavy et al. (2008) argued that uncompetitive government IT markets produce a double bind for large systems integrator firms. They come to rely on huge outsourced domestic government contracts for relatively unchanging services and running legacy IT systems, and the firms themselves are encouraged to invest in lobbying for contracts and other rent-seeking behaviours. Once the firms acquire very large blocks of work they do not have to be innovative, focusing instead on just curating old-fashioned IT systems over long periods, using proprietary solutions as much as feasible, implemented at huge scale and in very long contracts – stretching to nearly two decades in the case of the current CapGemini contract with HMRC. This way they can simultaneously maintain a high cost base to generate profits from, and yet help insulate their market share, an oligopolist's dream set up.

As an industrial strategy, allowing a closed oligopoly to develop in government IT is lamentably short-sighted, for both government departments and the firms involved. The privileged firms cannot grow their markets via exports, because their expertise is solely in running outdated and expensive à la carte systems, tweaked to indulge the conservatism of large bureaucracies and to respond to the (often uncosted) 'value guidance' (sometimes just whims) of politicians. The firms have no interest in promoting technologies that would produce low-cost, modular solutions that could potentially go on to win business in much larger-scale world markets. Where contractors attract lots of public criticism, as in the UK with the highest scrap rates of government IT projects in the Western world, they tend to hunker down defensively and become even more locked in to subsisting on domestic government contracts.

By contrast, the Netherlands, Canada and the USA suggest that a genuine competition of multiple providers, multiple solutions and approaches is always important, although each country secures it in different ways (Dunleavy et al., 2008). In the Netherlands and Canada, careful in-house regulation of government IT competencies and the maintenance of competitive balance have preserved IT sector competition, even in professionally concentrated policy systems. In the USA the sheer size of the public sector market, lower industrial concentration ratios and rules favouring small business bids have all helped to maintain far more vigorous competition amongst contractors – creating some periods and sectors of great advance, especially at the federal government level.

Interacting with the substantial problems of government–IT–contractor relations, it is important to recognize that bureaucratic conservatism in adopting digital technologies is not just a one-time problem, which can be easily broken down by e-government or other one-off initiatives, and thereafter marginalized. Instead, long-lived government bureaucracies have a capacity to adopt early technological changes in ways that erect new forms of obstacles to future change. When government organizations incorporate previous waves of innovation, usually with strong time lags, they tend to concretize them in forms that resist further developments. Even as UK government at last moves to 'digital by default' strategies in social security (Tinkler, 2011), problems are likely to remain.

For example, governments across the Western world have constructed tens of thousands of websites, which in the tradition of bureaucracy ('rule by offices') show an almost complete fascination with the written word. Every government website is awash with lots of complex text, and almost nothing else but text. There is still startlingly little use of any graphics or images, let alone simulations or games across government sites. Yet the massive online gaming industry has proved time and again that graphics-based communication can substitute for text very effectively, allowing people to complete complex tasks without having to be highly literate (or numerate). Such an approach would clearly have many benefits for people who are not educated to the post-university level that government websites are mostly written for. Government use of rich media is also still in its infancy, and the use of new technologies – such as low-cost remote interviewing via Skype – lags years behind civil society practice. At the most simple level, almost no government sites worldwide 'play back' users' views or behaviours to them in order to help their customers sort out what materials were found useful by other citizens, although business websites like Amazon have done so for a decade and a half. The production of these highly conservative government websites also uses a lot of staff to run expensive and conservative 'content management systems', and simpler-to-use alternatives are generally ignored.

Having slowly learnt how to do web content in conservative, risk-averse mode over the noughties, it will take most government organizations perhaps another five to ten years to recognize and adopt social media technologies already pervasive in the business sector and civil society. By the time government has adapted to this wave, another set of waves of change will certainly have occurred in the leading sectors of society. For instance, few if any government agencies yet realize (in late 2011 as we write) that their overwhelmingly text-based information could be generated far more economically (and altered far more flexibly) using blogging software than the more complex editing systems that government and its contractors have adopted (a blog is just a serially ordered website). Even if officials could be made aware of this shift, on past form it would take a lot of effort and perhaps five or six years to get agencies to accept a change from relying on their older website techniques.

If digital changes persist at the rate of the last 20 years, then a whole new set of younger staff, with a different education and socialization, will need to be recruited into government every three or four years in order to partly counteract bureaucracies' risk-averse mentality on investing in ICT changes. And severe organizational politics problems will typically recur in empowering each new generation to counteract government bureaucracies' wish to standardize on just one fixed, long-life template for handling digital change.

9.2 IMPROVING ORGANIZATIONAL LEARNING IN GOVERNMENT

The ability of government organizations to detect failings in current approaches, and to work out how to do things better, is always the fundamental driver for improved productivity within government, not least in the face of rapid digital changes. The capacity for users to shift their custom between suppliers is inherently much less in the public sector, despite the initiatives and perennial optimism about 'quasi-markets' reviewed in section 10.2, page 315. So the most pervasive key to creating sustainable productivity growth in government sectors is to foster more and faster 'organizational learning'.

A learning organization is one that is 'skilled at creating, acquiring and transferring knowledge, and at modifying its behaviour to reflect new knowledge and insights' (Garvin, 1993, p.110). This process involves:

'systematic problem solving; experimentation and the testing of new knowledge; learning from experience; learning from others; and shared knowledge and knowledge-spreading mechanisms'. There has been a long academic debate about how far 'organizational learning' differs from the simple aggregate of the individual learning undertaken by people within the organization (especially its leaders). Yet:

> although organizational learning occurs through individuals, it would be a mistake to conclude that organizational learning is nothing but the cumulative result of their members' learning. Members come and go, and leadership changes, but organizations' memories preserve certain behaviors, mental maps norms and values over time. (Hedberg, 1981, p. 6)

There is agreement also that a learning organization is one that is inherently agile: 'one that is quick to identify, digest and apply the lessons learned in its interactions with its environments. For public sector organizations, this involves developing innovative solutions to the constantly changing legal, political, economic and social environment' (McNabb, 2007, pp. 126–7). Many commentators have stressed the barriers to change in the public sector, including the reduced strength of competition processes and the difficulties of developing strong reward systems within restrictive government pay practices (Burgess et al., 2004; Moynihan and Landuyt, 2009). These observations certainly have force. But against them we need to recognize that government bodies are characteristically larger organizations, with elaborate internal capacities to search for and assimilate new knowledge, and often with strongly professionalized staff who embed individual and organizational learning into the whole definition of their occupational communities. At the least, there is no clear imbalance of these factors sufficient to suggest that government agencies are worse (or better) than the vast bulk of private sector businesses.

Figure 9.4 shows something of the complexity of the processes involved in determining how much organizational learning occurs in government departments and agencies, which have been exhaustively considered elsewhere (Gilson et al., 2008). Here we briefly work through the influences set out in the sequence numbered in the Figure, commenting on how they link to the problems of improving innovation and public sector productivity.

1   Organizational culture   This is the broadest framework within which organizational learning takes place. In cultural theory terms most public sector agencies are resolutely 'hierarchist' organizations, marked by a high level of 'grid' pressures (formal rules that determine individual behaviour) and by a high level of 'group' pressures (strong surveillance of individual behaviours and inter-personal requirements to conform to group norms),

Figure 9.4   Situating organizational learning in government sector organizations within external influences

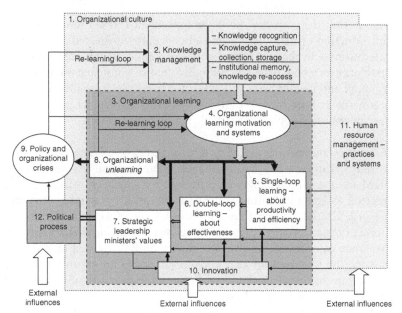

especially in machine bureaucracies and technocratic and regulatory agencies (Hood and Dunleavy, 1994; Hood, 1998).

Professional bureaucracies push this model towards a far more 'egalitarian' pattern where group pressures are strong but grid influences are reduced, especially in agencies dealing face to face with clients (as hospitals do with patients, and schools with pupils). Inherently greater levels of work autonomy for professional staff here also foster more small-scale, individual innovation in the treatment of clients. And when solutions are proven to work, professional bureaucracies are often adept in ensuring that micro-innovations are quickly absorbed and accumulated into a persuasive (often binding) concept of 'professional good practice'.

At another extreme, hierarchist practices in bureaucracies can degenerate into a 'fatalist' culture where grid (rule-bound) pressures are very strong, but where group cohesion is absent and organizational members distrust each other. With a deficit of collective resolve to sustain innovation, it is not surprising that the people involved in a fatalist organization become mentally defeated by the problems they face – so that the agency focuses simply on 'coping', implementing existing practices with little strategic direction or hope for improvement. Bastow (2012) presents an in-depth analysis of this phenomenon, focusing on the UK prison service's record of maintaining (but still managing) continuously over-crowded jails for more than three decades.

Despite the efforts of new public management (NPM) reformers, and the introduction of many practices and concepts transferred across from private business in the last four decades of public management reforms, few public agencies have the kind of 'individualist' culture characteristic of many small and medium-size private sector firms. Such businesses mostly have low (or at least lower) 'grid' (rule-bound) constraints, plus weaker 'group' inhibitors stopping individuals making innovations.

2   Knowledge management (KM)   KM is the most relevant aspect of the ways that organizational culture shapes organizational learning capacity. KM involves the complex of processes by which knowledge is first recognized as being of lasting value and relevance by members or units of the organization, rather than the information involved being classed as 'noise', or seen as only ephemerally relevant or as unreliable (Haynes, 2005). Once categorized, knowledge must then be captured. Yet at any given time the vast bulk of the 'knowledge' inside an organization will necessarily be 'informal', locked in the minds and practices of members of the workforce (Nonaka and Takeuchi, 1995).

Recognizing, formalizing and storing knowledge is only going to be effective if it is linked to a capacity to recall that this stored knowledge exists and could be relevant to a newly (or apparently newly) occurring problem. As the French essayist, Montaigne argued: 'Memory is essential to all the operations of reason' (quoted in Sertillanges, 1978, p. 186). If an organizational or institutional memory is missing then access to stored knowledge will not occur and learning cannot be effective. Indeed, without some memory capacity problematic phenomena will not be recognized and appropriately categorized, so that a learning process cannot get started. To look ahead a little, one basic chain of activities needed for learning is likely to be:

Memory → Problem recognition → Motivation to act → Capacity to act → Review

3   Organizational learning systems   These are formed within (and depend partly on) first general organizational culture influences, which largely determine what the organization seeks to achieve (Nevis et al., 1995). A second formative element is given by more specific knowledge management capacities – which fix how (and how effectively) the agency undertakes search behaviour when problems are encountered and recognized. Systems are most developed in organizations whose missions are dependent upon constantly changing their activities and outputs to respond to a rapidly changing environment, such as firms operating in highly dynamic industrial sectors. In concrete terms Finger and Brand (1999) suggest that the degree of commitment to organizational learning can be measured in terms of the resources devoted to, and the extent of, four main learning activities:

- educational and training activities;
- the active self-use of learning sources inside the organization by staff or units;
- the active use of learning sources outside the organization;
- the creation of an environment conducive to learning.

And six important learning capacities:

- individual learning capacities amongst staff members;
- collective learning capacities by units and levels;
- structural (triple loop) learning capacities (see below);
- cultural learning capacities;
- capacities resulting from the organization of work;
- the capacity of the organizational leadership to learn and promote learning.

On some of these dimensions, such as recruiting people with professional or graduate education and an emphasis on training, there are good reasons to believe that public agencies perform well – especially in professional bureaucracies like public healthcare and education systems where professional staff need to be continuously recertified. Modern public management human resources (HR) systems also assign a far higher priority to formalized professional development than many businesses, not least because public managers and skilled staff tend to stay in the government sector for long periods.

By contrast, Olsen and Peters (1996) argue that there are likely to be substantial barriers to organizational learning in public organizations, especially:

- an often common resistance to change amongst long-lived and rule-bound departments and agencies;
- a modest capacity to alter behaviour and organizational structures because of strong 'group' norm constraints, staff resistance and typically strong unionization; and
- a loss of learning continuities that occurs because of election cycles and party alternations in government.

*Figure 9.5   Greve's model of how an organization's performance set
against its 'aspiration level' triggers risk-taking activity*

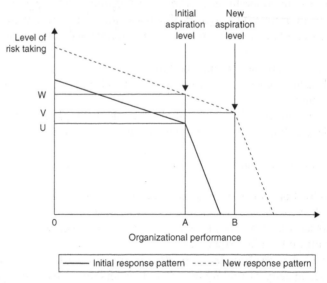

In addition, most organizational learning is done in 'ambiguous' conditions (March and Olsen, 1975) and by trial and error (Harford, 2011).
And yet government departments are often held harshly to account over
'errors' or expenditures on things that do not work out (see below). Trials
are acceptable, but not errors. Especially in the modern (24-hour news)
period, governments feel they must be seen by the public as continuously
successful. This often skews official stances towards proclaiming success
despite the actual results, and to quickly brushing 'lessons learned' under
the carpet, rather than analysing them carefully.

4   Motivations for organizational learning   Organizational learning
motivations have been linked in many different theoretical approaches
to factors such as the pace of change in the organization's environment,
and more controversially to organizational cultures and leadership.
However, the nexus of issues here is complex, and little evidenced.
Accordingly we follow one of the simplest yet most empirically grounded behavioural models of organizational learning within large firms
developed by Heinrich Greve in his book *Organizational Learning from
Performance Feedback* (2003). Figure 9.5 shows the basic framework,
with the level of organizational performance graphed on the horizontal
dimension, and the extent to which the organization undertakes risky

search behaviours for innovations or new solutions graphed on the vertical dimension.

Greve argues the following:

–   Organizations set a level of performance that they aspire to achieve – for instance, initially at A on the horizontal axis measuring performance here. Firms can choose different aspiration levels – for instance to be an industry leader, or to be a medium player, or to stick to a small niche within the market. Analogously, agencies can set aspiration levels that vary from being outstanding, through routine performance, to a fatalist coping-only strategy. A wide range of organizational structure and culture influences will combine to determine the aspiration level actually chosen.

–   When an organization is achieving its aspiration level it will have an equilibrium level of risk-taking activity, given here by U. If the organization is not achieving its aspiration level A then it will undertake more risky activities designed to boost its performance, shown by the thick solid line right of point A here. Organizations generally economize on risk-bearing activities whenever they can, and always need to be pushed if they are to do more than they have historically undertaken. The key thing to notice is that this response line rises to the left quite gently, so that under-performance triggers only a moderate willingness to incur extra risk-taking. On the other hand, if the organization is already performing above its aspiration level A the organization will tend to cut back quite sharply on its risky activities and research on innovative solutions, as shown by the thick solid line to the right of point A. This creates the kinked response curve focused at A shown in Figure 9.5.

–   Figure 9.5 also shows what happens if the organization is forced to increase its aspiration level, in this case to the new level B on the horizontal axis. In industrial contexts this can occur when another firm makes an invention or adds to the quality of its product, or when a new technology comes along, rivalling the firm's existing approach. The key analogy in government is the election of a new political party to power, where the new set of ministers or government executives demand that a government agency 'raise its game' and do better in delivering its core mission or a new mission. In the very short run, almost any organization will not be able to respond effectively to such disruptive developments – and so it will now have a deficit in the performance level it needs to aspire to, of B minus A. As a result, it is forced to trigger an exceptional level of risk-taking activity, shown as W on the vertical axis, in order to try and close this gap.

- However, in the long run the previous pattern of response lines will reform, but focused on the new aspiration level B, as shown here by the dashed line in Figure 9.5. Assuming that the organization can close up the performance gap via its initial, extraordinary level of risk-taking activity, then its R&D or other efforts will tend to decline back towards a new sustainable level V. This is higher than the original pattern at U, but it will be lower than the exceptional level (of W) achieved shortly after the new aspiration demands came into effect.

Thus in Greve's model the key things that will influence organizational learning and other expensive risk-taking activity (such as spending more on R&D, shifting business models, adopting new organizational structures, uprating training efforts and energetically seeking product innovations) will be the dialectic of the organization's aspiration level and its performance.

Various kinds of adaptive responses may tend to offset organizational learning – in particular a situation where an organization continuously adjusts its aspiration level downwards in response to its poor performance, rather than incurring the costs and risks of looking for new ways of carrying out its role. Pressures on firms from simple organizational survival may make them choose to adaptively reduce their aspiration levels as a response to radically new environmental pressures, rather than trying to raise their game (Greve, 2003). 'Permanently failing organizations' can live on for long periods in the private sector in protected niches (Meyer and Scott, 1992). This potential is even greater in the government sector for the reasons discussed above (see pp. 27–8).

Firms and agencies may well have previously rigorously eliminated all internal slack, under pressure to realize 'shareholder value' in the private sector, or because of NPM imperatives in government. Such organizations can run into particular barriers to being able to respond creatively to performance deficits that occur later on:

> Organizations practising lean management techniques may have so few resources that can be redirected to search activities that their capability of generating solutions is severely limited. Instead, they can imitate solutions available in the environment, but in a solution-poor environment, even this is difficult. (Greve, 2003, pp. 169–70)

5 *Single-loop learning*   Single-loop learning is an incremental improvement effort, orientated to improving efficiency. Here staff or units ask: 'How can we improve the activities that we are already doing? Or more cheaply produce the outputs that we already produce?' Such search is

often focused on error tracking and process monitoring. Organizations tend to hunt for solutions to problems (so-called 'problemistic' search) in the immediate neighbourhood of the problem itself. Alternatively they may look back to previous similar problems, seeking for either exact solutions, or for analogies and parallels that might apply to the current problem (Greve, 2003). By contrast, the 'garbage can' approach to organizational learning also emphasizes that often within an organization there may already be people who are advocates or enthusiasts for particular solutions; they are actively looking for ways of applying their preferred approach to new problems (Cohen et al., 1972). For instance, IT or web staff may be keen to promote new information systems or internet forms of working as ways of tackling problems to which they have not yet been applied. Some authors assert that public organizations in liberal democracies are often biased towards extant organizational practices, existing tasks and processes. Consequently they get stuck in incremental, single-loop learning, because only such issues unambiguously fall within the 'non-political' remit of the bureaucracy. But even here 'garbage can' processes can produce limited innovation.

6   Double-loop learning   Double-loop learning is more ambitious, asking: 'Are we doing the right things? Should we be undertaking different activities or producing different outputs?' Organizational leaders look more widely and inventively for permanent solutions to sources of error or under-performance, by varying their activities or outputs more fundamentally. In practice, the most knowledge about how processes are working is likely to be tacit and to be concentrated at the grassroots of the organization (Nonaka and Takeuchi, 1995). Yet often these staff are also shut out from asking broader-range questions about effectiveness by hierarchical structures. In government, double-loop learning may be especially restricted in those 'machine bureaucracies' where officials are most constrained to fit in with the political guidance on values from the governing party's ministers or executives (Ranson and Stewart, 1994; Romme and van Witteloostuijn, 1999). However, in professional bureaucracies the distinction between single- and double-loop learning is more extensively blurred. Here professional staff may be able to undertake so-called 'slack search' – where they can reflect more on what they are doing, experiment with different modes of achieving given objectives and come up with alternatives.

7   Triple-loop (or strategic) learning   Triple-loop learning is the most difficult and probably rarest form of response. The concept argues that organizations can only radically reframe how they look at their activities and roles by querying to some degree their underlying assumptions, principles and fundamental objectives. Yet critiquing the 'conventional wisdom' often calls into question strongly developed organizational beliefs and values. This stage is also one where an organization may self-consciously choose its aspiration level for performance anew, rather than simply operating with one that has been historically or conventionally accepted. Some authors argue that public sector organizations operating on their own can only be single-loop learners, because the double and triple loops considered here are seen as the reserved domain of political leaders (Common, 2004).

We turn next to a series of extra elements that seem to be very important for public sector agencies' organizational learning, but that have not been so extensively discussed in the relevant literature.

8   Organizational unlearning   Organizational *un*learning denotes a particular sub-dimension of performance in which there is conscious maladaptation to environmental stimuli, and in which unwanted outcomes are allowed to accumulate without countervailing actions being taken by management (Hedberg, 1981). Although some commentators (such as Easterby-Smith et al., 2000) are sceptical about the distinctiveness or value of 'unlearning', looking at how organizations lose or discard knowledge has considerable significance in contemporary government. Serious, inadvertent lapses of organizational memory have occurred in government across many major nation states. A good example was when the UK Department for Work and Pensions (DWP) forgot about a forthcoming change in pensions contributions that was legislated in 1986 but did not actually come into force until people began retiring in 2000. For many years in this period DWP misadvised people planning their retirements after April 2000 about their forthcoming pension entitlements – misadvice that resulted in the eventual accumulation of a £5 billion liability by the time that the mistake was discovered (National Audit Office, 2000a). A similar, more foreseeable but equally long-run instance of unlearning occurred following the phased decisions by UK ministers in the period 1994 to 1999 to remove exit controls from UK airports and ports. This meant that the Home Office (responsible for immigration matters) progressively lost all its ability to understand who was in the country from overseas. When a senior official finally confessed this to a Parliamentary committee, the roof fell in on the previous cost-saving policy. Exit controls were reintroduced, but will not be implemented until 2015 (National Audit Office, 2011c, p. 32).

Unlearning can also occur through departments or agencies failing to keep contextual information and planning assumptions up to date.

For instance, a 2001 outbreak of an agricultural animal disease (foot and mouth) in Britain was initially tackled by the department involved (Department for Environment, Food and Rural Affairs – Defra) using a fully prepared and thorough 'playbook' or manual –written up in 1968, when the last UK outbreak had occurred. Thirty three years late the same measures proved completely ineffective in halting the outbreak, chiefly because the Defra playbook assumed that farmers only moved their animals to local markets. In fact, because of better transport and more efficient markets since the late 1960s farmers had shifted over to moving animals much more extensively around the country, to wherever they could get the best prices. So the playbook's main remedies (local movement bans and local precautionary killing of animals around farms where outbreaks had occurred) no longer controlled the spread of the infection. Only a late intervention by PM Tony Blair, using independent modelling of the 2001 outbreak by outside scientific experts, finally allowed the problem to be brought under control, by imposing a nationwide animal movement ban and undertaking a mass slaughter of all animals at risk of infection.

9 *Policy and organizational crises*   These crises are the typical consequences of such mistakes. They are occasions where unlearning is especially large scale, intense or sustained. The seriousness of such problems is boosted by large organizational scale, weakly controlled organizational leaders, and a rapidly changing environment – all features that are common in many industrial sectors. In government terms, some factors most commonly magnifying crises include:

- centralized governments operating over large areas, with decisions affecting tens of millions of people at once;
- fast shifts in policy that are rapidly and reliably implemented (so that large-scale mistakes accrue quickly);
- an absence of constitutional checks and balances on the central government, especially in terms of weak legislative oversight;
- strongly nationalized media systems and adversarial party politics, both of which tend to fuel a lot of policy 'churn' when party control of government alternates, and there is strong political discounting of inconvenient evidence at other times.

These are all prominent features of the broader context of policy-making in the UK (Dunleavy, 1995).

Major crises often reveal the potential for large-scale 'policy disasters' or 'policy fiascos', where foreseeable or well-signposted mistakes nonetheless accrue on a massive scale. Such crises are then important triggers for major restructuring of the organizations involved. In the private sector, affected firms typically undergo bankruptcies, divestments and major restructuring, or hostile acquisitions. In the public sector the responses to crises often imply top leadership changes at the official level (and sometimes amongst politicians too), mergers or recombinations of agencies. Sometimes more fundamental changes of governance architectures occur (Rochet, 2007). A key US example was the establishment of the Department of Homeland Security, which brought together 28 previously separate US federal agencies, following the failure to prevent the 9/11 attacks in 2001.

10 Innovation   Innovation is the final key component of productivity change, and has been much studied in the private sector (as discussed in Chapter 1). No comparable degree of research has been carried out on innovation within government, although 'diffusion of innovation' in some analogous service organizations has been covered (Greenhalgh et al., 2004) and in decentralized agencies, along with cross-national convergence in how EU member states operate (van Stolk and Wegrich, 2008). However, the 2006 NAO report *Achieving Innovation in Central Government* focused especially on organizational-level innovations (Dunleavy et al., 2006b). It found that innovations were most often triggered either by an expenditure cutback or another need for savings (at that period in the UK mostly linked to the Gershon Review); or by a political intervention by a minister (and less often by top administrators). In the absence of such stimuli, government departments and agencies tended only to register possible innovations, but then to store them up unimplemented until such times as they were needed because of external demands for savings or similar pressures. Government organizations were also poorly set up to behave as serial innovators, which they seldom reported doing. Instead they tended to move erratically from one single-shot innovation to another. Every ten to 15 years they would also tend towards some form of 'big bang' policy change or reorganization, cumulating lots of unimplemented changes into a large, unwieldy transformation, often linked to an IT 'refresh' or re-contracting. Most depressingly of all, the overall scale of innovations identified to the study by major UK central departments and agencies was often low, with median values under £1 million (in 2006, a boom year for public spending).

The final two elements of Figure 9.4 may seem to have chiefly background implications for organizational learning. But both have been heavily emphasized in the conventional public administration literature, and often also in the rhetoric of day-to-day debates about governance improvements within liberal democracies.

11 Human resources practices and systems How agencies manage personnel can have a strong influence on organizational cultures, the extent and character of organizational learning, and on the rates and types of innovation undertaken by staff. In the public sector the imprint of exceptionally long-lived civil service characteristics is hard to underplay in explaining between-country variations in the character of national bureaucracies. Bernard Silberman (1983) showed how the modern Weberian model of bureaucracy was no sooner adumbrated in the late nineteenth century than it began to be differentiated into radically different forms. 'Professional' (or 'light touch') civil service systems emerged in the USA and UK, that relied on university education to socialize recruits before admission into public interest values, with thereafter only loosely coordinated public service systems. (The UK also fostered regular transfers of 'generalist' staff across central departments, whereas the USA developed separate, departmentalized HR systems, even for top staff.) By contrast, in France and Japan much more organization-centric, or heavy-duty versions of Weberian bureaucracy developed. Civil servants were extensively socialized into very strong departmental cultures in powerful and distinct ministries. These differences between countries remain remarkably enduring to this day. Recently, NPM changes have variegated the more hierarchical French and Japanese systems. And in the UK, recruitment to the senior civil service has broadened to include people from other parts of the public sector, plus some private sector late-entry staff. But these four countries' civil service cultures continue to show nationally distinctive features. In Whitehall a 'generalist' bureaucratic culture has remained strong and largely intact.

For organizational learning the key human resources management aspects are the extent to which officials normally work in flexible teams on projects (normally better for innovation), or instead manage separate 'desks' (which creates strong risk-averse incentives to 'keep your head down'). In many public agencies 'blame' cultures embedded in HR practices also inhibit innovation by penalizing those who try new approaches (of which a certain quota must fail). They lead to the marginalizing of people pushing entrepreneurial solutions. Most public sector contexts are a long way from the 'no blame' reporting of mistakes in safety bureaucracies (like airlines), or the rational approach to managing portfolios of projects (where some will fail) found in the most innovative private businesses, such as venture capital firms. Instead the government context tends to require proof in advance that projects will succeed; to be intolerant of any level of failure (and hence to lack any realistic notion of managing portfolios of projects); and to be slow to acknowledge that mistakes have been made or that policies have not worked – unless political changes intervene (when over-adjustments may occur).

12   Political and public discourse influences   These influences on organizational learning cannot function as the sources of detailed innovation that liberal democratic theory or the older public administration literature have conventionally assigned to them. Taken on their own, the stimuli from electoral politics, the interest group process and media scrutiny can easily hinder as much as they encourage effective organizational learning. Indeed, in especially partisan climates they may easily be counterproductive, although crises may also spur changes (Coopey and Burgoyne, 2000; Dekker and Hansen, 2004; Ferdinand, 2004; Rochet, 2007). Where a 'blame culture' is fuelled by opportunist politicians it typically encourages senior officials and public managers to adopt passive, highly risk-averse stances, that also often let steady productivity growth slide through organizational conservatism.

Yet, at the same time, it remains true that democratic politics and the deliberative processes in public discourse, construed more broadly to include a 'polyarchic' ('rule by the many') process, can create myriad triggers for learning by public agencies. This is usually stated more definitely than is merited: 'If the barriers to organizational learning in the public domain are to be overcome, it will be achieved through strengthening and widening access to the arena of public discourse and the political processes that relate to it' (Ranson and Stewart, 1994, p. 178).

Table 9.1 provides a full listing of the multiple sources of organizational learning (discussed in more detail in Gilson et al., 2008). The higher transparency of public agencies (relative to internal decision-making in private firms) is one key stimulus, an approach summed up by its most enthusiastic exponent, Robert Behn (2000), as '360 degree accountability'. In a well-functioning liberal democracy, political responsiveness and openness can provide a strong impetus towards continuous organizational learning, innovation and productivity – so long as these values are explicitly recognized by politicians and allocated some resources of attention, funding and support, and some space for trial and error processes to work out.

Political impulses are most distinctively involved in organizational learning after crises become manifest, or in cases of organizational unlearning emerging. In both cases political interventions usually focus wider external lesson-drawing on fostering relearning, and on a reorganization of knowledge management processes in the agency (the two 'political' flows shown in Figure 9.4). Yet Table 9.1 also shows that there are strong and specific mechanisms to back up, aggregate and condense,

Table 9.1 Six key sources of organizational learning for government organizations

Source of Learning	Key Component Influences	Time Period in Which Factor Operates
A Internal resources, experience, history	Organization's 'institutional memory', stored experience	Long term
	Staff expertise and 'ordinary knowledge'– staff renewal and culture change	Long and short term, all stages of projects
	Innovation record – e.g., transitioning to a serial innovations approach	Long term
B Citizens, customers, users	Citizen/consumer/user research and feedback	Short run only
	Learning from 'citizen redress' processes (complaints, administrative appeals, regulatory cases, legal actions by citizens or customers)	Long and short term
	Development of citizen/consumer choices and behaviours	
	Analysis of transactional activities and contact data	Mainly short term
		Mainly short term
	Experimentation, piloting	Short term
C Partners, rivals, close comparators	Main service contractors	Long term
	Major uses of consultants (and evaluations by consultants)	Short term
	Consultancy strategy	Medium term
	Other service partners (e.g., non-governmental or local bodies)	Long term
	Staff secondments, culture-sharing with other organizations	Long term
	Rivals or near-neighbour organizations	Long and short term
	Close comparators in home government or private sector	Short term
	Close comparators overseas	Short term
D Top-down controls	Scrutiny and interactions	Short term, post hoc
	Advice, intelligence and direction from 'core executive' departments (e.g., Cabinet Office, Treasury, PM's Office in the UK; Executive Office of the President or the Office of Management and Budget (OMB) in the USA)	Long term
		Long term
	Prime ministerial or presidential directives on how to implement trans-governmental change programmes	Short term and post hoc

Table 9.1   (continued)

Source of Learning	Key Component Influences	Time Period in Which Factor Operates
	(For agencies or other quasi-governmental bodies) overview by central government department/minister	Long term
	Centrally set rules for propriety, human resources policies and organizational management	Short term
	Centrally set crisis management or risk management rules	(but also longer-run learning)
E Critiques, advice, media scrutiny	Legislative oversight, especially departmental committees and general audit committee	Post hoc, mostly short term
	Main stakeholder consultations and critiques	Post hoc, short term
	Other interest or pressure groups, advocacy coalitions	Short term
	Media scrutiny and commentary	Short term
	External think-tanks	Medium term
	Academic research and criticisms	Medium to long term
	Other researchers' or consultants' commentaries	Medium to long term
F Testing interactions, crises, external review processes	Systematic learning from mistakes	Long term
	Departmental crisis management and response	Medium term
	Internal audit and review	Short term only
	Periodic reviews of department or agency strategy and leadership capabilities	Post hoc, medium term
	External audit and review (NAO and main sector review bodies, such as the Healthcare Commission)	Post hoc, often lagging a year or more behind implementation

and make effective the routine or 'normal' political and public inputs. Especially significant here are:

- the supervision of central or federal departments by 'core executive' agencies (responding to prime ministerial or presidential influences);
- the supervision of lower-tier (regional or local) agencies by national departments;

- the operations of external 'Supreme Audit Institutions' (such as the Government Accountability Office in the USA, the National Audit Office in the UK or the French Cour des Comptes); and
- the multiple institutionalizations of lesson-drawing embodied in internal control or internal audit rules (and sometimes in regular 'capability review' processes) within the government sector.

So, *if these political influences can be tuned with internal controls and arranged correctly* the combined effects of political and public discourse influences on organizational learning in government can be substantial forces for good. They are responsive to crises especially, but they can also provide a detailed discipline that is well-informed, specific and backed up by mechanisms to regularly and systematically capture and focus criticisms. The trick, of course, is to reach a point where effective institutional arrangements are in place, and chime effectively with an internal organizational culture receptive to learning and innovation.

Conclusions

There is nothing immutable about where productivity advances occur in advanced industrial societies. The long swing of change over three decades since 1980 has already seen rapid improvements in the actual and potential productivity of large-scale government bureaucracies. Productivity gains have followed especially from a series of often-ignored foundational changes – including the initial automation of office processes, improvements in measuring costs in outputs accounting, and the development of multiple key performance indicators. Taken together, these advances facilitated a shift to risk-based systems of administration that have significantly cut the staff needed to handle standard tasks (even as the complexity of tasks that governments are asked to do has *perhaps* expanded). In this process some long-lived and apparently static machine bureaucracies of the classic Weberian type, such as immigration agencies and tax agencies, have moved from IT laggards to operating large and relatively high-tech IT systems. In large countries like the UK, or even more the USA, these IT set ups are more complex and developed than those run by almost all businesses, except some of the world's giant corporations. Nor is there any reason to suppose that this potential for changes is played out or reduced. The current waves of IT and web changes offer manifold opportunities for redesigning public service delivery around 'essentially digital' processes.

Yet there is no simple technological determinism at work here, nor do shifts in technology on their own achieve the kinds of organizational re-envisioning and re-purposing on which the greatest advances in

productivity may depend. Like many large firms, public sector organizations may well initially pick up innovations in conservative and non-
forward-looking ways, making strategic mis-steps in their responses,
especially to disruptive technological change. They will tend to bend new
technologies and processes to serve their existing organizational culture,
rather than use them to critically reevaluate what they do. The 'politics
versus administration' dichotomy often strengthens such tendencies, with
politicians being risk averse and short-termist.

Systematically prioritizing and boosting organizational learning at *all*
of the 12 stages set out in section 9.2 offers strong prospects for converting
government services from productivity laggards into zones of continuous
advances in delivering services. Yet some confidence that the organization
will go on operating in a given functional space, along with an explicit and
consistent focus on productivity growth, are both needed if government
departments and agencies are to make the steady investments needed to
get better at organizational learning. And it is here that in the recent past
many problems of implementing productivity improvements have arisen,
to which we now turn in our final chapter.

10. Pushing through to productivity advances

Thinking about prescriptive strategies for improving public sector performance often gets side-tracked into a hunt for simple remedies, which turn out subsequently not to work as intended. We have charted here, for instance, the overall failure of new public management approaches to boost organizational productivity in UK government, despite being intensively applied for nearly two decades. In a closely congruent analysis, Hood and Dixon (2012) conclude that administrative spending and running costs increased sharply in Whitehall across the new public management (NPM) period (1980 to 2010) – making its reputation as a cost-cutting approach an ill-deserved one.

We turn in this final chapter to some better evidenced advice on coping with the complexity of achieving and maintaining sustainable increases in the productivity of public sector agencies, looking at four specific lessons:

1. Paying detailed, focused and consistent attention to boosting productivity, and putting in place strong and lasting institutional mechanisms to sustain this effort, are vital. You can rarely improve any aspect of organizational performance that has not been fixed and quantified in some degree. Nor has it been easy for politicians or top officials to sustain the necessary long-run focus on growing productivity, amidst a welter of different and often adversarial public management strategies. Achieving a consistent focus on productivity requires putting in place better organizational arrangements.
2. Strengthening provider succession, and the ability to shift users of public services from less productive to more productive providers could contribute strongly to productivity growth if it was achievable – but in fact it is very difficult to do. What is needed is a genuine analogue to the competition and succession processes (i.e., the transfers of output and activity from less efficient to more efficient firms) that account for half of all productivity advances in the private sector. A wide range of different NPM solutions have only transferred across superficial business processes in rather crude ways, without transferring risks. And constantly fiddling with the location of the interface

between the public and private sectors, or promoting quasi-markets, has been a waste of time in terms of generating more genuine provider succession. This service architecture tinkering mainly just displaces the nature of productivity growth problems. In most public services the key to securing more provider succession is to refocus on *substantive* changes of services, fostering innovations that can bring in new providers plus solutions. For instance, don't try to run the existing local public libraries system more cheaply. Set up a wholly e-book national lending library in competition, and then see how citizens really want to read books, and what books they want to read (Dunleavy, 2011a).

3. For productivity change to be continuous, and not a special exercise in a few episodic years, government staff need to be involved much more centrally and cooperatively in securing the future role of the state. Government managers and politicians need to counteract the often justified suspicions of state workers, trade unions and left-of-centre political parties that growing the productivity of government services is just a code for shrinking the state and degrading the working conditions of government sector workers. A non-opportunistic approach to productivity gains, one that shares gains more with state workers, is needed. Demonstrating such a commitment also entails liberating public sector organizations from artificial restrictions on intra-government competition. It will be important that successful public sector agencies can grow the scale of their operations and compete for work in the same way that contractors can – allowing them to build up expertise and capabilities to compete on even terms.

4. In the past the search for productivity gains was often passively obstructed or opposed by trade unions and allied parties on the political left. They have often been tolerant of slow or no productivity growth, and to this end insisted that the productivity of government services cannot be measured. Social democrats in Europe have especially seen a 'large-public-sector' strategy as a way of pursuing egalitarian objectives – for instance, expanding public sector employment as a way of involving more women, minorities and disabled people in the labour force. But in those countries where a large productivity gap chronically exists between public services and the private economy, a 'big state' no longer combats contemporary social inequalities effectively – and may even imperil the overall legitimacy of government. A smarter strategy for fostering genuine social equality is for unions and left-wing parties to cooperate in a push to create a high productivity public sector, while using the money saved in a generous welfare system – which evens out social gains far more effectively.

10.1 KEEPING FOCUSED ON PRODUCTIVITY

Many endemic problems in organizations persist because they are never directly identified, analysed in detail, mobilized against and attacked as a priority. We noted in Chapter 1 that a chronic diffusion of focus about organizational productivity in the government sector has been evident:

- in the decades-long inability to simply cost weight outputs to create whole-organization-level indicators for all government agencies;
- in the scarcity of high-quality, quantitative indices of organizational productivity across the public sector;
- in the tendency to give up on measuring productivity when faced with a need to make quality adjustments instead of coping with the issues involved;
- in the failure to develop and maintain good over-time indices of outputs/inputs; and
- in politicians' and top officials' constant lurching off from a precise outputs/inputs focus into wider (much less quantifiable) concepts like effectiveness or 'value for money'.

These patterns of behaviour have meant that public officials have not focused clearly, consistently and enduringly enough to keep the problem of productivity changes continuously in view over recent decades. Nor have government sector managers or professionals created a sufficient cumulation of information about how to sustain productivity growth, allied with practical experiences and strategies.

The good news, however, is that by analysing organizational productivity in the ways set out above, then in modern conditions most public managers should be quickly able to redress these gaps. They can learn a lot, quickly, about the productivity of their own agency, the dynamics of changes in its productivity over time, and the specific ways in which more generic suggestions for boosting productivity can be adapted to fit their own government organization.

In terms of *cost pressures*, the key factors to which managers need to pay attention include the following:

- The general dynamics from inflationary pressures on wages (since labour costs are often or usually dominant cost elements in government agencies). Although pay bargaining in the public sector is much more decentralized now than in earlier periods, it will nonetheless be hard for public agencies to avoid paying 'the going rate' of settlements elsewhere, most directly in the government sector, and less restrictively in the wider labour market.

- The costs of outsourced services provision by private contractors (and to a much lesser degree third-sector organizations) are equally wage driven.

- Other costs are usually smaller, but they may have significant influence at particular periods – as we demonstrated for the combined IT, construction and consultancy costs for major UK agencies in the 2000 to 2007 spending 'boom' period.

- Movements in materials costs generally only have visible impact on public agencies in special periods, or on those organizations that spend a lot on particular things, for example, periods of rapidly rising fuel costs for a police force with many squad cars. The biggest exceptions to this rule are the defence sector and government-funded 'big science'. In both these areas procurement costs always matter hugely.

- Major reorganization periods will normally raise capital and IT costs significantly, and have substantial opportunity costs in terms of normal productivity changes being put on hold and productivity levels degrading with unfamiliar new processes, as Chapters 3 to 6 repeatedly demonstrated.

The *level of demand for agency services* will always have implications for any government organization's productivity, in much the same way as it does for firms. Agency productivity will rise when demand increases faster than extra personnel can be recruited or facilities added to handle it – so, productivity usually grows in the early part of a demand boom. Existing offices and staff are worked harder, overtime is accumulated and part-time staff are hired in to cope with the extra demand, all at generally lower costs. Mostly these 'surge' hikes in agency productivity are not sustainable beyond the short term. As demand stabilizes at higher levels, so rather more 'normal' staffing and facilities levels are restored and productivity gains typically even off, as problems are fixed or procedures retightened. Less commonly, some of the innovations in business processes brought in to cope with the growth period become permanent, so that productivity levels stabilize at a new, higher rate.

When demand for an agency's services *falls off* suddenly or unexpectedly, productivity levels must decline, because in the short term the agency is left with too many staff or facilities for the new lower usage rate. Firms often 'hoard' skilled labour in shorter-term market downturns – because it is costly to lose key staff, but then have to rehire and retrain new people. In the same way public services managers are normally reluctant to overreact to potentially temporary conditions in ways that restrict their capacity irrevocably. But if a slump in service demand is too large or sustained, simply not replacing people who leave may not be enough to accommodate the change, and wider changes (like selling buildings or closing lines of activity) may become necessary. In the meantime, productivity levels must fall, because output levels are undersized relative to committed input costs.

Funding constraints may raise some similar problems, even in times of constant or rising service demands. If the budgets in an organization are cut or frozen across the board, the activity levels of many units may be constrained. In the otherwise buoyant or growing areas of the organization, productivity levels will thus decline for reasons that have nothing to do with demand, and everything to do with sharing the burden of adjustment across all parts of the organization. Managers may not wish to disband or downsize teams with otherwise strong demand, especially if they believe that a squeeze or freeze will lift in the near future.

Cross-public-sector changes can have both positive and negative implications for agency productivity. On the plus side, digital changes operating across the whole government sector, and other general modernization pressures, may push prevailingly conservative departments and agencies to look again at their business processes, and to adopt changes being demanded by politicians or by centre-of-government units (such as Prime Minister's Office). On the negative side, many 'fads and fashions' may be cycled through in ways that are not 'organic' to or 'authentic' for particular agencies. Changes happen in the agency only because the governing party or president alternates, triggering government-wide changes in the rhetoric or in the policy delivery styles of all public sector agencies at a given tier of government. Such imposed or 'inauthentic' changes, which do not arise from a department's or agency's individual context, may easily have counterproductive effects, boosting organizations' costs without helping their outputs or activity levels. A great deal of 'policy churn' (solely politically inspired changes in policy goals, implementation methods or regulatory approaches) may also have either zero or negative effects on individual agencies, despite being adopted government-wide with the aim of improving policy effectiveness.

Changes in the nature of service provision and in services quality may influence productivity, but in asymmetrical ways. Generally speaking quality shading is very easy to start doing in not very visible ways within public services. For instance, officials under pressure may degrade previous service standards, crowd facilities more, lengthen queues, shorten contact times in face-to-face or phone-based services, not pick up many phone calls and hope peole go away, and so on. Small changes here may help boost activity levels and for a time avoid falls in measured productivity. But after a while major declines of service quality need to be incorporated into productivity analyses. The cost-weighted output series has to be adjusted to reflect that we are no longer comparing provision of the same kind of public service output at time t_2 that was initially there at t_1.

On the other hand, productivity analysts need to reject the constant temptation inside bureaucracies for officials to tell each other 'good news' stories that hype up as exceptional achievements some wider improvements in service quality that are in fact occurring generally across the economy or society. Quality gains in public services should be identified only very sparingly. And non-specific or unquantified quality improvements should never be used as excuses for 'explaining away' rising running costs and falling productivity levels. In particular, transition periods where agencies are 'dual-running' an old business system and a new one in harness together are often more expensive and less productive than normal. It is much better to explicitly acknowledge something of a hit to cost containment in such circumstances, rather than to try to use intangible or contested quality gains as an excuse.

Policy changes can generally be expected to lower productivity. As new goals or policy instruments are brought in, agencies and staff inherently take time to fully understand and operate new things well. New business processes always create 'teething difficulties' for staff and customers. And a great deal of 'organizational learning' actually has to be experienced before lessons can in fact be understood and converted into responses (see section 9.2, Chapter 9). James Scott (1998) makes a powerful case for believing that policy-makers (both politicians and senior officials) will normally pursue rationalistic goals in ways that neglect what he terms 'métis', the practical experience of how given problems have been/ are being handled in the community by non-expert decision-makers, like firms, families, workers and communities, and by the agency workers dealing with them.

Major reorganizations often distract managers, creating by far the most directly adverse impacts on productivity levels in the public sector. Managers' attention is displaced away from making serial improvements in familiar and well-understood business processes. Instead they are asked to focus on 'big planning' for restructurings that may well create uncertainty and have adverse impacts on their career chances, perhaps endangering the position of their division within the organization. Some managers leave or retire early, using the reorganization as an occasion to decommit. Those who remain may be preoccupied by securing a role in the new set up, even with an initially ring-fenced labour market. All major reorganizations turn managerial attention inwards, and away from external linkages and cooperative relations with other agencies and stakeholders – which also become more fragile the larger the scale of the internal reorganization. All of these effects are generally strengthened the more 'inorganic' the changes are, that is, the less they are rooted in the specific development of the department or agency in question.

The dynamics of such developments normally cannot be prevented or controlled by department or agency managers because they originate in the agency's wider or political environments. For instance, how can an agency management that is keen to maintain or improve its productivity level respond to strong wage increases elsewhere in the government sector? A non-sensible approach might be to fiercely resist wage increases over a run of years, causing a flight of talent from the agency. Depressing relative wages in the agency might secure some temporary pause in the decline of productivity levels, but it will not be sustainable. Good staff will leave in a random 'Swiss cheese' pattern, and new staff will be hard to find or of lower quality. Add in short-term freezes of IT budgets and the agency's position within the mainstream of public sector advances could quickly be jeopardized after only two or three years of such policies. To respond in more sustainable ways to stronger wage pressures on costs, managers need to uprate and intensify their search for a wide range of serial improvements in their business processes, continuously bringing forward more innovations that could lead to increased output with the same levels of staff, yielding potential productivity increases that may counteract the costs bulge.

For a department or agency to be fully committed to continuously raising (or at the least maintaining) its productivity level, both managers and staff will need to have a wide menu of changes that they can push forward in a serial manner – typically a programme of linked incremental improvements where feasible changes happen regularly. Yet, empirical studies of government innovation strongly suggest another dominant pattern, reflecting the common absence of competition, and the relatively enduring character of most government organizations. In a study drawing on responses from 150 departments and agencies, Dunleavy et al. (2006b) found that UK national government organizations tended to become frozen into overly stable configurations that endure for long periods, during which productivity can decline gradually in response to wage or costs inflation. These periods of stasis are punctuated only by periodic 'large-scale' changes or reorganizations (during which productivity will normally decrease or be set back a few years). Many UK government organizations responded to a National Audit Office (NAO) survey about their innovations, by nominating very large-scale changes (designed to improve policy 'effectiveness' rather than productivity), or discussed projects taking five to eight years to complete. Dunleavy et al. (2006b) contrasted this with evidence from private sector comparator organizations, where large businesses almost never made innovations taking longer than two to three years to implement, instead adding many more but smaller-scale innovations, in a repeating manner, every year – mostly arranged in 'chain' sequences that led on from one to another. By contrast, UK government agencies mainly nominated only isolated or one-off innovations. In addition, some agencies had no, or very few, changes to report to NAO.

In the modern era there seems to be a considerable scope for government organizations to pick up and adopt many of the same types of changes undertaken by the giant private retailers (such as Tesco in the UK or Walmart in the USA), large insurance companies, some private healthcare providers and other reputable private firms with business processes that have some close analogies in the government sector. Table 10.1 provides a summary list of initiatives made within private services that have potential applicability in public sector services.

This list may seem a little specific and oddly focused when looked at from the perspective of most existing public administration or public management textbooks. The academic literature is preoccupied (one might say, obsessed) with two 'managerialist' topics – the design of organizational structures, and the selection, incentivization and socialization of staff. By contrast, Table 10.1 focuses on quite different kinds of generic change. It suggests that what matters is the *substantive content* of what a government organization is doing, especially in terms of the following:

- Simplifying policy to fit closely with the needs and preferences of customers, wherever possible delivering what it is that they need in a 'co-production' manner.
- Focusing hard on the nature of the substantive professional solutions currently deployed, and on innovations and upgradings of provision made possible by technological changes.
- Working creatively with contractors in competitive environments so as to help develop the role that other firms and organizations can play in completing the agency's key missions tasks.
- Paying close attention to customer interactions and to exploiting the huge potential for savings and quality improvements that modern digital era processes (run by more skilled staff) make feasible. Speeding up, simplifying and scaling up information flows between service providers and users, and expanding customer choices, are key here. Well-informed and often expert customers are often the first to identify new needs, or approaches that maximize their

Table 10.1 Twenty four generic suggestions for growing the productivity of all government services

Management suggestions	(a) Private sector examples	(b) Government sector examples
1. Shift to risk-based administrative processes (and away from volumetric checks)	Staffed supermarket checkouts replaced by customer self-checkouts	Adoption of risk-based checks for the processing of UK imports and exports (Customs)
2. Increase the scale of procurement to match technological change	Large supermarkets dominate modern retailing because of these economies of scale.	Consortia of government agencies often procure collectively to try to increase their buying power (but also often struggle with a 'not invented here' attitude).
3. Make suppliers do more of the work	Milk in supermarkets is delivered in trolleys suitable for immediate customer self-serve, going straight into chilled cabinets within the sales space. No transhipping by shop staff. Requiring suppliers to make staggered just-in-time milk deliveries means there's no need for 'back of shop' chill storage.	Some forms of business process outsourcing by government agencies work in similar ways, e.g. UK defence catering, even to forces on active field service overseas.
4. Increase the transparency and accessibility of information about stores and stocks to grassroots workers	A standard element of 'lean' manufacturing on the Toyota model	Assigning smallish delegated social care budgets to front line care workers, so that they can flexibly respond to client needs and ease immediate acute problems
5. Communicate key work flows progress against	Extensively used in manufacturing industries and most	Typically only deployed in minor ways in the public sector – e.g. staff in

Table 10.1   (continued)

Management suggestions	(a) Private sector examples	(b) Government sector examples
targets and achievements to grassroots workers; actively involve workers via incentives and information in achieving performance improvements	large private sector services companies	government call centres work with big screens showing call response times, and queues of waiting customers against expected response standards. Some police forces, schools and hospitals play back to staff accessible daily or weekly information on how their organization is performing.
6. Understand where costs and delays occur in the flow of business, then 'reverse engineer' so as try to eliminate costs and delays. Within any given service class, what's good for service quality is generally also good for costs and performance as well.	Standard practice in product redesign and service improvement in the private sector	Beginning to be used in large agencies, in customer understanding or communication units. A government-wide example was the PM's Delivery Unit, set up by Tony Blair (Barber, 2008; Kelman, 2006), but since abolished.
7. Stop doing unnecessary tasks	Airlines used to run separate ticketing systems and boarding card systems – now they rely on customers own ID documents and get customers online to pre-issue boarding cards with barcodes.	Eliminating the necessity different ID numbers for government services: NI, Tax codes, etc. Introducing 'digital by default' provisions that make online applications and transactions etc. mandatory unless there are very good reasons not to.
8. Scale up service provision, with 'network	Amazon dominates ebook marketing and dissemination	Hypothetically – a national ebook service could replace book lending

Table 10.1   (continued)

More management suggestions	(a) Private sector examples	(b) Government sector examples
products' displacing 'local products'	in a centralized way, partly displacing local bookshops.	by local public libraries (although not their community roles).
9. Develop more 'part-finished' or 'platform' products or facilities that users can then deploy to accomplish a very wide diversity of individual goals (Nooteboom, 2005).	e-Bay is a platform product that users can employ in very different ways. The Apps market for phones and tablet PCs is a classic example, along with Microsoft past strategy.	Like private systems, government labour market systems in UK and many EU countries let employers load job vacancies directly. Publicly funded wi-fi facilities, e.g. covering whole cities and providing free public Internet access.
10. Follow design/ prototype/ pilot/improve strategies, with rapid prototyping of multiple possibilities, online testing using randomized control tests, sifting from large menu to final solution	Standard 'big data'/ data warehousing methods of working, with online experiments of all elements of new market concepts and communications. Large numbers of transactions surface knowledge in depth of what works.	Government data warehousing and analysis is starting, but online experimentation is rare due to conservatism. Officials are reluctant to do prototyping and pilots for fear of 'political' problems, hence mostly still try to reach single perfect solutions, launched with big bang.
11. Design services so as to engineer customer 'returns' and bad service experiences out of the system. Aim for zero or minimum-feasible complaints.	In private services many of the most onerous costs attach to bad customer experiences, complaints and 'exceptions management'. Hence companies have strong economic incentives to minimize and try to eliminate avoidable costs generated this way.	Public sector processes almost never creatively aim to achieve 'zero complaints', but instead to achieve only a government-wide average level of problems. The average is often set too low for high-stress areas (like tax or social security), and here demotivates staff who respond by fatalistically normalizing complaints.

Table 10.1   (continued)

More management suggestions	(a) Private sector examples	(b) Government sector examples
	They focus intensively on – smoothing service experiences, removing checks, snags, irritations, and faults for customers; – removing difficulties and complexities for staff; – replacing points where unnecessary costs arise.	At the same time in low stress areas the overall average is too high and easily attained, so there is no continuous drive to eliminate remaining complaints, even where feasible (see Dunleavy et al, 2010a).
12. Phase out services for which demand has declined	Standard product succession strategies in the private sector.	'Creative de-commissioning' of public services where usage levels are dropping.
13. Use zero touch technology (ZTT) requiring no human intervention or checking for transactions	Most online e-commerce systems	Most online tax systems. Automated e-passport gates at airports.
14. Automate information-gathering	Combining store loyalty cards with fully electronic tills itemizing each purchase, especially in food and other product supermarkets, allow the auto-uploading of 'shopping basket' information overnight to fully automated re-ordering systems for chains. Data warehousing on a massive scale facilitates very sophisticated and	Hard to think of an analogous government use. Nor has government yet gained access to 'big data' piles in the private sector, because of privacy law and concerns. E.g. Walmart (in USA) or Tesco (in UK) control databases of purchasing behaviours that could be very valuable for government in fields like health care – knowing what people buy would hugely help government experts combating the adverse health or schooling effects of obesity

Table 10.1   (continued)

More management suggestions	(a) Private sector examples	(b) Government sector examples
	responsive trends and consumer targeting analyses, on a store-by-store basis, in real time.	or tobacco or alcohol addiction.

Customer focus suggestions	(a) Private sector examples	(b) Government sector examples
15. Automate permanent customer identification, and use 'one-time' customer identifications	Customer loyalty cards in retail as above	Having a unique ID number for all government transactions, as in Sweden, where banking sector IDs are also used for government purposes. The UK is moving towards a single number for social security and tax purposes.
16. Allow/persuade/ help customers to do more of the work tasks	Customer self-check-in at airports	Social care customers manage their own care budgets and choose how to allocate spending (within limits).
17. Segment customers more	Supermarkets that are able to offer tailored offers to customers based on shopping patterns	Online (intelligent) forms filter customers through relevant questions only, based on previous answers.
18. Feed back to users what other users find helpful	Standard in emerging social media marketing. Long record e.g. Amazon product reviews	Most government agencies give little or no customer feedback, and insist on tightly authoring all content on their websites in 'paranoid' public relations mode.

Table 10.1   (continued)

Customer focus suggestions	(a) Private sector examples	(b) Government sector examples
		solicits customer views of hospitals. UK schools and family doctors have less intensive scrutiny possibilities.
20. Capitalize on staff (and customer) knowledge	Some private companies run strong staff suggestion schemes, e.g. the Tesco mantra that suggestions should be 'Better for customers, simpler for staff, cheaper for Tesco'. This is backed up systematic collating of suggestions and rewards for changes adopted.	Very few government agencies run proper suggestions schemes. Changes have included 'innovation tournaments' with pilot funding for projects that come top.

Service design suggestions	(a) Private sector examples	(b) Government sector examples
21. Respect and release the expertise of front-line staff. Show continuously that the benefits from staff disclosing information to improve performance will be shared and that managers are trustworthy.	Large private firms aim to close fit their HR systems to rewards indicators of innovation and effectiveness of teams via promotions and incentive payments. 'No blame' systems for understanding problems have worked well in developing 'safety bureaucracies' (like airlines). Inventive 'talent management' strategies for key innovative personnel.	Many government HR systems still encourage staff to 'run a desk' and minimize the risk of mistakes and incurring blame. This can create a 'never volunteer, keep your head down' organizational culture. Introducing team working, scrapping tagged 'desks', requiring evidence of innovation for promotion, and introducing 'no blame' experiments and pilots, can all help change entrenched attitudes.

Table 10.1   (continued)

Service design suggestions	(a) Private sector examples	(b) Government sector examples
22. Use better service design.	There are developed professions and sub-professions in the private sector for all aspects of product and service design.	Service design professionals are less commonly employed in government, and often services are introduced by 'generalist' officials (and politicians) with little specific training.
23. Shift from 'Task once, use once' processes to 'Task once, use many times' processes	Engrained in cost minimization efforts.	Shift most government websites from inflexible content management systems to blogs, and use RSS feeds, permanent URLs etc. to cut maintenance costs and problems
24. Use fault-tolerant systems	Design websites for immediate use (no pre-registering or unnecessary IDs. Provide immediate remedies on lost log-in details.	Greater cross-use of same identities across government services e.g. 'Tell Us Once' programme in UK. Getting rid of pointless registrations and over-asking for ID is a long battle still.

Note: RSS is Really Simple Syndication.

satisfaction. Hence 'democratizing innovation' (allowing customers to drive or at least partly define the innovation programme) can offer service organizations a real competitive edge (Nooteboom, 2005; von Hippell, 2005). Conventional R&D efforts expensively seek to detect and then remotely 'model' or 'simulate' what customers want, and it speeds up the change process. In modern government involving customers more actively cuts these costs and may particularly stimulate the production of not-fully-finished products or capabilities, that customers can adapt to their needs (Nooteboom, 2006). However, while smaller innovative firms organized as fluid 'adhocracies' (Mintzberg, 1983) can fit this change into their organizational cultures relatively easily, this is a much harder adaptation for conventional 'hierarchist' public bureaucracies to adopt (Hood, 1998, Ch. 4).

- Constantly redeploying and developing staff and incrementally shifting organizational processes in much more flexible ways so as to maintain or develop outputs at lower costs. This process always entails retaining strong 'mission commitment' by staff and (if this is working well) high levels of trust by workers that managers will not behave opportunistically if they offer up information about where efficiencies can be made (see section 10.3 below).

It is worth briefly noting what is not included in Table 10.1, the kinds of things that although very fashionable in the recent period, and much practised in the era of new public management's predominance, seem to have little or nothing to do with improving government sector productivity. These include the following:

- Focusing on business process outsourcing, and forcing intragovernmental processes to be outsourced to private firms.
- Worrying about 'optimally' allocating the ownership of assets, so as to maximize the economic efficacy of their use.
- Obsessing about the 'realignment' of 'narrowly economic' or 'rational actor' incentives, or the notional transfer of risks in public services. These theory-based arrangements are often fragile. They can easily break down in a crisis, with any catastrophic cessation of services simply causing risks to revert to the state.

Occasionally, in response to particular policy problems or needs, it can be constructive to push the barriers between public and private sector activities back and forth. This is especially the case where the private sector markets involved are genuinely competitive and cost-lowering, and where supplier diversity can be increased. For example, these conditions can often be met by bringing voluntary or third sector organizations into play as possible local providers of particular services to customers, where they have particular organizational expertise or other advantages. But merely involving a few large private firms in service provision paid by government does very little to constrain costs or to save money (see next section). Instead it often freezes provision in a form that then becomes contractually specified for years ahead, slows down technological changes and creates stronger legal and contractual barriers to the organic, incremental and serial changes in services of the kinds recommended above.

10.2   STRENGTHENING PROVIDER SUCCESSION

Over-polarized, partisan debates about the role and operations of government have been amongst the most debilitating and persistent influences tending to blunt the optimal development of productivity in government services. In this section we focus especially on why right-wing parties, business interests and neo-liberal commentators tend to undermine efforts to improve government productivity in several dimensions. The public statements of such groups often seem to insist that government activity is inherently ineffective and repugnant, and somehow doomed to be wasteful and chronically inefficient (Haldenby et al., 2009).We need only note here how incredibly unlikely it is that the productivity patterns of a private hospital and of a public hospital, or of units undertaking highly analogous administrative tasks in firms and in government agencies, must somehow *necessarily* diverge across sector boundaries. If organizations carry out the same activities, with the same technologies, within a common societal culture, their productivity levels should be reasonably convergent.

At the same time, the generally right-wing colouration of 'new public management' (NPM) has focused on creating market-analogue processes within government. This approach has a certain theoretical resonance, but its effects in increasing government productivity remain at best unproven. The theory argument starts from the proposition that in competitive private industries, less productive firms have higher costs, charge higher prices or offer only lower-quality products. Hence they should progressively sell less than their more productive rivals. So long as the market concerned does not have monopoly or oligopoly features, or restrictive regulation protecting incumbents, then the competitive process will automatically tend to transfer business from less productive to more productive firms over time, accelerating the changes in industry productivity following from internal improvements in each firm. In the private sector generally, including many sectors that are far from perfectly competitive or are not impartially regulated, this transfer of business effect is nonetheless resilient and recurs regularly. Across many different business sectors it usually accounts for around half of the observed improvements in industry-level productivity.

Trying to reproduce analogues of this effect within the government sector has stimulated one of the biggest and most intractable debates in modern public management. Responsibilities for delivering public services still tend to be allocated either to state monopolies (at national level, plus state governments in federations) or to decentralized local authorities. With national or regional monopoly provision, citizens and service customers have nowhere else to go if the only services available to them are poor or costly. The users of municipal services have some capacity to shift between local areas in pursuit of an efficient tax/service mix. In the well-known Tiebout (1956) model, the marginal effects of citizens moving to more efficient areas can theoretically be magnified in ways analogous to the marginal shifts of customers between suppliers in private markets, thereby generating positive welfare effects. But the transactions costs of moving house between areas are always high for citizens. And any efficiency differences between local authorities anyway tend to be amortized into the capital values for properties in their areas (Dowding et al., 1994) in ways that negate both the signalling effects and the direct positive market effects of people moving areas.

The oldest models of public administration placed their reliance on political control at the local and national levels to create stimuli that would regularly energize government officials, generating new political impulses for them to be efficient and to introduce innovations in timely ways. Responding to public choice theories deeply distrustful of public bureaucracies (especially Niskanen [1971] 1995), the NPM wave from 1985 to 2005 advocated a wide range of methods that it was claimed would inject more competition between providers, cut costs and bring in new capital and organizational cultures to sustain increased innovation. Such effects have been claimed in turn for privatization, mandatory outsourcing, contracting out services, introducing private finance (PFIs) and private–public partnerships (Dunleavy et al., 2006a). Many NPM advocates on the right believed that bringing in private sector providers would automatically increase the rate of technological change and innovation because new suppliers would put pressure on incumbent government providers. As market maturity deepened, so the 'contestability' of huge blocks of work previously securely 'owned' by single suppliers would increase – creating lasting positive welfare effects beyond the cost savings achieved at the initial transfer.

With hindsight, much of this NPM prospectus has proven to be hopelessly optimistic and ill-grounded in organizational realities. In the IT sector, for instance, contracting out in strong NPM countries simply transferred monopoly power from public agencies to oligopolistic, multinational system integrator companies, every bit as conservative and uninnovative as the (maligned) civil servant operators before them (Dunleavy et al., 2008). The recurring difficulties with defence procurement oligopolies in the USA, UK, France and other high-spending countries also provide ample testimony that outsourcing or privatization in many circumstances does not effectively transfer risk away from government, nor create any strong pathways for cost-reducing innovations to be effectively developed. In both legacy IT systems contracting and defence procurement, contractors have faced a choice between modularizing capital good and service provision into low-cost forms that can be generalized and competed for more effectively – or retaining high-cost, à la carte models of service delivery (which lend themselves well to proprietary lock-in by oligopolistic suppliers). Not surprisingly they chose the security of the latter route, aided by the fact that politicians and government bureaucracies also share strong and myopic preferences for the à la carte model (Dunleavy et al., 2010, Ch. 9).

A quite different area of outsourcing has been for services that are not capital intensive and are often small scale, such as cleaning services and catering in small institutions. Here unsophisticated contract specification by government clients often led to an initial 'race to the bottom' as small businesses competed by cutting costs to the bone, in the process quality-shading in dozens of hard-to-capture but nonetheless often vital ways. In the UK lowest-cost cleaning contracts in hospitals contributed to a scandal of hospital cleanliness. Partly as a direct result, and partly because NPM management practice encouraged 'bed-cramming' and unrealistically high levels of usage, UK levels of hospital-acquired infections in the early 2000s reached the highest levels in Western Europe – at one point being 40 times greater than those in Denmark (NAO, 2000b).

Similarly, the outsourcing of school catering led to scandals of 'junk food only' school lunches contributing to rising obesity levels, as contractors sought more customers by lowest common denominator, fattening menus (Belot and James, 2011). And even contracts for refuse collection have proved problematic, with many winning bids proving to be under-funded. Penalty clauses have frequently been activated over quality-shading by contractors, and there have often been contract breakdowns and terminations (sometimes preceded by many months of inadequate service). Many of the new contractors in all these cases were under-capitalized firms and there were few signs of increased specialization or superior management practices (beyond cost-paring).

The main solutions adopted to stem quality declines in all these cases partly involved better contract writing, in which quality levels became more restrictively set out, recreating the 'iron cage' of government regulation that NPM originally wished to dispense with (Gill, 2011). A secondary solution has been to re-foster industrial concentration of even 'ancillary' roles in the hands of fewer, bigger companies with more assured quality-control capacities. The cost here though is in reduced competition and the emergence of oligopolistic markets dominated by two or three providers in cleaning, catering, refuse collection and many other services – such as Serco and Capita who now dominate the UK market. In the USA too 'there is evidence that competition, in and of itself, leads to some contractor turnover . . . [But] it does not appear that competitive vendors are held to higher standards than their noncompetitive counterparts regarding performance (as measured by adherence to contract terms)' (Lamothe and Lamothe, 2009, p. 164).

In the UK, the archetype of NPM provision was the massively used Private Finance Initiative (PFI), which increased procurement costs substantially and produced an oligopolistic initial market for most major projects, with very few viable bids per contract, even in the supposedly competitive construction sector (NAO, 2011a). Public agencies have repeatedly got trapped into dealing repetitively with tiny numbers of feasible providers, especially on the highest-value and most complex contracts, where only the largest contractors can insure against the risks involved. Again, deficiencies in contract writing led to scandals of UK public sector clients being charged tens or hundreds of pounds for simple maintenance tasks (like changing light bulbs). The government sector also lost out to the tune of hundreds of millions of pounds when PFI contractors succeeded in refinancing their projects (once built) at much lower interest rates, without initially having to pass on any of the gains made to their government sector clients (NAO, 2006).

An increasingly oligopolistic secondary market in PFI contracts was also created, where service delivery responsibilities are at permanent risk of being shuffled repeatedly across multinational firms in ways that government cannot even monitor effectively, let alone control (NAO, 2006, Part 3). Asset values are often stripped away at each transaction in ways that are exceptionally hard to regulate. Contract sizes are routinely aggregated massively in ways that re-pool risks. Ownership often transfers away from initially resting with firms with sector-relevant expertise towards hedge funds, banks or other financial entities solely motivated by short-term shareholder value.

In the UK in mid-2011 a social care provider looking after 31 000 elderly people (Southern Cross) went bankrupt after being successively owned by hedge funds that re-aggregated and remortgaged its assets (hundreds of old people's care homes) and took capital value out as dividends before selling the services contracts on. This event reflected the cartelization of provision rapidly achieved in the social care market (Scourfield, 2012). It created a huge risk for the UK national government, one that was many times greater than had care services remained under direct local authority provision – for then any provider difficulties would have only affected a few homes or areas at the same time.

These developments culminated in 2011 in the virtual abandoning of the previous crude models of PFI and public–private partnership (PPP) projects in the UK. If they are to revive, then very different and sophisticated models for involving private capital funding will need to be evolved (Treasury Select Committee, 2011; Hellowell, 2012a). Similarly, although the UK government has promoted quasi-markets heavily as a means of reorganizing the NHS, the future likelihood of success will depend heavily on achieving genuine competition that is fruitful in terms of innovation (Hellowell, 2012b).

The dwindling band of NPM advocates have placed great hopes in the creation of quasi-markets within the vast government education and health services, by decentralizing provision to thousands of micro-local providers, such as individual schools, colleges or hospitals (LeGrand, 2007, 2012). Here national government provides principally a regulatory framework and a national funding formula that allow local facilities to compete with each other to attract users or activities, with each user or activity attracted bringing with them a 'virtual pack' of financing. The regulatory structures of quasi-markets need to be set up so that users or customers can compare nearby or feasible providers easily using 'league tables', showing their comparative performance on key performance indicators (KPIs). Digital era developments have greatly simplified the information-giving process. And for many (fairly well-off) people living in urbanized areas, the transaction costs of moving between nearby micro-local providers can be much less than they would be for people moving across whole municipal areas. Offsetting shifts in house price capitalizations might also be lessened if detailed local geographies ('catchment areas') become less of a determinant of who can gain access to which services. The initial impacts of quasi-market systems are also often positive in terms of attracting entrepreneurial professionals and managers to 'first-mover' opportunities.

Yet, as with other NPM effects, the benefits of quasi-markets often quickly dwindle away as the changes involved become generalized to apply across whole policy sectors. The initial round of benefits experienced here may primarily reflect a selection bias, with innovations being picked up first by the most innovative leaders and organizations (compounding with the effect of the policy shift). Positive effects on staff and customers may also owe a good deal to 'Hawthorne' effects, where people initially respond to the occurrence of management interventions, largely irrespective of their actual welfare gains from the intervention. Over time, however, staff, competing providers, and contractors all learn how to 'play' the new system.

A range of club-type effects may also emerge, with 'good' schools progressively able to pick their students selectively from pools of the 'best' children, a process appropriately called 'client shaping' (a version of bureau shaping) (Dunleavy, 1991, Ch. 8). Client shaping is highly rational since teachers in a 'good' school need to work less hard to get good marks from brighter and parentally supported children than from those with lower IQ levels or unsupportive home backgrounds. Often the costs here are counted in increased expulsions of 'difficult' children; more banding; more class-based and ethnic segregation of students across schools; decreased social control in the worst schools; declining levels of cooperation across schools; and reduced community linkages or influence over schools. Such client-shaping processes are often subtle and cumulative in school systems and hospitals, and hence they can be very hard to detect early on and to counteract before problems become intense.

A key overall constraint on the effectiveness of quasi-markets is the extent to which competition for clients between providers is real or fake. Real competition depends upon there being significant levels of slack in the numbers of school places or hospital beds that are available at any given time. If customers (like parents or patients) are to have a genuine choice of providers then they need to be able to move relatively freely across providers without joining long queues for access to the facilities they want to reach. Yet this entails governments being willing to support slack capacity in the system, to somehow fund empty school places, or hospital beds and operating theatre slots left unfilled. Both the traditional public administration focus on avoiding duplication in provision, and NPM's obsessive stress on maximizing usage levels of school premises or hospital beds, militate against the provision of slack capacity.

Yet without significant amounts of unused capacity in the system, competitive effects are highly blunted (and may dissipate altogether in worst case set ups) because poor schools and hospitals know that they will tend to fill up anyway, despite their inadequacies. The clients of failing schools will be the least successful children (making it hard to recruit good teachers); or for poor hospitals they may be patients with the worst prognoses (making it hard to retain good doctors and nurses). But still these institutions will have 'customers' and their leaders and staff will be employed – and they will have a strong exculpatory story to tell about their abnormal difficulties. The conventional optimism of economists that club competition will improve welfare levels assumes that there are an optimal number of (good) clubs; that users are allocated efficiently but impartially across them (with no capacity for incumbent club members to exclude or tax new joiners); and that no one is left out of being a member of a viable club (Cornes and Sandler, 2006). Always hard to realize in practice, these onerous conditions are necessarily especially rare where the number of school places or hospital beds is closely linked to actual demand levels.

What this review of all forms of NPM shows is essentially that the problem of provider competition and succession is little addressed by most NPM solutions, once some one-off positive 'shock' effects have worn away. Ensuring that provision moves over time from less productive to more productive providers within the government sector is instead a complex problem, one that requires sustained attention over decades. It cannot be addressed by gimmicky or ideology-driven solutions, designed to reap short-term political returns from lobby groups or to help win a particular election by 'magicking' up short-term savings in the apparent costs of complex services.

10.3   INVOLVING GOVERNMENT WORKERS AND SECURING THE FUTURE OF GOVERNMENT

Over-polarized partisan debates are not confined to right wing parties and commentators. Social democratic parties, labour unions and left-wing commentators often tend to deny or indulge evidence of slow-growing productivity in public services, lining up instead behind the defence of anachronistically organized services. Workers and unions commonly oppose or reject many forms of services change that foster increased productivity or lower costs, using foot-dragging tactics to try to bargain for higher wages. Without a reappraisal of left attitudes to government productivity, such stances risk maintaining low-productivity performance into a digital era where fundamental improvements in the economic competitiveness of government provision would otherwise be feasible.

There are several powerful reasons for these historic attitudes and we discuss some broader and longer-run political factors involved in section 10.4. Here we want to focus on the main engine for reproducing and constantly updating resistance by state workers and public sector unions to productivity advances. As in private business, public sector workers and unions worry that if they offer up information to their managers about how to improve efficiency and productivity then they could be dealing with managers (or political controllers) who will not treat the information given in good faith. Instead, opportunistic managers will exploit information on how improve efficiency very selectively, using it to secure only one-sided, short-run gains at the workers' expense (Miller, 1992).

This was the central problem addressed by the so-called 'humanistic' forms of NPM, of which the leading example was the Clinton-Gore 'National Performance Review' period in the early 2000s (Kelman, 2005), with some parallels under the Australian Labour governments from 1985 to 1996 (Halligan, 2011). Miller stresses that managers have to show that if cost-saving information is volunteered by workers, they will use it in fair-minded ways to enhance the long-run viability and efficacy of the organization (thereby securing jobs and maintaining or potentially increasing wages and conditions). This is always a difficult line to walk, but Kelman (2005) stressed that the best staff in any organization typically want it to work more effectively. Managements that prove themselves worthy of trust in Kelman's view can normally draw on the strong commitment of around 30 per cent of staff keen to push ahead improvements in government agencies. They in turn will tend to bring along with the reform efforts the next half of the staff, who are potentially positive but normally quiescent. This process also tends to marginalize the perhaps fifth of employees who are highly resistant to changes for ethically bad reasons (self-interest, or reluctance to learn new things).

In the modern world, public sector workers' interests are best served by encouraging the emergence of a new, largely high-tech government sector, where the maximum range of activities are undertaken in 'inherently' or 'essentially digital' ways that are sustainable over the long term (Dunleavy, 2011a). Only a higher productivity route can offer public sector workers the opportunities to be better paid, to work in a clearly modern and efficient workplace, and to deliver services in a fashion that commands societal respect. The onset of austerity conditions in many advanced industrial societies after 2008 has greatly strengthened these imperatives.

As the realization spreads of the need to reappraise attitudes, it is important to look also at positive solutions to enhancing productivity, competition and provider succession within a government sector that continues to be a strong player in society and a key source of societal innovations. Here strategies to maximize productivity growth are likely to revolve around five key points:

1. *Creating strong and robust private–public sector competition processes*, where government always retains a real capacity to undertake service provision itself if private sector solutions are unattractive in cost or service quality terms. There are many different ways of sustaining such cross-sectoral competition, including:
   - a deliberate effort by government to sustain multiple private contractors;
   - government running its own centrally funded IT, procurement or other business;
   - service agencies operating in competition with contractors, to keep them up to the mark; and
   - local governments especially retaining the capacity to set up their own direct operations either individually or in coalitions across areas (especially in low-capital service areas).

2. *Fostering intra-public sector competition* involves allowing successful operators inside the public sector to quickly grow to scalable levels and to compete on fair terms with other government or private sector providers. This could be either on an occasional basis (for instance, one agency taking on service provision tasks or procurement handling for a nearby or similar agency), or on a cross-governmental basis (for instance, a centre of excellence within a tier of government regularly competing with private firms across a wide range of contracts). Regional or local agencies with a comparative advantage must be freed up to compete for work outside their own spatial areas. A range of intra-governmental contractors is needed that are of viable size, and are not artificially constrained by spatial or sector boundaries, in order to create continuous competitive tension with private sector providers. At least some government providers need to be able to obtain capital and professional expertise on comparable terms to large private competitors.

3. *Strengthening intra-public sector 'competition by comparison'* involves freeing up existing limited methods for public feedback and evaluation of decentralized providers of all kinds (for example, schools, local family doctors, clinics, hospitals, refuse collection providers, roads providers, transport providers) so that there is immediate (if moderated) online customer feedback about how service provision is going. The necessary concomitant is full transparency by the provider or contractor about its service levels and costs. Public agencies' governing bodies and contractors would both be required to show that they have paid regular and sustained attention to comments, complaints and customer feedback. In cases of long-standing problems, or underperformance on objective indicators relative to comparable services, the governing bodies of agencies would be required to consider bids from alternative providers (including for instance, neighbouring facilities or next door municipalities) to take over running their services.

4. *Making genuine differentiation of public services more flexible* entails allowing government sector providers who have a proven advantage to specialize in what they do and to appropriately scale up their operations (if they succeed). However intra-government competition is organized, it is important that some operators there can be of the right scale to attract the best professional expertise and high-quality management. If a government agency can develop excellent services, it should also be able to grow the scale of its operations in a fair competition environment.

5. *Capitalizing on professional advances more quickly* also requires changing how public sector agencies are staffed and organized, so that

organizational heads or management teams of proven worth within government could develop scalable operations to extend the reach of their expertise. Much of this might be small scale and cooperative between decentralized areas or authorities. For example, the UK has already seen some experiments with the heads of successful schools also taking on leadership roles in running another, nearby but less successful school. With more flexible provision for management teams to develop within government sector, similar but wider processes might mean successful management teams taking over failing hospitals, prisons or other facilities to seek to accomplish turnaround transformations.

6.   *Analysing carefully what is to be centralized or decentralized* in public policy systems will be critical if all the initiatives above are to help create a digital state. Local or sub-regional control over policy-making may have been most appropriate in the past, and is still needed in services where it is important to vary policy choices so as to respond to differing circumstances and political priorities across areas. But this older pattern may not be needed in some services because of digital changes – and here trying to retain it may only lead to an extensive duplication of facilities and costs.

For instance, in England there are 110 local councils that are library authorities, providing access to books and other information services for citizens, but 80–85 per cent of their book stocks are exactly the same, and they are still organized into only around 70 consortia for book-buying purposes. Mainly small councils are all independently contracting now for e-book provision, even though a national contract menu for e-book services would clearly be a much cheaper alternative for digital provision. Little wonder that digital or e-book provision is lamentable, and many councils are threatening to cut their library services drastically. Obviously, a national digital books service could operate without any local branches at all – whereas the many defenders of public libraries stress their vital social and community roles. But should not such roles be directly facilitated and staffed by appropriate staff (community or youth workers, rather than librarians, not renowned for their social skills)? The book provision role could then be undertaken in the most effective and cost-minimizing digital form. This example shows that separating out what is best done centrally (supplying books to citizens) from what is inherently decentralized (libraries' current half-developed community roles) is going to be a continuously important task in the digital era. 'Creative decommissioning' will increasingly mean being able to run down declining demand services, while opening up new ones (Bunt and Leadbeater, 2012). Virtually free marginal provision of e-services is continuously revolutionizing the organization of government (Dunleavy, 2011a) and the implications for cultural institutions are especially significant (Leadbeater, 2010).

10.4 PRODUCTIVITY AND COMBATING SOCIAL INEQUALITY

The political left and labour movements in many liberal democracies have also favoured 'big state' solutions for some broader reasons. They have often seen the public sector as an area of society where templates for the more civilized and humane treatment of workers and employees can be initially developed, and from this base can then be exported to the rest of civil society. Unionization itself, extensive employee consultation, better wage rates and progressive human relations policies are now all closely bound up with public sector employment in advanced industrial societies. As a result, the left is reluctant to see this bridgehead of more constructive employee relations reduce in size. The largest labour unions especially have a strong vested interest now in safeguarding the numbers of public employees, on whom their membership levels increasingly depend.

In addition, however, and more altruistically, the left has correctly regarded a 'big state' strategy as an important post-war means of incorporating first manual workers, and latterly women, ethnic minorities and gender minorities into full participation in the labour market. Large-scale government, on this view, has directly fostered major reductions in social inequality by opening up employment opportunities for minorities. When minority members get decently paid government sector jobs, then this helps to reduce income disparities and to break down centuries-old restrictions on the advancement of the most socially disadvantaged groups. Those who were economically marginal to employment, especially women and ethnic minorities, have moved into near parity in wages in many large-state countries, largely through the expansion of public employment, especially since the 1960s.

However, the 'big state' strategy has increasingly yielded diminishing returns in reducing inequalities, according to Lee et al. (2011, p. 117), with the widening gap between high productivity business sectors and low-productivity state agencies as a key culprit:

> The role of public-service expansion in decreasing income inequality by providing job opportunities for the economically and socially marginalized has been significantly diminished by an increasing inter-sectoral productivity gap and structural imbalance between sectors. [W]hen increasing productivity

differences arise between private-manufacturing and public-service sectors, a public-sector-expansion strategy could disrupt an important institutional mechanism of wage restraint – coordinated wage bargaining – that had undergirded the dominance of corporatist politics after the postwar period . . . Once the coordinated wage-setting institutions are weakened, wage flexibility in highly competitive sectors severely worsens distributional outcomes . . . [A] decline in employment potential and wage coordination leads to increased income inequality. Our findings demonstrate that our public sector–sectoral productivity gap interaction model accounts for the variations in within-country income inequality over the past three decades . . . [T]he conventional wisdom stating that public-sector employment will decrease income inequality . . . has been taken for granted as a formal, macroeconomic formula for equality projects in many countries. We found that the effect of equality projects based on public-service expansion is conditional on a structural factor: the inter-sectoral productivity gap.

Low productivity growth in a large state sector limits the reduction of social inequality in a second key way, by creating an increasingly 'leaky bucket' for redistributing via welfare state payments. If public service costs rise over time, then the economic surplus available for welfare payments is restricted, and the overall economic growth rate becomes impaired. This causes the sums available for welfare payments to first stop increasing and later to shrink back against indicators such as median wage levels. Yet there is clear evidence that it is the generosity of welfare payments that has the closest and most substantial effects in reducing social inequality across different countries (Lee et al., 2011, pp. 117–18). Over time, defending a low-productivity, 'big state' strategy will only erode the capacity of welfare states to ameliorate the most acute forms of disadvantagement.

Abandoning a tolerance of lagging government productivity does not mean giving up on the pursuit of social equality, nor does it entail that the left and social democratic movements should abandon their traditional objectives to reduce inequalities. It instead recognizes that privileging the employment conditions of only public sector workers, in ways that confer few real benefits on those workers over time (in terms of higher wages or real job security), is an unsustainable solution. Especially when government sector productivity increases far less than that in the private sector, this approach will tend both to erode public support for state intervention and to reduce the societal resources available for welfare state redistribution – on which the real reduction of inequalities most depends. As Lee et al. (2011, p. 100) conclude: 'Severely uneven productivity gaps due to different degrees of technological innovations significantly weaken and limit the effectiveness of left-wing governments' policy interventions through public-service expansion'.

The current austerity push in many European countries and the USA has underlined the importance of reaching a more sustainable basis for government's role in liberal democracies. The extraordinarily strong 'backlash against the state' that accompanied the onset of austerity policies (Dunleavy, 2010b, 2010c, 2011c) has acutely dramatized the political unsustainability of maintaining a long-term productivity gap between the public and private sectors. A smaller, leaner and high productivity public sector can be a powerful force for reducing social inequality – if it efficiently levies taxes, uses digital methods to regulate scrupulously in the public interest, provides transactional public services in robust ways, and uses diversely contestable methods for delivering remaining face-to-face services, co-producing an increasingly large range of outcomes with citizens themselves.

Conclusions

There is no single prescription for enhancing the organizational productivity of government agencies. The four routes to better performance set out in this chapter probably all need to be followed *at the same time* if the relative costs of public services are not to rise sharply over time. Government leaders need to take workers and professional staff along with them, boosting productivity in an atmosphere of active cooperation and mutual trust, where agency leaders' long-term commitments both to securing change and to distributing productivity gains fairly are not in doubt. Parties and unions on the left need to exorcise their fears of management opportunism and a slowing of social progress with a smaller state, in order to embrace more fully the scope for digitally-based modernizations that will increase the legitimacy of and demands for state involvement.

At the same time parties and interest groups on the right need to recognize that doing without the state in modern conditions is a throwback mirage, like the Tea Party hankering in the USA for a simpler, pre-modern world (Bernstein, 2010). Constantly raising the spectre of somehow (against all evidence) doing without the state only serves to distract attention from the continuous effort needed to make it better. Previous NPM strategies focusing on outsourcing, privatization and constantly fiddling with the boundaries of the public and private sectors have typically made surprisingly little positive difference to the long-run productivity of government.

Instead, to get government productivity growing month by month, and year by year, the changes needed are more varied and more subtle. The fundamental steps are:

1. collecting good-quality and stable data on government services' inputs, outputs and productivity growth;

2. focusing consistently on productivity trends within major organizations over long periods;
3. understanding what drives advances, stasis and declines in productivity;
4. normalizing pervasive increases in efficiency; and
5. committing to organizational learning and faster digital change (as discussed in the last chapter).

Creating genuinely competitive processes within and between government organizations can greatly increase the tempo and acceptance of transferring activities from less productive to more productive government organizations and community providers.

Overall, this is a huge change agenda, on which it is scarcely surprising that previous progress has often been confused or fragmentary. Yet this book shows that public sector workers, professionals and managers can generate the information, knowledge, expertise and opportunities needed to reverse the historic neglect of organizational productivity within government. The struggle to do so is certain to remain one of the defining challenges of the early twenty-first century.

Appendix: Data and methods

SOCIAL SECURITY PRODUCTIVITY

For the main outputs series for the 1997–08 to 2007–08 series we relied on information provided by the Department for Work and Pensions (DWP) from its own productivity work and covering a total of 14 benefits. These include both the number of benefits paid (load) and the number of new applications for benefits processed (claims): Each benefit was weighted according to the total costs of administering each benefit. Weighted benefits were then added and converted into a total index of output.

Benefits analysed for 1999 to 2008 period
Both load and claim measures unless otherwise stated:

Income Support	State Pension
Jobseeker's Allowance	Minimum Income Guarantee (until 2003)
Social Fund Payments	Pension Credit (after 2003)
Incapacity Benefit	International Pension Credit
Other Working Age Benefits	Future Pension Forecasts
Carers' Allowance	Attendance Allowance
Child Support Benefit (here we used a DWP measure for the number of children benefiting)	Disability Living Allowance

The index of total inputs for the 1997 to 2008 total factor productivity (TFP) analysis was based on deflated expenditure data (pay, procurement and capital) from the DWP (and before that the Department of Social Security, DSS) for the period under analysis. Specific deflators were used to deflate each expenditure components. These components were then

*Table A.1   Staff numbers in the Department for Work and Pensions, and
before 2001 in the Department of Social Security, in FTEs*

Year	1997/ 08	1998/ 09	1999/ 00	2000/ 01	2001/ 02	2002/ 03	2003/ 04	2004/ 05	2005/ 06	2006/ 07	2007/ 08
FTE staff (000s)	115.8	118.5	114.6	116.1	124.1	131.4	130.8	126.9	118.3	112.7	105.9

Source: Authors' calculations assembled from data supplied by DWP, DSS and relevant
agencies.

added and converted into the index of total inputs. The index of full-time
equivalent (FTE) staff was built according to the total number of FTE
staff for DWP/DSS, with key results shown in Table A.1. Staff productivity was the ratio of the index of output to the index of staff. Our staff
measure draws on data from the DWP, DSS and other DWP-predecessor
agencies.

The 20-year social security index (covering 1988 to 2008)
For our longer time series we used outputs data on the benefits described
in Table A.2 that were taken from the Abstract of National Statistics. We
checked the reliability of these data with the Work and Pensions Statistics
(for the 1988–99 period) and with the Work and Pensions Longitudinal
Study from DWP (for the 1999 to 2008 period). For this series we included
only 'payments' (that is, the total number of benefits paid or 'loads').
Unfortunately 'claims' were not reported in the public sources referred
to above for this period. For *the index of total inputs*, we used data from
the Abstract of National Statistics on 'General Government Total Final
Expenditure on Social Security Administration'.

We also calculated staff productivity by constructing an index of staff
costs by using data on the deflated paybill costs during this period. This
is slightly different from the approach we have taken in other services
where we use the total number of FTE staff, but unfortunately consistent data on FTE staff are not available dating back to 1987–08.

Paybill data was deflated using the GDP deflator and an index of staff
costs was calculated using 1987–08 as the base year. Staff productivity
was the result of the ratio of the index of total output to the index of staff
costs.

Table A.2   Benefits analysed 1988–2008

Benefits	

Working age
benefits
	Income Support (introduced in 1988; IS for unemployed
	    people is included until 1996, after which it was replaced
	    by Jobseeker's Allowance)
	Jobseeker's Allowance (before 1996 the Unemployment
	    Benefit was considered)
	Social Fund Grants and Loans (introduced in 1993)
	Incapacity Benefit (before 1995 data include Invalidity and
	    Sickness Benefit)
	Other working age benefits: Maternity Allowance, and
	    Widow Bereavement
	Child Benefit

Disability and carers' benefits	Attendance Allowance Disability Living Allowance (since 1993) Invalid Carers' – Carers' Allowance

Benefits for
elderly people
	State Pension
	Pension Credit (before 2003 Minimum Income Guarantee
	    was considered; between 1993 and 2000 data are for
	    people aged 60 and over and on Income Support)
	War Pensions

Housing	Housing Benefit

CUSTOMS PRODUCTIVITY

For the 1997–08 to 2007–08 output series we relied on data provided by Her Majesty's Revenue & Customs (HMRC) statistical teams. The output data covers the total number of import and export consignments processed by HMCE (Her Majesty's Customs and Excise) and HMRC since 2005. The output data was then weighted year on year, using the share of administration costs for each type of output.

Expenditure data for developing the input series were obtained from HMCE and its successor HMRC Annual Reports. It was necessary to estimate from these sources the total expenditure on staff (paybill) and other expenditure (procurement) for the customs area. It was not possible to separate out capital consumption for the customs and tax activities, so this expenditure category was excluded for the calculation of the index of total inputs. However, since this item tends to represent less than 10 per cent of total expenditure we do not believe that its exclusion will bias the results significantly.

The data was then deflated using the GDP deflator and a total index of inputs was established, using the same base year as for the index of outputs: 2001–02. The ratio of the index of output to the index of input constitutes the best approximation to TFP in the Customs area, but readers need to take into account that capital consumption is not included.

To calculate staff productivity, it was necessary to develop an index based on the number of FTE staff focused on the customs area. These data were obtained from HMCE and HMRC Annual Reports and special care was taken in isolating the number of staff relevant to customs.

An index of FTE staff was then developed, with the base year of 2001–02. The FTE staff productivity index results from the ratio of the index of output to the index of FTE staff.

TAX COLLECTION PRODUCTIVITY

1997–08 to 2007–08 analysis

For the output series we relied on data provided by statistical teams at HMRC. The data covers the total number of taxes processed for the different taxes listed below. It is important to note that this measure is different to the amount of money collected by each type of tax:

Income tax (includes Self-Assessment total, and number of PAYE live schemes)
Corporation tax
Capital gains tax
Inheritance tax
VAT

Excise duties and other indirect taxes (including insurance premium tax, air passenger duty and tobacco duty)

The data was then weighted according to the share of HMRC administration costs employed in processing each type of tax. An index of total output was then calculated, using 2001–02 as the base year.

Expenditure data for the series of inputs were obtained from Inland Revenue and its successor HMRC Annual Reports. Special care was taken to separate out the expenditure that corresponded to the tax effort during the whole period. The administrative costs data was composed of expenditure on staff (paybill) and other expenditure (procurement). It was not possible to estimate capital consumption. These data were then deflated using the GDP deflator. An index of total inputs was then calculated, using 2001–02 as the base year. The ratio of the index of output to the index of total input is the TFP index.

Alternative analysis

To gain more insight, we employed publicly available data to construct an index of output for the 1987–08 to 2007–08 period. Here, rather than relying on the total number of taxes collected we used the total tax amounts collected by each type of tax. The amount collected by the different taxes listed above was first deflated in order to have comparable yearly data using the GDP deflator. The deflated volumes were then weighted using the share of administration costs for each type of tax.

As with the main 1997–08 to 2007–08 series above, expenditure data on paybill and other expenditure from HMCE/Inland Revenue and HMRC Annual Reports were employed. These data were deflated using the GDP deflator and an index of total input was calculated using 1988–89 as the base year. TFP was the result of the ratio of the index of output to the index of input.

References

Adam, Stuart and James Browne (2011), 'A survey of the UK tax system', Briefing Note No. 9, London: Institute for Fiscal Studies.

Agarwal, Reeti and Ankit Mehrotra (2009), 'Developing global competitiveness by assessing organized retail productivity using data envelopment analysis', *International Journal of Business Science and Applied Management*, **4**(2), 1–16, accessed 29 September 2012 at http://www.business-and-management.org/download.php?file=2009/4_2--1-16-Agarwal,Mehrotra.pdf.

Allison, Graeme (1971), *Essence of Decision: Explaining the Cuban Missile Crisis*, Boston: Little Brown.

Al-Shehab, A.J., R.T. Hughes and G. Winstanley (2005), 'Facilitating organisational learning through causal mapping techniques in IS/IT project risk management', *Professional Knowledge Management*, **3782**, 145–54.

Aral, S., E. Brynjolfsson and Marshall Van Alstyne (2007), 'Information, technology and information worker productivity: task level evidence', NBER Working Paper No. W13172.

Ashworth, R., G. Boyne and R. Delbridge (2009), 'Escape from the iron cage? Organizational change and isomorphic pressures in the public sector', *Journal of Public Administration Research and Theory*, **19**(1), 165–87.

Atkinson, A.B. (2005a), 'Measurement of UK government output and productivity for the national accounts', *Journal of the Statistical and Social Inquiry Society of Ireland*, **XXXIV**, 152–9.

Atkinson, A.B. (2005b), *Final Report. Measurement of Government Output and Productivity for the National Accounts*, London: HMSO, accessed 14 September 2012 at http://ons.gov.uk/ons/about-ons/what-we-do/programmes--projects/completed-projects-and-reviews/atkinson-review/final-report/index.html.

Audit Commission (2011), 'Comprehensive Area Assessment', accessed 10 August 2011 at http://www.audit-commission.gov.uk/inspection-assessment/caa/Pages/Default.aspx.

Bailey, M. and R. Gordon (1988), 'The productivity slowdown, measurement issues and the explosion of computer power', *Brookings Papers on Economic Activity*, **19**(2) 347–432.

Barber, Michael (2008), *Instruction to Deliver: Fighting to Transform Britain's Public Services*, London: Methuen.

Barros, C. Pestana and P.U.C. Dieke (2007), 'Performance evaluation of Italian airports: a data envelopment analysis', *Journal of Air Transport Management*, **13**(4), 184–91.

Bartel, A., C. Ichniowski and Kathryn Shaw (2007), 'How does information technology affect productivity? Plant-level comparisons of product innovation, process improvement, and worker skills', *The Quarterly Journal of Economics*, **122**(4), 1721–58.

Bastow, S. (2010), 'Measuring productivity in the England and Wales prison system, 1979 and 2009', paper to the UK Political Studies Association Annual Conference, Edinburgh, 30 April, accessed 17 September 2012 at http://www.psa.ac.uk/2010/UploadedPaperPDFs/1323_1201.pdf.

Bastow, S. (2012), 'Over-crowded, as normal. Governance, adaptation and chronic capacity stress in the England and Wales Prison System, 1979 to 2009', PhD thesis, London: London School of Economics.

Bastow, Simon, Patrick Dunleavy and Hala Yared (2003), *Public Sector Agility: Data Appendices*, Annex to *Government Agility: Report to A.T. Kearney*, London: LSE Public Policy Group.

Baumol, William (1967), 'Macroeconomics of unbalanced growth', *American Economics Review*, **57**(3), 415–26.

Baumol, W.J., S.A.B. Blackman and E.N. Wolf (1989), *Productivity and American Leadership*, Cambridge, MA: MIT Press.

BBC News (2011), 'MRSA rates fall to record level', 3 August, accessed 19 September 2012 at http://www.bbc.co.uk/news/health-14390038.

Becker, Gary S. (2003), 'A theory of political competition amongst interest groups', *Quarterly Journal of Economics*, **XCVIII**(3), 371–400.

Becker, Gary S. (2005), 'Public policies, pressure groups and deadweight costs', *Journal of Public Economics*, **28**(2), 329–47.

Becker, Gary S. and Casey B. Mulligan (1998), 'Deadweight costs and the size of government', NBER Working Paper No. 6789, Washington, DC: National Bureau for Economic Research, accessed 16 September 2012 at http://www.nber.org/papers/w6789.

Behn, R. (2000), *Rethinking Democratic Accountability*, Washington, DC: Brookings Institution Press.

Behn, R. (2003), 'Why measure performance? Different purposes require different measures', *Public Administration Review*, **63**(5), 586–606.

Belot, Michèle and Jonathan James (2011), 'Healthy school meals and educational outcomes', *Journal of Health Economics*, **30**(3), 489–504.

Bernstein, J.M. (2010) 'The Very Angry Tea Party', *New York Times*, 13 June. Available at: http://opinionator.blogs.nytimes.com/2010/06/13/the-very-angry-tea-party/.

Bevan, Gwyn and Christopher Hood (2006), 'Have targets improved performance in the English NHS?', *British Medical Journal*, **332**(7538), 419–22.

Bhansali, S. and Erik Brynjolfsson (2008), 'Digitizing work: measuring changes in information worker time use and performance with a quasi-experiment', Paper No. 235, The MIT Center for Digital Business.

BIS (2008), *Public Services Industry Review. Understanding the Public Services Industry: How Big, How Good, Where Next?*, London: Business, Innovation and Skills.

Bloom, Nick and John van Reenan (2010), 'New approaches to measuring management and firm organization', CEP Discussion Paper No. 969, February, London: London School of Economics, Centre for Economic Performance.

Bloom, N., R. Sadun and J. Van Reenen (2005), 'It ain't what you do it's the way you do IT. Testing explanations of productivity growth using US affiliates', discussion paper, Centre for Economic Performance, London School of Economics.

Bloom, Nicholas, Carol Propper, Stephan Seiler and John Van Reenen (2009a), 'Management practices in hospitals', HEDG Working Paper No. 09/23, July, York: Health, Econometrics and Data Group, York University, accessed 1 October 2012 at http://www.york.ac.uk/res/herc/documents/wp/09_23_Removed.pdf.

Bloom, Nicolas, Luis Garicano, Raffaella Sadun and JohnVan Reenen (2009b), 'The distinct effects of information technology and communication technology on firm organization', CEP Discussion Paper No. 927, London: Centre for Economic Performance.

Bloom, Nicholas, Carol Propper, Stephan Seiler and John Van Reenen (2010), 'The impact of competition on management quality: evidence from public hospitals', CEP Discussion Paper No. 983, London: LSE Centre for Economic Performance.

Borzekowski, Ron (2009), 'Measuring the cost impact of hospital information systems: 1987–1994', *Journal of Health Economics*, **28**(5), 938–49.

Bosworth, Barry P. and Jack E. Triplett (2003), 'Productivity measurement issues in services industries: "Baumol's disease" has been cured', *Economic Policy Review*, **9**(3), 23–33.

Bowcott, Owen (2008), 'Up to 200000 ID documents may be false', *Guardian*, 8 October, accessed 18 September 2012 at http://www.guardian.co.uk/money/2008/oct/08/identityfraud.immigration.

Bozeman, Barry (2004), *All Organizations Are Public: Comparing Public and Private Organizations*, San Francisco, CA: Beard Books.

Brambor, T., W.R. Clark and M. Golder (2006), 'Understanding interaction models: improving empirical analyses', *Political Analysis*, **14**(1), 63–82.

Brandt, Loren, Thomas Rawski and John Sutton (2008), 'Industrial development in China', in Loren Brandt and Thomas G. Rawski (eds), *China's Great Economic Transformation*, New York: Cambridge University Press, pp. 569–632.

Bratton, William J. and Sean W. Malinowski (2008), 'Police performance management in practice: taking COMPSTAT to the next level', *Policing*, **2**(3), 259–65.

Bresnahan, T., E. Brynjolfsson and Lorin Hitt (2002), 'Information technology, workplace organization, and the demand for skilled labor: firm-level evidence', *The Quarterly Journal of Economics*, **117**(1), 339–76.

Breton, Albert (1998), *Competitive Governments: An Economic Theory of Politics and Public Finance*, New York: Cambridge University Press.

British Medical Journal (2010), 'Reorganization of the NHS in England', *British Medical Journal*, No. 341, Editorial 16 July, accessed 1 October 2012 at http://www.bmj.com/content/341/bmj.c3843?ijkey=2e0f56fdd5 e0603b9b679142b319254146c9c9c6&keytype2=tf_ipsecsha&linkType =FULL&journalCode=bmj&resid=341/jul16_1/c3843.

Brown, M.L. (2000), 'Scientific uncertainty and learning in European Union environmental policymaking', *Policy Studies Journal*, **28**(3), 576–96.

Brynjolfsson, E. and L. Hitt (1996), 'Paradox lost? Firm-level evidence on the returns to information systems spending', *Management Science*, **42**(4), 541–58.

Brynjolfsson, E. and L. Hitt (2003), 'Computing productivity: firm-level evidence', *The Review of Economics and Statistics*, **85**(4), 793–808.

Bullock, Jane A., George D. Haddow, Namon Copola, Erdin Yegin, Lissa Westermann and Sarp Yeletaysi (2006), *Introduction to Homeland Security*, 2nd edition, Burlington, MA: Heinemann-Butterworth.

Bunt, Laura and Charles Leadbeater (2012), *The Art of Exit: In Search of Creative Decommissioning*, London: NESTA.

Buratti, Simone, Dennis Keller, Yoojin Ma and Sara Young (2012), *Public Internal Financial Control: Composite Indicator Development for the Comparison of Internal Financial Control and Internal Audit in the Public Sector across OECD Member Countries*, London: LSE MPA Programme Capstone Project.

Bureau of Transport Statistics (2008), 'Table 4–2: licensed drivers: 2008', accessed 18 September 2012 at http://www.bts.gov/publications/state_ transportation_statistics/state_transportation_statistics_2009/html/tab le_04_02.html.

Burgess, Simon, Carol Propper, Marisa Ratto and Emma Tominey

(2004), 'Incentives in the public sector: evidence from a government agency', Working Paper, March, Bristol: Centre for Market and Public Organizations.

Burke, James (2007), *Al-Qaeda: The True Story of Radical Islam*, Harmondsworth: Penguin.

Businesslink (2011), Description of HMRC CHIEF system, accessed 15 September 2012 at http://www.businesslink.gov.uk/bdotg/action/detail?itemId=1078145531&type=RESOURCES.

Butler, David, Andrew Adonis and Tony Travers (1994), *Failure in British Government: Politics of the Poll Tax*, Oxford: Oxford University Press.

Cabinet Office (2009a), *HM Revenue & Customs: Progress and Next Steps*, Capability Review, London: Cabinet Office.

Cabinet Office (2009b), *Benchmarking the Back Office: Central Government*, London: Cabinet Office.

Caroli, E. and J. Van Reenen (2001), 'Skill-biased organizational change? Evidence from a panel of British and French establishments', *Quarterly Journal of Economics*, **116**(4), 1449–92.

Carrera, L., P. Dunleavy and S. Bastow (2009), 'Understanding productivity trends in UK tax collection', LSE Public Policy Group Working Papers, LSE Public Policy Group, London School of Economics and Political Science, accessed 14 September 2012 at http://eprints.lse.ac.uk/25532/1/UnderstandingTaxcollectionproductivity.pdf.

Castelli, A. et al. (2007), 'A new approach to measuring health system output and productivity', *National Institute Economic Review*, **200**(1), 105–16.

CBI (2009), 'World class public services', London: Confederation of British Industries, accessed 29 May 2011 at http://www.serco.com/instituteresource/subjects/UKmkt/PSI/index.asp.

Census Bureau (USA) (2012), 'Table 1096, State motor vehicle registrations', accessed 1 October 2012 at http://www.census.gov/compendia/statab/2012/tables/12s1096.xls.

Centre for Economics and Business Research (2009), 'The UK's public sector productivity shortfall is costing taxpayers £58.4 billion a year – in other words, not far short of half our income tax is paying for public sector inefficiency', press release, London: Centre for Economics and Business Research.

Charnes, A., W.W. Cooper and E. Rhodes (1978), 'Measuring the efficiency of decision making units', *European Journal of Operational Research*, **2**(6), 429–44.

Cho, Wendy K. Tam and James H. Fowler (2007), 'Legislative success in a small world: social network analysis and the dynamics of congressional legislation', Social Science Research Network paper, accessed 1 October 2012 at http://papers.ssrn.com/sol3/papers.cfm?abstract_id=1007966.

Christakis, Nicholas A. and James H. Fowler (2008), 'The collective dynamics of smoking in a large social network', *New England Journal of Medicine*, **358**(22), 2249–58.

Christakis, Nicholas A. and James H. Fowler (2010), *Connected: The Amazing Power of Social Networks and How They Shape Our Lives*, London: Harper Collins.

Christensen, Tom and Per Lægreid (eds), *The Ashgate Research Companion to New Public Management*, Farnham, Surrey: Ashgate.

Clement, Jan P., Vivian G. Valdmanis, Gloria J. Bazzoli, Mei Zhao and Askar Chukmaitov (2008), 'Is more better? An analysis of hospital outcomes and efficiency with a DEA model of output congestion', *Health Care Management Science*, **11**(1), 67–77.

Clory, Jonathan (2009), 'Managing public expenditure in a time of fiscal constraint', record of 'Innovating out of Recession in Public Services' seminar, 22 June 2009, pp.4–7 cover Patrick Dunleavy's presentation, accessed 18 September 2012 at http://www2.lse.ac.uk/government/research/res groups/LSEPublicPolicy/pdf/Innovating_out_of_recession.pdf.

Cohen, Michael H., James G. March and Johan P. Olsen (1972), 'A garbage can model of organizational choice', *Administrative Sciences Quarterly*, **17**(1), 1–25.

Common, Richard (2004), 'Organizational learning in a political environment', *Policy Studies Journal*, **25**(1), 35–49.

ComputerWeekly (2010), 'NPfIT spend rises to more than £6bn', 8 January, accessed 21 September 2012 at http://www.computerweekly.com/Articles/2010/01/08/239876/NPfIT-spend-rises-to-more-than-1636bn.htm.

Cooper, R. (1994), 'The inertial impact of culture on IT implementation', *Information and Management*, **27**(1), 17–31.

Cooper, William W., Lawrence M. Seiford and Joe Zhu (2011), 'Data envelopment analysis: history, models and interpretations', in *Handbook on Data Envelopment Analysis: International Series in Operations Research & Management Science*, Vol. 164, pp.1–39.

Cooper, Zack, Steve Gibbons, Simon Jones and Alistair McGuire (2010), 'Does hospital competition improve efficiency? An analysis of the recent market-based reforms to the English NHS?', Working Paper No. CEPDP0988, London: LSE Centre for Economic Performance.

Coopey, J. and J. Burgoyne (2000), 'Politics and organizational learning', *Journal of Management Studies*, **37**(6), 869–85.

Cornes, Richard and Todd Sandler (2006), *The Theory of Externalities, Public Goods, and Club Goods*, Cambridge: Cambridge University Press.

Dekker, S. and D. Hansen (2004), 'Learning under pressure: the effects of politicization on organizational learning in public bureaucracies', *Journal of Public Administration Research and Theory*, **14**(2), 211–30.

Department for Work and Pensions (DWP) (2008), *An Analysis of DWP Productivity 1997/98–2007/08*, London: DWP Corporate Document Services, Research Report No. 355 by DWP SPEAR project team covering 'Strategic Understanding of Productivity and Efficiency based on the Atkinson Review'.

Department of State (2012), 'Passport statistics', Washington, DC: Department of State, accessed 1 October 2012 at http://travel.state.gov/passport/ppi/stats/stats_890.html.

Department of Transport (2011), 'Vehicle licensing statistics', London: Department of Transport, accessed 1 October 2012 at http://www.dft.gov.uk/statistics/tables/veh0103/.

DiIulio, John J. Jr., Gerald Garvey and Donald F. Kettl (1993), *Improving Government Performance: An Owner's Manual*, Washington, DC: Brookings Institution Press.

Dohrmann, Thomas and Gary Pinshaw (2009), *The Road to Improved Compliance: A McKinsey Benchmarking Study of Tax Administrations – 2008–2009*, London: McKinsey and Co.

Dowding, Keith, Peter John and Stephen Biggs (1994), 'Tiebout: a survey of the empirical literature', *Urban Studies*, **31**(4), 767–97.

Dunleavy, Patrick (1982), 'Quasi-governmental sector professionalism', in A. Barker (ed.), *Quangos in Britain*, London: Macmillan, pp. 181–205.

Dunleavy, Patrick (1989a), 'The architecture of the British central state: Part I Framework for analysis', *Public Administration*, **67**(3), 249–76.

Dunleavy, Patrick (1989b), 'The architecture of the British central state: Part II Empirical findings', *Public Administration*, **67**(4), 391–417.

Dunleavy, Patrick (1991), *Democracy, Bureaucracy and Public Choice: Economic Explanations in Political Science*, Hemel Hempstead: Harvester-Wheatsheaf.

Dunleavy, Patrick (1994), 'The globalization of public services production: can government be "best in world"?', *Public Policy and Administration*, **9**(2), 36–65.

Dunleavy, Patrick (1995), 'Policy disasters: explaining the UK's record', *Public Policy and Administration*, **10**(2), 52–71.

Dunleavy, P. (2010a), 'New worlds in political science', *Political Studies*, **58**(1), 239–65.

Dunleavy, Patrick (2010b), 'Falling back on the (nation) state – and hating it', *British Politics and Policy at LSE* blog, 29 November, accessed 1 October 2012 at http://eprints.lse.ac.uk/41409/.

Dunleavy, Patrick (2010c), 'Hating the state – and exploiting the shock',

British Politics and Policy at LSE blog, 7 December, accessed 1 October 2012 at http://eprints.lse.ac.uk/41462/.

Dunleavy, Patrick (2011a), 'Essentially digital governance – four principles for the next decade and five current examples of their salience', presentation to Australian Prime Minister and Cabinet Department seminar, 21 April, previously given to UK Treasury and HMRC seminar, 9 June 2010.

Dunleavy, Patrick (2011b), 'The anatomy of a service delivery disaster: how the UK's tax agency goofed up. And what it means to one of their "customers"', *British Politics and Policy at LSE* blog, 10 November, accessed 29 September 2012 at http://eprints.lse.ac.uk/41477/.

Dunleavy, Patrick (2011c), 'The backlash against the state', *Political Insight*, April 2011, pp. 4–6, accessed 1 October 2012 at http://www.politicalinsightmagazine.com/?p=593.

Dunleavy, Patrick. (2012a) 'Getting Whitehall to incorporate new IT developments in public services remains an uphill struggle. The government now lags ten years behind the private sector in its use of social media and lack of feedback to users', *British Politics and Policy at LSE* blog, 27 January. Available at: http://eprints.lse.ac.uk/44035/

Dunleavy, Patrick (2012b), 'With a likely cost of £4 billion, the Health and Social Care Bill has all the hallmarks of an avoidable policy fiasco', *British Politics and Policy* blog at LSE, 24 January, accessed 21 September 2012 at http://blogs.lse.ac.uk/politicsandpolicy/2012/01/24/hsc-bill-policy-fiasco/.

Dunleavy, Patrick and Helen Margetts (2010), 'The second wave of digital era governance', *Social Science Research Network*, paper to the 2010 Annual Conference of the American Political Science Association, accessed 14 September at http://papers.ssrn.com/sol3/papers.cfm?abstract_id=1643850.

Dunleavy, Patrick and Paul Rainford (2011), 'Moving social security systems online: comparative experiences', Conference presentation to LSE Public Policy Group Conference, 'Moving Social Security Online', 29 June, accessed 30 September 2012 at http://blogs.lse.ac.uk/politicsandpolicy/moving-social-security-online/.

Dunleavy, Patrick, Helen Margetts, Steve John and Don McCarthy (1999), *Government on the Web*, National Audit Office 'Value for money' study, HC 87 Session 1999–2000, London: The Stationery Office.

Dunleavy, Patrick, H. Margetts, S. Bastow, R. Callaghan and H. Yared (2002), *Government on the Web II*, London: The Stationery Office, HC 764 Session 2001–2002, accessed 15 September 2012 at http://eprints.lse.ac.uk/597/.

Dunleavy, Patrick, Helen Margetts, Simon Bastow, Françoise Bouçek and Rosemary Campbell (2003), *Difficult Forms: How Government Agencies Interact with Citizens*, HC 1145 Session 2002–2003, London: The Stationery Office, accessed 24 September 2012 at http://eprints.lse.ac.uk/596/.

Dunleavy, Patrick, Martin Loughlin, Helen Margetts, Simon Bastow, Jane Tinkler, Oliver Pearce and Patricia Bartholomeou (2005), *Citizen Redress: What Citizens Can Do if Things Go Wrong in the Public Services*, 9 March 2005, HC 21 Session 2004–2005, London: The Stationery Office, accessed 14 September 2012 at http://www.nao.org.uk/whats_new/0405/040521.aspx?alreadysearchfor=yes.

Dunleavy, Patrick, Helen Margetts, Simon Bastow and Jane Tinkler (2006a), 'New public management is dead. Long live digital-era governance', *Journal of Public Administration Research and Theory*, **16**(3), 467–94.

Dunleavy, Patrick, S. Bastow, H. Margetts, O. Pearce and J. Tinkler (2006b), *Achieving Innovation in Central Government Organizations – Main Report* and *Volume II – Detailed Research Findings*, HC 1447-I and HC 1447-II, Session 2006–2007, London: The Stationery Office.

Dunleavy, Patrick, Helen Margetts, Simon Bastow, Oliver Pearce and Jane Tinkler (2007), *Government on the Internet: Progress in Delivering Information and Services Online*, HC 539 Session 2006–2007, London: The Stationery Office.

Dunleavy, Patrick, Helen Margetts, Simon Bastow and Jane Tinkler (2008), *Digital Era Governance: IT Corporations, the State and e-Government*, revised edition, Oxford: Oxford University Press.

Dunleavy, Patrick, Helen Margetts, David Raraty, Jane Tinkler (with D. Dorrell, T. Escher, S. Goldchluk, L. Hinds, M.K. Khan and S. Reissfelder) (2009), *Department for Work and Pensions: Communicating with Customers*, HC 421 Session 2008–2009, NAO 'Value for money' report, London: The Stationery Office.

Dunleavy, Patrick, Simon Bastow, Jane Tinkler, Chris Gilson, Sofia Goldchluk and Ed Towers (2010a), 'Joining up citizen redress in UK central government', in M. Adler (ed.), *Administrative Justice in Context*, London: Hart, Ch. 17, pp. 421–56.

Dunleavy, Patrick with Jane Tinkler, Chris Gilson and Ed Towers (2010b) 'Understanding and preventing delivery disasters in public services', paper to the Political Studies Association Conference, Edinburgh, 30 March, accessed 24 September 2012 at http://www.psa.ac.uk/journals/pdf/5/2010/1003_1311.pdf.

DVLA (2007), *DVLA Annual Report and Accounts 2006–07*, HC800, 19 July, London: The Stationery Office.

DVLA (2011), *DVLA Annual Report and Accounts 2010–11*, HC1105, 30 June, London: The Stationery Office.

Easterby-Smith, M., Mary Crossan and Davide Nicolini (2000), 'Organizational learning: debates past, present and future', *Journal of Management Studies*, **37**(6), 783–96.

Escher, Tobias, Helen Margetts, Ingemar J. Cox and Vaclav Petricek (2006), 'Governing from the centre? Comparing the nodality of digital governments', paper to the Annual Meeting of the American Political Science Association, Philadelphia, 31 August–4 September 2006, accessed 1 October 2012 at http://www.governmentontheweb.org/access_papers.asp#J.

European Court of Auditors (2010a), *Improving Transport Performance on Trans-European Rail Axes: Have EU Rail Infrastructure Investments been Effective?*, Special Report No. 8, Luxembourg: ECA, accessed 15 September 2012 at http://eur-lex.europa.eu/LexUriServ/LexUriServ.do?uri=OJ:C:2010:326:0016:0016:EN:PDF.

European Court of Auditors (2010b), *Are Simplified Customs Procedures for Imports Effectively Controlled?* Special Report No. 1, Luxembourg: ECA accessed 29 September 2012 at http://eca.europa.eu/portal/pls/portal/docs/1/7912988.PDF.

Eurostat (2001), *Building the System of National Accounts*, Luxembourg: Eurostat, accessed 29 September 2012 at http://epp.eurostat.ec.europa.eu/statistics_explained/index.php/Building_the_System_of_National_Accounts.

Ferdinand, J. (2004), 'Power, politics and state intervention in organizational learning', *Management Learning*, **35**(4), 435–50.

Fernandez, S. and H.G. Rainey (2006), 'Managing successful organizational change in the public sector', *Public Administration Review*, **66**(2), 168–76.

Finger, M. and S.B. Brand (1999), 'The concept of the "learning organization" applied to the transformation of the public sector: conceptual contributions for theory development in organizational learning and the learning organization', in M. Easterby-Smith, L. Araujo and J. Burgoyne, *Developments in Theory and Practice*, London: Sage.

Galbraith, John K. (1969), *The New Industrial State*, Harmondsworth: Penguin.

Gallagher, Mark (2005), 'Benchmarking tax systems', *Public Administration and Development*, **25**(2), 125–44.

Garicano, Luis and Paul Heaton (2010), 'Information technology, organization, and productivity in the public sector: evidence from police departments', *Journal of Labor Economics*, **28**(1), 67–201, accessed 1 October 2012 at http://works.bepress.com/psheaton/5 and http://www.rand.org/content/dam/rand/pubs/reprints/2010/RAND_RP1409.pdf.

Garvin, D. (1993), 'Building a learning organization', *Harvard Business Review*, **71**(4), 78–91.

Gill, Derek (ed.) (2011), *The Iron Cage Re-created: The Performance Management of State Organizations in New Zealand*, Wellington: Institute of Policy Studies.

Gill, Jit B.S. (2003), 'The nuts and bolts of revenue administrative reform', Washington, DC: World Bank, accessed 16 September at http://site resources.worldbank.org/INTTPA/Resources/NutsBolts.pdf.

Gilsing, V. and B. Nooteboom (2006), 'Exploration and exploitation in innovation systems: the case of pharmaceutical biotechnology', *Research Policy*, **35**(1), 1–23.

Gilson, Christopher H., Patrick Dunleavy and Jane Tinkler (2008), *Organizational Learning in Government Sector Organizations: Literature Review*, Report to the National Audit Office, 3 March, London: LSE Public Policy Group, accessed 22 September 2012 at http://www 2.lse.ac.uk/government/research/resgroups/LSEPublicPolicy/pdf/PPG_OrgLearninginGovLit_review.pdf.

Giuri, P., S. Torrisi and Natalia Zinovyeva (2008), 'ICT, skills, and organizational change: evidence from Italian manufacturing firms', *Industrial and Corporate Change*, **17** (1), 29–64.

Greenhalgh, T., G. Robert, F. Macfarlane, P. Bate and O. Kyriakidou (2004), 'Diffusion of innovations in service organizations: systematic review and recommendations', *Millbank Quarterly*, **82**(4), 581–620.

Greve, Heinrich R. (2003), *Organizational Learning from Performance Feedback: A Behavioral Perspective on Innovation and Change*, New York: Cambridge University Press.

Grönroos, Christian (2007), *Service Management and Marketing: Customer Management in Service Competition*, Chichester: Wiley.

Guardian Professional (2009), 'DVLA doubles annual contract spending', 23 November.

Haldenby, Andrew, Patrick Nolan, Lucy Parsons and Greg Rosen (2009), *The Front Line*, London: Reform.

Hall, Emma, Carol Propper and John Van Reenen (2008), 'Can pay regulation kill? Panel data evidence on the effect of labour markets on hospital performance', CEP Discussion Paper No. 843, January, London: Centre for Economic Performance, accessed 21 September 2012 at http://cep.lse.ac.uk/pubs/download/dp0843.pdf.

Halligan, John (2011), 'NPM in Anglo-Saxon countries', in Tom Christensen and Per Lægreid (eds), *The Ashgate Research Companion to New Public Management*, Farnham, Surrey: Ashgate, Ch. 6, pp. 83–96.

Hannan, Michael T. and John Freeman (1993), *Organizational Ecology*, Cambridge, MA: Harvard University Press.

Harford, Tim (2011), *Adapt: Why Success Always Starts with Failure*, London: Abacus.

Harris, Michael and Richard Halkett (2007), *Hidden Innovation: How Innovation Happens in Six Low Innovation Sectors*, London: NESTA.

Hasseldine, John (2010), 'The administration of tax systems', Working Paper No. 10-21, Atlanta: Georgia State University, International Studies Program.

Hatry, Harry P. and Donald M. Fisk (1971), *Improving Productivity and Productivity Measurement in Local Government*, Washington, DC: National Commission for Productivity.

Hayek, Friedrich (1944), *The Road to Serfdom*, London: Routledge and Sons.

Haynes, P. (2005), 'New development: the demystification of knowledge management for public services', *Public Money and Management*, 25(2), 131–5.

Healthcare Commission (2007), *Investigation into Outbreaks of Clostridum Difficile at Maidstone and Tunbridge Wells NHS Trust*, London: Commission for Healthcare Audit and Inspection, accessed 19 September 2012 at http://news.bbc.co.uk/1/shared/bsp/hi/pdfs/11_10_07maidstone_and_tunbridge_wells_investigation_report_oct_07.pdf.

Healthcare Commission (2009), *Investigation into Mid Staffordshire NHS Foundation Trust*, London: Healthcare Commission, March, accessed 21 September 2012 at http://www.nhshistory.net/midstaffs.pdf.

Hedberg, B. (1981), 'How organizations learn and unlearn', in P.C. Nystrom and W.H. Starbuck (eds), *Handbook of Organizational Design*, New York: Oxford University Press, pp. 3–27.

Hellowell, Mark (2012a), 'Private financing for public infrastructure is here to stay despite "PFIs" being consigned to history', *British Politics and Policy at LSE* blog, 18 January, accessed 23 September 2012 at http://blogs.lse.ac.uk/politicsandpolicy/2012/01/18/pfi-private-finance/.

Hellowell, Mark (2012b), 'Meeting the demand for care will mean ensuring the private sector health market is fit for competition', *British Politics and Policy at LSE* blog, 1 February, accessed 23 September 2012 at http://blogs.lse.ac.uk/politicsandpolicy/2012/02/01/private-sector-health-market-competition/.

Her Majesty's Treasury (HMT) (2009), *Public Expenditure Statistical Analyses*, accessed 17 September 2012 at http://www.hm-treasury.gov.uk/pespub_index.htm.

HM Revenue & Customs (HMRC) (2006), *HMRC Annual Report 2005–06* and *Autumn Performance Report 2006*, London: HMRC, accessed 16

September 2012 at http://customs.hmrc.gov.uk/channelsPortalWebApp/downloadFile?contentID=HMCE_PROD1_026500.

HM Revenue & Customs (HMRC) (2007), *Evaluation of PaceSetter: Lean, Senior Leadership & Operational Management within HMRC Processing, Final Report*, September, written by Dr Zoe Radnor and Giovanni Bucci from AtoZ Business Consultancy, London: HMRC.

HM Revenue & Customs (HMRC) (2009), *Autumn Report 2009*, London: HMRC, accessed 19 June 2011 at http://www.hmrc.gov.uk/about/autumn-report-2009.pdf.

HM Revenue & Customs (HMRC) (no date), *Detailed Findings of the Customs Information and Processing Requirements in the 21st Century (CIPR21) Scoping Study Report*, London: HMRC, accessed 5 April 2012 at http://customs.hmrc.gov.uk/channelsPortalWebApp/channelsPortalWebApp.portal?_nfpb=true&_pageLabel=pageLibrary_MiscellaneousReports&propertyType=document&columns=1&id=HMCE_CL_001504.

Hood, Christopher C. (1998), *The Art of the State: Culture, Rhetoric and Public Management*, Oxford: Oxford University Press.

Hood, Christopher C. (2006), 'Gaming in targetworld: the targets approach to managing British public services', *Public Administration Review*, **66**(4), 515–21.

Hood, Christopher and Gwyn Bevan (no date), 'The governance of health care by targets and indicators: can it be both proportional and transparent?', PowerPoint presentation, Oxford: ESRC Public Service Programme.

Hood, Christopher and Ruth Dixon (2012), 'A model of cost-cutting in government? The great management revolution in UK central government reconsidered', *Public Administration*, forthcoming.

Hood, C. and Patrick Dunleavy (1994), 'From old public administration to new public management', *Public Money and Management*, **14**(3), 9–16.

Hood, Christopher C. and Helen Margetts (2007), *The Tools of Government in the Digital Age*, Basingstoke: Palgrave Macmillan.

Horn, Murray (1995), *The Political Economy of Public Administration*, Cambridge: Cambridge University Press.

Hughes, Andrew (2002), 'Guide to the measurement of government productivity', *International Productivity Monitor*, No. 5, 64–77.

Hunt, B. and T. Ivergard (2007), 'Organizational climate and workplace efficiency – earning from performance measurement in a public-sector cadre organization', *Public Management Review*, **9**(1), 27–47.

Identity and Passport Service (2010), *Annual Report and Accounts, 2009–10*, London: The Stationery Office.

Iorwerth, Aled (2006), 'How to measure government productivity: a review article on "Measurement of Government Output and Productivity for the National Accounts (the Atkinson Report)"', *International Productivity Monitor*, No. 13, 57–74.

Jackson, P.M. (1982), *The Political Economy of Bureaucracy*, Deddington, Oxford: Phillip Allan.

Jackson, P.M. (ed.) (1995), *Measures for Success in the Public Sector*, London: Public Finance Foundation.

Jackson, P.M. (1997), 'Productivity and performance of public sector organisations', mimeo, Leicester: Leicester University Management Centre.

James, Oliver (2003), *The Executive Agency Revolution in Whitehall: Public Interest versus Public Choice Perspectives*, Basingstoke: Palgrave Macmillan.

Jenkins, Lin (2006), '10,000 a week have passport applications rejected over new photo rule', *Mail on Sunday*, 11 June, accessed 5 October at http://www.dailymail.co.uk/news/article-390116/10-000-week-passport-applications-rejected-new-photo-rule.html#ixzz28M3bbSQz.

Jones, Lawrence R. and Fred Thompson (2007), *From Bureaucracy to Hyperarchy in Netcentric and Quick Learning Organizations*, New York: Information Age Publishing.

Jorgenson, Dale W., Mun S. Ho and Kevin J. Stiroh (2007) 'A retrospective look at the U.S. productivity growth resurgence', New York: Federal Reserve Bank of New York, Staff Report No. 277, February.

Kaufman, H. (1976), *Are Government Organizations Immortal?*, Washington, DC: Brookings Institution Press.

Kelly, Gavin (2011), 'The Liberal Democrats' intended tax changes are about to cause trouble for the Treasury', *British Politics and Policy at LSE* blog, 6 April, accessed 16 September 2012 at http://blogs.lse.ac.uk/politicsandpolicy/2011/04/06/liberal-democrats-tax-treasury/.

Kelman, Steven (2005), *Unleashing Change: A Study of Organizational Renewal in Government*, Washington, DC: Brookings Institution Press.

Kelman, Steven (2006), 'Improving service delivery performance in the United Kingdom: organization theory perspectives on central intervention strategies', *Journal of Comparative Policy*, **8**(4), 393–419.

Kelman, Steven (2010), 'If you want to be a good fill-in-the-blank manager, be a good plain-vanilla manager', John Gaus Lecture, 3 September, American Political Science Association, Washington.

Kerr, J. and J. Slocum (1987), 'Managing corporate culture through reward systems', *Academy of Management Executive*, **1**(2), 99–107.

Kim, H.J., G. Pan and S.L. Pan (2007), 'Managing IT-enabled transformation in the public sector: a case study on e-government in South Korea', *Government Information Quarterly*, **24**(2), 328–52.

Kippin, Henry and Ben Lucas (2011), *From Big Society to Social Productivity*, London: RSA Projects, 2020 Public Services Hub and Citizen Power Peterborough, accessed 11 September 2012 at http://2020psh.org/wp-content/uploads/2011/04/RSA_BigSoc_A4_04. pdf.

Kleven, Henrik Jacobsen, Claus Thustrup Kreiner and Emmanuel Saez (2009), 'Why can modern governments tax so much? An agency model of firms as fiscal intermediaries', Working Paper No. 15218, Cambridge, MA: National Bureau of Economics Research, accessed 24 September 2012 at http://www.nber.org/papers/w15218.

Krueger, A.B. (1999), 'Measuring labor's share', Working Paper No. 7006, NBER, accessed 29 September 2012 at http://www.nber.org/ papers/w7006.

Lamothe, Meeyounge and Scott Lamothe (2009), 'Beyond the search for competition in social service contracting: procurement, consolidation, and accountability', *American Review of Public Administration*, **39**(2), 164–88.

Leadbeater, Charles (2010), *Cloud Culture: The Future of Global Cultural Relations*, London: Counterpoint.

Lee, Cheol-Sung, Young-Bum Kim and Jae-Mahn Shi (2011), 'The limit of equality projects: public-sector expansion, sectoral conflicts, and income inequality in postindustrial economies', *American Sociological Review*, **76**(1), 100–24.

LeGrand, Julian (2007), *The Other Invisible Hand: Delivering Public Services Through Choice and Competition*, Princeton, NJ: Princeton University Press.

LeGrand, Julian (2012), 'Both economic theory and evidence from the UK shows that state-funded healthcare which incorporates market-type incentives will save more lives and reduce more suffering', *British Politics and Policy at LSE* blog, 9 March, accessed 23 September 2012 at http://eprints.lse.ac.uk/43774/.

Lehr, W. and F. Lichtenberg (1998), 'Computer use and productivity growth in federal government agencies, 1987 to 1992', *Journal of Industrial Economics*, **46**(2), 257–79.

Levi, Margaret (1992), *Of Rule and Revenue*, Berkeley, CA: University of California Press.

Levi, Margaret, Tom Tyler and Audrey Sacks (2008), 'The reasons for compliance with the law', paper for the Workshop on the Rule of Law, Yale University, 28 March.

Levinson, Marc (2006), *The Box: How the Shipping Container Made the World Smaller and the World Economy Bigger*, Princeton, NJ: Princeton University Press.

Levitt, Steven D. (2004), 'Understanding why crime fell in the 1990s: four factors that explain the decline and six that do not', *Journal of Economic Perspectives*, **18**(1), 163–90.

Lewis, David E. (2002), 'The politics of agency termination: confronting the myth of agency immortality', *Journal of Politics*, **64**(1), 89–107.

Lichtenberg, F. (1995), 'The output contributions of computer equipment and personnel: a firm-level analysis', *Economics of Innovation and New Technology*, **3**(4), 201–17.

Local Government Improvement and Development (IDEA) (2010), *Productivity: Getting the Best Out of Your People*, London: Local Government Improvement and Development, accessed 11 September 2012 at http://www.idea.gov.uk/idk/aio/12252052.

LSE Identity Project (2005), *The LSE Identity Project Report*, London: London School of Economics and Political Science, Department of Information Systems, accessed 18 September 2012 at http://eprints.lse.ac.uk/726/.

LSE Public Policy Group (2008), 'Complaints handling in the Department for Work and Pensions and its agencies: research report for the National Audit Office', London: LSE Public Policy Group, May.

March, J.G. and J.P. Olsen (1975), 'Organizational learning under ambiguity', *European Journal of Policy Review*, **3**(2), 147–71.

Margetts, H. (1991), 'The computerization of social security: the way forward or a step backward?', *Public Administration*, **69**(3), 325–43.

Margetts, H. (1998), *Information Technology in Central Government: Britain and the United States*, London: Routledge.

Margetts, Helen and Patrick Dunleavy (2002), *Better Public Services Through E-government*, HC 704-III, London: The Stationery Office.

Margetts, Helen and Patrick Dunleavy (2012), 'Web science, public management and the second wave of digital era governance', *Philosophical Transactions of the Royal Society: A*, forthcoming.

Margetts, Helen, R. Eynon and T. Hicks (2006), 'Research into barriers and incentives for businesses filing returns online', article to accompany NAO value for money report *Filing VAT and Company Tax returns*, London: The Stationery Office.

Margetts, Helen, Patrick Dunleavy, S. Bastow and J. Tinkler (2008), 'Australian e-government in comparative perspective', *Australian Journal of Political Science*, **43**(1), 13–26, Special Issue, edited by R. Gibson and S. Ward on 'Australian Politics: the e-Politics Experience'.

McKinsey and Company (2010), *Achieving World Class Productivity in the NHS 2009/10 to 2013/14: Detailing the Size of the Opportunity*, London: Department of Health.

McKinsey and Company (2011a), 'The public-sector productivity imperative', paper written by Martin Neil Baily, Karen Croxson, Thomas Dohrmann and Lenny Mendonca.

McKinsey and Company (2011b), *Big Data: The Next Frontier for Innovation, Competition, and Productivity*, London: McKinsey Global Institute.

McLaren, Craig H., Bella Saunders and Carmel Zammit (2008), 'Comparing the perpetual inventory method and the whole of government accounts for depreciation', London: ONS.

McNabb, David E. (2007), *Knowledge Management in the Public Sector: A Blueprint for Innovation in Government*, Armonk, NY: M.E. Sharpe.

Meyer, John W. and Richard Scott (1992), *Organizational Environments; Ritual and Rationality*, London: Sage.

Meyer, Marshall S. and Lynn G. Zucker (1989), *Permanently Failing Organizations*, London: Sage.

Millar, Jane (2008), 'Making work pay, making tax credits work: an assessment with specific reference to lone-parent employment', *International Social Security Review*, **61**(2), 21–38.

Miller, Gary J. (1992), *Managerial Dilemmas: The Political Economy of Hierarchy*, Cambridge, UK: Cambridge University Press.

Mintzberg, Henry (1983), *Structure in Fives*, Englewood Cliffs, NJ: Prentice-Hall.

Moore, Gordon (2006), 'Excerpts from a conversation with Gordon Moore: Moore's Law (Intel)', accessed 29 September 2012 at ftp://down load.intel.com/museum/Moores_Law/Video-Transcripts/Excepts_A_ Conversation_with_Gordon_Moore.pdf.

Moore, Mark H. (1995), *Creating Public Value: Strategic Management in Government*, Cambridge, MA: Harvard University Press.

Moynihan, D.P. (2005), 'Goal-based learning and the future of performance management', *Public Administration Review*, **65**(2), 203–16.

Moynihan, D.P. and N. Landuyt (2009), 'How do public organizations learn? Bridging cultural and structural perspectives', *Public Administration Review*, **69**(6), 1097–105.

Mukhopadhyay, T., S. Rajiv and K. Srinivasan (1997), 'Information technology impact on process output and quality', *Management Science*, **43**(12), 1645–59.

National Audit Office (NAO) (1999), *United Kingdom Passport Agency: The Passport Delays of Summer 1999*, 27 October, HC 812 Session 1998–1999, London: The Stationery Office.

National Audit Office (NAO) (2000a), *State Earnings-related Pension Scheme: The Failure to Inform the Public of Reduced Pension Rights for Widows and Widowers*, HC 320, Session 1999–2000, London: The Stationery Office.

National Audit Office (NAO) (2000b), *The Management and Control of Hospital Acquired Infection in Acute NHS Trusts in England*, HC 230 Session 1999–2000, London: The Stationery Office.

National Audit Office (NAO) (2001a), *Regulating Freight Imports from Outside the European Community*, London: The Stationery Office, HC 131 Session 2000–2001, 2 February, accessed 15 September 2012 at http://www.official-documents.gov.uk/document/hc0001/hc01/0131/0131.asp.

National Audit Office (NAO) (2001b), 'Press release – Income tax self-assessment', London: NAO, accessed 16 September 2012 at http://www.nao.org.uk/whats_new/0102/010256.aspx.

National Audit Office (NAO) (2002a), *e-Revenue*, HC 492, Session 2001–2012, London: The Stationery Office.

National Audit Office (NAO) (2002b), *Better Public Services Through E-government*, HC 704 I-III, Session 2001–2002, London: The Stationery Office, 4 April, accessed 24 September 2012 at http://www.nao.org.uk/publications/0102/better_public_services_through.aspx.

National Audit Office (NAO) (2004), *Improving Patient Care by Reducing the Risk of Hospital Acquired Infection: A Progress Report*, HC 876 Session 2003–2004, 14 July, London: The Stationery Office.

National Audit Office (NAO) (2005), *Filing of Income Tax Self-assessment Returns*, London: The Stationery Office.

National Audit Office (NAO) (2006), *Update on PFI Debt Refinancing and the PFI Equity Market*, HC 10400, Session 2005–2006, 21 April, London: The Stationery Office.

National Audit Office (NAO) (2007a), *The Efficiency Programme: A Second Review of Progress*, HC 156 I & II, Session 2006–2007, London: The Stationery Office.

National Audit Office (NAO) (2007b), *The Management of Staff Sickness Absence in Department of Transport and its Agencies*, HC 527 Session 2006–2007, 8 June, London: The Stationery Office.

National Audit Office (NAO) (2008a), *Department for Transport: Electronic Service Delivery in the Driver, Vehicle and Operator Agencies in Great Britain*, HC 204 Session 2007–2008, 16 January, London: The Stationery Office.

National Audit Office (NAO) (2008b), *Department for Work and Pensions: Progress in Tackling Benefit Fraud*, 23 January, HC 102 Session 2007–2008, London: The Stationery Office.

National Audit Office (NAO) (2008c), *The National Programme for IT in the NHS: Progress Since 2006*, HC 484 Session 2007–2008, 16 May, London: The Stationery Office, accessed 21 September 2012 at http://www.nao.org.uk/publications/0708/the_national_programme_for_it.aspx.

National Audit Office (NAO) (2008d), *HM Revenue & Customs'*

Transformation Programme, HC 930 Session 2007–2008, 18 July 2008, London: The Stationery Office, accessed 17 September 2012 at http://www.nao.org.uk/publications/0708/hm_transformation_programme.aspx.

National Audit Office (NAO) (2008e), *HM Revenue & Customs: The Control and Facilitation of Imports*, HC 942 Session 2007–2008, London: The Stationery Office.

National Audit Office (NAO) (2009a), *Reducing Healthcare Associated Infections in Hospitals in England*, London: The Stationery Office.

National Audit Office (2009b), *HM Revenue & Customs' Estate Private Finance Deal Eight Years On*, HC 30, Session 2009–2010, London: The Stationery Office, accessed 29 September 2012 at http://bit.ly/6PoKfR.

National Audit Office (NAO) (2010a), *Revenue and Customs: Handling Telephone Enquiries*, 15 January, London: The Stationery Office, accessed 16 September 2012 at http://bit.ly/7piLi6.

National Audit Office (NAO) (2010b), *Reorganizing Central Government*, HC 491 Session 2009–2010, 18 March, London: The Stationery Office, accessed 14 September 2012 at http://www.nao.org.uk/publications/0910/reorganising_government.aspx.

National Audit Office (NAO) (2010c), *Department for Work and Pensions: Minimizing the Cost of Administrative Errors in the Benefits System*, HC 569 Session 2010–2011, 17 December, London: The Stationery Office, accessed 24 September at http://www.nao.org.uk/files/1011569.pdf.

National Audit Office (NAO) (2010d), *Department of Health: Management of NHS Hospital Productivity*, HC 491 Session 2010–2011, 17 December, London: The Stationery Office, accessed 24 September 2012 at http://www.nao.org.uk/publications/1011/nhs_hospital_productivity.aspx.

National Audit Office (NAO) (2010e), *Department of Health: Management of NHS Hospital Productivity – Regression Analysis Methodology*, 17 December, London: The Stationery Office.

National Audit Office (NAO) (2010f), *Department of Health: Management of NHS Hospital Productivity – Methodology*, 17 December, London: The Stationery Office.

National Audit Office (NAO) (2011a), *Lessons from PFI and Other Projects*, HC 920, Session 2010–2012, 28 April, London: The Stationery Office.

National Audit Office (2011b), *PaceSetter: HMRC's Programme to Improve Business Operations*, HC 1280, Session 2010–2012, London: The Stationery Office, accessed 29 September 2012 at http://www.nao.org.uk/publications/1012/pacesetter.aspx.

National Audit Office (2011c), *Home Office, UK Border Agency –*

Immigration: The Points Based System – Work Routes, HC 819 Session 2010–2011, 15 March, London: The Stationary Office.

Nevis, E.C., A.J. DiBella and J.M. Gould (1995), 'Understanding organizations as learning systems', *Sloan Management Review*, **36**(4), 73–85.

NHS Confederation (2002), 'Turning around failing hospitals', Briefing Paper December, London: NHS Confederation.

Niskanen, William ([1971] 1995), *Bureaucracy and Public Economics* (originally published as *Bureaucracy and Representative Government*), Aldershot, UK and Brookfield, VT: Edward Elgar.

Nooteboom, Bart (2005), *Learning and Innovation in Organizations and Economies*, Oxford: Oxford University Press.

Nooteboom, Bart (2006), 'Private sector lessons for government innovation', in National Audit Office, *INNOVATION Focus*, London: NAO, pp. 12–14.

Nonaka, I. and H. Takeuchi (1995), *The Knowledge Creating Company: How Japanese Companies Create the Dynamics of Innovation*, Oxford: Oxford University Press.

O'Donnell, Gus (2004), *Financing Britain's Future – Review of the Revenue Departments*, Cm 6163, London: HM Treasury, accessed 16 September 2012 at http://webarchive.nationalarchives.gov.uk/+/http://www.hm-treasury.gov.uk/media//FBAA7/odonnell_fore_ch1_245.pdf.

Office for National Statistics (ONS) (2000), *Transport, Travel and Tourism*, London: The Stationery Office.

Office for National Statistics (ONS) (2007a), *Measuring Quality as a Part of Public Service Output – Strategy Following Consultation*, London: The Stationery Office, available at: http://www.statistics.gov.uk/cci/article.asp?id=1831.

Office for National Statistics (ONS) (2007b), *Quality is the Key to Measuring Public Sector Productivity*, July, London: UKCEMGA.

Office for National Statistics (ONS) (2008a), *Public Sector Productivity: Health Care*, January, London: UKCEMGA.

Office for National Statistics (ONS) (2008b), *Public Service Productivity: Social Security Administration*, June, London: The Stationery Office.

Office for National Statistics (ONS) (2009), *Total Public Service Output and Productivity*, June, London: The Stationery Office.

Office for National Statistics (ONS) (2010a), *Blue Book*, London: The Stationery Office.

Office for National Statistics (ONS) (2010b), *Social Trends*, 'Households with regular use of a car', London: accessed 1 October 2012 at http://www.ons.gov.uk/ons/publications/re-reference-tables.html?edition=tcm%3A77-131202.

Office for National Statistics (2011), 'Quarterly travel and tourism 2001 to 2010', in *Transport, Travel and Tourism*, London: The Stationery Office.

Olsen, Johan P. and B. Guy Peters (eds) (1996), *Lessons from Experience: Experiential Learning in Administrative Reforms in Eight Democracies*, Oslo: Scandinavian University Press.

Olson, Mancur (1993), 'Dictatorship, democracy, and development', *American Political Science Review*, **87**(3), 567–76.

O'Mahoney, Mary, Marcel Timmer and Bart Van Ark (2010), 'ICT and productivity growth in Europe, an update and comparison with the US', in Mario Cimoli, André A. Hofman and Nano Mulder (eds), *Innovation and Economic Development: The Impact of Information and Communication Technologies in Latin America*, Cheltenham, UK and Northampton, MA, USA: Edward Elgar.

Organisation for Economic Co-operation and Development (OECD) (2010), *Public Administration after 'New Public Management'*, part of *'Value for Money in Government'* series, Paris: OECD Publishing.

Osborne, Alastair (2011), '"Sweetheart" tax deals come under scrutiny of auditors', *Daily Telegraph*, 17 December.

Osborne, Evan (2002), 'The keys to the kingdom: income tax and the state', mimeo, Dayton, Ohio: Wright State University, Department of Economics.

Oxford Economics (2008a), *The Public Services Industry in the UK*, Oxford: Oxford Economics.

Oxford Economics (2008b), *The Market for Public Services: International Comparisons*, Oxford: Oxford Economics.

Peñaloza, Maria-Cristina, Michael Hardie, Richard Wild and Katherine Mills (2010), *Public Service Output, Inputs and Productivity, Healthcare*, London: Office of National Statistics.

Peters, B. Guy and Brian W. Hogwood (1982), 'The death of immortality: births, deaths and metamorphoses in the US federal bureaucracy 1933–1982', *American Review of Public Administration*, **18**(2), 119–33.

Petricek, Vaclav, Tobias Escher, Ingemar J. Cox and Helen Margetts (2006), 'The web structure of e-government – developing a methodology for quantitative evaluation', *Proceedings of the 15th International Conference on World Wide Web in Edinburgh, Scotland, 2006*, accessed 1 October 2012 at http://www.governmentontheweb.org/downloads/papers/WWW2006-Web_Structure_of_E_Government.pdf.

Phelps, Mike G., Sophia Kamarudeen, Katherine Mills and Richard Wild (2010), *UK Centre for the Measurement of Government Activity: Total Public Service Output, Inputs and Productivity*, London: ONS.

Pollitt, Christopher (2011), 'Technological change: a central yet neglected feature of public administration', *NISPAcee Journal of Public Administration and Policy*, **3**(2), 31–53.

Pollitt, Christopher, Colin Talbot, Janice Caulfield and Amanda Smullen (2004), *Agencies: How Governments Do Things Through Semi-autonomous Organizations*, Basingstoke: Palgrave.

Polsby, Nelson (1985), *Political Innovation in America: The Politics of Policy Initiation*, New Haven, CT: Yale University Press.

Pritchard, A. (2003), 'Measuring productivity change in the provision of public services', a paper produced for the NIESR Conference on 'Productivity and Performance in the Provision of Public Services', London, 19 November, accessed 25 September 2012 at http://www.niesr.ac.uk/event/pritdoc.pdf.

Protopsaltis, G., N. Fulop, R. Meara and N. Edwards (2002), *Turning Around Failing Hospitals*, London: NHS Confederation.

PSSRU, Kent (2007), *Unit Costs of Health and Social Care 2007*, Canterbury, Kent: Personal Social Services Research Unit, compiled by Leslie Curtis, accessed 1 October 2012 at http://kar.kent.ac.uk/2785/1/uc2007.pdf.

Public Accounts Committee (2011a), *Management of NHS Hospital Productivity: Twenty-Sixth Report of Session 2010–2012*, London: House of Commons, accessed 25 September 2012 at http://www.publications.parliament.uk/pa/cm201011/cmselect/cmpubacc/741/74102.htm.

Public Accounts Committee (2011b), *Reducing Costs in the Department for Work and Pensions: Forty-Seventh Report of Session 2010–12*, London: The Stationery Office, accessed 18 September 2012 at http://www.publications.parliament.uk/pa/cm201012/cmselect/cmpubacc/1351/1351.pdf.

Public Administration Select Committee (PASC) (2011), *Government and IT – 'A Recipe for Rip-offs': Time for a New Approach, Twelfth Report of Session 2010–2011*, London: The Stationery Office.

Quinn, James Brian (1992), *Intelligent Enterprise: A Knowledge and Service Based Paradigm for Industry*, New York: Free Press.

Ranson, Stewart and John Stewart (1994), *Management for the Public Domain: Enabling the Learning Society*, London: Macmillan.

Roberts, Alasdair (2010), 'Harris's mirage: the positive service state', *Public Administration Review*, December Special Issue on 'Part VI: The Past as Prelude: Were the Predictions of Classical Scholars Correct?', S268–S272.

Rochet, C. (2004) 'Rethinking the management of information in the strategic monitoring of public policies by agencies', *Industrial Management & Data Systems*, **104**(3–4), 201–8.

Rochet, C. (2007), 'Making crisis a momentum for change within public services', *International Journal of Public Sector Performance*, **1**(1), 5–28.

Romme, A.G.L. and A. van Witteloostuijn (1999), 'Circular organizing and triple loop learning', *Journal of Organizational Change Management*, **12**(5), 439–53.

Rowlinson, A. and R. Wild (2009), *Public Service Output, Input, and Productivity: Measuring Police Inputs*, London: ONS.

Sargent, T.C. and E.R. Rodriguez (2000), 'Labour or total factor productivity: do we need to choose?' *International Productivity Monitor*, **1**, 41–4.

Savage, Mike and Roger Burrows (2007), 'The coming crisis of empirical sociology', *Sociology*, **41**(5), 885–99.

Savage, Mike and Roger Burrows (2009), 'Some further reflections on the coming crisis of empirical sociology', *Sociology*, **43**(4), 762–72.

Schein, E. (2010), *Organizational Culture and Leadership*, San Francisco, CA: Jossey-Bass.

Schreyer, P. (2001), *OECD Manual on Productivity Measurement: A Guide to the Measurement of Industry-level and Aggregate Productivity Growth*, Paris: Organisation for Economic Co-operation and Development.

Scott, James (1998), *Seeing Like a State: How Certain Schemes to Improve the Human Condition Have Failed*, New Haven, CT: Yale University Press.

Scourfield, Peter (2012), 'Cartelization revisited and the lessons of Southern Cross', *Critical Social Policy*, **32**(1), 137–48.

Sertillanges, A.D. ([1920] 1978), *The Intellectual Life: Its Spirits, Conditions and Methods*, trans. Mary Ryan, Dublin: Mercer Press.

Sharples, A. (2010), 'The government's response to unemployment', London: Department of Work and Pensions, paper to the LSE Public Policy Group seminar on 'Innovating out of the Recession: New Strategies in Human Resources', 29 January 2010.

Shleifer, Andrei and Robert W. Vishny (1998), *The Grabbing Hand: Government Pathologies and their Cures*, Cambridge, MA: Harvard University Press.

Silberman, Bernard S. (1993), *Cages of Reason: The Rise of the Rational State in France, Japan, the United States, and Great Britain*, Chicago: University of Chicago Press.

Simpson, Helen (2006), 'Productivity in public services', Working Paper No. 07/164, Bristol: Centre for Market and Public Organizations.

Simpson, H. (2009), 'Productivity in public services', *Journal of Economic Surveys*, **23**(2), 250–76.

Solà, M. and D. Prior (2001), 'Measuring productivity and quality changes using data envelopment analysis: an application to Catalan hospitals', *Financial Accountability & Management*, **17**(3), 219–45.

Solow, R. (1957), 'Technical change and the aggregate production function', *Review of Economics and Statistics*, **39**(3), 312–20.

Solow, R.M. (1987), 'We'd better watch out', *New York Times* (12 July), Book Review, 36.

Statistics New Zealand (2010), *Measuring Government Sector Productivity in New Zealand: A Feasibility Study*, Wellington: Statistics New Zealand.

Steering Committee for the Review of Commonwealth/State Service Provision (1997), *Data Envelopment Analysis: A Technique for Measuring the Efficiency of Government Service Delivery*, Melbourne: Steering Committee for the Review of Commonwealth/State Service Provision.

Street, A. (2003), 'How much confidence should we place in efficiency estimates?', *Health Economics*, **12**(11), 895–907.

Taha, Roshaiza and Nanthakumar Loganathan (2008), 'Causality between tax revenue and government spending in Malaysia', *The International Journal of Business and Finance Research*, **2**(2), 63–73, accessed 16 September 2012 at http://ssrn.com/abstract=1543911.

Tiebout, Charles (1956), 'A pure theory of local expenditures', *Journal of Political Economy*, **64**(5), 416–24.

Tinbergen, J. (1942), 'Zur Theorie der langfristigen Wirtschaftsentwicklung', *Weltwirtschaftliches Archiv*, Band, **55**(1), 511–49.

Tinkler, Jane (2010), 'Benefit fraud is already low – to save real money the government should concentrate on the errors', *British Politics and Policy at LSE* blog, 11 August, accessed 17 September 2012 at http://eprints.lse.ac.uk/39684/.

Tinkler, Jane (2011), 'Ten years after tax, social security departments in the USA and elsewhere are moving cautiously online. The UK is pioneering "digital by default" services and the advent of a universal credit at DWP could be an opportunity for breakthrough progress', *British Politics and Policy at LSE* blog, 28 June, accessed 25 September 2012 at http://eprints.lse.ac.uk/37227/.

Treasury Select Committee (2004), *The Merger of Customs and Excise and the Inland Revenue*, HC 556, Session 2003–2004, 11 November, London: The Stationery Office.

Treasury Select Committee (2010), *Administration and Expenditure of the Chancellor's Departments, 2008–09*, HC 156 Session 2009–2010, 24 February, London: The Stationery Office.

Treasury Select Committee (2011), *Private Finance Initiative*, Seventeenth Report, Session 2010–2012, 18 July, London: The Stationery Office, accessed 23 September 2012 at http://www.publications.parliament.uk/pa/cm201012/cmselect/cmtreasy/1146/114602.htm.

UHY Hacker Young (2010), 'HMRC staff morale plunges to a new low after PAYE scandal', blog, 20 December, accessed 16 September at http://www.uhy-uk.com/resources/news/hmrc-staff-morale-plunges-to-a-new-low-following-paye-scandal777/.

UK Government (1998), *Green Paper: New Ambitions for Our Country: A New Contract for Welfare*, London: HMSO.

Van der Torre, Ab, Jedid-Jah Jonker, Frank van Tulder, Theresa Steeman and Gerard Paulides (2007), 'The judiciary: productivity in perspective', *Social and Community Planning*, 147–55.

Van de Walle, S. (2008), 'Comparing the performance of national public sectors: conceptual problems', *International Journal of Productivity and Performance Management*, **57**(4), 329–38.

Van Dooren, W. and S. Van de Walle (eds) (2008), *Performance Information in the Public Sector: How it is Used*, Basingstoke: Palgrave.

Van Dooren, Wouter (2010), 'After Atkinson: the implementation of measurement innovations', paper to the UK Political Studies Association Conference, University of Edinburgh.

van Stolk, Christian and Kai Wegrich (2008), 'Convergence without diffusion? A comparative analysis of the choice of performance indicators in tax administration and social security', *International Review of Administrative Sciences*, **74**(4), 589–614.

von Hippel, Eric (2005), *Democratizing Innovation*, Boston: MIT Press.

Waldo, Dwight (1948), *The Administrative State: A Study of the Political Theory of American Public Administration*, Piscataway, NJ: Transaction.

West, Michael A., James P. Guthrie, Jeremy F. Dawson, Carol S. Borrill and Matthew Carter (2006), 'Reducing patient mortality in hospitals: the role of human resource management', *Journal of Organizational Behavior*, **27**(7), 983–1002.

White, Anne and Patrick Dunleavy (2010), *Making and Breaking Whitehall Departments: A Guide to Machinery of Government Changes*, London: Institute for Government, 2010, accessed 14 September 2012 at http://www.instituteforgovernment.org.uk/publications/making-and-breaking-whitehall-departments.

Willetts D., N. Hillman and A. Bogdanor (2003), *Left Out, Left Behind: The People Lost to Britain's Workforce*, London: Policy Exchange.

Wilson, James Q. (1989), *Bureaucracy: What Government Agencies Do and Why They Do It*, New York: Basic Books.

Wittman, Donald (1995), *The Myth of Democratic Failure: Why Political Institutions are Efficient*, Chicago: University of Chicago Press.

Work and Pensions Select Committee (2006a), *The Efficiency Savings Programme in Jobcentre Plus: Second report of Session 2005–2006*, 18 March, HC 834-II, Session 2005–2006, London: The Stationery Office.

Work and Pensions Select Committee (2006b), *Benefits Simplification: Government Response to the Committee's Seventh Report of Session 2006–07*, 16 November, London: The Stationery Office. World Bank (2010), Copy of NAO 'International Benchmark of fraud and error in social security systems', accessed 25 September 2012 at http://www.nao. org.uk/publications/0506/international_benchmark_of_fra.aspx.

World Bank (2010), 'Toolkit on Tackling Error, Fraud and Corruption in Social Protection Programs'. Washington: World Bank. SP Discussion Paper No. 1002. Written by Christian van Stolk and Emil D. Tesliuc.

Yip, George S., Timothy M. Devinney and Gerry Johnson (2008), 'Measuring long term superior performance: or how to compare apples with oranges', London: Advanced Institute of Management Research, Working Paper No. 063, accessed 14 September 2012 at http://www. aimresearch.org/uploads/pdf/working_papers/063-January-2008_ YipandJohnson.pdf.

Index